A Compendium
of **Musky
Angling
History**

A Compendium of **Musky Angling History**

Second Edition

By Larry Ramsell

Musky Hunter Publications
St. Germain, Wisconsin

© 1997 Larry Ramsell

Designed and edited by Steve Heiting

Published by
Musky Hunter Publications
P.O. Box 340, St. Germain, WI 54558

For information on Musky Hunter magazine or other books by Musky Hunter Publications, call 1-800-23-MUSKY.

ISBN 0-9660416-0-7

Printed in the U.S.A.

Contents

Acknowledgements

Acknowledgements are very difficult with a book of this type because so many people play a part. Perhaps the most important are all of the writers, who by doing their job have contributed various bits and pieces of this history; also, we must not overlook the publications that printed those works and are the ultimate sources for a vast majority of the research material contained herein. In addition, several personal friends and contacts have contributed importantly to this book. As is always the case, I probably will miss a name or two, for which I apologize.

Special thanks to:

Peter Haupt, Rod Ramsell, Ken Schultz, Harold E. Herrick Jr.,
Lou Spray, Homer LeBlanc, Al Skaar, Tony Burmek,
Dr. Ed Crossman
The National Fresh Water Fishing Hall of Fame
In-Fisherman magazine

Dedication

To my Dad, who taught me how and made my early trips possible;

To my Mom, who never gave up her quest;

To all the wives and children of musky nuts who tolerate the disease;

And to you, the reader, to help fan that small ember or add to the raging fire of desire for more knowledge of the king of fresh water.

Foreword

My first contact with Larry Ramsell came through an exchange of letters several years ago. I was trying to determine what was the largest musky that was caught the previous year and where it was taken. A mutual musky-fishing friend in Wisconsin told me to ask Larry. "If anybody knows, it'll be Larry Ramsell," said my source. He was right.

Not only did Larry know about the top fish that year, he knew what the top ten fish were and from whence they came. And he had this information for many prior years. Which is a bit remarkable when you think about it.

Who knows what the biggest bass caught in any given year were? Or walleye? Or brown trout? Sure, it is well known when a state or world record has been set, but for all those off-years, who has the facts? And who is going to take the time to verify reports and dig out the information that must be known to authenticate such matters?

That's why it surprised me to find an individual who had gone to extreme lengths to document particular aspects of one branch of sport fishing. Particularly since he is somewhat of a layman in the writing, tackle industry, and fisheries science professions.

Since our initial correspondence, Larry and I have come to know one another. We've been together in such diverse places as Ft. Lauderdale, Florida, and Hayward, Wisconsin, and have had many communications on musky fishing, world records, Muskies, Inc., the *Field & Stream* Fishing Contests, and other matters.

Knowing Larry, I think it is apt to describe him as an angling historian. That's a general description. He is foremost a musky fishing/musky lore historian, which is a bit more specific and of direct concern to readers of this book. If the Smithsonian Institution had a branch for musky lore, Larry Ramsell would be the executive director.

I suppose that such work is endearing to Larry, not only because it provides a service to the angling community, but because it is one way in which the mysterious affliction of musky fishing presents itself in him. It is no accident that such words as mania, mystique and fever are often used to describe the obsession of anglers who pursue what is likely the least predictable, least understood freshwater sport fish. It is only natural, given the whims of the fish and the peculiarities of the fishermen, that an assortment of myths, legends, happenings, and unexplainable phenomena, not to mention controversies over large and/or record catches, should be part of the history of this fish, more so than that of any other species.

In the following pages you'll learn about these fascinating bits of lore. You'll learn about the few anglers who stood above their colleagues in an ability to outwit many, and large, muskies. I once wrote that being close not only counts in horseshoes, but also in musky fishing. And while this is true for the majority of musky hunters, history tells us that there have been some successful anglers for whom "close" was not in their vocabulary.

You'll also learn about the fish. And perhaps most important of all, about the values of releasing. As an expert musky angler, Larry Ramsell knows whereof he speaks. As an angling historian he has a perspective on the past and the present that few others can match. I respect his work and the fact that he has produced this valuable contribution to the world of angling literature. This book is destined to be a reference source for many, and I know that after reading it, you will possess a profound affinity for all that is part of the world of musky fishing.

Ken Schultz
Associate Fishing Editor
Field & Stream Magazine

Introduction

While this is a compilation of musky history, it is by no means complete. To do this subject complete justice would take several volumes (I intend to write another book soon). In addition, there is some history being made in the 1990s that cannot be written for one reason or another. This "new" history will find itself in a future update or complete new book.

Readers of the first edition of this book will find many changes as much new information has been added and many additional large muskies have been caught (and some released). During the years since that first edition there have also been several major shake-ups in the hallowed halls of musky records. The stories of many previously-recognized world record muskies now reside in a chapter of their own, Musky Crimes of the Century. In addition, some of the fish that initially were listed as "should have beens" have now been upgraded to their rightful place in musky history.

As was the case with the first edition, my sole purpose for this book is to set the record straight again. I certainly didn't do it for the money I will realize from it, which will barely cover expenses.

Again, one does not write a book of this type, rather one attempts to compile this multitude of facts and information into some semblance of order ... enjoy!

Larry Ramsell

Chapter 1:
The Musky
Mystique

In trying to decide what chapter order to write this Compendium, I thought perhaps it would be a good idea to set the stage by finding out the different viewpoints from over the years that caused anglers to become so interested and excited over this torpedo-shaped fish. I felt it best to include as many viewpoints as possible for two reasons. First, they are all accurate (I love 'em); and second, to reinforce my conviction that the musky has, over the years, created more romance and insanity than any other of mother nature's finny creations!

Just what is this thing called "Musky Mystique?" What is it that turns normal people into maniacs? What is it that causes many anglers to dream of catching a musky, even though they have never ever seen one? Why do outdoor writers consider the musky a glamour fish? As all knowledgeable fishermen know, a musky is a fish governed by the laws of nature, isn't it? Well, maybe yes and maybe no. Let us delve back into the archives starting in the 1920s when musky angling was fast becoming popular, angling equipment was improving, and outdoor writers found an exciting subject to write about and, of course, exaggerate about.

As we proceed through the years, I will use quotes from the writers/musky anglers of the day. Many of the reasons for wanting to pursue King Esox will be similar, but many will also be unique to the angler. All are fascinating. One of the earliest books on musky fishing (if not the earliest) entitled *Muskellunge Fishing* by Ben C. Robinson, in 1925, sees it this way:

> Wherever anglers of the lakes and rivers meet, there you will hear yarns and arguments over *Esox masquinongy*, the musky of the wild northern lakes, and

the rivers of the mid-west and mid-south. muskellunge talk is among anglers as measles among youngsters, and the man who has not had some experience on casting rod and silk line with the "Tiger-Fish," as many delight in calling the pugnacious old warrior of the weed fringes and the windfall of the lake coves, will find that he has yet something to experience before he can well hold up his end with the "gang" in tent, shanty, or on the hotel veranda of the fishing resort.

All of the stories that have come down the watertrails about this eccentric and peppery old warrior of the northland and the Ohio valley of the Great Smokies and other isolated sections — no matter how lurid and highly colored they may seem to be — cannot very well overdo the real characteristics of the muskellunge. Without any doubt, in the mind of the writer, there is no other fresh water game fish that compares with him in pure viciousness and savage brutality as displayed when hooked and played on the proper tackle.

In 1928, William C. Vogt, who was probably the foremost angler of his time. wrote a book called *Bait Casting*. Although he didn't promote the mystique, his writing touches on it, to wit:

One afternoon I had six strikes that would have sent any man's blood rushing to his head ... It was a great thrill to feel those big fish strike the bait. Two of them, however, took hold of it very gently, then held it very still — so that you could hardly realize that a fish had touched the bait. But you got the feeling a real fisherman could never forget when they made the strike.

In his chapter "Muskalonge" in a Doubleday fishing book printed in 1937, Ernest G. Poole had the following to say:

The muskalonge is surely the prize trophy of the pike family to which it belongs. The muskalonge is an exceptionally hard fighter, and without a doubt, puts up the best and toughest battle of the larger, fresh water fishes. I will recall the first muskalonge I ever caught. I had never landed a muskalonge, but was very much interested in them: so much so, that I used to watch and admire an old French Canadian who spent most of his summers on the river and lake. After losing a big musky, Ernie has this to say: Apparently all the fish had to do was open his mouth and let the lure go." This is one of the problems that the bait caster, with light outfit, has to contend with. Unless he can sink the hooks in the hard mouths of the heavier fish, he has very little chance of landing one. Sometimes, however, a fish will sink the hooks into its mouth in its leaping struggles, and a fisherman will have better luck, but one can be sure that no muskalonge will attempt to swallow an artificial lure. Once it puts its teeth into an artificial lure; it apparently can readily tell that the lure is not made for consumption, and will endeavor in every possible way to rid itself of the bait. This is one reason why I consider that the muskalonge is probably one of the sportiest of our fresh water fishes, and in addition to this, I maintain that muskalonge fishermen using light bait-casting equipment get a great run for their money.

I have referred to the muskalonge fisherman as being more or less similar to the big-game hunter who looks forward to getting a record heavy fish for a trophy probably more than do the other types of game fishermen.

In his article "Musky Madness" in June 1942 issue of *Outdoor Life*, John Alden Knight (of solunar tables fame) sees it thusly:

The head of the Esox family is a screwball — but in him it's a virtue. Family traits, more often than not, pass from one generation to the next. Eccentricities of the forefathers often are discernible through-out an entire clan. Great-great grandfathers may have come to an untimely end at the hands of a vigilantes' posse, caught red-handed at horse thievery. His name may have been mentioned in whispered tones — he's held up as the family "horrible example." Even so — little Elmer is almost sure to evidence an early tendency towards the unlawful possession of his playmates' toys. It's too bad. but there it is, and nothing can be done about it.

An outstanding example of the persistence of family traits is found in the Esox family. From the lowliest grass pickerel to the grandiose muskellunge, three outstanding characteristics persist. One and all, they are insatiably hungry, entirely unpredictable, and radically eccentric.

Old man musky, being big, husky enough to be the king of the tribe, has perhaps more opportunity than the others to indulge his whims. His size and armament give him little to fear in the line of natural enemies, so there is almost no caution in his make-up. This lack of fear, combined with a devouring curiosity, may account in part for some of the strange things he does. The fact remains that his capacity for eccentric behavior seems to know no bounds.

In the first place, boats and canoes, oars, paddles, and outboard motors, mean little or nothing to a musky. If he is interested in some new and unusual bait, he will follow it right up to the side of the boat, frequently seizing it as it is lifted from the water. Occasionally, the charge of a musky after a rapidly retrieved bait carries him right into the boat, to the consternation of its occupants. A twenty pounder, in good health and vigor, does not make a comfortable boat companion.

Because of his eccentric behavior, there are few — if any — rules that can be set down for the enlightenment of those who would angle for the musky ...

... Last summer, while fishing in Lower Twin Lake, Wisconsin, my companion let his reel overrun. While clearing the backlash, he allowed his oversize plug to float on the surface about forty feet from the boat. There it sat, motionless, looking more like a piece of pulpwood than anything edible. For no reason evident to us, a monster musky struck it with a savage rush that left a boil in the placid water the size of an automobile. Unfortunately, my friend had his lap full of slack line, and the plug drifted back to the surface before the hook could be set. Meanwhile, mind you, before and after the strike, I had been casting an identical plug over the same water, and reeling rapidly according to custom ... Somewhat nettled at this breach of piscatorial etiquette. I spoke — feelingly and with some well-chosen adjectives to Harvey, the guide.

"That's nothin'," he said. "About a month ago, right here on Lower Twin, an old socker took a smack at a bait that was being lifted out of the water. He missed the bait. but he hit the oar. Knocked it up in the air, out of my hand, and the blade conked me over the head as it came down. You never can tell about muskies. They're just plain daft."

"Another time," he went on. "I was fishin' two men over there by the point. One was casting inshore and the other was fishin' out over the weed bed. A big fella followed a bait out from shore, right up to the boat. Instead of grabbin' that bait, he shot under the boat and nailed the plug that was comin' in from the other side."

The behavior of a musky that follows a bait up to the boat is interesting to watch. Usually the fish will swim directly behind the bait, subjecting it to close scrutiny, Sometimes he will strike it just as it leaves the water. At other times he will turn and swim away as the bait is lifted.

... "Followin' muskies have a tendency to nibble at the tail of a bait, evidently just to see how it tastes." ...

The tendency of a musky to break all the rules is not restricted to his methods of taking a lure. It also shows up in his fight after he has been hooked. When the hooks are first driven home, he usually will start away on a hard, powerful, driving run. To attempt to stop him is usually a tackle-smashing venture. But not always does this run come directly after the strike. Sometimes your musky will sulk, bulldogging against the tension of the rod, as though thinking it over. Look out for these sulkers. Action is likely to come when you least expect it, and a musky is lightning-fast.

Another thing about fighting a musky — you never can tell when you have him licked. Not being afraid of the boat, he will come in right-side-up, only to dart away again just as you think he is surely your prize. Sometimes he'll turn acrobat, and his frantic, twisting, somersaulting jump is something you will think about on a long winter night.

Eccentricity on the part of the fish seems, somehow or other, to be transmitted to the men who fish for him. It may be that a succession of days, where one surprise follows another, has its effect on the mental outlook of the angler. Again, perhaps the size of the fish and the excitement of fishing for him has an influence. Possibly the lack of exact knowledge of a musky's preference in baits or methods may have something to do with the angler's frame of mind. The fact remains that musky anglers, as a group. are like no other fishermen I ever met. They also break all the rules.

Of course, there is no trace of agreement among musky anglers. This is true, to a certain extent, of other fishermen, but in a musky camp similarity of ideas goes by the boards completely. Very few salmon or trout anglers will listen intently and sympathetically to the tale of a fish that was hooked and lost. But nearly all musky anglers will give such a story their undivided attention.

Propane tank bearing a musky in Boulder Junction, Wisconsin, the copyrighted "Musky Capital of the World."

Musky "creation" in Nevis, Minnesota.

The big fish in Bena, Minnesota.

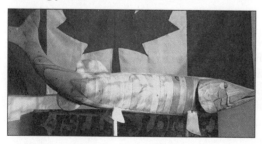

Release trophy from Island Lodge, Eagle Lake, Ontario.

The musky, as idolized throughout Musky Country

A musky carving by famed artist Pablo. It was a Cape Vincent, NY, contest trophy.

Husky the Musky at Kenora, Ontario.

A thirty-seven pound musky was once taken on a newly developed bait, and both the fish and the lure were exhibited outside a tackle shop. Within twelve hours, not a single bait of that variety was available in northern Wisconsin. musky fishing has its grapevine telegraph, and it operates quickly and completely.

The search for the perfect bait leads men to do strange things. Consider

The Musky Mystique

the case of a man who was fishing Chippewa Flowage, Wisconsin, one day last year. The boat near him seemed to be experiencing unusually good luck, having had many fish follow the lure, with three hooked and landed. Inquiry revealed that this boat was using a bait that neither he nor his guide happened to have. Accordingly, he had his guide start the motor and run him back to camp. There he got in his car and drove twelve and-a-half miles to a tackle shop, where he bought one of these perfect lures. Then he drove back to camp — twenty-five miles in all.

Waving the bait triumphantly, he arrived at the fishing grounds, attached the new spoon to a leader, and tossed it over the side of the boat. With feverish eyes he watched it sink out of sight as he picked up his rod. Then he discovered that he had fastened the bait to a leader that was not tied to his line.

The excitement of musky fishing often makes perfectly normal men do queer things. I know a fellow who knocked the bottom out of a guide boat with a hand ax while he was trying to kill a big musky that had followed a bait into the boat.

One fellow at our camp seemed to be particularly keen on musky fishing. His tackle shone resplendently and abundantly in his kit. He started out early and returned late. The spring of his step and the look of intent pleasure on his face was noticeable even in that gathering of enthusiasts. I spoke about him to Harvey.

"He's keen, all right," said Harvey. "The musky bug bit 'im about four years ago. Caught his first one by accident sort of. Seems like he come up here on his vacation. Lives in Missouri and never did much fishin'. After a couple o' days sittin' around, he bought some minnows, hired a boat, and went after panfish. All he had was a cane pole and a short, heavy line.

"Well, he was sittin' there in the boat, catchin' a crappie now and then, when he felt a heavy tug on the line. He reared back and set the hook, but the fish just about out-pulled him. Lucky for him the tackle held together, and he and the musky he'd hooked had quite a time for a while. The only way he knew to land a fish was to yank him into the boat — and a musky don't yank so easy. After a while he got excited and stood up so's he could get a better lift on the fish. He set himself and heaved — and just then the musky jumped. Well, our friend heaved the fish into the boat, alright, but as the musky came in, he went out over the side. After awhile he managed to climb over the end where the musky wasn't. Then he grabbed an oar and hammered the fish with it till it was quiet. They tell me he was the proudest man you ever see when he come in, wringin' wet, at the dock. Right then he started buyin' tackle and fishin' for muskies in earnest. Harvey looked out across the lake and then chuckled to himself. 'I hate to think,' he said, 'just how much that accidental musky has cost him up to now'." (Amen)

In the summer of 1939, two young men came to northern Wisconsin to fish for musky. Luck smiled upon them the first morning. One of them hooked a twenty pounder (estimated by their guide), and after a vigorous fight the fish was brought to boat, where the guide shot it. Away it darted on its last, dying rush. As so often happens, the fish swam in a circle, coming back to the boat. As it passed under the bow, the line caught in the brass sheathing over the prow and the weight of the fish broke the line as though it were a cotton thread. Almost immediately the fish turned on its side, died, and sank from sight. Dead muskies do not float. Now without hesitation, these two youngsters stripped down to their underclothes and went over the side. For nearly three hours they slogged about, up to their ears in muck and weeds, trying to locate the dead fish. Finally the guide prevailed upon them to get back into the boat. Both were blue with cold and had to be given treatment for shock and exposure back at camp.

Not infrequently has it been said that angling enthusiasm often verges on dementia. This — if it is true at all — is especially true of musky anglers. The size of the quarry and the excitement of its pursuit brings out the cave man in all of us. Call it madness if you will; that makes it none the less pleasant. If, in the life of every man, a bit of this musky madness should fall. I'm not at all sure that the world would not be all the better for it.

Yes! Muskies do cause musky fishermen to do strange things; this must be included as part of the mystique!

In 1948, noted musky angler and outdoor writer, Bert Claflin wrote a super book; *Muskie Fishing*. (I have read it about 60 times!) If I were to pull all of Bert's mystique from the book it would take several pages. I feel that part of the preface and part of his chapter "My First Muskie" pretty well covers it:

Millons of persons from all walks of life enjoy fishing with rod and reel, yet many of them have not experienced the great thrill of taking a muskellunge, the king of many lakes and streams, whose savage strikes, fighting ability, and almost unbelievable stamina places him among the first of our freshwater game fishes ...

"Hold him! You've got a musky! Don't give him any slack line!" These words came rapidly from my companion who was more excited than I. The fish was a big one. I wondered if my line would hold him. During the ensuing fifteen minutes I learned much about the fighting ability of a musky, accounts of which I had treated rather lightly theretofore.

Several times the old warrior broke water. Following each leap, he swerved about in a sharp turn and performed other tricks for which his species is noted. There was not an idle moment from the instant he felt the hook until he lay on the surface of the water, exhausted by his violent efforts to free himself. We weighed him that evening. He pulled the scale marker down to twenty-one pounds. Not an unusually large musky, but on my line he felt like a whale.

Capturing this fish, my first musky, marked my transformation from a trout fisherman to a devoted follower of what I believe to be the greatest fresh water fish that swims.

The Musky Mystique

I began fishing when I was not more than ten years of age. It has been my chief hobby from that time. During the years that passed I have caught nearly every species of fish common to the inland lakes and streams of the North American continent.

Up to thirty years ago, most of my angling was confined to taking stream trout with a fly rod. It still has a fascination for me, although I no longer catch as many of the beauties as I did in the golden days before it became necessary to make the long journeys to Canadian waters to find them in sufficient numbers.

Up to the time I landed my first musky, I disdained lake fishing. I had never seen a musky. I had heard tales concerning the size they attained and their fighting qualities, but I considered the accounts greatly exaggerated. The memory of that day will remain green as long as I live.

In 1952 *Outdoor Life* put together a book entitled *Secrets of Successful Fresh Water Fishing*. In the chapter "How to Catch Muskellunge," the mystique comes out as follows:

Persistence counts as much as skill when it comes to catching this elusive game fish ...

The muskellunge, an excellent gamefish, is not widely distributed. For that reason a large proportion of anglers never get a chance at one. Often it would involve an expensive trip to the northern lake country or to Canada, and not everyone can manage it. That' s a shame, because every fisherman deserves at least one musky trip in a lifetime.

I speak from experience. My first musky expedition took place in 1932, after I had saved several years to make it possible, and I've done considerable musky fishing since.

It takes plenty of food and the right kind of habitat to produce large muskies, which may run as heavy as 60 or 80 pounds. You won't find them beside every rock or close to every weed bed. In fact, most of the time you won't find them at all. Even skilled musky fishermen do not get a fish every time they go out. Frequently, Like you or me, they don't even get a strike.

The fact is, musky fishing is extremely unpredictable. You may get one fish in a week of intensive fishing or you may get several in one day. It is not unusual for a musky enthusiast to spend his entire vacation without raising a single fish. Yet the sport is so fascinating he'll be back next year trying again ...

Uncertainty is the key note of musky fishing. Some experienced men say that springtime is the most productive, others favor August, while still others prefer mid autumn before it gets so cold that you can't fish unless you are extremely hardy. Evidently one part of the season is as good as the other — if the fish are in the mood for the taking.

One thing is certain: you should plan to have at least seven full days on the water, from 10 to 14 would be better. A two week stretch should guarantee you at least one fair musky. unless you are very unlucky ...

A Compendium of Musky Angling History

To the initiated, musky fishing in a lake can become very boring. It's a matter of casting hour after hour over places where fish are supposed to be hanging out. Since strikes are infrequent, the beginner may lose interest. But one good tussle can make up for the boredom, especially if you win ...

In his 1953 book, *The Pike Family*, Robert Page Lincoln devoted nearly one half of the book to muskies. In many ways he touched on the mystique. Following are several:

There were six or eight of us sitting on the porch of Calvert's Cedar Island Camp, in Lake of the Woods in western Ontario. For over forty years this camp has been known to fishermen the length and breadth of the continent. To it have come famous men, industrialists, doctors, lawyers, and men from every walk of life. There have been hundreds of them who have come here throughout the years, all attracted as though by a magnet to this outstanding habitat of the muskellunge.

As I have stated above there were six or eight of us: and as was natural the subject being discussed and turned inside out was that of the muskellunge, its habits, its weight, its sub species, its coloration, methods of fishing for it and experiences met with during years of following this great sport. There were some interesting theories propounded. and possibly some questions were answered. Maybe that evening we talked enough to fill a book should a stenographer have been at hand to put down the remarks pro and con ...

Maybe I always have hoped to write something on the subject that could be preserved between book covers, which would probably do half-way justice to the taking of one of our most noble game fishes and which apparently seems to be the least understood. This I will state in regard to the fish, that during all the time you are fishing for it your interest in the pursuit never lags. It never lags because you know full well that any time when you least expect it all hell will seem to have broken loose and a fish of the grey warrior breed will have glommed onto your plug or spoon.lure. There is no slackening in interest when you are musky fishing. Virtually, you have to be on your toes all the time and be prepared for most anything.

As I write these lines I can hear in my memory the waters of a northern lake lapping on a rocky shore. I am casting a heavy duty musky spoon with a ganghook on it masked in red bucktail hair. It hits the water with a splat and is almost instantly started outward as it is reeled toward the boat. It has hardly gone more than a few feet beyond that patch of musky weeds when the big fellow strikes. In fact the impetus of his strike is such that he is carried upward free of the water, a huge fish, one of those remarkable finny creatures that are always a mystery and an endless source of interest.

Yes, there is something about musky fishing that brings you back to it time and time again. In fact you never get enough of musky fishing. If you hook and lose one, you figure that you will come back next year and take another whack at him. And the funny thing about it is that you do come back just as sure as you are at least a foot high. In musky fishing there is intrigue, adventure, uncertainty, never-failing interest, and a magnetic pull on the imagination that will not quell ...

It is doubtful if any fish outside of the tarpon and the Atlantic salmon have been more greatly, even voluminously popularized than the muskellunge, "the tiger musky" and the "grey warrior" that we have heard so much about for the last thirty or forty years. That the fish deserves the need of praise which has been accorded it as a fighter can be taken for granted, as fact. Possibly at times it has its fault and is slow on the draw, as it were, but by and large it is certain that when you are hooked into a lively specimen of the species Esox masquinongy you know that you are on the receiving end of a dramatic and pugnacious battle. You know that the battle is likely to be nip and tuck. Yes, there are chances in plenty that you will lose that fish, and there are many ways in which this can happen. It is for this reason that every avenue of approach to taking this great fish should be weighed and it is knowing these things that one may successfully land the fish of his dreams. But, just as there are men who have fished for tarpon for years without landing one, so are there fishermen who have failed in counting coup on the grey warrior. It just does not seem possible that this can be so, but experience and observation along these lines have proved

*Musky postcard: "One day's catch in Chautauqua Lake circa 1896."
Postcard courtesy Ed Maturek*

the truth of the assertion.

The muskellunge is one of those strange. odd fish that has always been, in the sense of things, mysterious and apart from other fish species. For instance, one can acquire an excellent knowledge of the black bass: in fact, many possess a close acquaintance with the species, but this is not true so far as the muskellunge is concerned. One never really gets to know the fish. They roam the waters in which they are found like a silent menace, rarely being seen, stalking their new prey with all the cunning of a wolf, or lying in wait among the rocks or lily-pads, as the case may be, to fall upon the unwary ....

Its presence seems to be masked from sight, which makes the fish all the more strange and mysterious. Feeding and operating inshore much of the time it goes about its inshore cruising operations with such stealth, in spite of its size, as to practically blot it out from human sight. Bass and other fish you may see now and then, but as a rule you will rarely see the muskellunge in its native haunts. Indeed I have known fishermen in the north who have fished the muskellunge waters year after year and claim they have yet to see the fish alive swimming about ...

There are instances where fishermen in a day of fishing on Lake of the Woods have had as many as thirty muskies follow their lures. An experience of the sort practically leaves the fishermen nerveless as he watches him idly following a lure and inspecting it at close range. I might mention that it is things like this that carry one back to the scene time after time and year after year ...

It was of course the application of the title "tiger musky" to this fish that probably accounted for the fierceness of the fish when in action. While this "tiger" appellation originally applied only to these muskies having the perpendicular stripes, it was not long until all muskies, regardless of the color or markings became "tiger muskies." It only served to give the muskellunge an added and more substantial build-up and increase its prestige among the greatest of all fighting fish to which even the tarpon must take second place ...

Much humor is brought to bear in muskellunge fishing, both in the fishing and in the landing of the fish. One year three fishermen from Texas had come to Mantrap Lake in the Park Rapids region of Minnesota to take what is called in the region a "tiger" musky. I am quite sure that the stories they had heard of the struggle one of these fish puts up had very nearly unnerved them and made them, at the outset, almost incapable of meeting with the famous fish. But they persevered and one day while trolling on the west shore of the lake a musky was hooked. So far, so good. Three men in one boat, with one musky for them to land. How were they to do this? They had read everything extant on how to hook a musky but never once had anyone said anything concrete as to how to land the fish. It seemed obvious that the fish should be gotten into the boat. There was a sand beach right before them, but it never occurred to them that the fish could be beached. They felt, come what may, that they must get the fish into the boat. The sum total of their deliberations was that it would be impossible to land it off the side of the boat, as they would not be able to get the fish in that way anyhow, in which of course they may have been right. It was decided that all three should stand on one edge of the boat thus bringing the gunwale down sufficiently to draw water over the edge, after which the fish, by main strength of the line and manly muscle, could be skidded over the gunwale and so into the boat proper. So far, so good. But when they all stood on the edge something happened and all three fell into the lake. Luckily the water was not deep and the man holding the rod did not let go of it. He did the first thing that entered his mind when he found that he had a footing on the bottom. He held the rod with one hand and the line with the other and made for shore. Once on shore he continued on up into the woods pulling the fish after him. The line didn't snap because it was a thirty-five pound test line. On the return to camp with the fish (which weighed 21 pounds) the three men, well shaken and hardly able to talk and give a coherent description of their experience, had their picture taken with the fish. I believe that six or eight rolls of film were utilized before they were content with the deed.

There is another story of a fellow who brought a shotgun along on the boat to put the quietus to his catch. While the fish was jumping around in the boat the man fired a charge of shot at the head of the fish just as it made a side lunge. The charge missed the fish but blew an aperture in the boat bottom, and very nearly sank the boat. By stuffing his coat or a portion of it in the hole and shouting for help the brave fisherman was rescued from his distressing predicament.

Sid Gordon, in his 1955 book *How to Fish From Top to Bottom*,

Musky postcard: "A record breaking muscallonge caught in Edinboro Lake by T.T. Root. Weight 41 pounds." Postcard courtesy Dan Basore/Historical Fishing Display

A Record Breaking Muscallonge Caught in Edinboro Lake by T. T. Root. Weight 41 Pounds.

lets his title of his chapter on muskies start his view point of the mystique:

Muskies, The Fish of a Million Casts

Little Willie, my obstreperous nine year old whose mother spoils him, refused to go fishing with us yesterday which disturbed me quite a bit. Along about noon, when no musky should be thinking about food, Willie brings the largest musky of the week before the veranda sitters at the resort.

He had picked up an old rod that I wouldn't think of using. Tying on a hook that would hardly hold a sunfish, he put a gob of worms on the hook and threw it in the water at the dock. Something hit and Willie ran for shore, dragging the something up on the sand and then tromped on it. One musky, such as Poppa would have given his eye teeth to land, lay prostrate on the beach.

Two days before that, I.B. Greenhorn, who didn't know the difference between a pole and a rod, nor a musky from a sucker, was out with a guide. He hooked into something that nearly dragged him out of the boat. Greenhorn "drug" back and the horrified guide couldn't even reach for his gaffhook before Greenhorn had heaved the fish into the boat. No play, no science, just another prize musky.

And then there was Schultz, from Milwaukee. He had come up to Hank Koerner's Resort at Rest Lake, Wisconsin. The guides were all busy so Hank took him out. When Schultz tied into a big musky, Hank hustled the boat into open waters. The musky dove and as his huge head and body came out of the water at the stern, he almost drowned the bewildered Schultz with the splash. Schultz paled and his hands trembled like aspen leaves. Hank yelled telling him what to do, but out came Schultz's knife and he cut the line at the reel. Hank almost cried. "Why did you do that? He was a prize winner!"

Schultz leaned back on the seat and calmly said, "Vell, dere is lots of muskies in der vorld, but dere is only von Schultz."

Nothing like that ever happens to me. I have to go out and work for my muskies. I don't pretend to understand them and I have yet to meet a man who I think does. Sure, there are those who know where they are to be found, but as far as men who can take you there and show you how to get a legal size musky any old day like they can lead you to bass or trout in public waters, there just isn't any such person.

Usually the musky is the toughest fish to fool, the hardest to land, and is the greatest prize of all our freshwater fish. You'll find them mostly in the inland lakes and flowages of Wisconsin and from Canada to Kentucky.

Years ago I named him "the fish of a million casts," and rightly so I think. If all your casts and mine and the other fellows' were added up, I am sure we'd find a million casts actually made to each musky landed. But little Willie, Greenhorn and Schultz got theirs on almost the first cast.

I am very sorry that I can suggest no "sure fire" lure for muskies. My personal preference is a large bucktail with two pork strips added, or a feathered spoon. But I have never caught a world champion musky, so you had better use your own judgment as to what to throw at them.

My notes on the lures which they reported had taken muskies tell me not one thing! The lures were so varied from bucktails and spoons to wooden and plastic plugs, all the way to flies on a fly rod, that there is only one bit of advice I can offer the fishermen. Never fish for muskies. Make believe that your musky lure is searching for walleyed pike, northern, bass, or bullheads. Then if a musky happens to hit the particular lure you are using, you'll vouch for it the rest of your days and probably never get another on that same plug. That is why we change lures so often, with our bucktails as first choice.

There is so much confusion among the fishermen that I hesitate to attempt submitting any cut and dried rules, for the muskies will cross me up. I'm sure.

I have seen muskies look with contempt at my lure 20 feet down in a very clear water lake. There they lay, several of them, as immovable as logs and so still that algae formed over their great backs. Under such circumstances I never get excited. What if my hands do tremble while I'm fumbling with the tackle box? The dratted thing sticks, that's all, and I cannot get to my favorite lure. And supposing the wire leader does not snap on the lure at once. No, it isn't my shaking body or my quivering hands. It is the fact that I am looking at those enormous fish, hoping they will not be frightened by the shadow of my boat on that bright July day and go away.

Finally, I allow the boat to drift away from them, and at 50 feet I use a high looping cast to get it down there to them. I'm ready to set the hook instantly at the first touch. No touch, and I comb that spot with everything in that tackle box. Then I give the boat a little kick with the oars and I drift over the con-

Musky postcard: "Landing a muskellonge, Chautauqua Lake, N.Y."
Postcard courtesy Dan Basore/Historical Fishing Display

vention. There they are, the chairman of the board, the president, directors, and the stockholders, but no greeters! With such a dead organization, how do they expect to do business?

Desperately I look at the largest bare hook in the kit and I wish I weren't a good sportsman. I am almost tempted to lower the gang hook and snag the disdainful creatures, especially the 50 to 60 pound chairman. Well, at least I know they are in that lake, and that is something.

This much I can say definitely. Any fish which eats about 30 pounds of other fish in the fall to gain a single pound in weight is no mean adversary for any angler. And when one is caught, once in a million casts, it is like winning a share in the Irish Sweepstakes.

In "Muskies are Mean" by Harry Botsford in the August 1956 issue of *Field & Stream*, a slightly different approach is observed, to wit:

Beyond doubt it was just about the most fervent and eloquent oration I had ever heard. It was delivered by a pillar of the church, noted for his contributions to civic improvement. He was happily married, a devoted father to his two children. His kindness to animals was almost a legend.

His speech was wholly extemporaneous, yet he never hesitated for lack of words, all of them bitter. He stood up in his boat and waved his arms for emphasis. To repeat that speech, word for word, would be downright libel. His climax, delivered with passionate conviction of a camp-meeting evangelist,

Musky postcard: "Chautauqua Lake, N.Y, 28 pound muscallonge."
Postcard courtesy Dan Basore/Historical Fishing Display

summed it all up. "The musky," he declaimed, "is the meanest damned critter that swims in the water."

He had a point. I could have enlarged on it myself, amplified it extensively. He presented his evidence, around a dozen minnows and suckers bitten and partially stripped of flesh. He'd been fishing with live bait, a method of taking muskies that is often successful. It appeared that this particular musky would grab the bait and take the traditional short run. Usually this means that the musky will scale the bait, take a longer run, then swallow it with gluttonous dispatch. But not this one. He was, as most muskellunge are, whimsically cruel. No wonder the man was indignant!

The musky is more than unpredictable. He is the largest freshwater game fish and the most cunning. His strength and agility are amazing. He probably inspires more profanity than any other game fish, yet he also provides great sport. If he smashes valuable tackle, it's usually because he's fighting hard — and against someone who doesn't know how to keep him within ordinary fighting bounds.

At times the muskellunge seems to have murderous malice built in him. He kills or maims ruthlessly. And when he is in that mood he will tackle anything that moves.

I have always believed that a bounty should be paid for big muskies. Their appetites are voracious. Often they kill for the sheer fun of it, and the destruction they can do in an hour is appalling.

Yet the muskellunge has sterling virtues as a game fish. Part of his indubitable charm lies in his size, his cunning and a stamina that is supreme among freshwater game fish. The ruffian is handsome, even though sinister. At times he is as wary and elusive as a brook trout, a fleeting shadow. Again, he will display rare boldness and a rowdy contempt of the angler. I have caught muskies with as many as five rusted hooks in the tough lips, evidence of their fighting ability and cocky willingness to come back for more.

In his book, *Hook, Line and Sinker*, Ralph Seaman decided to do a write up of a musky film he tried to make. The film and the chapter were titled "Musky Fever, a Delightful Disease."

Among veteran musky fishermen, a thirty inch 'lunge is certainly nothing to get excited about. Actually, among old timers, that 'lunge had better be in the forty inch plus bracket or, let's get into the big league, fifty inches plus before the hard bitten boys will begin to sit up and take notice.

On the other hand, to get back to earth, although a thirty inch plus musky may not be a big musky — by regular muskellunge standards — to fishermen who consider anything over, say, three pounds no matter what its species, as a big fish, that thirty inches becomes one whale of a big fish.

Besides, "I caught a musky!" becomes quite a statement to be able to make to the boys back at the office or plant, regardless of the musky's size. And, in addition, as time rolls on, probably the fish will get to be thirty-three, thirty-four or maybe even thirty-six inches in length, with commensurate increase in weight and girth, as the occasion demands!

In setting up plans for "Musky Fever," we decided to make an effort to tell, as far as possible, a realistic story of fishing muskellunge, including the problems, disappointments, frustrations and irritations we were sure to encounter. From our many previous years of having personally fished for this cantankerous fish, we know that thousands of embryonic 'lunge fishermen had a sad concept of what is often required before even one legal musky is caught.

Too many had seen advertisements in the sportsmen's magazines showing pictures of a lucky angler holding aloft a thirty or forty pound muskellunge, with a caption of "Come to Our Lodge For Giant Muskies." Many ads stated that "Last Year's Record Musky Was Caught in This Area ..."

But much had already been done. Many anglers, their imaginations fired by world record muskies and other impossible dreams of spectacular fish — "You go there," they would say to some friend, "and brother, you'll get a fish on every cast." — They saved their money for the big trip. Then were bitterly disappointed because possibly, in a period of a week's fishing, they saw neither hide nor hair of a muskellunge.

The story goes that these two young chaps, like thousands of others before them, had dreamed of one day trying for these big devils. They read the stories, they gloated over the pictures of thirty, forty, fifty pound muskies held in the hands of proud anglers, they heard about or saw pictures of Louis Spray's sixty-nine and three-quarter pounder (and then Louis had a standing offer to pay anyone 2,500 dollars in cash if he caught a bigger one) — they knew that any record fish in any one year — not necessarily a world's record — was worth a new automobile, a raft of outdoor equipment and a sizeable chunk of cash. So they wrote a number of resorts, finally selected one and in due time arrived, ready to go fishing.

Here, they figured, is where we pick up that new car! Without bothering to unload their various equipment — they merely dumped it unceremoniously into their assigned cabin — they addressed the resort manager. "Now, where do we go to catch one of those forty pound fish?" Just like that!

The resorter gulped, did a double take, but then decided to go along with the gag. "Well, I'll tell you, gentlemen," he said giving the problem his deepest and most solemn consideration, "the twenty-five pounders you'll get right off the dock — they may run a few pounds heavier off the left side of the dock rather than the right side. The thirty pounders you'll have to go out a couple of hundred yards for. The thirty-five pounders will probably require maybe a little more time. You may have to go as far as that point over there about a mile away."

"What about the forty or forty-five pounders?" one of them asked.

The resort manager stroked his chin and pondered deeply. "The forty or forty-five pounders," he told them sagely, "will take a little more time. For them, by all means go out to Pete's Bar."

This sounded like somebody's saloon but wasn't, Pete's Bar (Guide Pete

Peterson had discovered it and held its location a tightly guarded secret for many successful years of musky fishing) is still one of the most heavily fished spots in the Chippewa Flowage, in the Hayward area. "How do we get there?"

He told them the way. "And be sure to weigh your forty-five pounder in when you return," he told them. "You wouldn't want to miss all that dough."

Off they went to Pete's Bar. Casting a Lake Superior lake trout trolling spoon, one of them promptly latched onto a honey of a musky. Just like that. All the other boats rallied 'round to watch the fun. After the chap had the fish on for some time, he yelled to one of the guides in a nearby boat: "I've got a big fish on!" he said, "I'd like to beach him. Where can I beach him?"

"Sorry sir," the guide told him. "There's just no place you can beach him. This entire area is completely filled with stumps and snags. If you take the fish into shore I'll guarantee you'll lose him."

"Gosh! What'll I do then?"

"Do you want me to get into your boat and help you?" the guide suggested, reaching for his forty-five because he already knew the answer.

"Would you, sir?"

The guide changed boats, coached the fellow who followed his instructions

Lou Spray's "reward" poster, mentioned in Ralph Seaman's article.

most carefully and finally the big fish was brought along side, shot and landed. That musky, mounted, may be seen by anyone who visits Herman's Landing on Chippewa Flowage. I saw it next night in a display freezer in Johnson's Bar in Hayward. It was a magnificent fish. It weighed forty-six pounds plus some odd ounces!

The story has it, then, that the big musky, being brought in from the boat at the dock, was tossed carelessly aside onto the grass because the angler said: "I'm going back out to catch a bigger one!"

It might be noted in passing that no one had a camera along!

It was our ambition, in "Musky Fever," to illustrate some of the problems faced by the average angler, not to highlight some dramatic incidents such as we have described. So we did some research on how many casts a man could expect to throw before he caught a musky — any kind of musky. We came up with all kinds of answers, many of them highly conflicting, yet many musky fishermen seemed to feel that, over the long drag of say a week to ten days of solid and intensive casting (trolling with a motor is illegal in Wisconsin and who wants to row a boat?) — averaging between 300 and 600 casts per day, that you might expect some action of one kind or another on the average of once out of every 1,000 casts. Not once in every 1,000 casts, understand, but merely adding up that way over the whole period of your stay.

By "action" we mean that either you or the guide saw a fish, whether or not it was interested in your lure — you had one actually follow the lure — you had one actually make a pass at it — you had one hit it but failed to hook him — you actually hooked one but lost him — or you succeeded in landing one, legal size or not — that's what we mean by "action." Our checkup showed that, once in a 1,000 casts you might produce such action. Yet you might not or you might better that average tremendously.

One chap we talked to, with both he and his wife casting, put out, between them. a thousand casts per day for eight solid days, with not even a smell of action such as we outlined above. So, defeated, they went home. Later in the season they became steamed up again. They returned to the same waters and within the first hour he lost a nice one and shortly after landed an eighteen pounder. Less than an hour later his wife edged him out with a nineteen pounder. Total number of casts between them: probably not in excess of two or three hundred at the most.

In the 1958 book, *Musky Fishing*, by Joseph W. Jackson, a couple of notables were quoted:

Ernest Swift, then executive director, National Wildlife Federation:

Musky fishermen live in a world of their own. They feel that their sport is something special in the realm of fishing, and they have a right to that opinion. I have had zealots of the Rocky Mountains region with their cut-throats, dolly vardens, and rainbows, and the Pacific salmon fishermen ask, "What's a musky?" I felt truly sorry for them.

The Musky Mystique

Musky fishing is something special, in my opinion, very special; possibly because I was raised on it. It is hard work, it takes patience, there will be days of discouragement, and then all at once a month of fishing action will be wrapped up in a day or two, and the hard work and the lean days are forgotten.

Gordon MacQuarrie:

The musky's mean and almost brutal from the day of his birth. He never changes. He's cunning and strong. He's devious and unpredictable. He's "Jack the Ripper" of the inland freshwater lakes and streams of some 16 states and Canada, truly the royalty of his race of fish.

And an unknown angler from Pennsylvania:

That's my dream — a Wisconsin musky on light tackle. My fishing buddy is an FBI man and native of Wisconsin. Every third word he uses is "Wisconsin," and lord willing. someday I'll take him up on his threat to take me out there and scare the daylights out of me in a face-to-face meeting with a fighting, roaring tackle smashing musky.

And sometimes it takes more than an FBI man to catch America's most wanted fish.

Jason Lucas, former angling editor for *Sports Afield* magazine, wrote, "The Mighty Muskellunge" in June 1959. He sees it this way:

The muskellunge is our largest strictly freshwater game fish, and he' s generally considered also the tackle-smashingest. As a desirable trophy to show one's prowess he's been compared to the Kodiak bear. That's all wrong, since anybody with money, the trip and a good guide is about sure to see a Kodiak. But if old King Midas himself were resurrected and took to fishing, all his wealth wouldn't assure him of a fair-sized musky in reasonable time. Thus the

The ultimate musky — the 140-foot long, 4 1/2-story high walk-through musky at the National Fresh Water Fishing Hall of Fame in Hayward, Wisconsin.

musky's trophy value lies not only in his size and fighting qualities but in the grave uncertainties of fishing for him. It's people who fish for muskies who are crazy. And if they're not that way when they begin it, they soon ...

In his article "Musky Fever Strikes," John Scharf sees the mystique (musky fever) as follows after he had a follow from a musky:

"Well," said Bob with a knowing grin, "How do you like musky fishing?"

The truth was, I liked it fine. The musky didn't get hooked, but I was. I had a bad case of musky fever. And, just what is musky fever? Well, my fishing trips used to find me wading the Yellowstone River, casting a No. 10 Adams to rising cutthroats. Closer to home I was perfectly happy catching my limit of bass among the rushes of Minnesota's Lake Minnewaska. Now I spend my vacation time trying to just catch sight of a musky. You will notice I referred to it as just catching sight of a musky! That's musky fever.

Former angling editor of *Outdoor Life*, Wynn Davis, wrote in "Truth About Musky Fishing" in the special hunting issue of that magazine some years ago:

It takes a lot of know-how and a lot of fishing time to land a legal musky. This goes even for the experts fishing the best waters. There are exceptions, of course — times when the big fish seems to go on reckless feeding sprees — but such occasions are so rare they make newspaper headlines. In musky fishing, perhaps more than in any other fresh water angling, the odds favor the patient expert who thoroughly knows the water he's fishing.

Muskies grow big. And the average angler who goes musky fishing, especially the beginner, has a trophy fish in mind. I'd say the odds against a beginner landing a lunker are even greater than the odds against his winning the daily double at any race track in the country.

Only a few individuals, who fish often and hard for muskies in the top waters of the U.S. and Canada, can show records averaging one legal musky for every five or six hours of fishing. For most of us it's 100 hours, more or less.

Why in face of such odds, do so many fish for muskies? I think it's because these fish are a special challenge. We yearn for things rare and hard to obtain. Many men would rather spend a week or two fishing for the chance of landing one good musky than fish where they could land 100 or more good bass or trout in less than half that time.

In the 1961 book, *Muskie Fever*, by Bob Pinkowski, the mystique starts right out on the jacket write up by the editor quoting Bob ...

"Of all the game-fish that roam the fresh waters of this continent, the mighty muskellunge has been the center of more ridicule and disease than any other species," states Bob Pinkowski in his fascinating *Muskie Fever*. The disease is known as "Muskie Fever" and frequently becomes so virulent as to be incurable. Once you've fished for musky, you'll never go back to fishing for anything else. You've caught the Muskie Fever and you've started the most exciting fishing experience of your life. Muskies are real challenges to any fishermen. They are bold and temperamental. They have tricks that even the best of the other game fish haven't learned. Muskies are hard to hook for they have boney jaws and a habit of never taking the hook well. They are wily and will follow the bait for minutes, their mouth just two inches beyond the lure, and soon as they see the fishermen's shadow, they turn and swim away, their colorful bodies flashing in the sun.

In Pinkowski's chapter, "The Disease Takes Hold," the mystique is further promoted:

The "disease" is commonly diagnosed as "Muskie Fever," and, brother, when you contract it, you've had it — usually for life. Once a musky fisherman, always a musky fisherman. Such is usually the case, for this mad battler can get a guy so roiled up that he loses his appetite and can't sleep. Such was the case of this writer immediately after he encountered his first 'lunge sixteen years ago.

In Wisconsin, for example, Mr. Musky has created more excitement than did Gypsy Rose Lee when she stripped to her G-string one warm night in Hurley. From dawn on opening day to dusk of the day the season closes, the musky is pursued diligently by thousands of state and nonresident "hunters."

And that's what you have to do, hunt this fish. Unpredictable? He's just like a woman, only worse, when it comes to fraying your nerves. He can drive you mad with his favorite trick, shadowing the bait. And when you see him come cruising up behind your bucktail like a giant, spent torpedo, the adrenaline may fairly shoot through your system. He's the most exciting, this giant freshwater tiger.

Accordingly, the musky is rated first as the prize big game fish throughout the nation. Bass and trout fishermen will cuss you out and argue that pound for pound, either of those two species will outwit a musky. Perhaps they are right. But you forget about this pound for pound hogwash when you fish for musky, for here is a fish with more unadulterated color and legend behind him than Wyatt Earp. Stories of muskies and their capture can make even the most devout smallmouth bass fisherman's hair stand on end.

This bold, game member of the pike family is as temperamental fish as there is. Perhaps that's one of the reasons that will send you back for more, again and again. Nobody that I know understands muskies thoroughly. That takes into consideration the top guides, oldtimers, and even fisheries biologists, who practically sleep with the fish. Everybody says that you've got to keep fishing for them to even get the slightest idea of what they're about to do next. Even where abundant, muskies are full of devilish tricks contrived to drive many fishermen daffy.

In 1962 Bob Pinkowski wrote the chapter, "Fishing for

Muskellunge," in the book *Fishing Secrets of the Experts*. There he added to the above:

> So you are dead set on catching a musky, are you? Brother, have your head examined. It's not the musky that's a maniac, it's the people who fish for them that are nutty. Or if you aren't nutty when you start this game, you'll have a head start over everyone else in a relatively short time.
>
> The musky is a ferocious thing with more glamour than a Hollywood movie star. It is a tricky, temperamental, unpredictable devil that can lure you into a false sense of security by continually following your bait but not striking. And when you have run out of cuss words and are dead tired and ready to throw in the towel, he will hit. And 99 out of 100 times he will catch you napping. You will lose the fish but you will return home with a fish story and vow revenge. You will have contracted the musky bug. There will be no stopping. You will have to whip this insolent dog to save face and erase frustrations.
>
> Getting back briefly to what a musky will eat, and how fast, when he is hungry, try these three stories from the Boulder Junction area for size. They are true:
>
> On slicing open a 23 pound musky just a few hours earlier, a young man and his wife were astounded to find a 24 inch musky inside the larger fish's tummy, which just goes to show you what a large cannibal will tackle when his appetite calls for it.
>
> Here's a case of visa versa, going back on what I said earlier on fishing for muskies with pike minnows early in the season. The opening day at Boulder Lake recently found two anglers working hard — one fishing for walleyes with 4-inch minnows, the other for muskies with a pound sucker. So what happened? The walleye angler got a 42-inch musky, and the musky man got a 10 pound walleye.
>
> Two other men fishing the Boulder area on the same lake, within spitting distance of each other, each had a strike at about the same time. Both set the hook and started to reel in. A few yards short of their respective boats, their lines crossed. No wonder! Both had hooked the same 19 pound musky on opposite sides of the mouth and both on walleye bait of about the same size.
>
> Odd things like outboard motor hub caps, forks, various denominations of small change, key chains, parts which slipped loose from outboard motors, Langley De Liars, a man's wedding ring, a woman's bracelet, along with other goofy items have been discovered in musky stomachs.
>
> I personally am waiting for the day I'll catch one of these gluttons with a bottle of Canadian Club in its belly so that I can work off the frustrations encountered thus far.

In his 1962 book, *Man Against Musky*, Howard Levy starts things off right in the dedication:

> This book is not dedicated to any one individual, but is, instead, dedicat-

ed to a group of individuals — men who spend hundreds of hours, some of them lonely, some of them filled with the greatest of thrills — hours in the darkness of a frosty fall night, in drenching rain, on wind whipped waves and in the unrelenting glare of a hot summer sun, seeking a strike from the King — The Muskellunge ...

... Yes, we musky fishermen know just how exclusive the fraternity really is and just how tough it is to join it. Race, creed, color, sex, social standing, and college degrees have no bearing on the requirements for this fraternity. And though we musky fishermen spend hundreds and hundreds of hours without success, waiting for that bid to come, and though we may be wary and oft times disgusted, still we carry on knowing that the fish are here and that the very next minutes may be our time for the fraternity rushing to commence. I say the fraternity rushing, for even after the strike is made, you still must prove your mettle before the fish is finally boated and your fraternity pin is handed you.

In the article, "The Musky Fever Strikes," by Byron Dalrymple in the June 1962 *Fishing World*, the mystique is disguised as musky fever, to wit:

But the first thing one must learn about muskellunge fishing is that there is no such thing as "orthodox." There are, to be sure, patterns that muskellunge follow, general behavior patterns. But muskies are, just as they've long been advertised, most particular characters. That is undoubtedly what lends them such awesome appeal.

You can, for example, find a place where walleyes are feeding and you can take one on every cast, if you do exactly what you did every time. But you have difficulty even determining when muskellunge are feeding, if indeed they do all feed on the same day, and once you have found one feeding, he may not react at all like the last one you enticed into biting. And that is why the "musky fever" hits so many anglers so severely. When there is something you just can't fathom, you simply have to keep trying and trying.

I know at least two anglers from Milwaukee who spent ten consecutive summer vacations up in northern Wisconsin, trying desperately with top notch guides to catch muskies. It was the tenth season that each finally connected. There are undoubtedly hundreds more who experience this: it is an agony like nothing else.

There are some very general rules that can be helpful in bringing the musky fever down to a bearable degree, even if they will not work a complete cure. Some of these I offer here as a palliative to those in dire suffering.

However, the catching of a muskellunge will do not one whit to lower your temperature. It may just be one of the worst things that can happen to you. For even though the one you finally boat may be a poor fighter and come in like a limp rag, still you are addicted. The next time — you just know — will be different.

Erwin A. Bauer gets right to the point in "A Case of Muskellunge Madness" in the October 1963 issue of *Sports Afield*:

> You don't have to be crazy to put up with the labor of musky fishing — but it helps ...
>
> There are many fishes in sweet waters (and many, many more in salt) which are, pound for pound, more game and exciting than the North American muskellunge. The musky isn't especially fast, as game species go, and the brutes do not generate as much horsepower as some other fishes of equal size. Worst of all, they' re not really abundant anywhere — not even in the best musky waters in the best, and highly touted, musky country.
>
> To tell the truth, there are times when musky fishing becomes hard work as well as sport. Eventually every musky fisherman wonders why he isn't somewhere else, casting for some other kind of fish.

Even P.A. Parsons, noted trout angler, had a few words for muskies in his *Complete Book of Fresh Water Fishing*, published in 1963. To quote:

> It is a doughty, stubborn fighter — a grand game fish. Muskies run so large that your tackle should show respect for their size, strength and vicious disposition. Musky fishing is a sport for those with patience. Many men fish for them for years before they land one.

In the book, *Muskie*, by James A. Lind in 1964, we again start right on the dust cover.

> Catching a tiger musky, like bowling a 300 game, or shooting a hole-in-one, is one of the greatest thrills in the world of sports.

The first chapter of *Muskie* continues:

> Consider the unique place this saber-toothed brute reserves entirely for himself among the hundreds of freshwater fish found in North America. He's absolutely alone in his class, a king without a challenger. The legends of the awesome size and savage nature of the muskellunge are not figments of modern fancy. They stretch solidly back through the history of the New World, through the exciting discoveries of French missionaries and furtraders, and into the lore of the Indians who ascribed links with evil spirits to the ferocious fish.
>
> So important is the great game fish to so many people that, for the better or worse, it has completely changed their lives. For some it has taken lives bent like a sunflower toward the dollar and made the world about appear in different perspective. Some, consumed in the passion of the hunt, have lost their happy homes, many have lost their lives while musky fishing. Others have found new and better ones.
>
> Many men, and I am one of them would unhesitantly lay ten thousand

dollars on the line to the man who could truthfully say, "Come with me tomorrow and you will catch the biggest musky in the world." Nor would this be an irreverent disregard for the value of money. Such a fish would well be worth its weight in gold.

In the 1969 book, *The Muskie Hook*, by Peter Zachary Cohen, the mystique comes forth:

Mr. Grilfurth, the banker from Oklahoma, has been coming to the Inn every year since before Aaron was born — for fifteen years — and he'd caught eleven muskies, mostly with spoons. But he could stay for a whole month in the fall when the water was low and the natural food in the bays were scarce. He fished all of every possible day. His skin grew sandpapery, for the fall days could be as raw as the springtime. The man had fished, Aaron had noticed, feeling embarrassed, over four hundred days for nothing.

"But you haven't counted the five times they've broken my line, and the twenty two times I've seen them charge my bait Eighteen times they've struck at my bait and missed," Mr. Grilfurth had laughed, as he spoke.

One man with thick grey hair had said he'd saved for three years to come fish for muskies for two weeks. Aaron could remember him standing on the lawn of the Inn and crying plainly in the lamplight after his day last darkened and he'd come in without a catch. Other people had gotten angry and not returned. Then new people always came, wanting to try.

But Aaron was more and more uncomfortable living where grown men cried, or bragged of fights they had lost. And where it didn't bother his father or his brother to go out day after day and come back empty and take pay for finding nothing.

"The musky is king," his father would say, "and a king doesn't come to town very often."

In the June 1970 *Sports Afield*, Homer Circle even had an article entitled "The Musky Mystique."

Some fishing is addiction; this sport is an obsession.

What is there about that miserable muskellunge that compels so many fishermen to travel so far, spend so much money, and fish so hard to catch a few?

Some call it madness, but I call it the Musky Mystique. It's an obvious and mysterious fanaticism that blinds a comparatively small but dedicated band of fishermen to this hardest of all fish to catch.

How hard are they to catch?

Well, what other fishing do you know of where fishermen measure a day's success by the number of follows they had, not by the number of fish caught? I have listened to one musky fisherman after another tell in detail just what took place as each "follower" stalked, but refused their lures. And not one of these men caught a fish.

I talked with one school teacher who had been fishing muskies for over 27 years, and had caught a grand total of 13. He was unquestionably satisfied to spend each year's vacation period pursuing this will-o'-the-wisp, and settle for one musky every other year.

"Why?" I asked.

"Well, I'd rather catch one musky than a hundred other fish," he replied.

"Why?" I persisted.

"Oh, I dunno. Anybody can catch bass, perch, pike and walleyes. But a musky ... well, when you bring in one you can tell the way people look at it — it's something special. It's an accomplishment. I feel great when I catch one, that's all."

Yep. I thought. He gets to feel "great" once each two years. What a fish, to do this to a guy and make him like it. And yet, this teacher's record was far above the average musky fisherman.

And surveys show that a bare ten percent of fishermen buy a license to fish for muskellunge only. But, what a loyal, unilateral, fervent, dedicated, opinionated, hell-bent-for musky ten percent this is.

A normal fisherman can't be expected to understand or accept the abnormal attachment these narrow gauged nuts have for this fiendish fish. I won't join them because I enjoy too much the challenges that come from each sporting species.

But, I'll tell you this. I could become one of them.

Again why? Well, let me digress a bit to draw an analogy for you.

To me a musky is much like a house cat. I know no animal that appears to hold humans in such contempt despite their solicitous ministrations to it. When a cat is hungry the owner is the object of its attention, affection, leg-rubbing and meowing. Once that feline is fed, it couldn't care less about the existence of humans. And yet, millions of households wouldn't be without one. A fascination is there that's impossible for a noncat man to accept, but it's there, friend, it's there.

So it is with musky malaise. Being a dog man, I can't rationalize the cats for you. But, being a fishing man, I believe I can analyze this musky mystique because it has come close to grabbing me.

You might catch a musky. The odds are against it, so be sure to look surprised if you do. Then, again you could latch onto a world record. That's those miserable muskies for you.

But whether you catch one or not, these's always that certain inexplicable, deep down, inner urging that stirs in your loins each year when you start looking over your tackle. As you finger those outsize lures, your mind flicks back to that monster that followed six times, but never unlocking its jaws.

You wonder. Is he still there? Would he take it this year? And you start checking the calendar with a feverish glint in your eyes.

Some call it madness. I call it Musky Mystique.

The Musky Mystique

Tom McNally wrote "Mania for Muskies" a few years ago. Some quotes:

There are two kinds of freshwater fishermen: those who fish for muskies. and those who don't.

The muskellunge has been cussed and discussed from Canada to the Mississippi Valley. Arguments for and against "Old Needlenose" rise in executive suites and over back yard fences. Nothing is ever resolved by such debates except possibly all agree that "once a musky fisherman, always a musky fisherman!"

One day following some great bass fishing on Lac Courte Oreilles near Hayward. Wisconsin, Bill Weaver and I strolled down to the dock. A lone fisherman was just pulling in. He had the most elaborate tackle I ever saw. as well as the longest face I ever saw on a fisherman.

"Any luck?" Bill asked.

"Naw!" snarled the incoming angler. "Fished all day. Started before sun-up. Not one lousy strike."

"That's funny." I said. "Bill and I got a couple dozen smallmouths apiece."

"Smallmouths!!!" roared the unhappy fisherman. "Who the hell wants bass? I'm a musky fisherman."

We learned later that the guy damn well was a "musky fisherman." The camp owner told us that the man had started fishing exclusively for muskies 10 years ago. Each season he fished for muskies at every opportunity from the day the season opened in May until it closed in November. The guy fished for muskies on week-ends, on holidays. and throughout his three-week annual vacation. In those 10 years our wild-eyed "musky fisherman" had caught a total of three muskies. They weighed 8 1/4 pounds. 11 pounds and 13 1/2 pounds. That's a total of 32 3/4 pounds of musky meat in ten years of angling!

That's how addicted musky fishermen are. They figure the sun rises and sets in the musky bays and nowhere else. They are convinced that in all the world there is only one fish ... *Esox masquinongy*...The Great One, Himself, the Mighty Muskellunge.

Sport fishing (and writing about it) is my business. It has made me a top living for 20 professional years. In the course of my work it has been my duty to fish around the world for all the major gamefish species. But the hardest fish of all to catch, in my opinion, is that old Hardhead, the musky.

I've known musky addicts who lost their jobs over musky fishing. One discovered a musky he believed to be a new world's record. He kept trying for the fish day-after-day, long after he was due back at work. Consequently. he lost a top job.

Saddest of all, though, was a friend who lost a wife over musky fishing. His wife used to call my wife and complain that "all he does is run up to lake so-and-so and fish muskies. We never see him because he's always off after muskies. One of these days I'm going to tell him that he'll have to make a choice, either it will be muskies or me."

She did ... And he did ... That's right ... He chose muskies!

In the early 1970s I had the chance to see a beginner, Dennis J. Van Patter, get hooked. He later wrote "A Beginner's View of Musky Fishing." He started it this way:

People have often asked me how I became interested in musky fishing. I answer them quickly and truthfully when I say, "Who knows?" I do remember one fishing trip with my family to Ontario's massive Lake of the Woods on which our resort owner impressed me with stories about muskies being taken off the dock of his Miles Bay Resort. I know I was impressed because I still remember the conversation vividly and I was not older than ten at the time and was not interested in any sort of fishing at all.

The more I think about it and try to remember, the more I am sure that the muskellunge fascinated me first because of the unknown aspect and the powerful stories surrounding him and, of course, because I had never even seen one, much less caught one. So, I read more and learned more and the folklore surrounding this crazy fish amazed me. It does not take a genius to realize the muskies are a prize worth going after ...

Muskies materialize where there was empty water before. They disappear just as mysteriously. They rob the unwary, they tease the righteous. They are the prize of those who know what they are doing — and, every once in a while, those who don' t ...

In the back of his mind everybody wants to catch a musky. It's sort of like getting an Oscar. It takes an exceptional set of circumstances and an exceptional performance by the angler. You have to play your cards just right to get the fish to hit and you have to play your cards just right to get him in ...

If the musky you catch is sublegal in length, there is no question. If he is legal, but not a trophy-sized fish, return him to the water unhurt; although he is good to eat, he is just too exclusive for that kind of fate.

If you have caught a trophy fish, one that is larger than 30 pounds, and you want to have him mounted — fine. You have caught the fish of a lifetime.

Any fish returned unhurt increases the chances that we will always have excellent musky fishing. Maybe there is a message in the fact that muskies are hard to catch. To those who value this type of fishing, no price is too great.

If we are smart, we will be able to fish for muskies into the future. If we use our heads anything is possible. Who knows? I might even catch one. Look out, sonabitches. Here I come.

In *Carte Blanche* magazine, May/June 1971 issue; Norman C. Padgett wrote "The Tiger of Northern Lakes." To quote briefly:

Fishermen catching the magnificent muskellunge must use precautions, stamina, and patience unknown to the anglers of other freshwater fishes. But the successful muskellunge fisherman has the reward of our most treasured trophy fish and an experience not offered by other fishes.

The muskellunge is the most unique, mystifying and dangerous sporting fish of all those which inhabit the lakes and streams of the United States and Canada ...

The famous Homer LeBlanc saw it as musky fever in his book, *Muskie Fishing — Fact and Fancy — Lore and Lures.* To quote:

From my first day of musky fishing. I've fished for them at every opportunity, matter of fact, almost daily. I've neglected business, given up other sports, made a musky widow out of my wife ...

I was a mad musky fisherman with musky fever. However, I'm not alone as there are now hundreds of fishermen with Muskyitis ...

This musky fever or madness is hard to explain, once you've contacted the fever of tying into one of these fresh water tigers, whether you have caught him or not, from then on you' re a goner, you've contracted the fever and you'll find it hard to shake off. Other types of fishing will be more productive, but all you think about is a big musky.

I hope this will serve as a warning. Don't mess with muskies unless you want the thrills of a lifetime. You'll notice I didn't say thrill. Thrills you'll get. buddy, and you'll often dream and see yourself catching a world record musky. There will be times when your wife will be talking to you, you' re in a daze, she may only be a few feet away and you won't hear a thing she says. She will think you are losing your hearing, but you'll only be thinking about musky fishing.

Muskyitis is another such disease, some fishermen actually become muskyholics. Many will never be cured, they become addicted from the day season opens till it closes year after year.

At a musky club meeting, while addressing the group, I said I had come to the conclusion that musky fishermen are crazy. Someone remarked, "You're crazy too, you're one of us." I answered, "Yes, but I make a living at it and besides, I boxed professionally for nine years, what's your excuse?" He answered, "Because I've got Muskyitis."

Here is a different view, written by a Muskies, Inc. member back in November of 1973, entitled "What Muskies and Musky Fishing Means to Me."

It was Labor Day of 1963 that I first became acquainted with musky fishing. and little did I know then that this three-day weekend was to be the start of a new lifestyle for me. It began on that Friday night, sitting around my Uncle Lawrence's kitchen table in Madison, Wisconsin, and I was deep in wondering as to what this talk of tomorrow held in store for me. I kept trying to picture what this "superfish" would look like in my own mind, a fish which had stolen the usual conversation of relatives and converted it into "battle plans" for the following day.

Well, the eleven o'clock p.m. departure time did not bother me in the slightest as I was going to sleep the first 250 miles anyway. However, the talk of cold fronts, feeding periods, structure, wind, etc., that I overheard while trying to close my eyes did manage to arouse some curiosity and make me think to myself. "What's all this crap got to do with catching a fish?"

Five-thirty a.m. Saturday morning came sooner than I had expected, and with eyes half closed I piled out of the car in Park Falls, Wisconsin. and stumbled over to a white freezer on the sidewalk in front of an old building in the center of town. I remember peering over the edge and down inside where I saw fish the likes of which I had never seen before. These were muskies? At last, real visual contact with one of these "creatures" to erase the illusions that I had formed in my mind's eye. The weights I do not remember, but I do recall that they ranged between 32 and 44 inches in length. But the thing that impressed me the most was the eyes of the largest musky. Words fail me even now to describe what I saw when I was 10 years old. The eyes almost seemed to be alive, even though the fish had been dead for hours. They seemed to follow me as I walked around the case. No matter where I stood, they were still staring at me as if I was the cruel person that put him there. I became hypnotized and was perfectly content to just stand there and try to probe into the mind of this fish and understand the message his eyes were trying to convey to me!

Well, I was finally broken out of the trance I was in and headed into a near-by cafe by my father for breakfast before the last 50 miles to the lake where we were to start our expedition in search of a musky of our own.

But from this moment on, as I gazed into the eyes of a musky with my own, the seed was planted in my mind that would eventually make me what I am today. A seed so small and minute that it could not be seen with the most powerful electron microscope, but yet, one that is so powerful that it could mold the destiny, goals, and life of a living human being. This seed, being a highly contagious spore, has implanted itself and grown to the point that it has completely possessed my way of thinking so that the thought of muskies and musky fishing outweighs everything else combined! There has been a name tacked on to this disease that hits people the way it has myself, it is called "musky fever" by some, or "musky mania" by others. But, either way, it is an "itch" that just has to be scratched!

Why has this fish "possessed" me in the way and magnitude it has? Only "eye of the musky" knows the answer to that question, and that is one secret that is likely to never be learned. And that "eye" also contains the key to unlock the reason for the unusual personality and the "unpredictable" nature of this creature, the undisputed king of fresh-water, the muskellunge! In the meantime, there is no known cure for "musky fever," only temporary relief by making frequent trips can be achieved. This is the only way it can be, till I discover what the mystery or the secret of the musky's "eye" holds for me. And because of this, I treat the muskellunge as my equal, and when I do defeat him in battle, I'll show him the respect that a warrior of his caliber deserves ... the utmost care and subsequent release alive so that he may realize that I value what he has done for me!

The Musky Mystique

In a segment of his TV show "The Fisherman," Homer Circle asked Tennessee musky record holder, Dr. Hugh Holman, why, if it took him an admitted 70 hours per fish to catch one musky, he fished for them. His reply: "Because it is fun to catch one!"

In *Field & Stream*, February 1977, Jim Bashline put mystique in the title: "How to Catch a Musky Maybe — If you want a sure thing, look somewhere else." The text continued ...

Musky fishing is not a game for the impatient angler. If large stringers of fish, pounds of fillets, and continual action constitutes your idea of piscatorial fun, then you'd best stick to perch, crappies, bass, or party boat fishing. The catching of ten muskies per season puts one into the expert class. Most anglers would do well to catch ten in a lifetime. With muskies being introduced into new waters each year, the odds of catching one are perhaps better today than ever, but it's still a time consuming operation. It isn't that the muskellunge is such a clever creature: it's that the fish is so totally unpredictable. All worthwhile gamefish can be moody and hard to second guess, but the musky has earned the reputation of being the most enigmatic of the lot. Many casting reels have been worn out slinging lures that never get tested on something alive — which is the chief reason that anglers find the musky so intriguing.

The old saw about 10 percent of the anglers catching 90 percent of the fish certainly applies when discussing the muskellunge. In fact, the percentages may be even more lopsided. The anglers who decide to make the pursuit of muskellunge their exclusive fishing avocation could be counted in fractions of 1 percent. Oh sure, there are a lot of fishermen around (like you and me) who periodically decide to concentrate on muskies for a time, but after three or four days of chucking big lures into the cabbage weeds, our thoughts begin to stray. Some other species will give us more action, so we shrug our shoulders and head for other parts of the lake or different scenery entirely.

In spite of the lofty challenge a musky offers, I'm beginning to suspect that there is another advantage gained from pursuing them. At dockside, the angler who has spent the day (or week) fishing for other species is expected to show some results. The anglers within earshot who have spent some time fishing for *esox masquinongy* will immediately understand why our hero has no fish in the boat ...

In his excellent book *Muskie Mania*, Ron Schara devoted the entire first chapter to "The Mystique"; here are a few quotes:

In all of fresh water, there is no other fish like it. Musky!

Even the sound of its name has an urgency, a sense of excitement. To experienced musky hunters. the name symbolizes boldness, strength, jaws of needle-like teeth, obstinance, giantism. And — to many of the same veterans — the name also means ultimate frustrations.

To others the musky is a secretive fantasy, a torpedo-shaped cross between a slinky alligator and a cunning woman, a fish that lurks in watery depths, seldom to he seen.

Nelson Bryant of the *New York Times* once wrote, "Fishing for muskellunge is like writing love letters that are never mailed. Your chances of success are limited but there is pleasure in the ritual."

Yet others see the musky as a bold master of all fresh water, patrolling its domain with but one objective: to combine all smaller fish into one. Itself. And it does. Almost from day one. Hatchery-raised muskies consume thousands of lesser fishes within days. Muskies — 55,000 of them — only two to three inches long have been known to eat as many as 700,000 carp fry in three days.

Its prey must be alive. The musky seldom, if ever, will touch dead food. In fact, muskies will starve rather than scrub the bottom leftovers. With a nickname like "Tiger of the Lakes," would you expect any less?

What's more, fishermen expect nothing from the musky. They contract such things as "Muskyitis," a disease of addition. They'll spend 10 hours a day for a week and call it success if but one musky lands in the boat. Others are happy seeing a "follow" — a musky behind the lure. And still others question whether muskies really exist. A Pennsylvania study once concluded that the average angler — even in a good musky year — spent 75 to 100 hours of fishing to waylay a keeper.

But even those who subdue the real thing cannot contain their nervous excitement. Their eyes do not want to believe. And when it happens it's seldom accidental. You have to chase muskies to catch one. Occasionally panfishermen — particularly in the spring — will tie into a musky quite unintentionally. But such blind luck is definitely not a shortcut to putting a lunker on the wall.

The best fisherman in the country need an average of about 10 hours per fish. And it gets longer if you're not the best. A Minnesota school teacher once admitted fishing for muskies for 27 years and catching 13. But he was happy. For he clearly preferred to take one musky over 100 other fish species.

Of such things are mystiques made.

But what is this fish, the one known as *Esox masquinongy*? Why is this it an obsession to select fishermen? What hold does it have? Noted naturalist writer Jack Denton Scott calls the musky the "greatest prize nature can bestow upon a fisherman."

Bob Hill, a Minnesota angler, once recalled an incident to which a small musky got hooked lightly right at boatside.

The surprised fish leaped, twisted and crash landed into the boat, knocking itself out. Hill weighed the nine pound musky and released it after the fish regained its senses.

"Did I catch a musky? No. But then, they didn't get me either," he said later of the incident.

Why does a fish receive such accolades? The musky is just a fish, you know. Though an impressive one. A long, sloping snout covering a massive set of den-

The Musky Mystique

tures gives rise to a pair of wide set, penetrating eyes. Its large head, representing nearly a fourth of the body length, is flat or even concave on top and of iridescent green. The back is broad and muscular. The remaining body, ranging in color from green-gold to brown-gray or even silvery, is streamlined.

Nature-designed for sudden bursts of speed up to 30 miles per hour, the musky is propelled by a long, and powerful, V-shaped tail.

And to further fool the other fish of the water, the musky is usually camouflaged almost melting into a weed bed. Its body sides contain dark spots or bars on a light background, like so many stems of aquatic pondweed.

The musky even has a nasty grin, helped by a protruding jaw. The grin is real, however, as both jaws hold teeth, including the tongue.

Not even the northern pike, a close relative, is so finely tuned and equipped to dominate its water world. And for sure, no fish demands as much of a fisherman's time. Not only in the water, but in his thoughts and dreams as well.

There's an old rule of thumb: it takes 10,000 casts to catch a musky. Novices chuckle at such an absurd estimate. But novices soon learn. This is one old rule that has more fact than fancy. It is all too accurate. Some grown, rational men and women have spent years of honest searching for a musky. Not days. Years.

Of course, the opposite happens, an occasional musky fisherman will catch a lifetime of memories on the first attempt. But it does no good. The mystique lingers. There always was a bigger musky to catch.

This challenge alone perhaps generates the mystique of the musky. Only two other fish in the fresh water — sturgeon and paddle fish — obtain a larger hulk than a musky. But neither the sturgeon nor the paddlefish possesses its personality and spirit. The musky wins hands down on all the attributes that turns normal anglers into bumbling idiots.

The fish is curious but cautious. You can see a dozen muskies in an hour and come home empty-handed. Pro-fisherman Gary Roach, of the Lindy-Little Joe tackle makers, and I once raised 23 muskies in an afternoon on Wisconsin's Deer Lake. Yet we only hooked three. And two of those spit the treble hooks.

Muskies almost seem to enjoy following lures or plugs. Like it was a game. So much so that the measure of an angler's prowess is often counted in 'follows.'

But do not think it's foolish. If you can't catch a musky, the next best thing is seeing one. Few other fish have the nerve to trail an angler's lure to the boat, then stare at the source of the false meal. It almost appears as if the musky had a hunch the fishy-looking plug was a fake. And as the clever fish sinks slowly out of sight, it appears to say, "I thought so."

Meanwhile, on the surface, the angler, momentarily shocked at the sight, goes into a dither and awkwardly thrashes his lure in crazy figure-8 patterns. He's hoping the musky will reconsider, the musky seldom does.

I do not know why muskies exhibit such bad habits. And I hope no one ever does. To see a long, dark shadow with greenlike penetrating eyes trail inches behind your ready hook is a breathtaking, heart-stopping, knee-shaking, one hell of an experience.

Perhaps, above all else, it is the musky's elusiveness, the close follows, the near misses, the massive sizes that make musky fishing for most addicts.

But whatever the ingredients, the musky mystique is real. It exists in the minds of the muskies' adversaries, the fishermen. And it will continue to exist far beyond the day when each angler has made his own last cast, beyond the day when the smartest musky falls to a hook.

For in the end, and through eternal memories, the musky does it all: It can snap 30 pound monofilament the way the wind parts a twig, or it can fall to the delicate strength of an ultra-light rod and reel.

It will leap like an ornery marlin or dive like a sluggish catfish.

It will strike at high noon in a blinding sun or clobber a muskrat by the light of the midnight moon.

It will pulverize a plug on the surface or inhale a jig at 80 foot depths. It will thrive in lakeshore weedbeds or lurk in river's boulders. It will fight like an alley cat or surrender like a watered log.

But of such things is the mystique made. For every angler who has ever tossed a musky plug will come away impressed. He may become an addict. He may become bored. He may become exhausted or uncontrollably ecstatic. He may wish he'd never heard of a musky. Or he may regret not having met such a fish earlier in life.

Whatever, the fisherman will feel something about this magnificent pike, good or bad, sad or happy. And for that, generations of fishermen yet to come can be assured that the mystique of the musky will live on. And that my angling fellows, is good.

In August, 1977, I introduced my friend, Bruce Hopping, to muskies. He was hooked. I asked him why. His answer:

Why — I've been on only one musky trip with you — and here's what I felt.

18 hours of driving from my home in Galesburg, Illinois, to Eagle Lake, Ontario. My wife telling me how beautiful the scenery was and how nuts I am.

Going from the car to the boat in 20 minutes after arriving — Larry had already arrived.

Larry throwing me out of his boat with my 6 1/2 foot spincast outfit. Then giving me a rod that I could pole vault with and a winch of a reel with rope on it for me. Amazing how well they cast after a little practice.

3 days of practice — using plugs bigger than most fish I normally catch — into wet, windy, miserable conditions.

Learning to watch for the follow, and trying to master the figure-8.

Sore arms and back, blistered hands, but no fish of my own.

The good company, food, drink and stories and strategies of the evening before an early bedtime.

The Musky Mystique

One fish in 3 days of a million casts that Larry hooked, it jumped, was landed, measured and released all in about 30 seconds, but I can still tell you the exact color, time of day, and location of that fish. Unreal! And, oh yes, Larry's exclamation of "Musky! Son of a bitch!" At first I thought he had completely flipped out on me. Then I saw the fish — Magnificent!

Am I complaining? Maybe a little. Will I go back? You bet! Because with every cast my muscles tense in anticipation, with every strike my heart stops. Is this a musky? Larry tells me there won't be any doubt when that happens, but I've got to know that feeling.

In his "Travel" column in the June, 1978, *Sports Afield*, Robert Deindorfer helps mystify the 'lunge:

The musky happens to be considerably more than a fish. It's a gamester, a gargoyle, a meal, a trophy, a stew, a status symbol, and a bidding flutter of folklore, as well as America's biggest, most belligerent fresh water sportfish.

Along with everything else, the musky — Old Dynamite — suits our chronic sense of bigness. This fish isn't even legal unless it measures at least 30 inches, which would set the church bells ringing if it were a trout or bigmouth bass. At 69 pounds 11 ounces and 5 feet 3 1/2 inches, the existing world record somewhat exceeds the dimensions of my ten-year-old boy, who sometimes has to be carefully played himself, come to think of it.

The musky is always the topic of conversation for driven people who gather together at the bar in resorts. Sooner or later, they're likely to get around to talking of epic fish hooked, hooked and broken off, fish so familiar they've been given nicknames: Simple Simon and Dirty Ernie. that don't yet measure up to a new world record: Buckets and Big George, that, at an estimated 75 to 80 pounds. emphatically do, if and when someone hooks them with a gaff as well as a bucktail combination.

A tidbit from John Powers is a brief mention of musky from the book, *A Fisherman's Summer in Canada* by F. G. Aflalo, published in London, England in 1911:

The muskallonge is taken trolling; more often indeed. it is not taken at all though a fish of 19 pounds which I saw killed right opposite the camp within ten minutes of my arrival promised the realization of my ambition to kill one of these leaping pike, a dream still unfulfilled. The troll in general use is a frightful hors d' oeuvre which mav he purchased at Boyd's in Montreal, at prices ranging between half a dollar and a dollar; according to size. It consists of an enormous red and silver spoon (or of two, dressed tandem fashion) revolving about a brass bar and by way of garnishing, with a huge triangle dressed in red and white feathers As if this omelet of imitation food were not enough it is usual to hang a frog or a pound white perch on the triangle the whole forming surely the most appalling lure used in fresh water This is trolled slowly up and down the rocky shore and particularly round the edge of bays overgrown with reeds and the muskallonge dashes out and swallows the whole thing after which it heads for the horizon and puts up a wonderful fight. There can be no doubt about the sporting qualities of the 'lunge, as Americans usually call it, and one of 38 pounds was caught at Pickerel in 1909, which I saw in the C.P.R. pavilion at the Toronto Exhibition. One party of six rods took twenty-five of these monsters in a week's fishing this summer eight miles above Fenton's Camp.

The mystique has even captured well known personalities such as President Dwight D. Eisenhower and his brothers, Gypsy Rose Lee, Ted Williams, and Gunsmoke's "Doc" and "Festus" (Milburn Stone and Ken Curtis).

After pulling together and rereading the previous quotes, I again ask, "What the hell is the musky mystique? What is the magnet of mystique in my mind? Just what is it that has caused me to pursue muskies, almost exclusively, for over four decades throughout 12 states and two provinces of Canada? During which time I have guided many anglers to their first legal musky and have introduced many others to the sport. In all instances I have prewarned them of the possibility of contracting Musky Fever.

I know that Al and Ron Lindner of *In-Fisherman* magazine think the musky is just a fish and is governed by the laws of nature just as are other species. They are controlled by demands for food, protection and reproduction. As an *In-Fisherman*, I too should think this way, but I know, as a musky fisherman for these many years, that It just ain't so! I feel that I keep abreast of new techniques, methods and waters as closely as anyone. I'm not too hard-headed to try something new. But just when you think you have it figured, the SOBs put you in your place — again! In several seasons I spent literally hundreds of hours on the best waters in North America and had my poorest fish/hour average ever! Granted, I was concentrating on trophy size fish, but I should have "stumbled" into a few more than I did.

I defy anyone, including Al and Ron, to put a legal musky in the boat on any given day. In fact, I would be willing to put anyone on one of my favorite lakes (one of the best in North America) and defy them to average one legal musky every three days throughout the season! Granted they sometimes come in "bunches" like one three hour period that "Lucky" Jack Klein and I experienced when we caught six muskies up to 32 pounds, but the overall average is tough.

Is pursuing muskies the ultimate challenge? Yes, it is for me, but the mystique goes even deeper than that. Over the years I have spent thousands of hours researching popular and scientific literature and writing several articles on my findings. If you were to ask my friends they would probably tell you that I live, eat and breathe muskies; I often think that I get more enjoyment out of the damn critters reading about them and their colorful history than I do in the actual pursuit. Let's face it, if you fish intentionally for muskies, it is darn hard work. The stories and previous quotes you have read about spending long hard hours to even catch a small musky are true; I know, I have been there many, many times! On the other hand, I have, as I did Sunday, May 28, 1978, gone out and got one right away (second cast). Another time after arriving at the fishing grounds, I dropped my lure in the water in readiness preparation, and had an immediate strike! An exception to the rule? No. I don't think so, for you see, muskies have no rules. They do as they damn well please and when they please! Many times, after long, hard and discouraging hours; just when you wonder, "What in the hell am I doing out here beating my brains out?", one will follow or roll or strike and maybe (once in a while) even jump on ... often it is just enough to tease you into continuing to be a musky maniac and usually will cause you to stay and cast just a little longer.

Don't get me wrong. There are lakes where just about anyone can go and catch a musky, but almost exclusively smaller non-trophy fish and there is still no guarantee on a given day.

My conclusion is that the mystique is many things in combination, but nothing concrete.

Chapter 2:
Record Muskies?

The Could-Have-Beens, Should-Have-Beens, Might-Have-Beens, Legends and Hoaxes

O ne of my favorite pastimes in the slow part of the musky season (there is no off- season when you consider the possibilities of the expanded musky range in the east and south) is to dig through the archives of the old musky literature. Particularly favorite times are prior to 1911 when no formal records were kept, as well as the early days of record keeping (1911-1940) when several record size fish were taken, but due to one reason or another never made the "official" record list. I marvel at the legends as well as the verified tales. The legends often have much imagination, but the sad tales are the near misses. Most often angler ignorance in record application procedures (certification of scales, etc.) was the primary cause of record fish not being accepted, but failure to enter the *Field & Stream* contest also prevented the fish from making the official list. As we travel back in time, I will give you as much information as is available to me on each fish. Undoubtedly I will miss a few and lack full information on others. I will go back and start in 1774. I will list the year and if it is a legend, a reference, not verified not sport caught or just a plain hoax.

Although no sizes were mentioned, one of the earliest references, credited to Jones in 1774 and Scott 1793-1794, referred to "prodigious large pike" and stated that they were taken by spearing. In 1788 there was supposedly a 4th of July celebration in Ohio with the main dining attraction a baked 100-pound musky that had been netted in the Muskingum River (a legend from *Muskie Mania* by Ron Schara.)

From the National Fresh Water Fishing Hall of Fame comes the following:

"Would You Believe Five Feet?"
(circa-1824)

In the month of February 1823, there were two brothers by the name of Obediah and John Leneve who came to Father's and stayed two days and two nights. When they went home I went with them as they were living near my land. When we got to the Big Vermillion River we saw the ice was froze over the water. There being no snow, the ice was very clear and I saw a large fish start and run. I run after it, and when I could get close to it, I would strike the ice with the poll of my ax that I had taken with me. I kept on till the fish run where the water was shallow. He finally appeared to become weaker, stopped moving and settled down to the bottom of the river.

I then struck several blows over where it laid, as hard as I could strike, to see if it would run or not, but it laid still. So I cut a hole in the ice and throwed the ice out of it. The two Leneve boys stood by the hole watching the fish while I went to cut a sapling. I trimmed the limbs off it and left a hook close to the butt end. Then I came back to the hole, put the pole into the water, snagged the fish by the gill, and drawed it out of the water. When we got him out we saw that it was a pike fish six foot long. That was the largest pike fish I ever caught or saw caught in any way, or by any person, whatever.

Forest and Stream, May 6, 1899 refers to a report from the early 1800s:

In 1815 DeWitt Clinton knew the fish as the Muscalinga, and his account, in the first volume of the Transactions of the Literary and Philosophical Society of New York, published that year, is as follows: "The muscalinga, a species of pike, is greatly esteemed, and is generally caught in rivers emptying into the lakes. It weighs from 10 to 40 pounds and in a few instances 45 pounds, and is generally very fat." This report failed to denote how they were "caught" or if the weights were verified.

In the March 9, 1899 issue of *The American Angler* we find an article on "The Mascalonge" by Emery D. Potter. Mr. Potter refers to his first introduction to this "game fish" as having been in the spring of 1836 at Toledo. A friend of Mr. Potter's was passing the hotel where he was staying, "dragging an immense fish, and carrying a gig or spear ... He said it was a mascalonge, that he had speared it in Swan Creek, a deep, narrow creek entering the Maumee in front of the hotel." Mr. Potter then proceeded to borrow his friend's outfit to try his luck. He went to the creek and "had not waited five minutes," when a large mascalonge approached the bridge where he was standing, "swimming slowly upstream near the surface." The conclusion was inevitable and the fish was taken to the hotel scales, "where it pulled down a little over fifty-six pounds."

The March 18, 1886, issue of *Forest and Stream* refers back to an editorial from *Forest and Stream*, Vol. 1 p. 236:

> The largest (Muscalonge) we have ever heard of is vouched for by our friend S.C. Clark, who says that in 1840 he saw one at the mouth of the Calumet River, Michigan, which had just been captured in a seine, that was six feet long and weighed eighty pounds. The mouth would have admitted a man's leg. It showed a perfect Chevaux defrise of teeth, the canines at least an inch long.

The June 1961 issue of *The Pennsylvania Angler* article on "Record Muscallenge — Fact or Fiction," by Keen Buss gives us the following:

> The Ohio drainage apparently had its share of large 'lunge. Dr. E. Sterling of Cleveland, Ohio, claimed to have speared one of these monsters about the year 1844 which weighed 80 pounds.

For our next three references we go to the book, *The American Angler*, by Thaddius Norris, published in 1864. In his chapter on "The Pike Family," we find a sub-heading entitled "Great Blue Pike" (which is what the mascalonge was known as in Pennsylvania in the mid to late 1800s). Here we find references to two large fish. To quote:

> I have the head of a specimen sent from Meadville, Pennsylvania, in a jar of alcohol, which measures twenty-five inches in circumference; after large slices of it being cut off, to get it into the jar" (Note: the circumference of a 40-pound musky is about 18 inches). It has been taken weighing as much as eighty pounds in Connaught Lake in Bradford County, Pennsylvania.

A further reference to this fish comes from the previously mentioned article by Keen Buss and helps clarify things somewhat regarding where the fish came from:

> In the first place, there is no Connaught Lake in Pennsylvania, nor secondly, there were never any muskellunge in Bradford County as now constituted. However, checking through history, one finds that Bradford County once extended as far west as what is now known as Conneaut Lake, which is still famous for its muskies. (Note: This lake still holds the official Pennsylvania record of 54 pounds 3 ounces) One of the stories alluded to, I heard many years

ago (prior to 1864) when detained at Wheeling, Virginia (Note: Wheeling was in Virginia at the time), waiting for the Cincinnati Packet. It was from the hostler of the hotel opposite the Steamboat landing. He told me that the proprietor, who was then on a fishing excursion to the Kanawha, on a former trip had taken a pike which reached clear across the dining table, after its head and tail were cut off; and that it was necessary to have a tin boiler made expressly to cook it.

It is interesting to note that many of the areas being referenced for big muskies no longer have muskies to any degree or size. Primary blame, I believe, can be attributed to man. The next two areas referenced are a perfect example. The May 14, 1891, issue of *Forest and Stream*, among the large examples recorded are the following:

In 1864 Mr. Fred Alvord announced his capture of a specimen in Maumee Bay (Ohio) which weighed 85 pounds and in 1865 Mr. Schultz claimed to have seined a muscalonge in the old harbor at Milwaukee weighing 100 pounds. The species reaches a length of 8 ft. and individuals weighing 50 pounds are moderately common.

This may have appeared to be the case in the 1800s but as I detail in a later chapter, Big Muskies: When? Where? and Why?, 50-pound and larger muskies are, and have been rare for many years!

According to Clark:

The Annual Report of the Ohio Fish Commission for the year 1873 states that before the erection of the state dam in the Scioto River, a few miles below Chillicothe, anglers frequently took pike (muskellunge) weighing 30 to 40 pounds from the Scioto.

Next we move to Quebec. In his story, "Fishing on the Ottawa (No. 3)," W.T. (some used only initials in those days) in *The American Field* of October 18, 1884, makes reference to a muskallonge (*Esox nobilion* — one of the many scientific names used in early days) nearly 50 pounds that was caught from the Ottawa River in 1876. This is one of the earliest references to large sport caught muskies.

Back once again to an area now devoid of muskies. In *An Annotated Bibliography of the Muskellunge*, by Crossman and Goodchild,1978, we find an annotation on a 1927 paper entitled "An Ecological Study of Certain Southern Wisconsin Fishes" by A.R. Cahn. The annotation reads:

The muskellunge has been extinct in the Oconomowoc-Waukesha Lake district of Southern Wisconsin for the last 30 years but there is little doubt that it once occurred in the Fox River. A 40-pound individual was caught in 1877.

From *Forest and Stream*, March 18, 1886, comes the following:

Forest and Stream, Vol. XI, page 324 "A Monster Muscalonge" Bellevue, Ontario, Nov. 12, 1878 — This morning (Tuesday, Nov. 11) the largest muscalonge ever captured in the Bay of Quinte, (north shore of Lake Ontario) and probably one of the largest ever caught in fresh water, was taken in a seine near Bellville. I personally measured the fish and found its dimensions to be as follows: Length, from tip of nose to end of tail, 5 feet 4 inches; girth at thickest part (after a five-pound pickerel had been taken from its stomach) 26 1/4 inches; weight 52 pounds.

In the chapter "The Technique of Fishing" from the book *The Picturesque St. Lawrence River*, printed in 1895, I found a reference to a fish caught by a young girl which could be construed as the first woman's world record. To quote:

A most unusual occurrence I would like to place on record. In August, 1883, Miss Annie Lee, at the time eleven years of age, while trolling near Clayton for bass, with a No. 3 gold fluted spoon, which size is fitted with a No. 2 hook, struck and successfully brought to boat a muscalonge weighing thirty-six pounds, measuring four feet six inches in length. In the effort to secure this large fish the guide's gaff was broken, showing the enormous strength of the fish, yet it was finally secured, brought in and exhibited with those slight hooks still fast in its capacious mouth — an evidence not only of good tackle, but of skillful handling. (See photo in Chapter 4.)

In the same aforementioned book, I found some nice pictures of angler-caught muskellunge (on Page 55). These are the first pre-1900 musky pictures I have been able to locate and date. I would sure like to know the weight of the fish in the picture with the lady! Undoubtedly it was record class!

We now return to "Fishing on the Ottawa" by W.T. in the October 4, and October 18, 1884 editions of *The American Field*. On this trip W.T. took a musky of 40 pounds a short distance downstream from Ft. William and one of 41 1/4 pounds at the mouth of the Conlonge River, which flows from the north in Quebec discharging into the Ottawa (ten miles from the Noye River). It was caught on a spoon and hand line.

Record Muskies?

James H. Manning of Albany, NY, with a 37-pound, 54-inch St. Lawrence River musky (Holiday Bay) caught Aug. 31, 1885. The fish had a 19-inch girth.

A nice 45-pound musky and possible world record contender when caught, sometime before 1885, from the St. Lawrence River.

Lady captor and her prize — undoubtedly another record class fish from the St. Lawrence River before 1885.

The July 1, 1886 issue of *The American Angler* brought forth a very controversial letter written by General J. Garrard which helped at the time to add confusion to not only the various strains of muskies, but also to the scientific nomenclature. In fact, he was of the opinion that the unmarked muskies:

... from the headwaters of the Ohio to the headwaters of the Wisconsin differs from the mascalonge very distinctly in several important characteristics ... This is the fish that has just and rightful claim to the name of great northern pike ... There is fairly reliable authority that one was taken two years ago (1884) in Lake Courte Oreilles, headwaters of the Chippewa, that weighed 110 pounds. Those of 30 to 80 pounds are freely spoken of as common in the lakes of the Wisconsin pineries. In the parlance of a hunter who camps in those woods "They are as big as a man." In comparison with this grand fish the spotted pickerel, *Esox lucius*, with its maximum weight of about 38 pounds has but small pretensions to this name of "great northern pike" which is usually given to it by the writers of books.

What Garrard was trying to do was establish the Wisconsin musky as a separate species in a niche between the St. Lawrence spotted musky and the pike, *Esox lucius*. In my opinion, the slow communications of the late 1800s helped add to the overall confusion, and even yet today, many of the errors of that day have many people confused.

The next few references will point out the need for, and lack of, record keeping in the early days of musky angling. The September 12, 1885, issue of *The American Angler* carried a short story entitled "A Monster Mascalonge":

We had a pleasant call last Saturday from Mr. James T. Story, of Albany, who has added to our piscatorial picture gallery a photograph of the immense mascalonge (*Esox nobilior*) he had the good luck to capture in the St. Lawrence River, opposite Clayton, N.Y., on October 5th, 1884. We have no record of the catch of any larger St. Lawrence musky. We should like to hear from any fisherman who claims to have captured a bigger one. Mr. Story' s prize measured 56 1 /2 inches in length and 24 inches in girth, and weighed 46 pounds. He had out 260 feet of line, in 70 feet of water. when the fish struck and only a 2/0 triple hook below the spoon. The hooks were fastened in one corner of the fish's mouth. The photo Mr. Story left with us is an excellent one, which we would be pleased to have our angling friends inspect.

While penning these lines a letter has been received from Charles A. Walradt, Secretary and Treasurer Theresa Fish and Game Club, reporting the catch last Saturday, by Wm. Sharp. in the Indian River, of a mascalonge weighing 35 3/4 pounds — a larger fish for that stream than Mr. Story' s 46-pounder was for the St. Lawrence. It will undoubtedly be many years before either record will be raised.

In the September 26, 1885 issue a follow-up story entitled "Error Corrected" by A.N.C. was mentioned as follows:

I did not get *The Angler* before I left home (yesterday), but I find it here on arrival today and upon reading it discover that I must jog your memory. I have a photo of Mr. Story's forty-six pound mascalonge, which *The Angler* thinks to be the largest fish of the species ever caught on the St. Lawrence and it is one of the best fish photos I ever saw, but — if you will search the archives of *The Angler* office, provided there has been no serious upturning of the sanctum during the past few years, I think you will find a photo of a mascallonge caught in the St. Lawrence, near Clayton, by Capt. James Millward and J.B.

Spafford. of New York, that weighed forty-seven pounds. At least I sent you such a photo, and have since seen it in that little room where you keep your shears and paste pot; I refer to the temple in which you display some fine feats of horsemanship when you mount winged Pegasis and jab him in the ribs with a steel pen. A pound more or less of flesh on the bones of a fish that approximates in weight half a hundred pounds can make no earthly or watery difference to the fish, still the angler whose fish is shrunk a pound by figures in type might not exactly bless you. A.N.C.

This still didn't end the problem, though, as the October 21, 1885, issue shows. "Little Indian vs. Big St. Lawrence" by H.H.T:

We called attention in our issue for the 12th ult. to a photograph left at this office by Mr. James T. Story, of Albany, of a forty-six pound mascalonge caught by him in the St. Lawrence River, opposite Clayton, N.Y., and at the same time made mention of another one recently taken in Indian River of thirty-five and three-fourths pounds weight. As we made acquaintance with *Esox nobilior* in the latter streams many years ago and have taken a great number from its waters we felt a little nettled over the superior weight of the St. Lawrence fish, though a comparison of the two rivers as to size would justify the claim that Indian River made the best showing after all. Then our esteemed friend "A.N.C.," who revels in throwing big piscatorial weights at our heads, came to the front with a forty seven pound mascalonge, caught in the St. Lawrence by Captain Millward and J.B. Spafford, a photo of which he had sent to Mr. Harris soon after the capture-see Angler of 26th ult. Of course the one pound better relegated the Albany fish to the background and his back fin seemed to wear an additional droop every time we looked at the photo.

Now something had to be done in behalf of Indian River as against both of these large fish. We descended into our inner consciousness and brought to mind something we had heard from Theresa, N.Y. about a very large mascalonge having been caught below Black Lake two years ago by a man, whose father, Charles P. Ryther, of Ryther & Pringle, Carthage, N.Y., iron founders and machinists, we had known from his boyhood. The letter of inquiry addressed to him was handed over to his son and this is his reply:

H.H.T.

Father handed me yours of the 11th and requested me to answer. As to the exact date I cannot inform you. but it was sometime in the latter part of August 1883. We started from Theresa in the morning and arrived at Black Lake that evening. The day was bright and we only caught three mascalonge, which averaged about eight pounds each. Fishing was said to be better at the foot of the lake, in what is called Lower Indian River. It connects Black Lake with the Oswegatchie River. It was here we caught our prize.

We started from camp about six o'clock in the morning and rowed directly to the point where the Indian and Oswegatchie Rivers unite. Just before reaching the point Mr. H.K. Greene, the gentleman who accompanied me on that trip, exclaimed that he had a heavy.strike, I looked back of the boat and saw a huge mascalonge jump full length out of the water and swim off up the Indian River. He had missed the hook. But his mate was not so lucky. He got hooked and it required good work on our part to keep him from breaking away. First I towed him and then he towed me. We had him well hooked, however, and in about an hour and a half Mr. Green worked him up to the boat and I shot him through the head with a Winchester rifle. We rowed to Heuvelton and from there shipped him to Carthage. At Heuvelton he weighed forty-nine and one half pounds and having been out of the water two hours and bleeding so much as he did when I shot him, I think it safe to put his weight at fifty-one or fifty-two pounds.

We used Chapman's No. 3 pickerel bait and forty feet of ordinary strong linen braided line on a stiff side rod. The fish was a perfect beauty and was free from any marks. He was four and a half feet long, fourteen inches from back to belly and eight inches through the shoulders. Many large ones are caught here every season, but that was the finest one I ever saw. I have fished a great deal in the St. Lawrence and Indian Rivers, but I can positively say that for genuine sport Indian River and Black Lake are by far the better fishing grounds. Geo. D. Ryther Carthage, N.Y. Oct. 24.

The year of 1885 would have to be considered a banner year for big muskies. The July 11,1885, issue of *The American Angler* makes mention of two big muskies to wit:

A fifty-pound mascalonge was caught in Coal Lake, Todd County, Minnesota on June 21, 1885 by Charles Laningsga. (Note: Although not impossible, I have doubts on this one. The Minnesota DNR list of musky waters published 10-16-75 lists Big Swan and Maple Lakes in Todd County but makes no mention of Coal Lake. Perhaps since it is within about 25 miles of the Mississippi River it has/or had access.)

The second mention:

The capture of a forty-five pound mascalonge, measuring over fifty-four inches in length and twenty-two inches in girth, is reported from the Eagle Lakes (area) of Wis. Mr. E. B. Sanders of Wausau, Wis. caught the fish.

The October 10, 1885, issue presents us with the following earth shaker:

Eagle Waters, Wisconsin (via Milwaukee, Lake Shore & Western Railway. H.F. Witcomb, G.P.A., Milwaukee, Wis.) Sept. 9th Mr. Ellwood, from DeKalb, Illinois, in company with Frank Carr as guide, took one mascalonge in Little St. Germain Lake — length 56 1/2 inches, girth 27 1/2 inches. They were unable to weigh him on account of not having a scale that was sufficient to hold the fish — weight was estimated at 60 pounds. He was without doubt the

Record Muskies?

largest mascalonge ever taken in the Eagle Waters.

Comparing the length and girth of that fish against a list of known weights with similar length and girth measurements would put the weight of the above fish nearer to 50 pounds and certainly not over 55 pounds unless the fish was unusually heavy throughout its length. Nevertheless, it had to be a super fish!

Again it's time for the ladies to get in the picture! The October 3, 1885 issue of *The American Angler* makes the mention of a lady angler. Again, under the heading of Eagle Waters, Wisconsin:

> Each of the ladies of the party had the good fortune to hook mascalonge, and with some coaching and little assistance each one killed her fish. Miss Josephine DeMott handled her tackle with skill borne of experience and killed and brought to boat a twenty-five pound mascalonge by an hour's plucky fight, with the coolness of a veteran.

It is interesting to note that these members of the Acme Rod and Gun Club who camped on Stone Lake, made a big issue of sport as evidenced by the following statement:

> The Acmes don't fish with hand line and drag these (fish) into the boat by brute strength. Every mascalonge hooked by us that can beat the steady spring of a 9 ounce rod and gentle persuasion of an F or G silk line is welcome to his liberty. It takes time to kill fish in this way before they can be boated. Greater numbers can be taken by hand lines — mere pot fishing — and we do not care to compete with that style of slaughter.

Also, all of their fish were weighed "in presence of witnesses on a Fairbanks standard scale." It would appear that members of this club were far ahead of their day in both sportsmanship and honesty! If only someone would have realized that there was not a never-ending supply of muskies and started a release program, as they killed many muskies!

"Angling in the Middle West" by Emereson Hough in the August, 1901 issue of *Outing* Magazine indicated that already in 1901, the "handwriting was on the wall." To quote:

> In regard to the angling for muscallunge, one is obliged to write somewhat in the past tense. We still have muscallunge fishing in Wisconsin, though little or none in Michigan. Minnesota has a number of muscallunge waters within her borders and indeed is today attracting the greater portion of the attention of the trolling cult. Yet, prolific as are these waters. there is no comparing the

59

results of today with those which were common ten, fifteen or twenty years ago. Pen cannot chronicle the unspeakable butchery which took place over all the Wisconsin wilderness when the railroads first penetrated that virgin country. Never has the brutishness of human nature been more fully exemplified than it was up in the dark forests of the pine country, which was at that time but little known. It was exceedingly simple. One went up the railroad to almost any little logging town, took a little used trail to almost any little lake tributary to the Mississippi River system, anywhere in the Manitowish, Turtle Lake, Tomahawk Lake, or St. Germaine region, indeed on any one of those lakes which drain into the Wisconsin or the Flambeau River, and having secured any kind of a boat from a birch bark to a lumbering bateau, he simply took to trolling almost any kind of a spoon hook in almost any part of the lake. The merest novice might take a dozen, a score, indeed two scores of magnificent muscallunge in a day's fishing, if he did not tire out. One party composed of men from Louisville, Ky., and from Chicago, on one trip piled up over a ton of muscallunge on the sandy shores of one of the lakes near Three Rivers, Wis. They returned year after year and repeated their shameless performances, until at length even the guides revolted and told them that they must come there no more. A great deal of this was hand line fishing, with out the first element of sport attached to it. One learned gentleman, who adorns the medical fraternity in the city of Chicago, invented a sort of spring box. so arranged in the stern of the boat that when a muscallunge struck the spoon he found himself played automatically on a big coiled spring, like a mammoth watch spring. By means of this contrivance, with the hand line in one hand and a couple of poles sticking out over the side of the boat, this gentleman angler managed to satisfy his idea of sport. No one can tell how many tons of fish this one party of ruffians has killed. Members of the party used to boast of their performances, up to within a few years back, at which time they began to hear so much plain talk regarding themselves that they now never refer to those distant days.

Today we do not hear of thirty and forty pound muscallunge as a common thing in Wisconsin. The fish run very much smaller and very much fewer. It is the same old story. If a good fish, say an eighteen or twenty pounder, is taken at any of the summer resorts the size is multiplied by two and sent to the news-papers and sporting goods stores of the city. Really I doubt if there was a fish taken over forty pounds in Wisconsin last season, and perhaps not half a dozen, recorded or unrecorded, that went over thirty pounds. The largest muscallunge of which I have heard in these waters weighed fifty-five pounds and it was taken some fifteen years ago (1886).

The April 14, 1888, issue of *The American Angler* reports on "A Noble Mascalonge" by Geo. S. Marsh:

I send you today a photograph of the big mascalonge caught in the Eagle Waters by Mr. Saunders, of Wausau (in 1887).The fish was 4 ft.11 inches long (59 in.), 2ft. 4in girth (28 in.) and 50 pounds weight.

Record Muskies?

In *The American Angler* in 1891 we once again see the lack of early record keeping, even within that publication. An article entitled "The St. Lawrence Mascalonge Record," points this out vividly:

> Lascar is informed that the best record within our knowledge of Muscalonge caught in the St. Lawrence River is that of Mr. S. Dexter Pillsbury, who caught in one forenoon several years ago, three fish weighing respectively 46, 38, and 23 pounds. If this has been beaten we do not know it. Do you?

Yes, and they would have too, just by referring back to their September 12 through October 31 issues of 1885!

Muskellunge Management in Michigan by John D. Schroeder, inland fisheries specialist for the Michigan DNR, reports of a giant musky:

> One fish reportedly caught in a pond (pound) net off Sleeping Bear Dunes in Lake Michigan in the 1880s was said to have weighed 162 pounds and measured more than seven feet long. The skull of that fish, which was retained by Alvin Westcott of Glen Arbor, measured about 13 inches long and 20 inches in circumference more than seventy years later.

Knowing that bones shrink minimally, how would those measurements vs. supposed weight, compare with known weights and measurements? This very question went through the head of Dr. E.J. Crossman, curator — Dept. of Ichthyology and Herpetology, Royal Ontario Museum and Professor of Zoology, University of Toronto, when I sent him the above information; so he and a student went work on it. The results follow:

Authentication or Debunking Old Fish Stories
By E. J. Crossman

Anglers, and their relatives after them, have a notorious reputation for inflating stories associated with their catches. Some of the most far-fetched are part of the folklore on pike in Europe. It is always those species with a potential for greatness which are the subject of these "enlargements."

Stories of muskies over 100 pounds are legion and I attempt to track each one down in order to learn whether the animal ever did, or can break that 100-pound barrier. Most people know of authentic cases but it is very interesting how most of these records recede into the mists of story, hearsay, mistaken memory, etc., when traced back. North America is not without its folklore.

To illustrate just one of these, I will use the 162-pound musky referred to me by Larry Ramsell. The story was included in a report (Muskellunge Management in Michigan, by J.D. Schrouder, Fish. Div. Pamphlet #45, 21 pp.) on the [now disqualified] record muskellunge for Michigan (62 pounds 8 ounces , Lake St. Clair). The article went on to say, "Larger Great Lakes muskies have been reported, but were not officially authenticated. One fish reportedly caught in a pound net off the Sleeping Bear Dunes in Lake Michigan in the 1800s was said to have weighed 162 pounds and measured more than seven feet long. The skull of the fish. which was retained by Alvin Westcott of Glenn Arbor, measured about 13 inches long and was 20 inches in circumference more than seventy years later."

To check the story we must have muskies from which we can derive all of the following: head length, maximum head circumference, total length, and total weight. The extensive records of fish caught by anglers are of no use as they will not include the head measurements. This problem constitutes one of the many ways in which specimens of fishes painstakingly cared for in reference collections can be utilized. These specimens have all the information we need.

Luckily the skull of a muskellunge is massive, and is rigid enough that we can assume that a dried skull, measured 70 years after capture, would not have shrunk enough to differ significantly from that of more recent, preserved specimens.

To solve the problem, as many specimens as possible are measured and weighed. In a full scale research situation specimens from several collections would be borrowed to derive a maximum of information for greater accuracy. For the purpose at hand only specimens at the Royal Ontario Museum, and available published information, were used. Luckily these included head sizes which exceed those of the mystery fish and this allows for greater confidence in the findings of the exercise. The data and rough figures for this note prepared by Erling Holm at the Royal Ontario Museum.

The relationships between head (skull) characteristics and body characteristics of museum specimens can be expressed on graphs (Figures 1-4) as points (solid dots) for each fish. A line is drawn to fit these points, and on that line we can plot a point (a solid dot within a square) representing any known information for the mystery fish. Other information about the mystery fish can then be determined from that point. Points denoting the claimed length or weight of the mystery fish are plotted as an open square (Figures 3 and 5).

In Figure 1, Head Length is plotted against Total Length of the reference specimens. Once the relationship and line are established the point representing the mystery fish (the point inside a square) is put in and the unknown facts read off the graph. In this case the relationship suggests that a skull 13 inches long should come from a musky approximately 53 inches in length. When I extended that line to a point representing an animal 84 inches. or 7 feet long, the relationship indicated that head length of a 7-foot muskellunge should have been at least 20 inches, not 13 inches. Only in Figures 3 and 5 are the extensions that were made for the other lines but were deleted when the final form of those figures was prepared.

In Figure 2, Maximum Head Circumference is plotted against Total Length of the reference specimens. From that relationship we can estimate that a skull 20 inches in circumference should have come from an animal approxi-

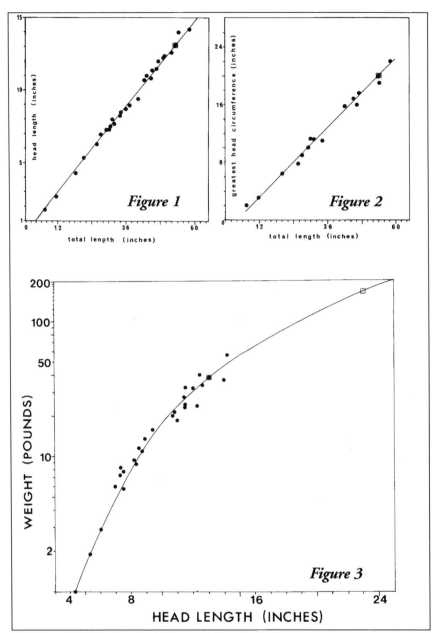

Figure 1

Figure 2

Figure 3

mately 54 inches in length. When I extended this line to a point representing a musky 7 feet long it indicated that the head circumference of a 7-foot musky should have been 32 inches, not 20 inches.

Figure 3 indicates the plotted values for the relationship between Head Length and Total Weight. These data suggest that the skull was from a fish of approximately 39 pounds. This figure includes the extension of the line to the point representing a musky of 162 pounds (open square). The relationship indicates that the head length of such a musky should have been 23 inches not 13 inches.

Figure 4 indicates the relationship of Maximum Head Circumference to Total Weight. in this case the skull size (20 inches) is that of a fish weighing 44 pounds. If we extrapolate this line to 162 pounds it indicates that the circumference of the skull of a musky weighing 162 pounds should have been at least 29 inches, not 20 inches.

A lack of consistency in results obtained as above is inherent in extrapolation and the problems of not knowing what the curve should look like after it

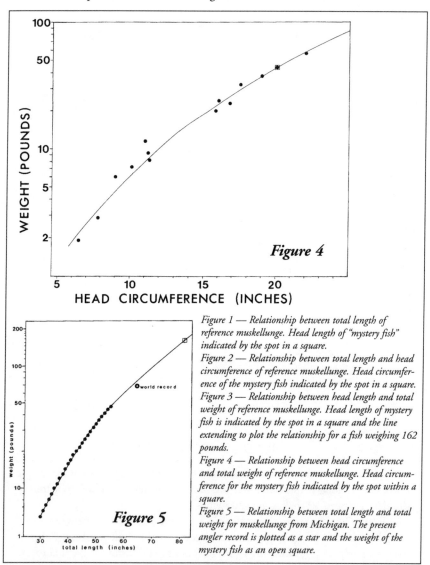

Figure 4

Figure 5

Figure 1 — Relationship between total length of reference muskellunge. Head length of "mystery fish" indicated by the spot in a square.

Figure 2 — Relationship between total length and head circumference of reference muskellunge. Head circumference of the mystery fish indicated by the spot in a square.

Figure 3 — Relationship between head length and total weight of reference muskellunge. Head length of mystery fish is indicated by the spot in a square and the line extending to plot the relationship for a fish weighing 162 pounds.

Figure 4 — Relationship between head circumference and total weight of reference muskellunge. Head circumference for the mystery fish indicated by the spot within a square.

Figure 5 — Relationship between total length and total weight for muskellunge from Michigan. The present angler record is plotted as a star and the weight of the mystery fish as an open square.

is extended beyond the section represented by real data. However, even the 5-pound spread in calculated total weight is not unreasonable, and the calculated lengths are amazingly close.

It is interesting to compare the results achieved against a plot of the length x weight relationship of present day muskies. The points plotted in Figure 5 are from *In-Fisherman* magazine (See SR4: p. 11). They were labeled "Michigan Average" and I chose them as representative of very good growth. This is an attempt at a fair comparison of the mystery fish from "the good old days," which might have grown at a rate above that achieved by some populations today. Figure 5 indicates that a fish of 162 pounds probably would have been approximately 82 inches, or approximately 7 feet long. It is also interesting to note that the lengths and weights derived from the skull measurements (figures 1-4) compare favorably with those of present day muskies. A fish of 53 or 54 inches would weigh about 41-44 pounds.

The conclusions which might be drawn are as follows:

1. There was no fish 7 feet long weighing 162 pounds, which had a skull 13 inches long and 20 inches in diameter.

2. The skull, and the length and weight, represented two separate fish stories which somehow became entangled over 70 years.

3. Anglers and their antecedents perpetuate pernicious prevarications.

How true, and so rests another legend!

Returning once again to Clark's muskellunge in Ohio, we find the following reference:

The largest specimen recorded from the Ohio waters of Lake Erie was described by McCormick (1892) as being six feet long and weighing 78 pounds. It was caught (no mention of how) in 1891.

This reference comes from the weekly *Visitor* printed in Hayward, Wisconsin. The late Eldon Marple was a well-known historian in the Hayward area and has a regular column called "Historical Vignettes." It was his story entitled "Big Ones That Didn't Get Away," that I would like to quote from:

The Hayward Lakes Region has always been famous for its fishing waters. What was fishing really like in the days when its lakes and streams had few fishermen and these waters reportedly abounded with fabled big 'lungers who had never seen a lure? Were the "big ones" as plentiful as we are led to believe? The answer to these questions is without a doubt an affirmative according to what records I can find of these times.

In September of 1892, a *Fishing and Hunting Guide of Northern Wisconsin*, a twenty-page booklet authored by O.E. Rice, was being printed by the *Hayward Journal-News*. We will quote from it, with some editing:

> Near the terminus of a splendid turnpike carriage road built from Hayward in 1891 the justly celebrated Lost (Lost Land) and Tea (Teal) Lakes. Here is destined to be the favorite fishing resort of this section, as the waters are filled with the ordinary lake fish before named. In these waters the lover of sport realizes his greatest expectations, for the famous muskallonge fish are caught here in numbers. These cannot be landed with a pole because of their great size and strength. They run all the way from seven to sixty pounds and are taken on a trolling hook. Six hundred pounds of fish were caught in two days by a party of three about the middle of August, 1892.

Accompanying this article was a photo from a 1897 plat book showing four anglers with 12 muskies taken in one day!

In 1873, G.M. Skinner started perfecting his fluted blade spoon in Clayton. N.Y., a bait that was to become the standard trolling bait

in the late 1800s. On October 6, 1893 Mr. Skinner caught his "World's Fair Muscallonge." Caught on a No. 8 Gold Fluted Spoon, it weighed 42 pounds and was 55 1/2 inches long.

The June 13,1954, *Milwaukee Journal* reported an article from the June 11,1896, *New North* from Rhinelander, Wis. It had a report of a musky weighing:

> ... nearly 80 pounds and was just under six feet in length. There were 3 men involved; W.D. LeSelle, M.J. O'Reilly and Mr. Coon. The fish was first seen while trolling in St. Germaine Lake in early June. The fish was spotted swimming and when it came close to the boat, O'Reilly grabbed a club and smashed it onto the musky's head. The fish submerged in a swirl of water and was gone from sight. They went out again the next day and this time they were prepared as one of the men had an axe. They again saw the fish and the axe was brought down deep into the head of the musky. Four days later the body of the fish was spotted and the men notified. The fish was badly decomposed, but was towed to shore where the head was saved and taken back to Rhinelander as evidence of good faith. Coon and

"World's Fair Muscallonge," caught Oct. 6, 1893 by G.M. Skinner on Skinner's No. 8 Gold Fluted Spoon. Weight 42 pounds, length 4 feet 7 1/2 inches.

Record Muskies?

Early day group catch from Wisconsin. Courtesy of George Mattis & Wise Land Co., 1901, and Lou Spray

LeSelle said the musky was just under six feet long and round as a saw log (however round that is!?) Estimated weight: 70 to 80 pounds!

The May 21st, 1898 , issue of *Forest and Stream* brings us a report of a "Minnesota Fish, in Fresh Water Angling" by Fred Mather:

> A weird story comes down from Minneapolis telling of three muscallunge caught this month at Buffalo, Minnesota, the smallest of which weighed 44 pounds and the largest 61 pounds is heavier than any weight I ever heard ascribed to any 'lunge taken west of the St. Lawrence, I think we have license in asking verification of these weights. (Amen!) Messrs. Henry Weigand and George Taylor of Minneapolis are the lucky anglers to whom this rare good fortune is attributed.

One day's catch from the St. Lawrence River in the early 1900s.

Here we go again. Buffalo, Minnesota is close to the Mississippi River. Were these fish caught there? Are the weights accurate? Again no record keeping. Had the 61-pounder been real, sport caught and verified, it would have been the world record until 1940 and would still be the Minnesota record! Also it would have eliminated several of the muskies on the current world record list from 1911 to 1940!

Louis Spray sent me the following:

Probably the largest musky ever was netted about the turn of the century in Butternut Lake four miles from Park Falls, Wisconsin. It was netted with the "community net," which was used by the town people for obtaining fish for food.

No offense to Louis, but it would be impossible to judge size from the photo. It appears, as was the norm in those days, that the men in the picture are standing a considerable distance away from the fish. Also, if the fish was netted, why is one of the men holding a rod and reel?

At last we made it to the 1900s! I am sure there were many more possibilities in the late 1800s because there were voids of several years in the material I was able to find to research.

The turn of the century musky from Butternut Lake, Wisconsin, and reported by Louis Spray.

W.D. DeGroot, in *Forest and Stream*, May 4, 1901, speaks in general references:

It is said the specimens have been taken weighing 75 to 80 pounds, these giants have been captured in the St. Lawrence River in the earlier days. Weights of 50 to 55 pounds were not unusual in the early days of the muscallunge waters of Wisconsin and Minnesota.

I sure would like to know where he got his information as the earlier reference works, most written in New York, had no similar knowledge.

A potential "Ladies Record" from days of old in Wisconsin.

In all the research I have done, the story that is most often written about is the supposed 102-pounder from Minocqua Lake and the 80-pounder from Tomahawk (same lake chain) in Wisconsin in 1902. Supposedly, Supt. Nevin of the State Fish Hatchery Commission and E.D. Kennedy captured these two fish while netting for spawn. This story has been retold so often that it is almost taken as gospel. But — let's investigate the facts further and perhaps put one of the biggest fish stories of all time to bed.

In 1925, noted outdoor writer Cal Johnson (who held the world record briefly in 1949) contacted the Wisconsin fish authorities to try to verify the weight and actual record of the 102-pound musky and received the reply that neither one of the big female 'lunge were actually weighed on any scale, but the

A successful family outing from the early days of Wisconsin.

"estimated" weight was given. When Ray Kennedy, grandson of E.D. Kennedy, was interviewed by Tom Hollatz for Tom's book, *Guides of the Wisconsin Northwoods*, he was asked:

Didn't your grandfather, Eldorado Kennedy catch the biggest musky on record ... 102 pounds?

His answer: "Yes, when he was working for the conservation department. He had to return it to the lake (Minocqua) when the spawn was removed. After I caught a 50-pounder one year I just couldn't imagine a 100-pounder. There's no way I can stretch my imagination. I told my dad that I just can't imagine a fish that big. No way I can understand. My dad looked at me with a little bit of a smile and said, 'they say they made better whiskey in those days'!!"

Ironically, the 50-pounder that Ray caught is the largest ever caught and verified from the Minocqua chain.

The March/April, 1977, issue of *The Conservationist*, a New York D.E.C. publication, brings us our second and third possible women's world records. It is entitled "The Magic of Musky Fishing" by Harold E. Herrick Jr., who was a noted musky historian on the St. Lawrence River at Clayton, New York:

It was in August of 1904 that Grandmother Bacon tied into her large 40-

Grandmother Bacon's 40-pounder (left), and Mrs. W.F. Morgan's 43-pounder, both caught in the early 1900s.

Record Muskies?

Grandmother Bacon and Mrs. Morgan with boatman Colon and a 40-pound St. Lawrence musky caught in 1904 by Mrs. Bacon.

pound musky near the large tree at Joyce's — Wolfe Island. I was told that this 53-inch fish surfaced many times with runs away from the boat. Some 40 minutes later, the still lively fish was brought along-side the skiff. Boatman Colon handgaffed the gills and the fish was rolled into the boat and sat upon. The great moment of musky fishing — St. Lawrence River style — had arrived with the ritual raising of a white flag, still practiced today.

During the many years, those two grand old fisherwomen, Bacon and Morgan, fished together, many large 'lunge were boated with the largest Morgan catch being 43 pounds. The local newspapers reported the fishing exploits by these two summer resident ladies from New York City.

In "Muscallonge Fishing in Pennsylvania" by A.J. Van Sise in the July 1908, issue of *Outdoor Life* there is a picture accompanying the article showing a 44-pound 2-ounce musky from Lake Le Boeuf in Pennsylvania in 1902. Consider that the first recognized musky world

Three nice muskies and one hybrid from the old days.

record was established just 3 years later in 1911 at 48 pounds. This fish was also written about in *Field & Stream* magazine, and in the book, *The Pikes and Their Cousins*, documenting its weight and existence.

Peter Haupt passed on the following:

> In 1909 there was supposedly a 58-pound musky taken from Big Arbor Vitae Lake, Wisconsin. There is a nice clear large black and white photo of it in the Vilas County Museum at Sayner, Wisconsin.

This fish could have been the world's record until 1932! The only accurate and official list of musky world records that has ever been compiled is one that I put together a few years ago for my article, "Big Muskies, When! Where! and Why?," which first appeared in the August, 1973, Muskies, Inc., newsletter. This was done by researching the *Field & Stream* contest from its inception in 1911. This was the only source of verified (affidavited) muskellunge catches. There was a major flaw in this method. In order to be considered, potential world record fish had to be entered in the yearly *F&S* contest. As this article proceeds, several "should have, could have, or might have beens" will be pointed out.

In the 1930s The American Museum of Natural History was tied

Ladies caught many large muskies in the early days in Wisconsin.

in with the records, but to a minor extent as *F&S* published the yearly record list.

Another problem that evolved from the *F&S* contest was that in
order to make the *Field & Stream* record list the fish had to be a yearly contest winner. For instance when Lou Spray (three-time record
holder) wrote to *F&S* asking for a
list of musky record holders from
1939 on, *F&S* wrote back and stated: "Unfortunately, none of the
information in which you are
interested in is available because
records are not kept that way ..."
Lou then had a friend of his in
New York go there personally. The
return report was: "He said according to their (*F&S*) records, I (Lou
Spray) only actually caught one
world record musky, the one in

*A 21 1/2-pound hybrid from the
old days.*

1949." According to this type of thinking, Cal Johnson didn't hold the
record in 1949 with his 67 1/2-pounder, which is absurd! It appears
though, that their (*F&S*) writer, Dan Holland, thought differently in
the March, 1940 issue in his article "World's Record Muskies" as he
gave credit to Percy Haver, Lou Spray and John J. Coleman for setting
new world marks in 1939.

*Angler and
guide with
a good day's
catch (obvi-
ously, no
release pro-
gram back
then).*

With the aforementioned in mind, let us proceed. Let us move on to one of the most prolific bodies of musky water in history, Lake of the Woods. The material I wish to relay to you regarding Lake of the Woods comes from an excellent book entitled *Lake of the Woods, Yesterday and Today*, written in 1975 by Duane R. Lund. To give the reader an idea of size, Lake of the Woods includes: "1,980 sq. miles of which 1,485 sq. miles is water, a complete watershed of 27,000 sq. miles; 65,000 miles of shoreline (more than Lake Superior); 14,000 islands and is at the widest 65 miles north to south, and 55 miles wide from east to west."

The one primary quote I wish to relate from the book comes from page 83 following a picture on page 82 of the author's father, Richard Lund, holding two large muskies taken in 1912. The author's father told of catching muskies or large northerns "on virtually every cast here early in the 1900s."

Although it is possible that some of the previously-mentioned large muskies could have been hoaxes, we now come to a known hoax; perhaps the largest of all time! In the March/April 1973 issue of the *Michigan Natural Resources* magazine, an interesting article appeared entitled, "Off the Record Monster Musky." It refers to an August 24, 1940 article carried in the Detroit News with a picture of an unidentified fisherman circa 1908 posing beside a supposed 110-pound muskellunge! A supposed witness said he viewed the catch "and found it to be a 110-pound muskellunge, seven feet four inches in length, with a 51-inch girth. The fisherman who caught it was out alone trolling with a heavy chalk line and big spoon. It struck at 11:30 a.m.

Roughing it for ducks and muskies in the early days of northern Wisconsin.

and it took him until 1 p.m. before he landed the monster." Wow! Sounds fantastic, doesn't it? But not so. As it turned out, the hoax was perpetrated by two fellows from Bellaire, Michigan, aided and abetted by a commercial photographer. The fish was actually only a 54-pound musky speared in the Torch River. (Had this fish been sport caught it would have been the record for real!) It was hung by a hawser in front of a shed. A picture was then taken of the fish and another of the spearman standing with his arm extended. By carefully combining the two, it made the fish look huge! At least 10,000 postcards were supposedly sold of the picture.

The 110-pound hoax (actually 54 pounds) from Michigan's Torch River about 1908. The fish was speared.

In his section on "Muskellunge" in the book *The Pike Family*, 1953, Robert Page Lincoln writes about this same fish:

> Years ago one met up with statements by writers on the muskellunge, especially the "doctor authorities," who, without hesitation, would state that the muskellunge has been known to reach a length of eight feet and a weight of eighty to one hundred pounds. I found this statement in the Seventh Annual Report of the Game and Fish Department of New York State, a massive volume, put out at the turn of the century. It told of many one hundred pounders being taken. A hundred pound musky was said to have been taken in nets in Wisconsin by commercial fishermen many years ago, and the fish is said to be mounted and still preserved, though where it is I do not know. Certain waters in the northern part of lower Michigan have always produced large muskies. Some time ago in *Fur-Fish-Game* magazine I showed a photo taken over forty years ago, of a fish that was supposed to be in the hundred pound class. A man standing alongside of the fish seems rather dwarfed. The fish, I might mention, was hung up on a stable wall on a nail and the man was reaching up and had his hand on the jaw of the fish.

Earlier I made reference to a supposed 162-pounder from Lake Michigan in the 1880s. Dr. Crossman's article, "Authentication or

Debunking Old Fish Stories" did an excellent job of realism in debunking the legend of one of the heaviest muskies on record, at least from the information that was provided. Let's take the given data for this Michigan legend, the 110-pound hoax and see what can be done with it in a humorous light. The following is quoted from the *Michigan Natural Resources* magazine:

Fishing Is Dangerous

Dear Editor.

We would like to comment on the "Monster Musky" article in the March/April (1973) issue. You may draw your own conclusions from evidence offered.

From information given and the photograph shown (copy enclosed) some rather "hard" data may be inferred. Lines have been drawn on the photo demarking the massive part of the fish's body to include about 60% of the total length, or approximately 50 inches. This portion of the fish roughly comprises a cylinder, the volume of which can easily be found by using the girth (given as 51 inches) to find the radius (51 divided by 2π) or 8.1 inches and then applying the formula for the volume of a cylinder, $\pi r^2 h$.

Our calculations show this to be about 10,500 cubic inches or 6 cubic feet. We could also conservatively assume the remaining head and tail would increase this by about a fifth, giving a grand total of 7+ cubic feet of musky.

The stated weight of 110 pounds applied to the already determined volume gives the fish a density of 15.7 pounds per cubic foot and a specific gravity of 0.25 which compares favorably with that of dry cork (0.29) and is one-quarter that of the water the "Monster" inhabited.

We find it difficult to believe an angler could have battled 1 1/2 hours with a fish that could not possibly submerge, as 110 pounds of cork or its equivalent would have a buoyancy factor of an additional 325 pounds. The biggest, strongest man alive could not have pulled it under water.

Want to go a bit further? Le us now assume that all the given statistics are true except the reported weight. Logic requires us now to believe any adjustment must reflect accepted values relative to fish flesh, to wit, it closely approximates that of the water it inhabits. Seven cubic feet of musky weighs 436 pounds, give or take a fin here and there.

The laws of proportion and scaling can be flaunted no more than those of gravitation, a fact often overlooked by the gullible.

J.B.S. Haldane put it all together in a neat little monograph entitled "On Being the Right Size," and to the unconvinced, we recommend its perusal.

Sincerely,

John R. TenHave

Science Department, Grand Rapids

and George C. Vaughn

Physics Department, Educational Park, Grand Rapids

In January, 1978, I visited Dr. E. J. Crossman at the Royal Ontario Museum in Toronto. While there, I noticed an old mount of an obviously large musky. Yes, it was another "should-have-been." It was a 57-pound 10-ounce musky that had been caught in 1917 from the French River, Ontario. It was 59 inches long and had a girth of 30 inches. It was captured by a William Fulton. This fish followed by a year the second verified musky on the world record list. The 1916 world record was, at 51 pounds, the first verified 50-plus-pounder.

Claimed 60-inch musky from Wisconsin in 1917.

Now, on to the new references. One thing that helps my research is information passed on to me by fellow musky fishermen. In March 1979 at a meeting of the Headwaters Chapter of Muskies, Inc., that I attended in St. Germain, Wisconsin, Ray Bangs, owner of the Village Camera Shop in Minocqua, Wisconsin, had a pleasant surprise for me. It was an excellent picture of an angler with a large musky (see photo) reported to be caught from Muskellunge Lake at McNaughton, Wisconsin, in 1917. Etched on the picture are the length of 60 inches and the weight of 55 pounds, which would have been the world record had it been verified!

Moving to Robert Page Lincoln's *Guide to Best Fishing* in 1948, we find the following quote:

> Sabaskong Bay, the great bay of Lake of the Woods, has probably been harder hit by fishermen than any other section of the mighty water. Nevertheless, it still produces good muskies and the fact that you may see as many as 10 or 15 of the species during a week's vacation, some of them ranging up into the top brackets, is proof that the lake still produces some big ones. When we first fished here 25 to 30 years ago (1918-1923), the species were very numerous and the taking of a 35- or 40-pounder was not considered unusual.

In 1919 the third official world record was caught. This fish is an interesting story in that although it was accepted as a world record musky and stood for 10 years (second longest in history), it was in fact a hybrid "tiger" musky (musky-northern pike hybrid). This fact became obvious when a picture of the fish was dug out of the archives by Rod Ramsell in 1977.

Forest & Stream's October 1920 issue had an article by Ben Robinson entitled "The King of Our Inland Waters." His article refers to a possible giant of 75 pounds from the Ohio River drainage:

> I personally know of one musky that is yet to be taken from his home in the deep water that after due and sad consideration by a host of reliable — if there are such in existence — old timers which will bounce the scales at seventy-five pounds.

"The Three Muskieteers" by Larry St. John in the November 1920 issue of *Field & Stream* had listed 33 muskies that had been caught in 1920. The largest listed was a 54-pounder caught in Wisconsin on a semi-surface plug. No mention was made of the name of the lake or angler, and obviously it wasn't "entered and accepted" in the *F&S* Contest for that year or else it would have become the new world record.

August Ulman, in his article, "The King of the Tribe *Esox*" in the October 1921 issue of *Forest & Stream*, stated:

> The largest fish that the writer ever saw weighed fifty-five pounds, but there are reports of fish being caught up to eighty pounds and even one hundred pounds." Again — no facts or details.

In the September, 1958, in the West Virginia Conservation publication's section, "Our Readers Write," had the following:

> Big, big, big, musky. I thought you might like to see this picture of a musky taken from Elk River in 1921. It weighed 69 1/2 pounds and was six feet two inches long. The fish was caught by my father, Bill Stalnaker, near Frametown bridge ...

I received a letter from Jim Wetzel, president of the Elk River Musky Club of West Virginia, Inc.:

> Larry,
> Stumbled across a very interesting article in the Sutton, West Virginia, town paper (enclosed) about "a legendary muskellunge" from the Elk River about 12 miles south of Sutton in 1917. I am making every attempt to follow up on this musky; I desire to find a picture of this same fish but with something

in the picture with it for comparison!

No doubt, from the thick lower jaw, this fish is large, but I seriously doubt it will attain the length and weight assigned to it in the article. I believe this particular fish has been subjected to a faulty conception of proportions, as did W.E.R. Byrne's fish in the enclosed article taken from the book *Tale of the Elk*, written by Byrne. I'll stay in touch. Will contact you when I find something more or less substantial on this Stalnaker musky.

Jim

When I wrote the original *Compendium* I had no picture of this fish. In the following article, referred to in Jim's letter, a picture of this fish was included. So, with the help of Jim and the article's author, Steve Creasey, we now have a picture. Following is Steve's article, which appeared in the *Braxton Democrat-Central*, August 3, 1984:

Wild Things
By Steve Creasey

This week comes a letter from Mrs. Neva S. Wilson, a resident of Petroleum, WV, and with it a negative of a monster musky caught by her father, the late Bill Stalnaker, of Frametown. Bill was born in Progress in 1903 and was the son of John Bennet Stalnaker and Jerusha Ellen Frame Stalnaker. The Stalnakers lived in Frametown near the river and Bill, like most young boys, was an avid fisherman.

His wife, Lula Maysel Mitchell Stalnaker, a young 82 years old, who now lives in Petroleum with her daughter Neva, recalls that everyone down Frametown way had seen a huge musky in the eddy immediately below the bridge and everyone had tried to catch him without success until Bill reached the age of 14.

In March of 1917, Bill set upon the Elk with a white sucker seven inches in length in pursuit of the legendary fish. When he struck Bill was in for the fight of his life. With his father's help, Bill managed to boat the incredible *esox* after a three-hour

The legendary Frametown Musky.

battle that had he and his boat all over the Frametown Eddy of Elk. Now, you guys that have the incurable fever better sit down for what you're about to read will no doubt peel your socks back.

Bill took the monster fish to Roy Hardway's store in Frametown where he had it weighed and measured. Are you sittin' down?

74 inches (thats 6-2) and 69 (that's sixty-nine) pounds and eight ounces.

Now readers, I know there are two kinds reading this. Some of you are trying to regain your composure and some are saying "It can 't be. That's bigger than the state record." Well, you guys that stay on the river in pursuit of the elusive *esox* know that a musky can reach that size. And, pert' near every one of you has a story about one that size of your own so, why the skepticism? I'm here to tell you that I talked tonight with Bill's 82-year-old wife and she didn't make any bones about the weight or the length. She was quite matter of fact. She said he took the fsh to the Bollinger Studios in Gassaway where the photo was taken.

Bollinger was Bill's uncle. I asked her why Bill didn't register the fish as a record and she simply replied that people just didn't think much about records in those days. As for the picture, I have only a negative that is 67 years old and is in pretty rough shape so, I don't think it will print well but, use your imagination. If Mrs. Wilson can locate the original photograph, I will reproduce it and re-run the picture again later. Mrs. Stalnaker also recalled that Bill caught another musky in the same hole in the same month nine years later that he believed to be the big one's mate, it measured at 56 inches. Mrs. Stalnaker cleaned that one herself and measured the egg sacks which hit 18 inches themselves. She said she "sliced them off like bologna and fried them."

Bill retired in Ritchie County on the Hughes River, another dangerous musky haven and passed away there in 1972. His daughter and wife said he lived his life well though, having caught many, many muskies in addition to being a skilled and avid hunter. Mr. Wilson says that she and her sister Nova D. Hyer of Walker hunted and fished with their daddy many times and loved every minute of it.

I believe this man was one whale of a fisherman and wherever he is the legend of the Frametown Musky of 1917 lives on.

In "Muskying with a Champion" by Shegetaro Morikubo in the September 1924. issue of *Field & Stream*, the following conversation took place between Mr. Morikubo and Wm. C. Vogt, champion fly caster:

"Have you any more fish stories to tell?" asked Mr. Vogt, who would rather feast upon fishing stories than attend a banquet.

"Yes, two years ago last summer (1922) at Taylors Falls a muskalonge weighing sixty-five pounds was roped. One day when the dam was shut off, three men who happened to be walking on shore heard a racket and found the musky struggling in the shallow water. The men roped it and took it to shore."

"Listen Doc," cried Vogt, grasping my arm so tightly that it actually hurt me, "below Taylor's Falls where the deep water rushes may be found muskalonge so immense that they could swallow a cow whole for breakfast."

That may not be any idle dream of a fisherman.

Record Muskies?

In "Muskellunge Fishing in Wisconsin" by Fred Bradford Ellsworth in the April 1924, issue of *Outdoor Life*, we find a big fish list from 1923. The largest was a 52-pounder caught by John J. Hoogan from Shishebogama Lake near Woodruff. Properly verified it would have been a new record by 13 ounces.

In 1923 while "fishing for food and not records," Brendon Reid of the St. Lawrence River Chapter of Muskies, Inc. said he helped his grandfather kill a musky around 90 pounds. No records were thought of, no pictures were taken. It was divided up for food! Brendon stated that when the fish was placed in the boat it was so powerful that it tore the seats loose with its flopping. He said the fish was nearly 7 feet long! I'm glad the fish was not verified. It would have eliminated much musky history and put the record practically out of reach!

This fish is probably one of the most overlooked fish since records were first verified in 1911. In "Record Muskellunge" by Keen Buss, June 1961, *The Pennsylvania Angler*, we find a picture of the current Pennsylvania record. It was a magnificent fish that was 59 inches long and weighed 54 pounds 3 ounces. It was caught in 1924 from Conneaut Lake by Lewis Walker Jr. Had this fish been verified and accepted by *F&S* when caught it would have beaten the 1919 world record, but more than that, it would have preempted the next two world records caught in 1929.

In the December 1975, issue of the Muskies, Inc. newsletter, Andy Woolfries related a fish story that I thoroughly enjoyed. Andy was understandably perturbed by the presence of numerous northern pike in musky waters. His story:

> In a burst of unwonted ambition, my guide and I lugged boat and gear across Turtle Portage from Sabaskong into Whitefish Bay. That was before a sissier generation blasted a canal through the rock and sand. We had shore lunch on the south side of Sioux Narrows while watching a bear scoop blueberries on the north shore. (Advancing civilization has now turned that beautiful spot into a gaggle of souvenir shops, gas stations and assorted tourist traps). After lunch, we began to cast the likely looking spots. Suddenly, my bucktail was shadowed by the biggest musky I have ever seen. The guide estimated a weight of 60 pounds. The giant was moving up on the lure mouth open. He was set to hit! Then, from nowhere, a two-pound jack dashed for the bucktail and hit it hard. For an agonizing instant, the big musky hesitated, appearing to be debating the wisdom of taking jack and all. Then he swept away. The guide swore. I cried — but I was much younger then.

One fish, the mount of which can be seen at the Fresh Water Fishing Hall of Fame, in Hayward, Wisconsin is a 59-pound, 55-inch musky. This fish supposedly was caught in the 1930s from Lac Courte Oreilles and would have been a world record at the time if it was sport caught. Circumstances surrounding the "catch" are somewhat cloudy.

We again must thank Peter Haupt and Ray Bangs for providing us with information of a 52-pounder (caught by Gust Peterson from White Sand Lake, Lac du Flambeau, Wisconsin, on October 15, 1935. With this fish we have a reverse situation! In his article "Facts About Big Muskies" in the August 1952 *Sports Afield*, Cal Johnson

erroneously listed the Peterson 52-pounder a world record, which is not correct, as there were four verified muskies caught from 1929 to 1932 that were larger than Mr. Peterson's beautiful trophy.

In July of 1937 a Detroit, Michigan, man received a color post-card from New York with the following message:

Bert: I just came from town and happened to see this card (the 75 pound 'lunge) caught 22 years ago (1915). You doubted me as did *Field & Stream* so am sending one to them too. Yours for bigger and better fish. Helen.

The supposed 75-pounder from Lake Chautauqua.

A very nice fish and an excellent photo for that time; but 75 pounds? This fish was caught from Lake Chautauqua, N.Y.

Again in July of 1937 a big fish reference. The following letter was sent to the fishing editor of *Field & Stream*.

Dear Sir.

Last July (1936) while on my vacation at Minong, Wisconsin, I heard tales of an unusually large musky that had been caught in the vicinity.

This year I returned to Minong and the tale was verified. The fish was 71 inches long and weighed 69 pounds. While I did not see it, the fish is said to have been mounted. There were numerous people who had seen it weighed, willing to sign affidavits as to size and weight. Among them, and the man to whom I suggest you write, is Mr. Norm Adams, postmaster at Minong. Mr. Adams is a real sportsman and I know you will find him absolutely trustworthy.

My sole interest in this matter, if the tale is true, is to have the fish recorded as a record fish. I might add I do not know who the lucky person was, how it was caught; or from what lake it came. If the story is true I will certainly appreciate a copy of all the information that you care to give out.

Well, evidently nothing further came of this catch. Certainly a 69-pounder within 20 miles of the Hayward area should have made some noise, especially in light of the fact that the world record at that time was only 58 1/4 pounds!

The world records of 1931 (56-8) and 1932 (58-4) stood on their own merits, but a fish caught by Alfred Tietze from Eagle Lake, Ontario, about 1937 could have been next and would have wiped out the battle for the world record in 1939-1940. Mr. Tietze's fish reportedly weighed 62 1/2 pounds! It was reported to be 63 inches long and had a reported girth of 36 inches.

The chapter on "Muskalonge" by Ernest G. Poole in the 1937 book *Fishing for Bass, Muskalonge, Pike & Panfish*, refers to another 125-pounder:

It was not an uncommon experience some years ago to catch this species weighing up to and over one hundred pounds; at least old-timers and commercial fishermen operating on the Great Lakes and tributaries vouch for this. The St. Lawrence River between the Thousand Islands and Montreal, Bay of Quinte in Lake Ontario, and Georgian Bay in Lake Huron have produced over a period of a great many years the world's largest muskalonge. A commercial fisherman by the name of Gaunthier, operating in the vicinity of the Bustard Islands in Georgian Bay, Ontario, found one of these fish which weighed 125 pounds dead in a net. For some years the head of this fish was nailed up on the outside of one of his fish houses.

In the early 1940s another tale took place. To quote from a Heddon "Pal" rod ad:

Too big for the scales but not for his Heddon Pal Rod, a musky caught by Adolph Bockus, Canton, Ohio, at Grassy Narrows Camp, Morson, Ontario, Canada. No scales could be found large enough to weigh the whopper caught on his Heddon Pal rod. Six days later in Canton, the fish weighed 60 pounds measuring 59 inches long and 27 1/2 inches in girth. If weighed when caught, it would have set a new world's record.

From the looks of the picture, it very likely would have; however, later found information changed the possibility. In doing research, I ran across an item that makes one wonder if the truth may have been stretched somewhat; if not, Mr. Bockus must have been quite a musky man. In the article "Record Beaters," by Dan Holland in the March 1941 issue of *Field & Stream*, I found the following:

> There were many other fine muskalonge entered in the 1940 contest, but they were outclassed by the three monsters already mentioned (Haver, Spray and Walden's 60-plus-pounders). Two years ago, a 60 pound rod and reel muskalonge was unheard of; so when there are three of them better than this weight in one contest, it's no wonder that the other entries are overshadowed.
>
> Data on the remaining seven muskalonge prize-winners in the 1940 contest are as follows: Fourth prize — from the world-famous Lake of the Woods musky waters, this prize winner weighed 53 pounds 8 ounces. It was caught by Adolph Bockus while fishing with a Marathon Musky Houn. A Heddon Rod (a Heddon ad is where the original reference appeared of a 60-plus-pound Bockus fish), a Shakespeare reel and a Shakespeare nylon line made up the remainder of the tackle. Caught on September 16.

Well, you can make up your own mind; a *Field & Stream* Contest prize winner of 53-8 and no verification on the 60-plus-pounder. Just before the first edition of this book went to press, I came up with additional information on the Bockus fish. I was chasing down a blind lead on a 65-pound fish from Lake of the Woods, and it turned out to be the Bockus fish. However, some of the details were different! According to my new source, the Bockus fish did weigh 65 pounds (I wonder how the weight was obtained) and this person said that his uncle had been the guide when Bockus caught the fish from Sabaskong Bay. According to the picture postcard that I was able to obtain, the fish was caught out of Turtle Portage camp, rather than Grassy Narrows Camp!! Again, it seems strange that Mr. Bockus would enter a 53-pound 8-ounce fish in the *Field & Stream* contest and not one in excess of 60 pounds, especially when it may have possibly been a world record.

On June 15, 1947 a musky was caught that was nearly a new world record. *Field & Stream* received a contest entry blank from a Mr. Harry H. Bed. His letter that accompanied a witnessed and notarized affidavit was as follows:

> Enclosed affidavit of the big musky I caught: Weight: 65 pounds 5 ounces,

length: 53 3/4", Girth: 33 1/2", Caught at Minaki, Ontario, Canada, Rod: Heddon Medium, Reel: Pflueger Supreme, Line: Marathon Nylon, Leader: Allwyr, Bait: Trenton Spin Doodler. I am leaving tomorrow for a trip further north, where the big Northern Pikes congregate. Yours for better fishing.

Should have been a new world record, right? Wrong! It was caught a few days before the Ontario season was set to open!

Returning again to Robert Page Lincoln we find additional references in his book, *The Pike Family* in 1953:

The 65-pounder caught days before the 1947 season opened.

Even today the Big Fork River is a good producer of muskies and annually records many specimens in the thirty pounds. The stories of large muskies seen and lost to fishermen on this stream are quite numerous. At the time I was on the Minneapolis Tribune, some years ago I had occasion to write regarding large muskellunge as known to the state. A gentleman who had read this article came to see me and here is the story.:

He had gone north to the Big Fork River not far from Bowstring Lake (previously mentioned) and had taken a spear one evening, just after the ice had gone out, with the object in view of spearing pike. By shining his light into the water at the mouth of the stream where it left the lake to flow into the Big Fork River he was able to see into the water with great ease. He did not see any pike but what he did see as the beam of his flash lantern swept over the water was something that held him transfixed to the spot without taking his light from the place where the object had been spotted. And the "object" was none other than the largest muskellunge he had ever seen. I asked him how long the fish was and he said to the best of his ability to estimate, it must have been eight feet in length. He said when first he detected the fish Lying there in the water he had the flood beam on the approximate center of the fish. At that point he estimated that the fish was no less than a foot deep. Moving the light toward the back of the fish he was able to see that portion of the fish also. He estimated four feet either way from the center where the beam of his light had originally marked the fish

A Compendium of Musky Angling History

Of course I did not attach much credence to the size of the fish as related but when asked how he knew it was a musky he said he had taken a number of the species in his life and this one had the spots of a musky without the slightest doubt. It was just when he decided if he should spear the fish or not that it moved out of the area of light and disappeared. I am convinced that the man had looked upon an outstanding muskellunge, but that it was eight feet in length is something else again. It may have been six feet in length and at that length it would probably take the world's record prize.

Once in awhile a huge musky will wash up on shore in any musky waters. One such fish in Minnesota weighed almost sixty pounds.

This may be a reference to the same fish Louis Spray sent me a picture and information on, which was a clipping from an old newspaper. The copy under the picture was as follows:

The near 70-pounder found dead at Pokegama Lake, Minnesota.

There are larger fish in Itasca County waters than ever taken by a fisherman with rod and line. This was proved last week when the monster pictured here (see picture) was found floating near the shore in Pokegama Lake. The fish was found by Don McDougall and his brother ... the location was not far from the outlet of Pokegama, along a sandy beach.

While the monster had been dead several days, it still held together, so the boys brought it to town in their boat. Carefully measured, it proved to be four feet eight inches long. Weighed, it tipped the scales at 64 1/2 pounds, even though it had been dead some time. A true muskellunge, it has all the markings of this game fish.

Conservative fishermen who saw the big musky estimated that alive it must have weighed not far from 70 pounds. No indication of what caused its death could be noted. These big fish perhaps die of old age. A number of years ago two men found a dead musky on the shore of a small island near Stoney Point in Pokegama Lake. The fish was fully four feet long and estimated to have weighed nearly 50 pounds.

Record Muskies?

Some years ago Peter Haupt told me of a 60-inch "hybrid" musky that had been hooked, shot and lost by an excellent musky fisherman named "Musky Gus," who had a reputation as a catcher of big muskies. After the fish had been shot (it was legal then) and lost, a large hybrid was found washed upon the shore dead. This took place on Lac Vieux Desert, Wisconsin, which has produced the two largest hybrid muskies on record: the current all tackle world record of 51-3 caught by John Knobla in 1919, and a 50-4 caught by Delores Ott Lapp in 1951. After the fish had washed up on shore, expert taxidermist Fred Aman of Conover, Wisconsin, was notified. Mr. Aman then went to see the fish. In a phone conversation with him, he told me that it was "a full bodied hybrid, 60 inches long" — and it was his estimate that it would have weighed "a pound per inch" or 60 pounds. Unfortunately, the fish was too badly decomposed to save. What a shame!

In another sad tale of a near miss, Mel Ellis wrote of his misfortune in "Musky Madness" — "It gets you for sure, particularly if you are after a record breaker," in the March 1950 *Field & Stream*. We will quote from it as follows:

> The musky lay just out of the fast water in a pool several feet deep. From the bank where we stood looking down, he was as long as a fence post and big around as a watermelon. His fins were like the small fans the gals used to flirt over in Grandpa's day, and his ugly, jutting jaw was nearly as big as the lower lip of an Ubangi flapper.
>
> "Johnny," I said, finally tearing my eyes away from the fish, "I'd give a lot to get a hook into that guy."
>
> Johnny laughed a little. "Who wouldn't?"
>
> Johnny said he'd been seeing the fish every year for eight years. He thought it would probably weigh more than 75 pounds. And he added: "But I don't think anybody will ever land him ..."
>
> After several fruitless days I got back on the river the day after Labor Day, and it was something wonderful. An early cold snap had tinted the leaves. The water was up some and sparkling. The few bluewings that had been around were gone, but there was a strange flock of new-plumage sprigs resting in the pool.
>
> They took wing at my first cast, and as I watched them take on altitude to clear the trees my fingers slipped from a reel that had stopped dead. I tried to crank, and lifted my rod tip. I was snagged solid, and then the snag started to move.
>
> Now, there have been more than a few times in my life when fright has turned me into a pretty buttery sort of man. There was the time I'd fallen asleep

on a warm rock in the foot-hills above Malibu Beach to wake up with a rattler for a bed partner. The time I went through the marl of a spring hole with my hip boots on, not to mention that first raid over Berlin.

Yet I doubt if anytime in my life did my whole being take on the pure consistence of jelly as it did when I realized that I was probably hooked into what might turn out to be a world's record musky. For at least five seconds I stood as helpless as a snake-charmed frog. Then, when the full significance of what was happening socked me, I came out of it and set the hooks with a hard lift of the rod. Not once, but two and three times, hoping all the time the fish had a square enough grip across the plug to keep it from slipping.

The rod pressure sent him traveling, as I was afraid it would. To have tried to stop him would have been foolish as a man trying to stop a rhino with a slingshot. He traveled, and there was nothing to do but let him have his way. He went straight on up out of the pool and into the fast water. Which was his mistake and my good fortune. I leaned back, thumbed hard, and he slowed down.

When a fish loses some of its forward momentum, it usually is good business to lay it on as hard as tackle will permit if you want that fish to turn. The pressure and the fast water did it. The musky turned and whipped back into the pool as if he'd seen his own ghost coming downstream to get him.

Then like all big fish, he went to the bottom, which gave me time to grab a deep breath and remember my lessons. It was certain that I couldn't fight the fish. If I were to land him, it would have to be after a long-drawn-out push and-pull contest, with me keeping on just enough to pressure to make him work.

The fish stayed deep, swinging back and forth across the pool with almost pendulum-like regularity. I lost track of time, but it must have been an hour before I began to tire. This thing might keep on all day and into the night, I thought; so I began surveying the shore for a spot where I might beach him. As far as I could see, there was only a single sloping patch of sand in sight, and it was at the far downstream end of the pool.

I got out knee-deep into the water before starting a slow push toward the spit of sand. The musky wasn't very cooperative, but foot by foot — literally — I worked through the rocks around the edge of the pool. The sun was away past noon when I reached the spit, and I sank to the warm sand and worked the fish from a sitting position until I could breathe again. Then I stood up and began pumping the musky toward me.

Things went smoothly until he sighted the white sands. Then, in a single rush, he tore back out into the pool, taking every inch of line I had gained. With an almost childlike gesture I turned left and then right, looking over my shoulder as though for help. Of course, there wasn't anyone to help me. And, of course, there couldn't be anyone to help me. It was the musky and I. Even if there had been someone present, it would still have been just the two of us. It had to be that way now. Just the two of us, and the thought of it got me to shaking again.

There wasn't much to do except to start pumping again. I did, and it was something like walking a horse over a trestle bridge. The second time, the fish came a little farther up the sand spit before turning on the power for a run back to the depths of the pool. The fourth time in, and he was close enough for a good look. Johnny had said he would weigh more than 75 pounds, but on the end of my line, black and green against the white sand, he looked like a 175 pounds, and then in my eagerness I made the fatal mistake. I started walking down the spit toward the fish instead of keeping him coming toward me.

Never walk toward a fish. If he won't come to you, wait, but don't move toward him — whether musky, steelhead, black bass or a big German brown. Just don't walk down to the fish, hoping he will be there for you to net, gaff or shoot, because he won't be. And this musky wasn't. I hadn't taken two steps when he saw me, and it was as if I'd jabbed him with an electrified rod. He went straight to the top of the water. He didn't come all the way out, but sort of skimmed like a flying fish and then power-dived. The line sprayed water to my cheeks as it shuttled from the reel.

I guess I knew it was all over before he came to the end of the line. There was a terrific yank and I was turning limp line back on the spool. I picked up the plug. It was slivered, smashed and the hooks were straight as toothpicks. I don't remember much about walking back off the sandspit, or how long I sat on the banks of the pool, with the rod and the plug lying at my feet and my head in my hands. Johnny's arm around my shoulder awakened me. "He's a great fish, Johnny," I managed to say.

Johnny nodded. He picked up the plug and looked it over. Then tossing it to the ground, he said: "Well, that didn't hurt him any. He's still in there. But nobody'll ever fool him again."

Jason Lucas wrote about "The Maddening Muskellunge" in the January 1952 issue of *Sports Afield*:

Two years ago, some Ontario guides — quiet conservative men — told me of a musky that had washed ashore on the north side of Lake of the Woods. He had evidently died of disease, for he was little more than skin stretched loosely over bones. They said that, from his length, had he been even in fair shape he would unquestionably have weighed well over 100 pounds. They were too conservative to say so, but I believe most of them thought, that in good condition, he would have run well over 125 pounds.

This happened in 1950. As for the size, I can only let the record speak for me. There has never been a verified 60-pounder caught in Lake of the Woods and there has never been any verified proof of a musky bigger than the current world record from anywhere!

In the March 1958 *Fisherman* magazine, in an article entitled "The Mountain States' Unexpected Muskies," by Robert R. Bowers, we find another mention of a super big West Virginia musky:

> Diving back into the history of this underwater cannibal we find that perhaps the largest musky ever known was "Moby Dick," an oft-hooked, never landed muskellunge which haunted the waters of the Elk River. Much to the chagrin of those who challenged old Moby someone wanted that cannibal dead, and killed it the easy way — by dynamiting The fish measured more than 62 inches long, almost a foot longer than the state record! Moby Dick was never weighed, but from Musky standards there is little doubt he'd have reached the 50-60 pound bracket."

We now move ahead to the time somewhere near the early 1950s. Following up on a tip from Peter Haupt, I was able to learn of a very big musky found dead on the Eagle River, Wisconsin, chain of lakes. Thanks to the Alwards of the Chanticleer Inn there, the following dimensions were learned: "The head measured about eight inches across the forehead, and it was estimated to weigh over 60 pounds." (see picture) When the fish was found, it was badly decomposed and only the head could be saved.

The head of the estimated 60-pounder from the Eagle River, Wisconsin, chain, compared with a mounted fish.

In the August 1979, issue of *Fins & Feathers*, editor Steve Grooms wrote about the legend of "Pine Island Pete." It all started in the early 1950s:

> They love to talk about old Pine Island Pete up at Ross' Teal Lake Lodge near Hayward, Wisconsin.
>
> In the evenings, when rods are stowed and the boats bob gently by the docks, the evening cocktail talk drifts inevitably to stories about Pete. Pete's been gone now for about 14 years, but he's sure not forgotten.
>
> Pete was a musky who haunted a weed bar on the north end of picturesque Pine Island on Teal Lake for about a dozen years. A musky that big would necessarily have been a female, but "Pete" sounds better than "Petunia" or some other feminine name. For you see, Pete was a giant among muskies, a truly

Record Muskies?

heroic fish.

They talk about Pete often up at Ross', especially the veteran Teal Lake guides.

Paul Quail talks about him. Pete was the grandest musky Paul has seen in 61 years of guiding for Ross' lodge. During the famous dozen years when Pete roamed his bar, tearing up people's tackle and generally making fishing expensive in his area of Teal Lake, Paul saw more than a few lines broken on Pine island Pete. And Paul was one of the witnesses to Pete's final appearance.

Jesse Ross will tell you about Pete, too. Jesse, who is a couple years younger than Paul, has seen a few muskies in his fifty years of guiding. Jesse will tell you about the day he lifted a shiny new anchor after a session of casting to Pete's bar. Pete didn't challenge any bucktails that day. He attacked that anchor.

Nelson Ross, who represents the second generation of his family to supervise the elegant hospitality of Ross' Lodge, can tell you about fighting and losing Pete. Nelson was one of the first to have Pete on. That was back in the '50s when Pete was a smaller fish, less than 40 pounds. Nelson was winding in a walleye when Pete moved in to assert his claim on that fish. Pete and Nelson tugged in opposite directions on that poor walleye for over half an hour before Pete decided to let go. The walleye was a 16 incher.

From that point on it became widely known that a large fish was working the bar north of Pine Island, and soon the fish had a name. Lots of people had him on and always with the same result. The guides will tell you it wasn't so very hard to get a hook into Pete, but "he had a way of gettin' off." Mostly he broke lines. Over the years Pete ripped off enough bucktails and plugs to set himself up in the tackle business.

Tim Ross, Nelson's son and the lodge's business manager, saw the mighty fish roll near the surface one time. "I've seen a lot of monster muskies mounted and put on display in the bars in Hayward," he will tell you, "but I've never seen one as big as Pete." Pete, in fact, showed himself pretty regularly. Every now and then the giant musky would pop up beside a boat, scaring the wits out of some drowsy panfisherman half full of beer. Tim remembers Pete as "a good tourist fish."

As the years rolled by, Pete grew bigger and so did his legend. His personality gave a special character to the whole lake. Even non-fishing guests at the lodge could share in the excitement of the giant musky that could not be landed. Just as a castle is not truly a castle without a resident ghost, a musky lake is not quite a musky lake without a resident leviathan. Pete singlehandedly made Teal Lake a thrilling place to fish.

Then came the day of disappointment. Somebody was fishing Pete's bar when a big musky hit. After a long fight, the fish was landed and ultimately brought in to the lodge to be weighed. The guides watched with long faces as the scales balanced at 28 pounds. If this was Pete, it was sad to find that he was so small, and even sadder to think that he was now dead.

The very next day, somebody was casting a big lure out on Pete's old bar when a monster of a musky attacked it and popped the line as if it had been a spider web. Everybody smiled. Old Pete was still out there, doing what he did so well.

It was some time after that when one of Ken Eck's clients tied into Pete. This fellow had married a gal who had been fishing muskies all her life. Soon he was a musky fisherman too, full of convictions about how it should be done.

"We had been fishing Pete's bar," Ken recalls, "and he was reeling a Cisco Kid Topper through the weeds. The plug got hung up on the very last weed. When he jerked free, suddenly I saw these huge jaws coming down around the plug. I mean, there wasn't any big splash or showy strike ... just these monstrous jaws closing all around that plug.

He set the hook once, then Pete began to move away from the bar toward deep water. I kept hollering "Hit 'im again!" but he had this idea that he'd tear the hooks loose if he tried to set them a second or third time.

I thought we had Pete anyway. We were way out away from the weeds in clean water, and the fish had been on for some time. Once we had him come by the boat, right close. Suddenly that musky just stood on his head, with his body up in the air beside the boat. The guy's wife was so close to Pete that she could have touched him. I never saw a fish do anything like that before ... he just put his head down, with his body sticking straight up in the air, and then he went down. But we got a real good look at him, and I swear there was four feet of musky sticking up in the air, and if his tail wasn't at least twelve inches wide, I've never seen a ruler!

Pete was moving out to deeper water after that, when suddenly the Cisco Kid Topper came floating up to the surface all by itself. I guess that guy learned about setting a hook several times, but he learned one fish too late. You know, I couldn't eat lunch that day ... my stomach was just tied up in knots. I couldn't even eat supper. It isn't right to let a fish get to you like that, but ooh what a fish he was! I couldn't get him out of my mind.

Ken was never to see Pete alive again, and he has spent many hours since that day thinking about what would have happened if his client had set the hooks again. Maybe Pete would have snapped the line with one shake of his head, or maybe ...

Ken Eck is sure Pete's tail was over 12 inches wide, and he knows that the tail of a 38-pounder is nine inches wide. He's measured them.

Pete's last hurrah came not long afterward, on a day in 1965. None of the guides we spoke to were actually there that day, so we don't have all the details.

This time the man who hooked Pete was John Skruglund, the owner of a cottage on the lake. Maybe he had better tackle than anybody who'd hooked Pete before. Maybe he had better luck. Maybe he was more skillful. Maybe Pete had lost some of his strength that had served him so often in these encounters before. This time, anyway, he did not break free.

No one knows how long the man and the musky dueled. It went on long enough to attract the attention of Paul Quail, the lake's senior guide. The great fish was tiring when Paul cautiously approached Skruglund's boat to say, "Looks like you have a nice fish on. Would you like some help?"

Record Muskies?

"I think I have caught Pine Island Pete," came the answer, "and, yes, I do believe I'd appreciate some help getting him in."

The two boats came together on the water, with Pete Lying beaten on his side. The guides will tell you, "They had that fish for sure. Paul knows what he's doing He's landed hundreds of muskies. He would have gotten that fish in the boat."

Paul never got the chance. At that moment, John Skrugland's fishing partner, who was understandably excited by the sight of the monster Lying alongside the boat, planted a gaff hook deep in Pete's belly.

Water flew every which way, and suddenly Pete broke free and dove down into deep water, carrying the gaff hook in his stomach. He also carried the lure and a short section of fishing line ... the last line he'd ever break. Pete was never seen again, dead or alive.

And these days when the guides sit around the lodge in the evenings to reminiscence about Pete, you can sense a mixture of emotions as they talk. They still feel the loss of the great fish and deeply regret the fact he died at the bottom of the lake without bringing joy to the angler who finally beat him and without bringing the world record back to Wisconsin. Every man who ever tangled with Pete would have loved to see him come at last to adorn one of the walls of the lodge, impressing the tourists in death as he had in life. At the same time, you hear in their stories a strong undercurrent of respect for the fish that refused to be subdued. For Pete was a musky man's musky, the ultimate embodiment of the power, fighting spirit and unpredictability that makes muskies what they are.

Teal Lake still has great muskies, quite possibly fish which carry on the genetic inheritance of Pine Island Pete. Last summer, with no warning and for no apparent reason, a monstrous musky threw itself high into the air right beside a boat fishing not far in front of the lodge. Ken Eck was nearby and he is sure the fish weighed between 50 and 60 pounds. Perhaps there are others out there, too.

But up at Ross' Lodge, they still love to talk about old Pine Island Pete.

Following up a tip from Peter Haupt I came up with the following info. A friend of his had related that he had heard of a picture of a 70-pound speared musky at a tavern in a small town on Lake Winnebago's (Wisconsin) east shore. The fish was taken during sturgeon spearing season in February one year in the 1950s. I followed up with a few phone calls and got some additional information. The fish was supposedly 72 inches long and weighed 76 pounds! It was taken by a local farmer. It was rumored that the Wisconsin Conservation Department (forerunner of the DNR) offered amnesty if the spearer of the fish itself would come forward, hence promoting fund raising for stocking Lake Winnebago with muskies. They failed to lure him, it or the photo. There the trail ended. Further attempts to get information were in vain. I presume due to the fact that it was taken illegally. If it was a musky and not a sturgeon, it would be the largest ever taken by any method!

Another rumor from the 1950s concerned a musky that had been found dying along the shore near MacKenzies Camp on Eagle Lake, that was said to have weighed 62 pounds. I had a friend in the area, Bill Meyers, track it down for me. Bill caught up with the person who found the fish only to find that rumor had added many pounds to the fish, as it had only weighed 27 pounds! Well, that puts another one to rest.

One of the most controversial and sad stories in musky history took place in Wisconsin in 1954. For a year and a half, the late Peter Haupt and I investigated and researched this fish. We started in the newspaper archives of the *Sawyer County Record, The Milwaukee Journal, The Evening Telegram* in Superior, Wisconsin, and others. It was a reported 70-pound 4-ounce musky from Middle Eau Claire Lake, caught by Robert Malo of Port Arthur, Ontario.

I made a visit to the area to interview some of the people who lived there at the time and to get a general pulse of the area. I also had the privilege to view the mounted fish (before it was put on public display). Here are the highlights.

It was early morning June 6, 1954, when Malo, fishing with

The mounted remains of Robert Malo's huge musky.

Record Muskies?

George Cruise of Chicago, hooked the fish on a sucker. After beaching and shooting the fish, people at the resort were alerted. The fish was then taken to a taxidermist in Duluth, weighed and skinned for mounting. At the weigh-in the fish was thought to weigh 69 3/4 pounds. When opened for mounting, the fish had rolls of fat, a partly digested 5 1/2-pound pike and 8 1/4 pounds of eggs. The next day the Minnesota Department of Weights and Measures was called in to verify the scales. The inspector found the scales to be 8 ounces slow! Before going further with the scale, let me interject some thoughts and findings.

During my visit to the area I talked with Wilbur Smith who has been a guide there for over 30 years. Wilbur had gone to Madison the day the fish was caught and didn't get to see it. For a time he said that he doubted a fish that size came from Middle Eau Claire. (It is not a natural musky lake.) Then in a following year after the Malo fish, Wilbur saw one several times in Mid Lake that he thought would go nearer to 80 pounds! Later, he said " Someone broke a spear off in the fish and it was never seen again."

Taxidermist George Flaim called Malo's fish the ugliest musky he ever saw.

When Peter Haupt interviewed the taxidermist he was told: "Ugliest musky I ever saw." This taxidermist mounted at least one a year over 50 pounds, sometimes 55 pounds from Lake of the Woods and also mounted the first 60-pounder in history which came from Eagle Lake in 1939. Peter's statement after visiting with the taxidermist: "At this point I'm convinced Malo's fish weighed 70 pounds 4 ounces." As for myself, i'm convinced a tremendous musky was legally caught but the one thing that was uncertain, the accurate weight, is what kept it from being accepted. There seemed to be no disputing the fact that a big musky had indeed been caught, even by *Field & Stream*, although the letter of refusal from Hugh Grey, then *Field & Stream* editor, indicated the scale was indeed the key item. The utility scale that was used was marked only in pounds (no ounce marks). The estimate at the time of the original weighing ranged from 69 1/2 to 69 3/4, but of course there was no way to know for sure. The angler and the resort operator believed the fish tipped the scales at the 69 3/4-pound mark. When the scales were determined to be 1/2-pound slow they added this to the 69 3/4 and came up with 70 1/4 pounds. More information and the current disposition of the Malo fish will be forthcoming in Chapter 4.

The next reference is in regard to extremely long muskies from Leech Lake, Minnesota. In 1956, Roger Halvorson, a taxidermist from Fergus Falls, Minnesota, mounted a musky caught in Leech Lake that was 66 inches long (see picture), which is 2 1/2 inches longer than the current world record! The problem was the fish weighed only 43 pounds.

The mount of the 66-inch Leech Lake musky.

We now embark on an area that I had originally intended to stay from, that being fish stories. I have decided to enter this area anyway, for a couple of reasons. First of all the stories that follow have credibility. They are termed "stories" only because the fish is still swimming — not because they are lies. In most cases, the anglers involved have tremendous reputations as expert musky anglers. In all likelihood, had any of the fish involved been captured, they would have set a new world record. And secondly, it is stories such as these that keep us going and help add to the musky mystique!

In 1955, Fred and Tony Burmek, joined by Clayton Slack Sr., embarked upon a siege of musky catches that made musky fishing history. In recapping "The Twelve Days," we find that in 12 days of angling, these anglers brought in 17 muskies that totaled 553 1/2 pounds! They had 10 over 30 pounds with six of those over 35 pounds, and the two largest went 41 1/2 and 43 1/2 pounds, plus a 26-pound northern pike! In addition, they caught 25 others that were released! Suffice it to say then that the Burmeks know a big fish when they see one. In 1957 Fred hooked and lost a musky of mammoth proportions. For nearly 20 years he wouldn't write about it because "everyone talks about the big one that got away," but after years of persuasion by brother Tony, who was a witness, Fred finally agreed. Following then is Fred's story as it happened:

A World Record Musky ... Almost!

This traumatic experience began about 2 p.m. on a dark overcast day on October 30, 1957, on the Big Chippewa Flowage near Hayward, Wisconsin.

We were fishing along the drop-off of a big sand bar near the entrance of the west fork of the Chippewa River.

We were casting wooden lures that brother Tony had worked on for many years to perfect. Tony had already caught a 41-pounder that morning near Oscar Treland's resort, on the north end of the flowage, which is one of the best musky areas. We had raised several other big fish there. It was one of those days when you could smell the muskies!

Musky fishermen seldom talk when fishing is good because each man is concentrating on a potential strike.

The water was calm as glass, with a good visibility of our lures nearing the boat.

The air was very quiet with only the sound of a distant flock of geese and the loud splash of our lures on each cast.

Tony's lure was nearing the boat when I heard a sudden gasp and he said "look at that!" The hair on his head bristled and a chill went up my spine as I looked down at the huge fish following Tony's lure. At first glance, it looked like a shark!

Tony started working his lure in a figure 8; but the musky sank out of sight as it seemed to turn back toward the bar. The silence was now static!

We began to fan the area with casts when, all of a sudden, my plug stopped dead! I rocked the boat as I set the hooks, hard — again — and again! The huge musky came to the surface and rolled, the tail coming out of the water like a surfacing whale! Man! He was big!

Tony was on the oars, heading out for deep water. I felt line slipping out from under my thumb as I tried to pull that big fish — my heavy rod was bent and I could hear my loud breathing. Slowly I gained about three yards of line and then it seemed to stop. We were out in deep water and my line slanted down at an angle.

I was aware of Tony putting his rod out of the way and setting the gaff hook in a handy place. My hat seemed to be floating on sweat and this 40 degree day now seemed well up into the 80s! The minutes ticked by.

"He's coming up," I gasped as I saw the slant of my line rising. Suddenly, there it was! About 40 feet away, wallowing on the surface. The jaws of that huge fish opened and his gills flared wide as he shook his head in anger, trying to rid himself of that lure. It was actually a frightening sight. I glanced at Tony, who was shaking his head with an expression of awe and disbelief. He looked at me with sort of a sad expression for he knew that I was on my own, and could do nothing to help me, until I got that monster near the boat

With a sudden heart-stopping splash, that tremendous fish thrashed about for a few seconds and then disappeared. The slant of my line started going straight down. I could not gain a foot of line on it, even though my rod was bent and I put on all the pressure my line would bear.

The minutes seemed like hours as I worked on that fish, with Tony pushing the oars as we followed the fish, who was still down deep. I began to wonder who had whom — as that big fish had led us at least half a mile away from where I hooked it.

Every bone in my body ached and I was grateful to Tony for the sips of coffee, as he held a cup to my lips, and for the puff or two of a cigarette he also held for me.

It is impossible to describe the strength of that fish as we followed it. My arms and shoulders were numb with pain, especially when the fish would thrust forward on its short runs, taking line at will, in spite of my bowed rod and the constant pressure I had on it.

"How long is it now, Tony?" I asked. "About — well, close to two hours," he said in a hoarse voice. Suddenly I felt that something was wrong! The fish had been in the same spot now for quite awhile. I wondered if it was snagged. There it was again! That odd crunching feeling transmitted through my line.

Whoosh! The world came to an end. My line went slack. I reeled it slowly. It felt as if the line had torn. It seemed I reeled a long time when my leader appeared — and then — only the head of my lure was there! The big fish had ground my lure to splinters!

Gloom — We just sat there in silence — each man with his own thoughts — it was getting dark. Finally, Tony who had been gazing across the wide expanse of the Chippewa Flowage, looked over at me and said, "Nobody, but nobody, will believe this."

I was finding it hard to believe myself, and I had just experienced it. "How big do you guess it was?" I asked Tony.

He thought a moment and then said, " I would never tell this to anyone; but since we both saw it, I would say it would have weighed well over 80 pounds."

We motored back to the resort in darkness; and as we pulled up to the docks, the resort owner was there to meet us. "How did you do, fellows?"

"We got one, a 41-pounder," I said, "but you should have seen ..." and then I stopped.

The resort owner had a grin on his face; and I knew that Tony was right. Nobody would believe it.

Tony and I have, at various times over the past 15 years, tried to tell the story but in each case, you can see the doubt in the listener's eyes. However, in fairness, I cannot honestly say that I would believe anyone who tried to tell me about an 80-pound musky that got away!

But it did happen; and I'm glad I've finally told the story as it happened. It had to be told.

Someday, perhaps, you will hook into one of those big muskies out on the Chippewa Flowage, or wherever you fish, because there are fish that big in several lakes in northern Wisconsin.

But I hope you land it! Because it's hell to have the thrill of your life sound like a fish story!

Normally, most musky stories like the above end here, but not this one. Recently, while talking musky with Jim Kennedy Jr. and Sr., the elder Kennedy told a story about a set of very large musky jaws that Tony Burmek has. Although I forgot about it for the time being, I recalled the story as I was preparing this information, so I contacted Tony by phone and asked him to tell me the story about the jaws and where he found them. His story follows:

It was a year when the Chippewa Flowage waters were low, which made the beaches wide. I was guiding two men, when one asked to go to shore for a rest, not feeling well. So I pulled up on a shore where the West Fork of the Chippewa River came into the Flowage (but now part of the big lake). There were a lot of giant stumps along that shore with long roots in all directions.

Since the man wanted to rest, I decided to take a walk along the beach, to hunt for Indian artifacts. From where I walked, I could see the area where Fred hooked and lost that big musky. We never talked about it because it sounded like the old cliche, "you shoulda seen the one that got away!" But, after around 20 years later, Fred and I decided to write it as close as our memories could give an accurate account. You can understand, Larry, that we wrote it with the attitude that it happened, like that, and to heck with anybody who don't believe it (and believe us we didn't expect anyone to believe it!). But, surprisingly, we get nice letters about it saying, "That must have been quite an experience." Perhaps they believe it because we've caught so many muskies over a combined total of

70 years of musky fishing between us! The reason I've wasted your time in writing the above, Larry, is because I found those big musky jaws within 200 yards of where that big one hit! This was two years later! But that will be a mystery. We will never know if the jaws I found were that fish's.

But to get back to the jaw, I walked along that beach and alongside of one of those huge roots, I spotted the skeleton of the musky. When I first saw the odd looking thing, I didn't recognize it as a fish! I thought it was an animal skull. Too bad it was not up closer to shore on this wide sandy beach (as I said the water was very low) in dry sand. It was close to the water's edge, so as gently as I could, I scraped heavy, wet sand away from it, but it began to disintegrate like white powdered chalk.

At one point I did have the huge skull and part of the back bones, but as they dried they started to fall apart. I finally ended up with the two halves of the lower jaw. One half is shown on the enclosed picture (see photo). The hand holding the jaw is that of an 8 year old boy, small. The picture was taken lying right along the jaw of my 52-pounder. Don Johnson, sports writer

Musky jaw found by Tony Burmek held alongside the head of a mounted 52-pounder.

for the *Milwaukee Sentinel* saw the jaws and was really amazed at the size of them. (He mentioned them in one of his columns.)

Johnson's column in part: "... the best relief from the malady (cabin fever) I've had lately was just sitting around on a snowy afternoon and talking with Tony and Rudy Burmek of Milwaukee ... Tony handed me a plastic box containing only the jawbones of a fish. A musky. A monster. The jaws were huge. The teeth were like a dog's. 'Compare them with that 52-pounder,' Tony said, pointing to a mounted trophy displayed in his dining room. There was no comparison.

"'I asked a biologist to estimate what this fish must have weighed,' Tony related, peering pensively into the box as I handed it back. "He guessed it was at least 85 pounds,' he said."

Anyway, Larry, back to the day I found them, in the eve. I took the jaws to the bar in Hayward where Cal Johnson's former world record musky is on display. A 67-plus-pounder. When I held the jaw against the glass of Cal's muskie, the jaws' teeth were almost twice as long! The crowd that gathered around was amazed! I heard various estimates ranging from 80 to 100 pounds, from all the pros who have seen it, and guessed at the size. My honest opinion is that it was around 80 pounds. And, my guess is that the fish died of old age, or as you know, it could have hit some lure wrong that lodged in its throat, or tried to swallow a fish too big to go down its stomach. That too, is a mystery.

Was it Fred's fish? One additional note on the picture of the jaws from Tony:

I did something I shouldn't have, because at the time I found them, I considered them a souvenir! Note the back end of the jaw (see picture). It was longer, and had sharp jagged edges, so I sawed the ends off as you can see.

Before moving on, I wanted to relate one more story from Tony, regarding a 58 1/2-pounder he caught about 35 years ago (early 1940s) that he now thinks may have been a hybrid:

When I caught that 58 1/2-pound hybrid musky about 35 years ago, a guide's pay was $8 a day then. That was before I could afford to mount fish. I remember remarks about the "funny looking round tail ends," and the odd spots and stripes on its side. That fish caused such a sensation in the Hayward area because everyone thought it was a world record (genuine, as hybrids were unknown then). A crowd of us went to almost every scale in the town's meat markets! Its weight varied from 58 1/2 to 59 1/2 pounds. Later we cut off the head, spread the gills, and nailed it on a friend's barn. The rest of it we cut up and split among friends.

Ouch! Although Tony's fish was short of the world record at the time, if it was indeed a hybrid, it would still be the hybrid world record today!

A final note from Tony:

The big fish population has really gone down since those days. I think that I averaged at least 10 forty plus pounders a season. But, pollution, fishing pressure, big motors, etc., etc., are taking their toll ...

The next reference I have comes from the book *Musky Fishing* by J.W. Jackson, 1958:

A reliable man who was with the Wisconsin fishery service for 35 years — and whose word I respected — once told me that when a state fishing crew — spawn netters — seined the Fishtrap Lake in Vilas County area northeastern Wisconsin, they netted a musky so large it required three men to free it from the net. It was their combined judgment that it would weigh about 125 pounds — and they had handled a great many muskies.

We will now move on to a couple of incidents that happened to that "Grand Old Gentleman" of Wisconsin musky fishing — the late Bill Hoeft. I believed Bill when he said that he would rather catch a new world record than receive a tax-free gift of a million dollars! In an article Bill wrote entitled "I'll Tell You About Muskies" in the August 1970 issue of *Outdoor Life* he tells of a couple times he came close:

Bob was also fishing with me on a hot calm day in August of 1957. That's the day I saw the biggest musky I've ever seen on the end of a fishing line. We were working Big St. Germain Lake near the town of St Germain, Wisconsin. We'd been casting plugs from dawn to nearly noon without a strike.

I'd rowed our boat to within casting range of a stand of pipe grass edging the shoreline. The water was no more than three feet deep there. I wasn't enthusiastic about the location, because I haven't hooked many muskies in the shallows during the midday hours. But you just can't predict where a musky is going to be.

Bob was casting a huge black-and-white underwater plug. He flipped it along the edge of that pipegrass and made a couple of turns on his reel handle. Then Bob just about fell flat on his face when something belted his plug with a violence that almost ripped his rod from his hands. He was so surprised he couldn't speak. He just hung on and grunted.

The man on the oars is important when a big fish is hooked because he has to keep the boat away from the fish. When a musky is charging back and forth under the boat, you can kiss him goodbye; you can't keep up with his blinding speed. He'll out maneuver you and smash your rod or snap your line. I just about broke my back pulling on those oars to get away from the shore and the fish.

That move put some additional pressure on Bob's line and made the fish jump. I couldn't believe my eyes when he cleared the water. I've seen hundreds of jumping muskies, and I can judge their size quite closely. I've estimated the length and weight of many of my own fish quite accurately while I was fighting them. Later, my estimates proved out fairly well with tape and scales.

I'd bet my life that Bob's fish weighed well over 60 pounds, and I wouldn't be surprised if it topped 70. The musky's length was upwards of five feet, and his girth was like a fat man's He was a very dark brown, and that means something: the bigger the musky is, the darker his color. That one was the darkest musky I have ever seen.

The big brute jumped three times. Each time he came down he hit the water broadside. And each time, he blasted out a geyser of white spray as though somebody had dropped a railroad tie out of the sky.

The third jump ended the spectacle. The musky's massive weight and lunging power straightened out Bob's snap swivel as though it were made of well-cooked spaghetti. When his line went limp, we were the two most disappointed fishermen in the world.

Record Muskies?

I've encountered one musky that I'm sure was even larger. If I had caught that one, I'd have the world record. I don't see how that fish could have weighed less than 75 pounds, maybe a lot more. Perhaps I shouldn't give those figures, because I never actually saw the fish, but here's what happened.

Tom Olson and I were fishing Buckatabon Lake on a calm summer evening 13 years ago. We were casting large suckers, and it was nearly dark when the giant hit. Boy, did he hit! My rod tip shot forward, as though I'd hooked a runaway bronco. There was that one single smash, and that was all. I peeled out slack line in hopes that the fish still had the sucker, but I knew in my heart that he was gone.

Eventually I reeled in my bait. I've never seen a sucker so mutilated. It was completely disemboweled, and its flanks were deeply cut.

Those tooth marks astonished me. They were nearly 10 inches apart, and the only word for that dimension is fantastic. I couldn't wait to get back to my restaurant and measure the jaw widths of some of my mounted fish. It's still hard to believe what I discovered.

You have to assume that there's some shrinkage when fish are mounted, but the widest jaw width I came up with was 5 1/2 inches. Then I carefully remeasured the widest spread of the slashes in that sucker. It was an unbelievable 9 1/2 inches. You can draw your own conclusions about whether or not that musky would have hung up a new rod-and-reel record.

Bill also lost a big one in 1978. It was the first week in November and he and Jess had given up bait casting and had gone to live suckers as they do each fall. They fish with suckers big enough for people to eat and when they get a taker, they don't expect it to be a small one. Bill says that this taker was a real one and he told Jess to lay on the oars because it really must be a monster. He got her to the surface with a load of weeds on the line like a hay shock. They got her to within 15 feet of the boat with her dorsal fin and tail out of the water. Bill says she was better than 60 inches and he feels sure it was better than 60 pounds. Jess remembered the motor and ran to tilt it up out of the way, but when the pressure slacked on the line by leaving the oars, the big musky belched that sucker up and was gone. Bill said he camped on this spot until the weather ran him off, but all he got was one more sucker slashed up!

Bill Hoeft probably spent as much time as anyone in Wisconsin chasing big muskies.

In late 1979 a letter was received at the Muskies, Inc. office and forwarded to me. It was information on a large musky:

Dear Sir:

In 1962 I was fishing Big McKenzie Lake near Spooner, Wisconsin ... and I caught a musky the likes of which I will never catch again.

It was 57 inches long, had a 28-inch girth, and weighed about 60 pounds. It was a female musky with a large egg sac in it.

I've fished that lake for 25 years and finally caught my keeper musky. I am sending a picture for your viewing. (See photo).

If you are interested, I caught it on a 5-inch chub minnow using a #8 Eagle Claw hook with a split shot weight to get the minnow to the bottom. I was fishing 10 feet of water near a weed bed. The time of day was noon — 12 noon and it was cloudy.

The Wisconsin 60-pounder caught out of season.

Interesting I thought, how a 60-pound fish caught in the 1960s wouldn't be recorded anywhere, so I wrote to the angler and asked for more details. As it turned out the angler was ice fishing for northern pike or walleyes on December 30. Here's his account:

The season had closed November 15, 1962, I was alone when I caught it. The guys said you'll never catch one like that in a million years. Reason I kept it was because I grabbed it in the eyes to paralyze the fish and thusly blinded it. If I would have thrown it back, it would have bellied up and died under the ice. Took about 20-30 minutes to land the fish.

In September of 1979 I spent an enjoyable week at Lindmier's North Shore Lodge on Eagle Lake. During one of my visits to the lodge, I noticed a dried musky head on the mantel of the fireplace. Noticing it was from a very large fish, I inquired about it. I was told that it was from a dead fish washed up on shore in the beach area one spring, and that it weighed over 60 pounds. It didn't appear to be that big to me, but it was old and dried out and it sure is possible for Eagle Lake! At any rate, it makes for good fireside conversation.

In 1986 I had the opportunity to talk to George Moore about this fish. He had been there at the time and was able to provide a picture.

It was indeed a huge fish — George is well over six feet tall!

In recent years, stories of big muskies have become a rarity. The September 9, 1977, issue of *Outdoor News* carried a story of a 71-pounder that had been speared illegally in the Cass Lake area of Minnesota around 1965-1967. Of course no one knew who or where, just that it weighed 71 pounds. This same article made mention of the finding of the "decomposed remains of a musky which was well over 70 pounds on the north shore of Pike Bay." My only question is that if the fish was decomposed, how was weight determined?

Next I bring you an undated reference, a supposed 60 1/2-pounder. This fish is mounted and on display in a northern Wisconsin watering hole. The fish was caught by Harry Yarbrough from the Trego Flowage on the

This musky washed up on the shore of Ontario's Eagle Lake and was said to weigh over 60 pounds.

Namekagon River. No date of catch is listed, but the length is 58 inches. Its girth is not listed, but it appears average. Personal opinion, considering known weights vs. lengths and girths and considering that there is no verification of the listed weight; I would place the weight at closer to 55 pounds, especially in view of the fact that I have had the opportunity to see five mounted muskies (verified) over 60 pounds, and many in the 50-pound range (several of these were mounted by the same taxidermist as the fish in question).

From *Rod & Gun*, summer of 1970, comes an article by Zack Taylor entitled "What's The Truth About All Those Musky Lies?" Zack has a reference to a St. Lawrence River musky of 80 pounds. To quote:

A St. Lawrence ship channel was once deepened by dynamite and an unexpected result of the explosion was a belly-up musky. It weighed an even 80 pounds!

Thanks to the late Owen Chelf of the Kentucky Silver Muskie Club, I was able to track down a big musky that became the subject of a hearing in the Kentucky Court of Appeals. On March 12, 1965, a civil action was filed in the Hart County Circuit Court by Quentin Vance against Otha Durrett alleging that on February 18. 1965, he set two baited fishing hooks on poles in Little Barren River in Hart County, Kentucky, about 25 yards south of the confluence of Little Barren River with Green River, and he further alleged in said lawsuit that on February 20, 1965, that the said Otha Durrett, while fishing at this spot took from one of said lines a muskellunge weighing 51 pounds. The two baited hooks were attached to lines and some sort of stob or poles and had been visited about noon by Mr. Vance and when he left them they were both baited with live suckers. That same afternoon Mr. Durrett was fishing in the same vicinity with rod and reel.

A very large muskellunge fish took the bait on Mr. Vance's fishing line and Mr. Durrett began to pull it in. The line broke and the fish attempted to get back into deeper water. Mr. Durrett jumped into the water and caught the fish with his hands and with the help of Ernest Roundtree, who was fishing in the vicinity, the fish was dragged onto the bank and Mr. Durrett took it home. He had pictures taken of it, had it mounted and refused to return it to Mr. Vance. In a suit for damages, Mr. Vance recovered $750.00. Mr. Durrett then appealed the case to the appellate court. His story was that he was fishing at the mouth of Little Barren River with his rod and reel and he caught a small sucker fish about 10 inches long. He took his sucker and baited an unattended bare hook and line that was tied to a stob on the edge of the bank of Green River. As a result of this, he caught this large muskellunge about one hour later.

And, so it goes ... what was undoubtedly a very large musky ended up in court instead of the record books!

As the trail of big muskies from long ago grows faint, I have begun to pursue the credible stories of recent times. As stated, I had originally intended to stay away from fish stories, but opted to proceed in cases where the angler's credibility was such that the stories, in all likelihood, did happen! Following is one such instance. It involved the late Bill Tutt; I personally knew Bill to be a top notch musky hunter and sportsman, who had tagged and released many large muskies. His story is about "Big George."

Big George
By Bill Tutt

We bought the resort in the winter of 1966. It's located in north central Wisconsin's Iron County, about 12 miles out of Mercer, on the Turtle-Flambeau Flowage. Prior to that, I had been traveling for Bear Archery Company as a sales representative and this area was part of my territory.

I was introduced to musky fishing by a dealer of mine at that time, along with the resort owner where I usually stayed, both of whom were musky freaks. We spent many ten to twelve hour days together, "chasing the greens," and the bug bit me hard.

The thought of living on one of the best musky waters in the country was almost unreal, but I have learned to live with it. I looked forward to the season of 1967 more than I could describe, having visions of all those hours in the boat with our guests, or close friends, doing what I so loved to do. The only fly I was to find in the ointment was, none of the guests fished muskies, and neither did any of my friends, save for the two locals who I then saw much less of than when I'd been traveling.

Consequently, when I fished, which was at least a portion of every day, I fished alone. When I'd mention muskies in the bar, or hint around for someone to go with me, most of them would look at me like I'd fallen out of a tree, or like I should not be allowed out without a keeper of some sort. I soon kept my mouth shut, like most minorities, and quietly took to the boat alone.

The Flambeau is a large and often frustrating body of water to fish for the average fisherman, inasmuch as there is a distinct lack of weed cover. I, too, was accustomed to fishing over weeds, shorelines, bars, etc. in much smaller inland lakes. Immediately I was awed by the overall size of the pond which confronted me; 175 miles of shoreline; 18,000 acres of water — and very few weeds. In short, it scared the hell out of me!

Luckily, the best of the musky fishing lies close to our resort, so, I concentrated on a small area, approaching it as I would a comparable size lake, forgetting as best I could the vastness of the surroundings. It paid off. Almost at once I could literally weigh the results.

Very soon, too, I found the heat in the bar I'd been receiving much less intense. In fact, it did a complete reversal as I began to gloat and feed it back to the walleye fishermen who had been on my case originally. I found them mute, suddenly, if not downright surly.

I caught about 40 muskies that first summer, the largest of which was thirty-six pounds. Not once was anyone in the boat with me! But, herein lies the story.

That first summer alone, I raised not once but several times, a musky of trophy proportions.

I had worked sport shows with the archery company for years. At every

Sentinel Sport Show in Milwaukee, I had stood in awe, gazing at the former world record from Hayward to the point where I could see it with my eyes closed. I had caught one myself which weighed forty-one pounds, so a "good fish" was not exactly new to me. However, the one in Baraboo was something else again. She haunted a shallow sandbar, on the east side of, what was one of the original lakes before the dam was built in 1926.

With the fluctuation the depth over the bar varies from three to six feet on the average, with dropoffs east and west running to twenty-two and forty-five feet, respectively. Though basically void of weed growth, there were a few, and also scattered driftwood snags and deadheads strewn about randomly. It was next to one of these that Big George (as I named her) hung out.

The submerged portion was sizeable enough, but the limb protruding above the waterline was nothing more than a marker, a casting target, certainly no indicator as to what lurked below. It was, however, a godsend in rough water as it enabled me to pinpoint about where to brace my feet in anticipation of her "runs on the boat," which came on the average of seven out of ten times, believe it or not. And it was unbelievable if not incomprehensible, that a fish that size could be viewed so readily. She was a joy to have around, to say the least, and I can't begin to guess how many musky fishermen she helped me hook by just showing herself.

Many times in the bar at the resort I would casually invite some walleye nut to take a short ride to "see a nice fish," only to watch them go slackjawed in shock as she'd hit short or swirl near the bait. I've seen more knees give out, refusing to support the necessary body weight, than a football trainer in charge of running backs and wide receivers.

Between Big George and myself, (and yes, I realize the contradiction of name to sex, so no mail please) we slowly began to convert, even manufacture, musky fishermen.

In the four seasons I fished for her, attempting to induce her to hit, she was seen, literally, dozens of times by dozens of people. She became a legend in her own time, as they say.

My closest guesstimate of her size would be sixty-six inches, sixty-four pounds. I had her at arm's length more times than I can ever recount and I was looking ... hard! She was a "ton" more fish, so to speak, than my State Record musky in 1971, and that was a keeper at fifty-five inches, forty-five pounds. six ounces.

She was not at all fussy about what she chased. You could throw anything in the tackle box (or all of it for all I know) and here she'd come, just like a freight train. The lure would hit the water and I'd start the retrieve when suddenly this V-shaped wake would appear behind it. It would continue to swell and rise until it was about 5 or 6 inches high. My pulse would pound and increase along with the wake, as if they were one and the same.

Seldom, though, would she do the same thing two times in a row. One time she'd close with blinding speed to boil beneath a plug or around a bucktail, and the next time she'd merely keep pace to the boatside where she'd lie there, staring up with those all-knowing eyes, only to sink slowly from sight. At times I'd realize after such a display, that every muscle in my body was like a banjo string. Had someone placed a hand on my shoulder at the instant, I'm sure I would have either jumped completely out of the boat or fainted dead away.

It's hard to explain how you react, after a time, to that kind of thing. I suppose you could actually compare it to a game, of sorts. I fully expected to see her more often than not, but after a while I really didn't expect her to hit, although I had to play my part in the game and be ready just in case. We played it daily for four seasons, just that way: I'd throw, she'd show, and I'd go. Very seldom would she ever play twice in a matter of moments, but it was not uncommon to see her morning and evening of the same day. Numerous times she'd blast a surface bait clear out of the water or roll over one, but never did she actually hit a lure. This went on from June of 1967 until August of 1970.

Mel Johnson, a friend of mine from Peoria, Illinois, arrived on Saturday of that first week in August, He and his wife, Pauline, came for a week to just "lay around." He said he might fish walleye a little, if the mood struck him, but he had never tried muskies and really didn't care to, much to my chagrin. He did, however, relent to the point of going with me that first evening to watch.

To make a long story short, Mel saw a week of musky fishing that I dare say would stack up to anybody's, anytime, anywhere. He never fished the whole week, but he was with me from Saturday evening till the following Friday night when I caught nine muskies in ten trips out. They ranged in size from 26 1/2 to 38 pounds. Never once did he lift a rod to make a cast, he just watched. How 'bout that?

We were never out over an hour and a half at any one time, and never failed to boat a fish any time out, that is to say until Wednesday evening, when I finally hooked Big George.

It was cloudy all day with a chop on the water which worsened every hour.

Mel and Pauline went somewhere for the day and I occupied myself with routine chores around the resort, champing at the bit the entire time. By then Mel had become my good luck charm, or at least it seemed so.

Another friend of mine, Art Matthias, from Milwaukee arrived to spend the night as was his habit when he was in the area. At that time he too traveled for an archery company. Like Mel, Art was not a musky fisherman, in fact he did not fish and had never seen a big fish in the water.

Only one of our guests that week had even thrown for musky. Also from Milwaukee, Louie Hlavenka had been out with me one time some weeks before, to try his hand, but had not purchased any equipment as yet. He had been fortunate enough, however, to see Big George.

Louie came over to the bar that morning to look once more at the fish I'd caught the night before. It was 49 1/2 inches, 36 pounds. We shot the breeze for awhile and before he left he borrowed a rod and reel and one bucktail from me. He said he might give it a go, then left.

He was back within the hour with skin the color of parchment and hands that were still shaking badly. I almost passed out when he said it had been Big George that had hit him. She smashed the third cast he'd made with such violence that Louie was paralyzed. He said it never occurred to him to set the hooks. He simply locked both thumbs on the reel and held on as she headed off the bar toward deep water, towing the boat and Louie behind.

When she at last spit the tail, he said he then sat down for a long time, he never dreamed anything would hit his lure and hadn't even bothered to take a gaff or net; nothing but the rod, reel and one bucktail.

I almost spit up at his account of the happenings. I'd been after her for four years and nothing. He stumbles out and hangs her on the third cast not knowing whether he was afoot or horseback. By then I was really champing at the bit.

The wind kept increasing throughout the day as one by one our guests gave up the ghost and returned to the resort. They began gathering in the bar, settling in for the remaining hours, til bedtime after lashing down boats and gear in the rough water.

Art joined my wife and I for dinner and Mel arrived about that time. I gave him an account of Louie's harrowing experience as he sat shaking his head. Then I dropped the bomb. I casually mentioned that I was anxious to get over there to see if she was still hungry. Marj went into orbit, Art and Mel went pale, I went to the boat.

Of one thing I' m fairly certain. I'm very sure that mine was the only boat on the entire flowage that evening. We never saw a soul the whole time we were out there and I never talked to anyone after that who had gone out that night. It's easy to say now, but it' s true. I knew, with an inner certainty, that if I could get to Baraboo, she was going to hit. I can't explain it further, I just knew!

It was a hairy ride, even I'll concede that, and I've been in on a lot of them. Art and Mel are both big men. Art stands 6'6" and weighed 286, while Mel was 6'2" and 235.

I'm 6' 160 pounds. At the time I had a 16' Lund, with an 18hp Evinrude. We drove directly into the teeth of a southeast wind getting over to Baraboo and the sandbar. In open water it was no longer waves, but swells with troughs between the walls of water five feet high.

My admiration for Art's courage did not diminish during the trip; I knew he could not swim a stroke; I knew, too, that he had to be petrified. We made it at any rate and I headed the boat around the south end of the sandbar, next to the small island where it ends.

The way the wind was skirting the island we would drift almost directly across it, and at one hell of a rapid rate. The whipping of the treetops as the wind whistled through and the froth and foam on the water was nothing short of eerie, giving it sort of a greenish glow. As soon as I killed the motor we picked up speed as the wind shot us along.

I quickly picked up my rod which was already rigged with a yellow tail. The color did not please me at all with the cloud cover overhead, but I knew with the speed of the drift that there wasn't time to change then. I asked Mel to

Record Muskies?

dig out a black one as I spotted the snag. With the boat racing and the clouds rolling and tumbling, I shot the first cast toward her hideout. It hit right at the base of the snag and I retrieved it swiftly, deciding as it neared the boat that I had better change it. I lifted it free of the water, unscathed, and replaced it with the black one Mel had dug out.

Turning back, looking for the snag once more, I saw we'd drifted out of range already. Something different would have to be tried or we'd be here a long time, averaging one cast per drift.

Starting the motor, I ran back around the end of the bar to set another drift along the same line. The motor itself could be the problem I realized then, for the screw was not tight enough to hold the lower unit clear of the water, especially as rough as it was. A further consideration of the speed of drift prompted me to decide that the anchor was the only answer as much as I dreaded trying it. I had Art drop it and as it finally caught, I handed him my knife, with instructions to cut the rope if and when I told him. So, with Art hanging onto the bow with one hand, clutching my knife with the other and Mel riveted to his seat in the middle, I hurled the black bucktail toward the snag.

The hair parted and flared in the air as it settled to the surface, in about the same spot the yellow one had landed before. The result, however, was much different this time. Never will I forget the next twenty minutes!

No sooner had the tail hit the water, than Big George hit the tail. She was the kind of musky you dream about, and it was the kind of hit you dream, too. It was equivalent to a surface bait type hit, inasmuch as the tail did not sink at all. There was a tremendous eruption of spray and foam as she nailed it on a swirl, going away. After the boil of the hit there was a hole, a void as it were, where water had been but wasn't any longer. It was about half the size of a pool table top and it remained for far longer than you can imagine, even with the wind blowing it should have closed immediately, but it didn't. It was unbelievable!

From the hit, everything seemed to happen in slow motion. It's hard to explain, but Mel and Art said later that they recalled it the same way. I felt the awesome, solid jolt of the strike and the sheer feeling of power up the line as I set the hooks. It traveled up my arms and across my shoulders and back. After all those practical sessions we'd had, the message was now clear: this time we were playing for keeps: or rather, this time we weren't playing at all.

I set the hooks the second time as a matter of formality, as there was no doubt in my mind she was hooked hard from the start. She was in about four feet of water when she hit. I fully expected her to head out to a deeper hole and more room, but she didn't, she headed straight for the boat.

I yelled at Art to cut the anchor rope as I frantically picked up slack line. She was plowing along, just under the surface, leaving a wake like an arrowhead which pointed right at me. Her dorsal fin and tail broke water as she neared the boat, some eight yards away. Glancing quickly, I saw that the motor had, as I feared, dropped into the water, that' s where she was headed. Holding the rod high with my right hand, I jerked the lower unit clear just as she slipped under

111

the back corner of the boat on the left side.

I was conscious of the line literally singing through the water as she came past. The three of us heard it every time she got close to the boat, almost as if it was a sound of protest from the strain, and stress. She remained quite close to the boat the entire time I had her on. Never once did she show any inclination to leave the shallow bar. She was never further away than about ten yards and seldom out of sight under the water.

The line of least resistance for her was downwind, toward deep water, which lay a scant twenty yards distant. Had she chosen it she would have been in a depth of thirty-five feet, but she never once swung to the downwind side of the boat.

When I described earlier Art and Mel's size, it was for a reason, During the ensuing battle one of them, and I don't remember which one, made mention of the fact that she was holding the boat in a stationary fashion on the bar, which she continued to do throughout. She held that much weight in that much wind for twenty minutes. We never gained a total of eight yards the whole time. I'd bet my resort there's not a human alive who could do it: for two minutes, let alone twenty. It was the most awesome display of courage and sheer strength the three of us will ever see, I have no doubt.

Four times in all I worked her in alongside the boat only to have her spook and make a short run away. The effortless way she'd run was breathtaking. With a seemingly gentle stroke of that broomsized tail she'd rip line off the reel as though there were nothing attached at all. My thumb would smart as I'd attempt to snub her down. There was no way.

After gaining that few yards' breathing room she liked to maintain, she'd lay near the surface sweeping that tail back and forth as she faced away from us, holding a sixteen foot boat, motor, three grown men and gear in a fixed position, while the wind blew a gale across the lake we had all to ourselves.

With the weight of the fish, the pitching boat, and a motor that refused to stay put, I had my hands full. My arms began to suffer a burning sensation and felt leaden. I began to give thought to the gaffing process and knew it was going to be a sticky thing at best. I had visions of trying to hold her up with one hand while wielding the gaff with the other as she made a move at the motor: it made me shudder just to think of it.

I made a decision. Mel would have to handle the gaff. I didn't really like the idea, but it seemed to be the thing that made the most sense. He had watched me gaff some nice fish over the past four days. so that was the way it would be. To refresh his memory under pressure, I explained where I wanted him to hit her and that I didn't want him to worry about hitting her too hard: just a good, solid. sharp rap would do it.

Up to that point there had been no conversation in the boat the entire time I'd had her on. Art's comment now was, "I never dreamed a fish could get that big! I still can't believe it!" Mel made a remark about her ancestral background and let it drop.

She was really showing signs of fatigue by that time. so I told Mel to get set and we'd give her a try. He picked up the gaff and knelt in the bottom of the boat as I started applying additional pressure. Three different times she had thrashed about on the surface, shaking her head from side to side in an effort to throw the tail. Not once had she shown any inclination to jump if, indeed, she could have.

The last two times I brought her to the boat she came, head on, mouth wide open with the great gills flared and working. It looked roomy enough down the gullet to allow a man's head inside without danger of scraping his ears on either side. We could clearly see the bucktail on those occasions. It was buried through the gill plate on her right side. One hook of the front treble was past the barb, and two on the trailer. In short, other than breaking the line, she never had a chance.

Her coloration, compared to the majority of muskies taken from this body of water, was extremely brownish in tint, rather than the dark emerald shades of green we're used to. Then. too, the color covered more of her body toward the belly than occurs on younger, smaller fish: much less white on the underside.

Mel readied himself as I brought her closer. She was rolling partially over onto one side by then, her gills snapping in a final effort to gain strength. It was futile; however, at that point it was as good as over. As I stepped over the seat separating Mel and me, I glanced at Art. He had a deathgrip on the side of the boat, his fleshy face was chalk white as he stared at the trophy of a size few men will ever see.

Coaxing her gently, I pulled her head toward the transom end of the boat, positioning her broadside. She slid along the surface easily, all fight gone. As she drew even with Mel, he raised the gaff and I immediately realized the mistake I'd made, but, too late. Mel's left handed!

I had been so careful, done everything at a snail's pace to eliminate the chance of something like this happening and even then, I blew it. The only possible way he could have hit her first without hitting the line was to have swung the gaff backhanded. Under the circumstances, it was not his responsibility to think of it, it was mine. I blew it.

As he swung the gaff, the boat rose on a swell with the gunnel rising between Mel and the musky. The handle of the gaff made contact with the boat just prior to reaching the line or the fish. The result was the wooden handle splintered but did not break in half. The hook portion sliced cleanly through the cable leader as if one had cut it with a knife. Though the lower part of the gaff made contact with the skull, a considerable amount of impetus was spent. The blow did little. if any damage physically other than to stun her momentarily.

After the leader parted she lay awash on the surface, rolling over then on her left side. I shouted at Mel to gaff her. hoping he'd be able to at least get the hook into her, giving some chance. He was so shocked at the fact that she was free that my words did not register at all. I yelled a second time as I made a lunge for the side of the boat in an attempt to grab her with my hands, but I couldn't reach her.

We drifted quickly away then, but she remained on top and unmoving, simply floating on her side. I threw the rod down and started the motor, spun the boat into the wind and went back. She was still atop the water, making no effort to swim, but as the boat neared her she began to stir. Mel was crouched over the side with the splintered gaff at the ready as we closed on her. We were within a few scant yards of her when she at last spooked and went under. We could see her as we went over her, but Mel was unable to reach her with the gaff.

I kept circling the area in hopes she'd show again, which at last she did, but it didn't help us. She made one attempt to jump and throw the tail, but it was a puny effort.

I never saw her again. No one ever saw her again. I checked the area every day for about three weeks to no avail. There' s an old adage which says it all. I won the battle, but I lost the war!

The shame of it is the waste, not the fact that I lost her. Had she merely thrown the tail and gotten off, it wouldn't have bothered me very long. I'd have taken up the chase once again, as before. However, hooked as she was, showing blood from the gills when last we saw her, there's no doubt in my mind she died. With the wound and exhaustion, she probably went very quickly, but it's little consolation. She suffered more than was her due; she deserved better.

The way it ended took something out of musky fishing for me. A touch of something special that used to be there but isn't any more; and never will be. As I sit here, now, I know where other big fish are in the Flambeau, one of which is a much larger musky than the one just described, believe it or not. I heard accounts of sightings of it long before I was fortunate enough to see it close up for myself. The first time I had it follow to the boat until it was literally at boatside I was not in the least excited as I thought to myself, "Look at that stupid sturgeon, following a plug." Then I got a good, close look and damn near fell out of the boat.

My boat was 58 inches across the beam and on two different occasions she followed, to then sink, passing directly beneath it. Standing up, glancing quickly from side to side, I was able to see fish on both; she was huge.

She's not nearly as cooperative as Big George, however, for in all the times I've thrown at her, she's only shown twice. I'm reluctant to even add this, but I will at Larry's prompting.

There is as much difference in size between this fish and Big George as there was between Big George and my 45-pounder, and that's a lot!

But, I'll have to add, there was only one "Big George!"

In 1978, while fishing Lake of the Woods with Bob Kmitch and the late Art Lawton, and under the guidance of Dr. Jerry Jurgens, Dr. Jerry related a story about a very big musky that had been lost in the area we were fishing by other Muskies, Inc. members, the Rakows. I dropped Vince a line and asked him to relate the story in his words for this chapter. Following is that story:

Larry, I got your letter the other day. I knew Jerry would probably tell that story to you. We saw you fishing the exact spot where it happened with Doc Jurgens and Art Lawton in September '78, however, you didn't realize it was Elaine and I at the time.

It was my wife, Elaine, who hooked, fought and lost the fish you heard about. Let me make it clear, we do not think it was even near a record fish, however, it was very big. First a little background in my experience. I have caught three fish over 50" or over, up to 53 1/2 inches. I also have three others from 47 to 50 inches, so I am familiar with what a 50" fish looks like in the water. I am convinced this fish was approximately 60 inches long! I could not, in all honesty estimate the weight accurately, however, I am confident of the length.

From the beginning:

Lake of the Woods, mid-September, 1977. I won't identify the reef we were fishing, suffice it to say it was a typical reef. We had raised a fine musky on this reef four times earlier that morning. She was near 50 inches and surely between 30 and 35 pounds, however no huge monster. As we went around the reef for the umpteenth time, backtrolling and casting, we went on past the end of the reef. I told Elaine to throw one more cast at a submerged rock at the very end of the reef where it drops very sharply into deep water. About halfway in on her retrieve with a black Musky Fin and a pork rind, she had a good solid hit. If the fish followed from near the rock, it was probably lying in 6 to 7 feet of water. We immediately thought she had hooked the fish we had raised four times previously as it was seen in the general area earlier. The fish immediately ran for deep water which indicated to me it was probably hooked in the upper jaw which later proved to be correct. The fish continued to go deeper which really baffled us because we thought we should be able to handle the fish we thought we had. I thought there was something wrong with the drag on my wife's 5000 and twice I reached over and tightened it slightly. The fish still seemed to be able to pull off line at will when I reached over and tried to pull line off against the drag myself and found it almost tight. It was then we realized we had a bigger fish than we thought. After resetting the drag to our satisfaction, which is very difficult with a large fish on, we changed our tactics some and started treating it as a fish we wanted to keep badly.

It was still very deep and at one point a good 200 yards from where we had hooked the fish. I checked the locator and saw it was a steady 72 feet at that spot. Watching it closer, I backed the boat directly over the fish and was able to see it on the locator. At this point we had had the fish on approximately 10 minutes and Elaine was finally able to start gaining line. After a few minutes the fish was visible directly beneath the boat. I was flabbergasted at the size of the fish. Elaine was exhausted and couldn't comprehend what she had on and then the fish dove again. It didn't get too deep before it stopped and Elaine cranked it up again. This time it came up almost to the surface but about 10 or 12 feet away from the boat and despite her best efforts could not get it near enough to attempt a landing. Again it dove and held down for a few minutes at an unknown depth. Finally it came to the surface again so we had a third good look at it. This time it was only inches below the surface, but about 10 feet or so away. At this time we could see the bucktail and that there was probably only one hook now holding. We could see the spinner revolving, the bucktail hair and pork rind flutter alongside the fish's jaw. There was a mild breeze blowing us along at this time and I was standing ready with a gaff and club but the fish wouldn't come near the boat. Finally it sunk down to about 5 or 6 feet below the surface where it was just visible and at this time the hook just plain pulled out. The fish just laid there in sight for a very few seconds more, probably not realizing it was free, before finally sinking out of sight. We were both heartsick, heartbroken and everything else you could think of. But we both realized that was how that fish got that big in the first place, by beating fishermen fair and square. There was nearly 80 feet of water at the spot where she finally broke loose. but only 200 or 300 yards from some shoal waters.

We hope the fish survived. As near as we can estimate, Elaine had the fish on for slightly more than 20 minutes and we lost it about 400 yards from where it was hooked. The fish came up three times so we are reasonably certain of its length; however, I can't estimate its weight because I don't have anything to compare it to. I have a 40-pound 2-ounce fish mounted and it was considerably larger than that, but how much, I don't know.

Is there a world record musky in Lake of the Woods or Eagle? Or any surrounding musky waters? It is possible, but the chances of anyone getting it are slim. There are more muskies than we realize living among the good lake trout waters and these fish have an opportunity to grow large. Getting them or at them, that's the question, as Shakespeare said. "Some day we'll figure it out. Maybe."

Anyway, that's the story. Larry, one of the most exciting times my wife and I have had in the thousands of hours we've spent musky fishing together. It's also one of the reasons we now fish in spots where big ones like to hang out and don't see very many smaller fish, but we enjoy it. Hope to see you musky fishing.

Regards, Vince Rakow

The next reference I have is a hoax! I knew about this one several years ago, but had forgotten about it. Actually I had put it out of my mind because it was so obvious. The fish is claimed to have weighed 70 pounds 5 ounces. It was not claimed to be sport caught, but rather speared by Indians (so I was told).

According to the late Peter Haupt, this fish was an illegally-taken 62-pounder that was turned over to a taxidermist for alterations! It was then painted by a former northeast Wisconsin expert taxidermist.

Although the alterations were immediately obvious to me, it has fooled biologists. However, if one looks close enough at the mount the seams are obvious (poor job!) and the most obvious thing is the pectoral (front) fins. Not only are they eight inches behind where they should be, they are on at the wrong angle! (see photo)

The 70-pound 5-ounce hoax. Note the position of the pectoral fins.

In his newspaper article "Monster Muskie," Jim Lee had some interesting quotes in the March 29, 1974 issue of the *Wausau Herald*. His article start sets the stage:

> Every year the tale surfaces. The locale may be Lake Wissota, the Flambeau Flowage or Lake Minocqua. The setting may change, but the story remains pretty much the same.
>
> I hear the Department of Natural Resources netted a 100-pound musky out of (insert the name of the nearest large lake), an angler will exclaim.
>
> His fishing buddy knowingly nods agreement and eagerly recounts the time "just a few years ago" that the DNR also netted a 100-pound behemoth from another nearby body of water.
>
> While the tale makes for adrenaline pounding visions of boat length monsters lurking in state (Wisconsin) waters just waiting to smash the dimensions of the current world record muskellunge to smithereens ... unfortunately the stories are just that ... tall tales.
>
> "To my knowledge, DNR personnel have never netted or shocked any musky that would have broken the world's record of 69 pounds 11 ounces," Max Johnson, area fish manager for Lincoln, Langlade and Marathon counties, states.
>
> Dick Wendt, area fish manager for Vilas, Oneida and Forest counties, contends there is nothing in DNR files to substantiate claims of a monster musky, although he has heard of newspaper clippings about the turn of the century that allude to a musky of about 100 pounds being found.
>
> However, there is nothing in the past 50 years or more of DNR work in Wisconsin waters to back up the tales that continue to be told.
>
> Johnson said DNR personnel in the Northwestern counties of the state have told him of having seen huge muskies while netting or shocking lakes in that area.
>
> "They've rolled big muskies with their shockers, but have never been able to get their hands on the fish," he related. " Some of the men felt the muskies

might have exceeded the current record, but they were never able to contain the fish in order to get the data."

Wendt, a knowledgeable musky man in his own right, took several brawlers in the 30-pound class last summer. But there's one fish that will keep the summer of '73 in Wendt's mind for a long time ... the one that got away.

"All I saw was a big swirl and the fish took off," he recalls.

"Now I caught several 35-pounders last summer and had no trouble turning them. But this one, I couldn't do a thing with. It just kept right on going."

How big was it?

No one will ever know. That's the thrill of musky legend. There's just enough truth in the tale to keep visions of a 100-pound "monster" alive in the minds of all Wisconsin fishermen.

Again, I would like to interject here, as I have on previous pages, there are no verified reports of a musky having ever been taken anywhere that exceeds the current world record — by any means!

This next reference is somewhat obscure. Due to the circumstances surrounding the capture of the fish, my source wishes to keep himself and those involved out of the report. Since it is the fish we are concerned with, I gladly comply to get the information and in this case a picture. We are printing the picture (see photo) with the face of the person holding the fish blacked out to comply with the above.

This fish was reportedly shot from a dock in shallow water, I assume in the spring when fish this size would be shallow to spawn. This reportedly took place in northwestern Wisconsin some years ago. There have been reports of this fish weighing over 70 pounds. I don't believe the fish was ever weighed. My personal opinion of weight, after studying a poster size photo, is approximately 60 inches long and between 55 and 60 pounds. However, a fish of that

A potential record musky, shot in the shallows.

length and girth could weigh as much as 12 pounds more if it was full of spawn.

Kentucky too has its tales of big muskies from days gone by. The following account came from Owen Chelf, one of the founders of the Kentucky Silver Muskie Club:

> Regarding our telephone conversation about big muskies, I might tell you this ... Several years ago we were loading our boat onto the trailer on the ramp to the ferry at Mammoth Cave. We cordially passed the time of day with the old gentleman who operated the ferry for the Park Service.
>
> He asked "Where did these muskies come from?" My reply was that they had always been here and were native to the Green River. Then he asked, "Are they what the old timers call Jacks?" And my answer was yes. He said, "Well, my grandfather caught one in a basket (meaning trap) that weighed 75 pounds." There would have been no reason for him to misrepresent that to me and is probably as accurate as the method used to weigh the fish.

This next account puts chills down my spine. I'll explain later. To start, I will quote from an article by John Power that appeared in the November 24, 1978, issue of the *Toronto Star*. The story is centered around Brendon Reid of Gananoque, Ontario, veteran St. Lawrence River guide of some 55 years. Yearly, Brendon takes a busman's holiday to chase a big musky ..."My wife and I would chase after old Mossyback." The way he describes ol' Mossyback is it's a fish that would have to be seen to be believed. Which Reid did on five occasions.

Fish Story?

"I've caught umpteen muskies over 40 pounds and one that weighed 58 1/2 pounds," Reid related. "That Brobdingnagian made them look like fingerlings. It was at least seven feet long and its jaw measured 15 or 16 inches. Like an old snapping turtle, its back was coated with moss."

There are those who would dismiss his tale as just another fish story, except for the fact that Reid has substantiating evidence! After one encounter with Old Mossyback. he was left with a couple of enormous scales impaled on his hooks. Biologists who examined them estimated the fish's weight to be in excess of 100 pounds.

"His lair was off the beaten

Two verified musky scales and a quarter — the small scale is from a 44-pounder. The large one ...?

path and I never saw anybody else fish that spot," says Reid. "It consisted of a triangle of shoals, 32, 34 and 37 feet down, surrounding a 72 foot hole.

"He whipped me fair and square. In one battle, he broke water a dozen times, finally stripping my spool of 1,100 feet of line." He hasn't seen hide nor hair of the monster for three years.

WOW! Some creature that must be, and what about my chills? When I visited with Brendon in early 1978, I had the opportunity to see and hold this scale and believe me, it is huge! I'm sure it will send chills down your spine too! It has been identified as a musky scale by top biologists!

From the *Muncie Star* (Indiana) in 1976, by Bob Barnette:

The late Tom Graves, who operated the bait house at Big Chetec in the summer and ran the Tower Lanes bowling establishment in Muncie in the winter, told me that an Indian came one night to his cabin with a musky far larger than the giant that currently held the record. The Indian asked $100 for the fish, which had been taken in a Chippewa net. It was a chance for a world record and the attention and profit that goes with such a record. Tom decided that he didn't want that kind of record and the Chippewa, the huge fish cradled in his arms, turned from the door and was gone into the night.

Fish biologists agree that many species, given ideal conditions, may reach proportions far in excess of known records. Such a fish are not taken because they remain in deep water seldom fished and because their great strength enables them to smash tackle and rip nets.

It is to this mystery, this fascination for the unknown, that causes the sport fisherman to endlessly cast his lure into the big water. Who knows what is out there waiting?

The next fish story will be an article that appeared in the *Minocqua Times* (Wisconsin) on July 21, 1977. I have no other background on this happening, although I have previously covered the supposed 102-pounder referred to as not likely true. If the fish involved in this story "The Monster Musky is Back" by Steve McEnroe is real, it must certainly be a record. Some anglers expressed the feeling that it was a sturgeon, but ... they weren't there! Here's Steve's story:

In 1902, two men, including a member of the State Fish Hatchery Commissioners, reportedly captured a 102-pound musky in their net during a spawning operation on Minocqua Lake. After weighing it, they returned the monster musky to the lake. It was never seen again, and it's doubtful if the mon-

Record Muskies?

ster is still alive 75 years later, but perhaps one of his sons is haunting the lake — for on July 6, another giant musky made itself known.

David Assman, 29, of Waukesha, and his wife Sue were staying at the Knotty Pine Resort on the lake's southwest side. He has been fishing the lake since he was a child, as his grandfather owned a cottage in this area. Each year he comes north musky fishing, and he has caught his share. In fact, earlier that day, he had caught and released an undersize musky on Lake Kawaguesaga.

On the night of July 6, he and Sue were out fishing for walleyes on a rock bar on the south side of the lake, an area that usually provides them excellent walleye fishing. But nothing was hitting, and it hadn't been for three nights in a row. At about 10:30 p.m., Sue snagged her line on the rocks, or so she thought. "Sue was sure she was on the rocks," said Assman, "but then the rock began to move."

Sue surrendered her rod, a 6 1/2 foot spinning outfit. to her husband. She had been using a nightcrawler on a number six hook with no leader and a sinker shot about two feet from the hook — on 15-pound test line. Then began perhaps the longest six hours in Assman's life. "It was just unreal. The first time we saw him we were scared to death," said Assman. What scared them was a fish at least six feet long. Assman swears the fish was a musky, and it was further identified by Don Vicari of Hammond. Indiana, who has successfully fished for musky in this area for several years.

In all, 12 people in five boats watched the battle between Assman and the fish, with Vicari and his wife Judy staying till the 4:30 a.m. finish. During that period, the fish broke the surface 17 times, often jumping completely out of the water. Vicari kept a running count.

"It would just come out of the water. It was unbelievable," said Assman. " I'm positive it was a musky. We had a fairly good look at it as we were using spotlights on it. Once it jumped right at the back of the boat, which is four feet wide, and it hung out well over both sides. Another time it jumped along side and it was nearly half as long as the boat," which is a 15 footer.

But throughout the battle, "He had it his way," Assman said of the musky. The fish didn't tire, because it would sink to the bottom and rest. "I could barely get him off the bottom, unless he wanted to move," said Assman. "In fact, he actually pulled the boat at times. I used a half tank of gas trying to keep him positioned at the right front of the boat," he said. " I hoped I could tire him and get him close enough to the boat so I could gaff him or hit him on the head with the anchor or something, but when he wanted to rest, he just laid on the bottom and rested."

Neither man nor fish wore out, but the line finally did. "I had turned the drag down real loose, but the line just fatigued. There was nothing I could do. It just couldn't take it any longer. After it happened, it really didn't bother me too much. I know it was a thousand to one shot to begin with. We just went home, had a drink and went to bed," Assman said.

Assman will be ready next year though. He is stretching his usual one week northwoods' vacation to two weeks, and he hopes to drop those odds a bit.

A Compendium of Musky Angling History

Just how much does that fish weigh? If it is indeed a musky, and it is six feet long, it will undoubtedly be a world record. The fish holding that record now is a 69-pound, 11-ouncer caught in Wisconsin's Chippewa Flowage in 1949. This one is estimated at six feet, or 72 inches long.

His weight? Your guess is as good as mine! Not wishing to discredit any anglers or witnesses, but rather to look at these stories from all angles, I wish to relate the following. You will be the final judge!

First, does a sturgeon look like a musky? Especially after dark? If you will look at pages 14 and 22 of the June, 1979, *Fishing Facts* magazine, you will see pictures of Spence Petros holding a sturgeon, that, if you were to just glance at it, you could easily mistake it for a musky. The general shape of that sturgeon, as well as location of the fins is very similar to a musky.

In 1977 reports filtered down from Quebec that a 65-pounder had been caught in Lake St. Louis on the St. Lawrence River. I was finally able to get in contact with Jacques Tougas from Lacine, Quebec, for some more information on this fish. Yes, the report was true. Then the mystery deepened! The fish was taken to a Montreal paper and photographed. It was supposedly caught by a lady angler while livebait catfishing! — It would be a new Quebec record if registered! But, it has not been ... the anglers, the fish, and the original photos have disappeared! There are many rumors ranging from netting to dynamite. At any rate, while corresponding with Jacques, he related to me the following regarding big muskies several years ago: "Section 13-A (Bouchard Isle — between Lake St. Francie and Lake St. Louis on the St. Lawrence River) brings many memories as I was raised in Contrecoeur (Quebec). From commercial fishermen in the area (20 years ago — 1958) came many stories of 100-pound muskies."

Later Jacques was able to track down more information: "Last Monday (April 9), Mr. G. Savage of 65-pound musky fame called me. I set up a meeting for Wednesday night. Wednesday found Jacques anxiously at Mr. Savage's door. 'Where's the musky?' It was on the living room wall. There hangs the worst piece of taxidermy (or embalming) on a respectable musky I ever saw. Not fantastic, just respectable. Jacques took out his measuring tape and came up with the following measurements: Length — 53 1/2 inches; Head O.D. — 16 inches;

and reported girth 23 inches.

To quote Jacques, "Around here that's 40 pounds max!" He then took a couple of half-hearted photos, talked fishing a bit, then left. He further states: "Will this kill the mystique? Of course not, it' s all part of the game. For a period that 65-pound fish existed and I am kind of sorry I ever found it."

As for the weight of 65 pounds, Jacques was told to check with a local fishing club who weighed the fish and the taxidermist who also supposedly weighed it. The fishing club had no records and the taxidermist refused to comment!

In the fall of 1978, another huge musky showed up at Leech Lake. It was 62 1/2 inches long, but no accurate weight could be obtained as it was found dead and decomposed. Its weight was estimated at over 55 pounds, which would have set a new state record. The length of the head was 19 inches and it was 5 1/2 inches between the eyes! Thanks to Jeff Arnold and Jeff Lein of Reed's Tackle Shop in Walker, Minnesota, for help in obtaining the information and pictures of this fish.

In May of 1979 a fantastic happening occurred — it was a 59 1/2-incher that had been released! I had heard about this fish two days after it was released, and pursued the first hand story from the angler involved, Bill Meyers. I received a letter from Bill regarding the catch, and would like to pass it on to you, but first more about Bill. Between the time I received the letter and wrote this, I had the extreme pleasure of fishing with Bill.

Two views of the head of a 62 1/2-inch musky found dead on Portage Bay of Leech Lake, Minnesota, in 1978. The 19-inch head measured 5 1/2 inches between the eyes.

During this time I was able to learn much about both the man and the fish. Bill is what I would term an "old timer" at musky fishing and has caught his share of big ones. He guided on Eagle Lake for several years, but has since given up that "hassle" for the pure enjoyment of the sport. I can't recall a more peaceful and enjoyable three days on Eagle Lake. Yes, we fished hard, but we also enjoyed! .

Following is Bill's letter:

Dear Larry,

I am writing you a brief account of the release of the 59 1/2-inch musky that I hooked out of season on Eagle Lake. I was guiding two walleye fishermen on opening weekend of fishing season. Saturday opening morning, I went to the same bay I go to every opening (15 May) and we caught our limit of eighteen walleyes in about 2 1/2 hours of fishing. I noticed all the walleyes were males and still contained milt, so l felt spawning season had not been completed. Sunday we returned to the same spot, mouth of a shallow bay, 100 yard wide narrows, depth 3 to 6 feet all over the entire area, walleyes hold along a jut of land about 25 yards long at the mouth of this shallow bay. Every year I have seen musky at this particular spot for the past six years, usually following a hooked walleye to the boat. Bay is a spawning area for the musky. Anyway, we had been fishing this jut of land for about half an hour catching and releasing small male walleyes. When half way down the shore off a rock face, I felt a weight on my line and set. Then I felt movement, and told the fellows I was with, I was into a big heavy fish (I was using an ultra-light Garcia rod, 10 pound test line, and a blue and white Canadian jig fly and minnow). The fish moved off quite slowly, I was backing the boat and followed up the jut and about 65 yards into the bay, and circled and came back off an area with submerged rocks only about 3 feet deep. The fish came to the surface and cruised in a half circle about 15 feet from the boat. We and another boat that was following the action had a good look at a huge musky. She had 3 white scars on the top of the head and the back 1/3 of the fish had a series of scars to the tail (left side) which we could see when she neared the boat, and could also see that she was lip hooked. She rolled and submerged, I waited awhile. then strummed the line a bit, got musky moving again and slowly took in line, backing the boat toward her as she came to the surface again, maneuvering the boat and her along side, I had two fellows in the boat measure her with a paddle marked off in 1" graduations. They said 60", but to me it looked 59 1/2". The musky showed its agitation and swam off a bit and sounded. Another boat had come up and wanted to try and get a picture, but I couldn't raise her again. I put the boat over top of her and reeled in as much as I could, rod down in the water, and it broke off.

Larry, I promised myself never to kill another musky, but I believe if I had caught this one in season, I would have probably changed my mind. I've seen big musky on Eagle. but this one had to be near the top as we had lots of time to get a good look at her. Larry, if you wish to use any of this letter, please feel free to do so. Keep a tight line.

Sincerely, Bill Meyers

Record Muskies?

Release a 59 1/2-incher? Wow, even though it was out of season! However, after spending many hours in a boat with Bill and learning what a true sportsman he is, it is easy to understand. When Bill and I were fishing, he put me on a spot where he had raised a 50-plus-pounder several times. In the course of conversation, I learned that if he caught it, it would be photographed (in the water) and released! Bill has no use for them (other than the possible exception noted above) and merely enjoys seeing them. Yes, I sincerely believe he would release a 50-pounder or bigger for that matter!

Back to the 59 1/2-incher. When I quizzed Bill about the scars, they apparently were in a pattern that an outboard propeller would leave ... someone nearly killed that fish! When I asked him how big he thought it was, all he could talk about is the tremendous girth the fish had — obviously full of eggs. Bill is not a small man and it was his opinion that the fish was bigger around the middle than he was! Unquestionably, if caught during the season it would have been a new world record ... and he released it! My hat is off to Bill, one of several super sportsmen I have had the pleasure to associate with in my pursuit of the King of Fresh Water.

The following article by John Power appeared in the *Toronto Star*, Friday, November 23, 1979.

Seach for Incredible Hulk

Honey Harbour, Ont. — Yes, kids, there really is an Incredible Hulk. The ferocious, powerful, green gargantuan is alive and well, and living near Thompson Island, north of Honey Harbor.

That's the label laid on what may be the biggest musky ever to swim Ontario's seas. There's at least one cottager who won't let her kids go swimming "while that thing is out there."

An angler, who brought it alongside his boat before the beast popped the 40-pound line like it was store string, required medical attention when he got back to shore.

Another fisherman saw what he thought was a beaver swimming with a branch in its mouth. He nearly fell out of the boat when he got near enough to identify the "beaver" as the head of a huge musky and the "branch" as a two-foot pike!

Son hooked fish

Veteran Unionville piscator Bill Bridgeman was fishing with Jim (who has a 45-pounder to his credit), when the junior member of the team locked into a 'lunge that turned tail and emptied his reel.

"It had to be Hulk," said Bridgeman, who knows his muskies. His cottage is perched practically on the rim of that famous lunker hole.

Gunning for that brand of big game calls for heavy artillery. Bridgeman gave his nod of approval to the Conolon trolling rod, Penn reel, and 25-pound lead-core line. He looked skeptically at the 5-foot 40-pound monofilament leader.

It was a calculated risk. There are two options. Either go with a thick wire leader which deadens the action of the plug, or use mono that lets the lure step lively, resulting in more strikes. More losses, too, since a musky's razor sharp fangs can make short work of a nylon lead.

In view of the Brobdingnagian target, a 10-inch "Lunker Killer" saw the light of day for the first time in two years. It's a flat, jointed, wall-eyed bait made right here in Toronto by cabbie Frank Bauman, who used to operate Handcraft Tackle Co.

Bridgeman tied on the magnum Rapala that has caught a pair of trophies for him so far this season. He logically elected to stick with his winning horse.

As expected, Stan "Musky Man" Nowocin was already working the Thompson beat, along with Metro devotees Harold Cartwright, Ron Hewie and Frank Mariano.

As usual, they had fish. A 27-pounder, plus one which nudged the 35-pound mark. Cisco Kid and Swim Whiz were the winning tickets, according to Nowocin, who mentioned the fact they had been trolling their offerings 20 to 30 feet down.

That information confirmed the accuracy of Bridgeman's depth sounder, which had been flashing a few fish at the 25-foot level.

The "100 hours per trophy muskellunge" theory is bunk. At least, if you make the saw-off 25 pounds, as does Bridgeman. Otherwise, that master, along with his partner, were owed a few.

The boat was clipping across the center of the big bay at 11.2 km (7 mph), the tip of the trolling stick throbbing with the action of the pulsating plug, when the rod bowed and the reel bawled.

"It's a fish!," Bridgeman shouted, as he kicked the motor out of gear and started to crank his line. "There's 70 feet of water in this hole."

It felt like a great sunken log, as it was hauled in, heavy and steady. Finally it dove under the boat, still hanging deep and out of sight.

At long last, it surfaced some 20 feet off the stern. We stared in disbelief. "Migawd," Bridgeman gasped, "it's The Hulk."

Hulk or not, it was a mind-boggling beast that looked more alligator than fish. Bridgeman's oversized net, which he says "Is the biggest I could find in Toronto," looked inadequate, despite its 7 1/2-foot circumference.

It was. The net was too small — and too weak!

When he expertly steered the musky's head to the bottom of the 44-inch bag, fully one-third of the fish still hung over the rim. Which makes it 5 1/2 feet in length Bridgeman reckons 6 feet since the head and neck were bent.

Without lifting it from the water, he tried to steer the net near enough to the boat so the hoop could be grasped by hand. That's when the dead weight of the fish bent the frame at right angles to the handle, which, while boasting a 1 1/8-inch diameter, actually bent and crimped, too.

The Lunker Killer stayed in the mesh, while Incredible Hulk was dumped back in his lair, where he slowly swam into the shadowy depths. It left a lump in the loser's belly that refuses to leave.

It is tales such as this that help to keep both the mystique and legends alive! In 1980 in *Field & Stream*, Jerome Knap wrote of legends:

Wherever muskies swim, there are legends about the truly big ones. Lake Nobonsing reputedly holds a huge denizen of the deep named Ironjaw. It regularly straightens hooks, bends spoons, and makes toothpicks out of plugs. On one occasion it reportedly put the grab on a swimming dog.

Up on Lake of the Woods, near Kenora, they speak of the evil-eyed behemoth of a musky that's been christened Ol' Croc. Apparently, the Lake of the Woods leviathan habitually and unceremoniously makes off with walleyes which anglers were in the process of playing. One local musky fisherman tells about releasing a 16-pounder, then watching with amazement as a huge monster-like muskellunge rose from the depths and wrapped its crocodilian snout around its smaller brother.

Are all these tales of monstrous muskies just fish stories? I suspect not. A friend of mine diving in Eagle Lake claims he saw a musky that was longer than he is tall, and his height is 6 feet. Once in 1965 or 1966, as a young fisheries biology student working at the Fisheries Research Station in South Baymouth on the Manitoulin Island, I picked up the rear half of a dead musky floating in the North Channel, and that half weighed 45 pounds. (It was weighed on a commercial fisherman's scale.) We estimated that the live weight of this fish would have been close to 100 pounds!

Since dead muskies do not normally float, it is rare when a dead one is found, but for the second time in two years a monster was found dead on the shores of Leech Lake, Minnesota. The following story appeared in the July 4, 1980 issue of *Outdoor News* in the letters to the editor section:

To the Editor:

Two fishermen from the Twin Cities, Bob Draack and Jim McGowan, were fishing on Leech Lake on May 20 this year and found a very large musky floating dead in the water off Five Mile Point. The musky measured 59 1/2 inches in length and.we guess it was around 60 pounds in weight (live).

Bob and Jim are having the musky's head mounted by Roger Halvorson of Fergus Falls, MN, a famous musky guide and taxidermist.

As we have seen the fish that was found last year by Randy Anderson of Dillons North Star Lodge on Leech, we know this one is much larger.

We feel you would want to know this, because had this fish been caught it would easily have been the state record musky.

We would appreciate printing this in your paper. I' m sure all your readers would be very interested in this.

Jack & Judy Johnson,
Sugar Point Resort, Leech Lake
Federal Dam, Minnesota

Since this musky was picked up in May and had deteriorated as much as shown in the picture, could it have been one of those "mistake fish" that winter harpooners all too often take a shot at only to lose when it shakes off the spear?

B.F. Jones wrote in the August 1915 issue of *Forest And Stream* about muskallunge:

Just so with the muskallunge or nosconge as the Indians called them. What's the use of telling? But as I was in at the death and aided in the landing and killing of seventy-four inches of fight that weighed over eighty pounds of courage and spirit perhaps any experience is at least worth the telling. Were it possible for a muskallonge to retain its size and acquire the endurance of a five-pound black bass or a fifty-pound redfish in their own environment there would be no taking of him as he would have to be killed and all you would get would be the empty body.

The muskallunge has never been very plentiful — at least, I have hunted them for almost forty years, and have only been fortunate enough to bring two of immense size to the finish, and this is how one of them was killed.

Jim, Doc and I had been in the Kankakeee lowland between Torch Light and Grass lakes, two small tributaries of Traverse Bay. The first day we had landed several of indifferent sizes — mine of thirty five inches, eighteen or twenty pounds being the largest. The second day we took nothing; the third morning a light, warm, drizzling rain had set in about eight o'clock, and we had bright hopes. I had just pulled a small fish up to my boat when a yell from Jim notified me that he was hooked. When I reached him Jim's boat had been overturned with him in mud and water up to his armpits — the surface of the water for fifty feet around covered with pond lilies and cattails all torn to shreds, fighting with every ounce of his strength and skill to keep the monster out of a dense growth of pond lilies which was evidently the rendezvous of the brute. Rowing around I managed to place myself in front of the monster and by beating him over the head with my oar I managed, by the aid of Jim 's pull to drive him into shallow water; he showed fight gritting his teeth and snapping his ponderous jaws continuously, with an ominous sound that was terribly suggestive. Jim finally secured a firm footing and it was a case of "Go it fish! Go it man!" Only after I had hooked my gaff between his massive jaws were we enabled to drag seventy-four inches of fish to shore. He weighed eighty-seven pounds and I recall that we slew him with a hand-axe. This fight was over twenty years ago (1890s).

In the 1922 publication of the American Fisheries Society, a chapter was written by E.T.D. Chambers entitled "The Maskinonge: A Question of Priority In Nomenclature." From that chapter comes the following:

A few years ago, the Ontario Department of Fisheries at Toronto received a magnificent specimen of maskinonge, over five feet long and weighing fifty-two pounds. It was caught in the branch of the Rideau River, which passes through Kemptville, by Sam J. Martin, of Kemptville. Big as this specimen was, it has been cast altogether in the shade by a capture by a French Canadian, Mr. Alphonse Allard, at Chateauguay, on the border of the St Lawrence, a little west of Montreal. This monster, which was sixty pounds in weight, had a girth of twenty-seven inches. The length of the head from the tip of the snout to the back of the gill was exactly a foot.

Every year it seems, tales circulate through musky country about the world record size fish netted by the DNR during spawn taking operations. The tale told most often is the supposed 80- and 102-pounders taken from lakes Minocqua and Tomahawk, Wisconsin in 1902. I have come up with additional information. While helping Dick Rose research information for his book *The Complete Guide to Musky Fishing*, Dr. William Pivar corresponded with John H. Klingbeil, supervisor of Fish Production for the Wisconsin DNR

Mr. Klingbeil' s letter contained the following in regard to these fish:

Enclosed also is a picture of the article contained in the *Minocqua Times* regarding the two large muskellunge that we caught back in 1902. We have no other verification of any exceptionally large fish which were caught. I have gone through the annual reports for the Commissioner of Fisheries from 1902 and 1903 and no mention of either of these fish is made there. There is some question regarding the authenticity of these fish; however, we have nothing really to document the matter.

From: *The Magic of the Muskellunge* by Bob Cary, The American Fisherman's Fresh and Salt Water Guide:

... John Klingbeil, superintendent of the Wisconsin fish propagation program, says, "There are always stories about those 100-pound muskies going around, but we've never seen one."

Klingbeil's crew annually nets spring-run females for hatchery spawn.

They've never seen a 100-pounder, or even an 80-pounder. But that doesn't prove that such an old rod-wrecker doesn't exist.

From Ed Wodalski in the May 7, 1989 *Wausau Daily Herald*:

Minocqua guide E.D. Kennedy apparently took to his grave the story of the 102-pound musky caught in Minocqua Lake.

Kennedy and Supt. Nevin of the State Fish Hatchery Commission claimed to have captured the fish in 1902, along with an 80-pound musky taken from Tomahawk Lake. Both fish were returned to the lakes after milked of spawn, apparently never seen again. Or were they?

Jim Mcqueen, a Minocqua hunter, trader and trapper, reported finding a dead 78-pound musky washed ashore on Tomahawk Lake in the summer of 1923.

The fish measured 59 inches with a 25 1/2-inch girth.

Local musky experts of the time claimed the fish was a close descendant of "Old Mose," the 108 -pound (it apparently gained six pounds through the years) musky netted some 20 years earlier.

So much for those fish. Now on to facts. At the end of Mr. Klingbeil's letter he made the following comment:

Incidentally, during the spawning operations each year fish in the 52-56 inch bracket are caught annually. We have not come up with any fish of any particularly large size; however, this may be because of the type of net which is used or may be of course because of the very few extremely large fish present.

In the late 1960s I had the pleasure of watching the Wisconsin DNR spawning crew do some stripping of spawn from muskies from Big Arbor Vitae Lake in Vilas County. After they had finished, I visited with one of the supervisors. I asked him if they had ever netted any record class muskies during these operations. He stated that one of the crews had captured one that they estimated to weigh in the mid 60-pound range. The three of them couldn't handle it, so they let it go.

In the spring of 1982, I was visiting with Dick Wendt, area fish manager at Woodruff, Wisconsin. When I asked him the usual big fish question, he came up with a letter that was circulating within the DNR from Mrs. Clarence (Donna) Tischer of La Crosse, Wisconsin.

I not only got to see the picture, but they were kind enough to give me a copy of it, which I now share with you.

The fishery crew estimated the fish to be in the 100-pound class; my guess would be somewhat less. It is a huge fish and obviously heavy with spawn.

Apparently, in response to a DNR request for "information regarding a rumor of a fish being taken around the turn of the century by conservation people" (probably the Minocqua/Tomahawk fish) Mrs. Tischer contacted the DNR as she had a picture of a very large musky being spawned by a 1932 fishery crew. Following are some excerpts from her letter:

> ... As I wrote before — it is a very good picture considering it is about 50 years old but it is not a good picture of a fish because the head is away from the camera. On several different occasions my grandfather, G.F. Emberson (Floyd) told me the fishery crew that day May 20th, 1932, estimated the weight of the fish to be in the 100-plus class. Also a picture of the fish was in the Capitol building at Madison. He said it was caught at Three Lakes, Wis. but not which lake. Picture was taken by Bob Becker, Sports Editor of Chicago Daily paper. A man by the name of Bill Billings could have been with that crew (not sure). Fred Hewitt would have been my grandfather's immediate superior. Also a man named Webster, can't remember a first name, was a person who visited our home and I had the impression he was very important ...

The photo from Mrs. Donna Tischer. The picture was taken in 1932 as a fishery crew was taking spawn from muskies.

Moving now to New York's famous fish factory, Lake Chautauqua, we get some more photographic proof that spawn-taking crews do occasionally capture big fish. While visiting in the spring of 1982, I took time to visit the hatchery at Bemus Point. Upon my

A giant from New York's Lake Chautauqua.

return, Bob Bonar produced several pictures that had been taken of netting operations many years before. Several big muskies were taken.

Now on to the St. Lawrence River:

During the Muskies, Inc./Muskies Canada Challenge Cup II, October 1981, I had the opportunity to visit with D.E.C. biologist Bill Pearce. Bill, as a young biologist with the DEC, did some spawn netting for bass on the St. Lawrence River during the mid 1950s (circa 1954/55). One morning during his routine check of the capture nets he came upon a big surprise. The nets he used were six feet long and occasionally a musky was captured in these nets intended for bass. The big surprise came in the form of a musky in one of the nets that defied belief. Bill said the fish was in the net "on an angle, reached from one end to the other; and still had a bend in it." He said the fish was at least a foot across the head and his best estimate of weight was that it was in excess of 80 pounds! In fact over the years he has often thought it could have been close to 100 pounds! He stated that if he had it to do over again, he would have killed the fish to be mounted for the state's museum. Instead, he gently eased the fish from the net and watched it swim away!

A couple more photos of huge muskies netted by New York DEC crews.

Are any of these fish still alive? Doubtful, but perhaps they have descendants of like proportions. In fact, Ed Cheverette was doing some spawn netting for the Ontario DNR around 1980 when he came up with one he estimated at around 65 pounds. He has netted several just over 50 pounds also! So much for big muskies taken by fisheries crews before the season opens.

During my many years of researching musky history, one thing became painfully obvious to me. Fifty-pound (and over) muskies are (were) not caught very frequently. In fact only 94 have made the verified list. Of course more have been caught, but for one reason or another were never officially verified. Since publication of my book's

first edition, I have learned of a few more (If I were to make an edu-
cated guess as to the actual number of 50-plus pounders caught, verified and unverified legitimate, I would have to place the number
somewhere in the neighborhood of 150 to 175.)

From the August 12, 1932 *Minocqua Times* (Wisconsin):

There was a *Sports Afield* exhibit at which a record breaking musky, weighing 54 pounds, and caught in Carroll Lake, in these northwoods, was shown.

Anyone know more about this one?

Recently I received a call from Dr. Will Wright. He had returned
from Eagle Lake, Ontario, with a tale of a giant hybrid. It seems that
a lady guide and her client had hooked a monster a couple of days
before the musky season opened that would have weighed over 60
pounds. Will also said she had personally caught a 51-pounder some
years before. "More details please," I pleaded, "and a picture." He
came through in super style; not only a picture, but a complete story
by the lady herself, Ginny Tipton. Here is her story:

My story began quite a few years ago. More than I care to admit. Our family had been coming to Eagle Lake every spring for some time. My husband and
I had 4 children and of course one boat was not enough to take us all fishing at
once and so I took to running a boat and motor, while taking two, and Tip took
two. But then back to that big moment. Two of the kids had stayed in camp.
Tip had a boat with our youngest daughter (10) and I had my boat and the old-
est (16). We had fished all morning, casting the shores in hopes of snaring that
big one. Finally we drifted into Froghead Bay for a try at it and pulled into a
good sized bay with a creek at the bottom of it. My daughter Claudia and I were
casting one side of the bay and Tip and Bev were working the other side when
all at once a big jack hit Tip's plug and he was having quite a time, with it breaking water and thrashing around.

Claudia and I were so engrossed in watching them we brought our plugs
in without watching and when we both turned around at the same time here
laid this monster of a fish with its mouth open ready to take the plug on
Claudia's line. It scared her so bad she jerked the plug right away from him. I
said "My God, Claudia, why did you do that?"

Her answer was "I don't want that thing in the boat with me."

"Well I do," says I, so we took off casting our hearts out to raise him again.
We had made four passes up and down the same shore and had about decided
he wasn't going to raise to the bait again when all at once about halfway
between the boat and shore the water boiled, and up he came. Well, I had him
on my hook now what do I do?

He was so big that he went deep and ran and ran and ran. My reel was
singing, my thumb was hot and I was running out of line. This may sound

crazy, but is true. I did the only thing I could, I took chase with Tip shouting "What the hell do you think you're doing, he'll turn and go under the boat," which should have been true but wasn't. The run had tired him out and after that the big thing was getting him up off the bottom. Finally the struggle was about over, but the water was a bit rough and I was floating into shore. I told Claudia to paddle it out to open water and in her excitement she paddled me right into shore.

We should have lost this fish but didn't. He weighed in at 51 pounds and I never thought I'd see another one that size in my lifetime. It's a thrill, a sensation, that only a musky fisherman can appreciate.

But then came the spring of 1982. I had seen and had on my line more than a few musky that ranged from six inches to 15-20 pounds. People got pretty used to seeing me and my friends flying around the lake come rain or shine. One weekend I was asked to take two fellows from Quebec out to try and bring in a big northern pike or jack as we call them. It was an overcast day that looked as

Ginny Tipton's 51-pounder from Eagle Lake.

though the sky could open up at any time. I headed for an island where over the years had always been good to me when I was looking for northern. Pierre and his friend had worked one side of the island and we came around one end where there was a long reef that is under water. They had brought in several but of no size so were really getting into it. Pierre had a plug on that looked as though it would scare any fish out of the area and he was giving it his all. Jerking it up, down, to one side, to the other, wind it in 5 turns and start all over again.

As we came round the reef and on down the shore some 100 feet or so he dropped this terror not more than a foot from shore and immediately gave it a jerk. He never got a chance to give it the second jerk because the water erupted and I said, "Well, Pierre, you've got a big one now." It never did break water again, but went down and it was some time before he could lead it up to the top. We about fell out of the boat at the sight of that monster. We had him hooked, a monster tiger musky and not yet in season.

After admiring him the next thing was how we were going to get Pierre's super plug away from him. It was not a question of getting him in the boat. That couldn't be done without clubbing him and that would have killed him. We guessed him to weigh in the area of 60 pounds and a beauty to see. We had no gaff and no camera, so we took the net and slipped it over his head. Of course, he didn't like that and threw his head catching the barbs on the plug in the net and tore it loose from his outer lip. He didn't seem to realize he was free or was just too exhausted to move because he just laid there about 3 feet from the side of the boat Finally it just sank slowly out of sight and Pierre just sank down and said "My God, I probably couldn't have afforded to have him mounted anyway, but I know now there are bigger fish out here than I've seen hanging on the lodge wall. He'll probably never be the same again. Pierre went up to the lodge with a smile on his face, his plug in one hand and a net bent out of shape and I'm sure he'll dream all winter about getting back to Old Eagle again.

A great story by a lady legend. A very nice article entitled "Lady of the Lake" which was about Ginny's prowess as a guide, appeared in the May 1983 issue of *Ontario Out Of Doors*. A short quote from that article by John Wright is in order. John asked Ginny what was the biggest musky she had ever seen. It contains a little more insight to the huge tiger. "He was a monster musky. Biggest I've ever caught in Eagle Lake was 51 pounds. This was bigger. The teeth on him, you didn't dare put your hand anywhere near its mouth. We got him tired and beside the boat in fairly short time. When they're that big and that old, they tire quicker. We used the net and could just get it over his head. It chomped down on the twine and the plug came loose. So did he. I was glad to see him get away. He was out of season, anyway."

Boy, if they ever opened the season a little earlier on Eagle Lake there would be several more big fish on the list.

Of course we all remember the 59 1/2-incher caught and released by Bill Meyers a few years back. An old friend, Vern Carson, caught and released a 56-pounder fishing for walleyes before musky season opened several years back. And now comes yet another huge, out of season, Eagle Lake musky. Friend Gordy Euler, owner of Euler's Camp on Eagle Lake, related to me a story of a big one caught by a guest before musky season while fishing for smallmouth bass. Gordy's story:

The Fight — June 10, 1967

This true musky story goes back some fifteen years. I was guiding with another guide of many years experience on Eagle Lake and surrounding lakes. We had eight men whose main interest was walleye and northern fishing.

Being their last afternoon we had already limited out in walleyes and were slowly casting the shoreline for northern and scattered smallmouth bass. At 4:00 p.m. some of the fishermen had tired of casting and decided to head for home as they were leaving for the state of Wisconsin after the evening meal at 6:30 p.m. The other guide headed for home with one boat following. We decided we would fish for another 1/2 hour then we would also head in for supper.

A Compendium of Musky Angling History

As our time went quickly we soon headed for home up the back channel of Eagle Lake. Upon rounding a sharp turn in the channel we noticed one of the boats, which was supposed to have gone home, in the middle of the channel. Motor trouble naturally is the first thought. As we neared we noticed the one fisherman holding his rod as if he were still fishing The rod had a good bend pointing into the water.

Rather annoyed with the situation, I questioned why they had not gone home with the other guide? "One last cast for the year!" was the answer and, "We hooked a monster of a fish."

Realizing they were not joking I started questioning as to length, approximate girth size and color. They both stated half the length of the boat and a belly as large as a 45 gallon drum.

At this moment the other guide had returned and also was very curious as to the happenings.

The fisherman holding the rod stated he only has 12 pound test line and did not know how long his line could hold such weight.

The fish presently just lay on the bottom and did not move. The depth of the water was close to 35 feet. They had hooked the fish right on the shoreline in about 6' of water. Slashing the lure (a large Mepps — yellow willow-leaf spinner with no hairs or feathers), the instant it hit the water, rolling over and did not surface again, but headed for the middle of the channel away from the rocks and weeds along the shoreline.

I climbed into their boat with my landing net and asked if I could feel the line to test the weight on the end I took the line in my fingers and slowly lifted up. Whatever was at the end of the line was heavy and also alive, as I pulled up it moved slightly away with solid pressure I questioned whether his drag on the reel was loose or tight. He stated the fish had no problem pulling out the line when it moved quickly as it had done on a few occasions. He handed me the rod and said "You try and get him off the bottom. My arms are getting weak and tired."

I took the rod and almost felt lost just standing there doing nothing as the fish lay on bottom. I decided to slowly force this fish up to the surface by slowly raising the rod tip with full pressure and bring down the rod tip quickly and reeling up the slack to the water's surface. Doing this about six or seven times the fish realized it was being pulled off the bottom and was getting closer to the surface. He pulled the line real hard and headed right back to the bottom and lay there again. I repeated the same procedure and the fish came closer to the surface, but again went back down to bottom. This time it moved around more under the boat forcing me to move around and hold the rod on the other side of the boat. We had made up our minds we would not rush the fish and the 12 pound test line should hold and foremost of all things we wanted to see what kind of fish was on the line so long and would not surface.

The fish now was on the line an hour and the only time it had been seen was when it struck the lure.

I again started raising the pole and reeling quickly with pumping action to

136

bring the fish off the bottom. It was slowly coming up as it had done twice or three times before. This time we would get to see it. The fish had other ideas as it headed straight towards one of the boats that was in our group of 4. They quickly moved farther off and the fish slowly returned to the bottom of the channel. It had to tire soon as my arms were also getting tired from the constant heavy weight on the light rod.

I slowly started reeling again to get the fish off bottom. This time it came a little quicker with less resistance. The fish seemed to be tiring. This time I almost reeled steady with no slippage in the reel at all. We were now going to get our first good look at the fish which now had been on the line over 1 1/2 hours.

It surfaced! Almost 10' from the boat not rolling, not plunging, not fighting, just lay on the surface as a fish sunning itself. It was a huge musky. Now to land that huge fish or at any rate to unhook the fish and release it as quickly as possible. The musky season did not open for another 10 days — this being June 10th the season opened June 20th.

The lure was in the muskies' mouth out of sight and we could not see how deeply the treble hook was embedded. I handed the rod back to the fisherman who had hooked the fish and explained to him how I wanted him to slowly lead the fish back to us along side the boat. I would grab the musky with my hands. The musky was not halter broken and could not be led alongside the boat as I had expected. The fish kept well away from the boat almost 6' to 7' at all times and staying below the surface 18"-24".

I pushed the motor down and started it up and slowly idled the boat alongside the huge musky. It lay there now just under the surface. In a flash I picked up the landing net and dipped deep, head first the huge musky went in. I lifted up the net and fish. It was halfway into the net and filled it. The landing net handle broke. The fish lay there for a moment then shot for bottom again. I looked at the broken net in disbelief and set it back in the boat.

The spinning reel buzzed steady as the fish ran steadily away. The thought now struck us - was there enough line on the reel? There was, the fish stopped running and lay many, many yards away on bottom again.

This time I prepared differently for the fish. I got the other guide in my boat and two good landing nets from the other boats. We would land this musky if the line would hold or hook would hold. Slowly and methodically the fisherman maneuvered the fish to the surface. It again appeared about 30' from the boat rolled and raced about 18' straight down almost making the reel smoke. Again he slowly surfaced about 15' from the boat.

I laid one landing net in the rear of the boat and the other in the front of the boat. The guide slowly idled the boat close to the musky. The fisherman handed me the rod and reel. He grabbed the landing net. The fish lay perfectly still on the water's surface. I advised them to dip both nets and not miss — I would grab the fish in the mid-section and pull it over the side.

I set the rod and reel down with the reel on free spool. I said "O.K." They dipped! I grabbed the fish and he or she whatever the case! The musky now lay motionless for the moment in the bottom of the boat. I did not take time to admire its size. I quickly removed the hook with my pliers from its mouth. Only one hook of the treble hook had made contact inside its mouth. The musky was not injured and did not bleed at all from the wound. There was no blood at all in the boat from landing it or being hooked.

I slowly raised it up holding it by the inside of the gill covers. It was an extremely heavy fish well marked with absolutely no scars on any part of the body, with no broken fins or tip of tail. It was a perfect specimen of a musky. I stood upon the middle seat of the boat so all the fishermen would have a good look and then I slowly let the musky slide into the water through my arms.

The musky finned its way for about 8' and then there was a mighty splash and roll, and the musky disappeared.

The other boats headed for camp for cold beans. I waited around close to 15 minutes to see if the musky would surface again from the exhausting fight. It did not reappear so we also headed for home. The reason I waited was to make sure the musky would survive and would live to fight again another day. An exhausted fish is easy prey of the seagulls. They peck out the eyes firstly and then the tender flesh protected by the gill covers, killing the exhausted fish and making them food for the other birds.

The musky did make it. In August of the same year two experienced musky fishermen lost a huge musky about 1/4 mile down the shoreline from where this one was hooked They stated it did not jump — it just hit and rolled and got off. They both guessed 60 pounds or more because of its length and huge midsection, almost as round as a 45 gallon drum.

The musky we released we guessed weighed between 55-60 pounds. Its length was close to six feet long. The landing net I broke was 36" deep and all the fishermen said I had the musky in all the way down and it still stuck half out of the net.

You always hear about the one that got away. This musky was one lucky King or Queen of the Back Channel of Eagle Lake. It did not get away, but got its freedom due to good luck and timing on its part.

Over the years, a few 50-pound plus fish were caught that for one reason or another were not entered in contests. Therefore it is impossible in most cases to verify these catches. If true, however, they should be recognized; and if untrue the angler in question will have to live with his own conscience. At any rate, they all help add to the mystique!

One of the many dozens of fish mounts hanging in the National Fresh Water Fishing Hall of Fame at Hayward, Wisconsin, causes one to stop and look. It is a 59-pounder. This fish was supposedly speared by Indians in 1939. Several people owned it over the years and for many of those years the fish resided in a local supper club. The fish was eventually sold to a Mr. Bill Cook who then donated it to the

The mounted 59-pounder at the Hall of Fame.

Hall. The fish was mounted by famous (former) Field Museum Taxidermist, the late Karl Kahmann. If you wish to see what a near 60-pound fish would look like beside your boat, stop by the Hall and take a look!

On one of my trips to the St. Lawrence River I stopped by one of the local watering holes. Staring down at me from behind the bar was a huge fish. It is a 52-pound 60-inch monster caught by one of the famous local guides, the late Clay "Musky Ferg" Ferguson. The fish was caught during October of 1956, probably from the famous 40 Acre Shoal.

In the 1930s and '40s, Cal Johnson (a former world record holder) wrote an outdoor column for *Sports Afield* magazine. In one of his columns I ran across a picture of a big musky with the following caption: "Muskies that tip the scales to the tune of 55 pounds are an event — not a common occurrence. Above is pictured such an event in the form of a 'lunge caught by R.B. Piehler of Chicago in Hunter Lake, near Winter, Wisconsin. The waters are near the mouth of the famous Chippewa River."

Again no additional info and no record in contest lists, as was the case with the previous fish. Anyone in Chicago know anything about this musky?

R.B. Piehler with a 55-pounder from Hunter Lake, Wisconsin.

In an ad for Calvert's Camps in the July 1934 issue of *Outdoor Life* was this picture of a 54-pound musky caught from Calvert's.

While perusing the archives at the Fresh

Water Fishing Hall of Fame I came across many more gems. In an old Pflueger catalog #145 (undated), I found a picture with the following caption: "Hundreds of bystanders viewed the battle to the death between this 50 pound 3 ounce, 5 foot muskalunge and A.D. Hudson, at Conneaut Lake Park, PA. Hudson won — with a Lowe Star Bait and a Pflueger Reel." Obviously a very old photo!

In an old undated South Bend catalog I found the following: "A musky almost as big as a man, taken at Cedar Island Camp (Lake of the Woods) by E. S. Calvert, Rainey River, Ontario." Ernie Calvert was a famous pioneer resorter on Lake of the Woods and caught many, many huge muskies as attested to by Bert Claflin in his book musky Fishing (my favorite!) Although no weight is given for this fish, it obviously is in the 50 pound class!

Ernie Calvert with a 1930s fish from Lake of the Woods.

R.B. A 54-pounder from Calvert's Camps.

Of more recent vintage was a picture passed on to me by Bill Davis in early 1982. The picture was from an Illinois outdoor publication. The caption under the picture was: "Mike Crawley is holding a 57-pound 54-inch musky caught by Harold Firestein (background) of Naperville, IL. Harold landed this monster with 25-pound line and a Johnson spoon for bait while fishing at Nestor Falls Canada."

I called Mr. Firestein to gather more details. During my phone conversation with him I learned a couple of things: First, the paper had goofed on the weight and length. The fish was 54 pounds and 57 inches. Secondly, the fish was caught before the season opened and after being photographed, was released!

While on the subject of huge preseason muskies, I must tell you of recent info received from fellow sleuth George Pifer. Seems one of the locals was fishing for pike on the St. Lawrence and hooked "Mrs. Big." When brought boatside, he was able to lay his rod on the fish and later measured the rod — 63 inches! It was said to be very thick across the back.

During my visit to the St. Lawrence River I came across several interesting finds that I wish to share with you, plus some additional Wisconsin information.

My first find is an old picture captioned "A days catch on the St. Lawrence, Thousand Islands, N.Y." It appears to be a late 1800s or early 1900s picture. The fish in the center is of trophy proportions. I'll let your imagination establish the weight.

The next few pictures were obtained from one of the top guides on the St. Lawrence River, Jim Evans of Ogdensburg. He is a musky fanatic and his scrap book was like taking a journey back through recent history. The first photo that intrigued me was obviously very old. It was taken in Morristown in front of some buildings that were built in the very early 1800s. From the look of the man's clothing, I would date the picture around 1900. The fish? Huge! My guess is that it is in the neighborhood of 55 pounds.

Next we have a fairly recent photo of a fish from Black Lake. Black Lake empties into the Oswagatchie River which in turn empties into the St. Lawrence. This fish was reported to weigh 51 1/2 pounds. It was 51 inches long with a girth of 23 inches. The fish appears to be very heavy throughout its length. I can find no record of its ever hav-

ing been entered in any contest, so it belongs in the unverified category. As an aside, Black Lake has the potential to produce fish of this weight. Whether this is one remains a mystery.

Some early photos from the St. Lawrence River.

Now we come to a real bummer!

This fish is probably in the 60-pound class. It was taken by an Indian on a sturgeon set line. One has to wonder just how many potential world record fish meet their demise in this fashion. What a shame they have to go that way! At least here is proof that there are still some very big muskies available. There are additional tales that are told about the Indians, big muskies, etc.; but, since they are second- and third-hand I shall put them aside for further investigation.

The next fish comes as a result of correspondence received back in August of 1979 from Tom Maki.

Anthony Sommer of Cheektowaga, NY, caught this 51-pound 8-ounce musky from Black Lake (left). At right, a potential record lost forever!

Tom sent me the following letter:

I always enjoy your many stories of large muskies that are in the magazines. I recently returned from a fishing trip in Ontario, and I thought you might be interested in a musky that is mounted at the resort I stayed at.

The owner said that he caught it about 7 or 8 years ago and that it was 55 inches and 55 pounds. The mount is certainly a very large fish.

I am enclosing a brochure from this resort which includes a picture of this large fish.

I wrote Tom back and passed it off as probably a resorter's promotion, without bothering to check it out (shame on me!) Recently, when I came across Tom's letter and decided I had better follow through a little further before filing it for good. I wrote a letter to the resort — Cedar Lake Camp, Perrault Falls, Ontario, and received the following letter from the new owner, Mr. Clifford A. Milko:

In reply to your letter of recent date relating to the musky picture in our brochure. The fish was caught by the previous owner, Larry Johnson, during September of 1973 in 4 O'Clock Bay on Cedar Lake. He was using a Bobbie

This musky lost weight, from 55 down to 53 pounds. Nice fish, anyway!

Record Muskies?

Bait with a perch finish. The fish weighed in at 53 pounds even.

Although we don't have any pictures other than what's on the brochure, it was mounted in our office and I could take a picture and forward if you so wish.

From John Power of the *Toronto Star* comes the following:

Dear Larry:

Herewith an old photo of a musky hooked by a customer of Bill Brissette, a former guide at Macey's Bay near Honey Harbour. (The photo was unusable).

Bill swears it was seven feet long and was apparently lost beside the boat when he tried to subdue it with an axe.

Probably not much you can do with it but I knew you would be interested. Bill would like to have it returned when you're finished with it.

Still haven't checked out that 71-pounder per your request but will do so soon.

Best regards
John Power

And more from John:

Sorry no Hulk pix. (John's reply to my query if he had been able to get a picture of the "Incredible Hulk" monster musky on Georgian Bay). Who could focus at a time like that? However, have included a story relating to the incident and a photo of the net after the beast destroyed it. Note the handle is crimped, although no attempt was made to lift the fish out of the water.

Following is John's article as it appeared in *Outdoor Canada* in 1981 entitled "The Fisherman Who Got Away":

Bleak is the word that best describes Georgian Bay that raw November morning. Leaden skies hung low and heavy over black waters.

The few cottages on the rugged pine-studded islands were deserted and sightless, their windows shuttered and hatches battened. A bitter norther spat a mixture of rain and sleet to remind us that winter was just around the corner.

I burrowed deeper into my float suit, thankful for the long johns, woolen shirt and down vest beneath it. Lined boots, balaclava and gloves completed my ensemble which was duplicated by Bill Bridgeman's garb.

"Great weather," I remarked to my fishing partner

"It couldn't be better," he enthused, grinning with anticipation. "The Red Gods are smiling today."

Muskellunge monomaniacs are a breed unto themselves. Many are taciturn types, capricious creatures like their quarry. All are tough and dedicated. They have to be because it's on days like this — when the barometer is dropping as it was when we left Bill's cottage — that the majority of wallhangers are taken.

All 'lunge buffs share a common ambition: catching a world beater! And it isn't pie in the sky: Almost every musky beat boasts a resident monster which surpasses the 69-pound 11-ounce record.

For instance the upper St Lawrence harbors "Old Mossyback," a 100-pound-plus gargantuan which veteran guide Brendan Reid has tied into on five occasions.

Lake Nosbonsing is the home of "Iron Jaw" and Lake of the Woods is where "Ol' Croc" lives. Both are reported to be gator-like in size and ferocity.

"Beast" is the handle given the seven footer which skulks in Wabigoon Lake near Dryden. Lodge operator Craig Dawson (now known as the Wabigoon Woebegone) would have gladly traded the 31 he tallied in the 25- to 50-pound range last season for one Beast. After fighting it for more than an hour he lost it when he tried to beach it.

Which brings us to the object of our November exercise — incredible Hulk. That 's the monicker laid on the enormous muskellunge which lurks among the countless islands a few kilometres north of Honey Harbour not far from Bill Bridgeman's hideaway.

"Hulk would make two of this one," he had said pointing to the impressive mount of his son's 45-pounder.

Well, no, he hadn't actually seen the legendary leviathan himself; although he's almost certain that son Jim locked horns with it. Before Bill could turn the boat and give chase, whatever was on the line had taken a beeline for the horizon, spooling the reel in the process.

His neighbor, however, did get an eyeball on the storied giant. According to Bill: "He thought he had spotted a beaver swimming with a stick in its mouth. When he got a little closer, he realized that the beaver was the head of a musky and the stick was a two-foot pike!"

He related another chapter in the incredible Hulk saga. This one concerned a doctor who, along with his family, was spending the weekend with a colleague who has a cottage about a kilometre from Bill's.

"The medicine man and his 10-year-old daughter went out in a small boat to cast for bass in the bay. Darned if he doesn't hook the Hulk which must have been curious because it came straight in, lay on the surface and glared at them malevolently.

"The little girl became hysterical and her father figured that the only way he could land that monster was to tow it to shore. When he started the outboard the 'lunge took off so fast that it yanked the rod right out of his hand. I'm told they both required medication."

"Both?" I asked, puzzled.

"Yep. Hers from a pill bottle; his from a whisky bottle."

It's nice to fish with a kindred spirit. I believed Bill's Incredible Hulk anecdotes and he didn't smirk at the sight of my tackle bucket.

I've yet to find a tackle box which will accommodate musky baits of a size to match one's ambitions. A lipped plastic pail is dandy. Simply drill holes around the lip, stick one of the tail hooks through it and the lure hangs out of harm's way inside the bucket.

Record Muskies?

After steering us through a maze of channels and around countless potential boat-wrecking boulders, Bill said: "Get rigged. We'll start here." We were a kilometre or so from the mouth of the Musquash River which is one of the traditional musky hotspots in that corner of Georgian Bay.

Our outfits were similar. We both had chosen 1 1/2-metre rods with stout butt sections, heavy-duty levelwind reels and 12 kilogram lead-core line. It takes your lure down without the help of sinkers and is multi-colored so you know exactly how much line is out.

We didn't concur on the choice of a leader. Bill gave his nod to a one-metre braided wire lead while I fastened a 1 1/2-metre length of 22-kilogram monofilament to the end of my line.

While there's a chance it might be sliced by a muskie's shearing fangs it lets the lure dance a merrier tune which means more muskies on the line. Those predators prefer prey that's alive and kicking.

My partner started off with the largest Rapala plug, a lure that has produced well for him in the past. I snapped on a creation called the "Bauman Lunker Killer," a gigantic jointed plug.

No lure on the market is too large for 'lunge. They've been known to put the bite on fish which any angler would regard as keepers. Muskrats aren't uncommon fare and a guide I know swears he witnessed a huge musky dine on a small dog which chose the wrong swimming hole. My taxidermist discovered a mallard duck inside one that he was preparing for mounting.

The most interesting feature of this particular Bauman bait was its coloration. Its belly was dark blue and its back white, a reversal of nature's order.

That's a clever idea, when you think about it. After all, their light undersides and dark backs help camouflage fish from predators, be they above or below.

Although he kept one eye on his flasher-type depth sounder, it wasn't because he was worried about hitting rocks. Bridgeman is totally familiar with channels and bays for many kilometres around.

He was watching for muskellunge, and every once in a while he'd announce: "We've just passed over another." Then we'd usually work that weed bed or shoal for a while before moving along.

The waters of Georgian Bay are tricky to navigate, and the bottom goes up and down like a roller coaster. As a matter of fact, trolling in Bill's 16-foot boat is a little like riding on one, especially in rough seas. The wind was picking up, making the open stretches roily and dotted with whitecaps.

Bill maintained a nine- to 11-kilometre per hour pace and followed a zigzag course whenever possible. He explained that it enabled us to cover more water and varied the action of the plugs. When it comes to musky moxy, Bill heads the class.

We were passing a rocky point when his rod bucked and the surface boiled some 24 metres back of the stern. "Fish on!" he whooped, as he kicked the motor out of gear and drove the hooks deeper.

"Just a baby," said Bill, as he worked an 18-pounder near enough for me

145

to wrap the mesh around it. He compressed the gill covers between his thumb and finger, thus immobilizing the fish while he dislodged the hooks with the help of pliers. The fish was then released, none the worse for wear. The entire operation, from strike to finish, hadn't taken 10 minutes.

It's the consensus of the fishing fraternity that a musky shouldn't be kept unless it's going to be mounted. They're too rare and valuable to be taken for the table.

That's also a strong argument against the use of light tackle. The longer a 'lunge is on the line, the lower its chances for survival. Shock, exhaustion, injuries and hemorrhaging take their toll of an estimated 30 percent of the muskies that are returned to the water.

So, while it's possible to land a lunker with a whippy rod and gossamer monofilament, the chance of its living to fight another day is very slim.

It was near noon when I first tasted action. We were passing a dropoff when a vicious strike almost wrenched the rod from my hands. Unfortunately, the fish hadn't felt the hooks. An examination of the scarred plug indicated the lure had been grabbed from the top.

Some 30 minutes later, over a kilometre from that spot, it happened again. This time I felt the fish for about 10 seconds before the hooks pulled.

If there's any truth to the 200 hours per musky theory, I was well over my quota and should expect a lot of lean pickings in the days ahead.

Shortly after 1 p.m., we passed through a deep but narrow passage between two islands, where a slight current eddied the surface. "Look at this," Bill exclaimed, pointing at the dial on his depth sounder. The bottom reading was completely obliterated by an incredibly thick school of fish at the six-metre level.

He reckoned they were herring, which move from the depths to the inside waters at that time of year. "I'll be surprised if there isn't a musky hanging around the edge of such easy pickings," Bill remarked as he turned the boat for another run up the channel.

After half a dozen passes through that concentration of fish the helmsman suggested we try our luck elsewhere.

"Give it one more go," I suggested, "so I can test a theory. " It had suddenly occurred to me that the first fish to be devoured are the sick or injured which attract attention by abnormal or erratic behavior.

Instead of simply dragging the lure through the school below, this time I would pump the rod and make the plug dance a jog. I snubbed the spool under my thumb b so the king-size enticement wouldn't pull line from the reel each time it was jerked.

All well and good if I had just remembered to lift my thumb when the fish struck. The 12-kilo line popped like store string.

I cussed my stupidity and felt even worse when Bill, who knows his muskies, said: "Wow! Was that a heavyweight!"

I attached a new leader to my line and snapped on the last Lunker Killer, figuring I'd only be marking time for the rest of the day. I'd had my chance and

Record Muskies?

I blew it.

At 3:30, my rod bowed once more, and the reel howled a protest as line melted off it. "The devil's children have their father's luck," Bill muttered as he cranked in his line.

We were in a 90-metre wide pool which was the convergence of four channels. The fish had headed for the middle where it sounded and refused to budge.

Bill kept the boat clear of the line while I kept pressure on the fish and pumped the rod. Finally it moved slowly and purposefully for about 20 metres; then stopped again. There were no explosive antics or blue-busting leaps The really big muskies seldom do such things.

"I hope I don't jinx out by mentioning the fact that this is the same hole where the doctor tussled with Incredible Hulk," Bill remarked after 10 or 15 minutes had passed without our getting a glimpse of The Brobdingnagian.

I kept the rod high and gained a little line as the behemoth circled the boat. The line gradually angled toward the top until a huge back split the surface some 15 metres behind the stern.

"Oh migawd, it's him " Bill gasped in disbelief.

My knees went rubbery at the sight of that old warrior. It looked like a great golden log as it lay broadside to us. Then it took off again. Now that I'd seen it I was more nervous than ever.

At long last I was able to raise it from the depths and lead it toward the landing net which Bill had ready and waiting. It was a mind-boggling musky with a head like a crocodile and the girth of a pig.

Bill netted it masterfully getting its massive snout right to the bottom of the 44-inch *Better get a bigger net!*
bag. Even though the fish was curled somewhat at least one-third of it still protruded past the rim of the net.

When Bill attempted to swim it through the water so we could grasp the hoop it literally collapsed.

The hefty handle crimped and the hoop bent 90 degrees, dumping my dreams back into the drink. Only the plug remained.

That evening as we sat in front of the fireplace without enough heart even to drown our sorrows, Bill said: "Look on the bright side. Maybe this was your lucky day."

"How's that?" I asked.

"Has it occurred to you " he grinned, "that perhaps you were the one that got away?."

147

Scotty Elko sent me a clipping from the *Vilas County New Review* (Wisconsin) by Dan Satran. It contained a reference to a 50-pound musky caught in the early 1900s. I thought you might enjoy it.

Try Red Cabbage As Lure For Musky

The late George C. Dobbs of Conover published a little booklet on the history of Conover before he died. I finally got around to reading some of his anecdotes.

He doesn't exactly date the event but he recalls that in the early 1900s guide Al Adams suggested to his customer, Dr. Rohr, that he put on a bait consisting of a red cabbage leaf on a spoon hook which he used to catch a 50-pound musky. He writes that Al Adams told him the first person he guided (about 1903) was Denis Carroll of Chicago, who later built a home on Lac Vieux Desert. Al said he was paid $1.25 for his day of guiding, and they landed and kept six muskies. In those days there was no limit.

An interesting tidbit from the February 1938 issue of *Sports Afield*. It regards a 53-pound 2-ounce musky caught in 1937.

Prize Fish

Four Minnesotans won grand prizes for big fish they caught in a fishing contest, just closed, which attracted a total of 770 entries during the 14 weeks it was conducted. Open to anglers from all parts of the country, prizes were limited to fish caught in Michigan, North Dakota, Minnesota and Wisconsin. Fish entered in the contest in four classes averaged eleven and one quarter pounds apiece and represented a total poundage of 8,751, according to L.C. Dillon, sales manager of the Fitger Brewing Co., Duluth, which sponsored the competition.

Charles Leitch, 1277 Games Street, St. Paul, topped the muskellunge division with a specimen caught in Roosevelt Lake July 30th which weighed 53 pounds and two ounces. A total of 92 of this species, weighing 2,318 pounds and averaging better than 26 pounds apiece, was entered.

Where is Roosevelt Lake? If anyone can provide more clues and/or a picture of this fish please do!

While I am on the subject of help, there are a few others I could use help with if anyone is so disposed to take the time. In Joe Fellegy's wonderful book, *Classic Minnesota Fishing Stories*, (Waldman House Press, 525 N. Third St., Minneapolis, MN 55401), there were several references to big muskies I would like to get more on. In the *Minneapolis Tribune* of Sunday, August 26, 1951, there is a story (and perhaps picture?) of a 50-pound musky caught by Stanley Kroll. There is also a story about it in the Grand Rapids Herald Review of August

13, 1951. The fish was entered in the Fuller Contest in Grand Rapids. A picture there perhaps?

How about the picture in the Cass Lake Chamber of Commerce office of a speared 70-pound-plus musky. My letters to them have gone unanswered. Can anyone help?

Our next tidbit comes from Conover, Wisconsin, expert taxidermist (and super provider of musky research help), Ron Lax. Several years back a huge female musky was found dying in Lac Vieux Desert, Wisconsin. The huge fish was hung from a tree for a couple of days during which time most of the spawn in her drained onto the ground. Approximately eight to 10 pounds of it! Ron then procured the fish to mount. It still weighed over 50 pounds after draining and dehydrating all that time! What a waste!

Late last fall, through one of my informants, I learned Ron had another huge (60-inch) musky from Lac Vieux Desert to mount that had been hit by a motor. I wrote Ron and asked him for the story. He wrote back the following:

> Larry, I haven't forgotten about you. I'm just trying to get all the facts straight before I make any mistakes. I've had at least four people claim they hit and found the fish. You know how that goes, everybody wants to be in on it. I now know the person who hit the fish. He also has Polaroid pictures of the fish when he hauled it in the boat. As soon as I get all the exact facts and pictures (he said we could use them) I'll be sending them to you. Hopefully within a couple of weeks.
>
> Sincerely, Ron.

Some time later I received a second letter from Ron:

> Dear Larry,
> Sorry it took so long for the pictures. The picture of the musky between seats in the jonboat is the 60-incher.
> The fish was hit in August 1982 on Lac Vieux Desert by an outboard operated by Dr. M. S. Krupa ... I didn't receive the fish till two days afterward, which made it partially decayed. The fish was hit along the right side and up across the top of the back just in front of the dorsal fin. I never weighed the fish because of its decayed condition. I just tried to get the

The 60-inch musky hit by a prop on Wisconsin's Lac Vieux Desert in August 1982, shortly after it was recovered.

skin off as soon as possible. I would estimate the fish between 50 and 60 pounds.

Sincerely, Ron.

What a shame to see two huge muskies go that way instead of being caught. Makes one wonder how many other huge muskies die without being caught.

Time now to hear from one of the true legends of musky fishing — the late Homer LeBlanc. Homer revolutionized musky catching during his over 40 years and thousands of muskies from Lake St. Clair. Over the years Homer has written hundreds of articles and a couple of books on musky fishing.

From my files I found a letter from Homer with tales of a few of the big muskies he has caught, or hooked and lost. Homer's tales:

Big Thriller

My first big thrill was in my early days of musky fishing. I was trolling with a spinner and bucktail lure. The tip of my rod bent back and it felt like I had hit some weeds. I quickly reeled my lure to check it. As the lure neared the boat, the spinner blade broke the water by two feet and a huge musky grabbed it in mid air. I hadn't seen him and it must have come from nowhere, to grab that lure! Needless to say, it scared the heck out of me, and I jerked back and luckily hooked it. The battle lasted for about an hour in a pouring rain. It rained for two days. I had to go to work; the result was that it never got weighed. One of my neighbors had cleaned it. Estimated at about fifty-five pounds.

Big One Got Away

The biggest musky I ever had grab a lure gave me a sickening kind of thrill. That day, I was out fishing for charter with four fishermen. We caught two muskies. They had to be back at the dock by 2 p.m., as they had to catch a train back to New York. After they left, I decided to go out and try to catch a musky, since company was coming for dinner and had never eaten any.

I had trolled only a few minutes and this monster musky grabbed my lure. It held its ground and I kept losing line. I put the motor out of gear to stop the forward motion. The lake was fairly rough and the boat kept drifting away and I kept losing more line. The musky wouldn't give ground,

Homer LeBlanc and friends with a 50-pounder.

so I decided to put the motor in gear and turn the boat around, back to the musky. To make headway, I had to accelerate the motor. I gave it just a little too much acceleration. The result was that I wound up with a slack line for a few seconds. I got a tight line again and was gaining most of my line back. The musky was about forty feet away and definitely a world record. He violently shook his head and threw the lure a good forty feet. An observer in a rowboat saw the action and the musky. He came over to console me and said, "he was as big and as long as a railroad tie." This musky gave me several thrills, one was a very disheartening one. I felt like crying.

Biggest Thrill

Late one afternoon, I invited a neighbor to go musky fishing with me. We were trolling an area that had several heavy cabbage weed beds.

I hooked a giant musky with a casting size lure, and with a light flexible rod. All hell broke loose; the musky charged the boat and came flying out of the water by three feet and only about four feet back from the boat. There was nothing I could do to get him away from the boat and the weed bed. This musky made seven jumps in all, each time he would head for bottom. The musky hooked the lure into the base of a big stalk of cabbage weed and tore himself loose. The lure was well embedded into the weed and I pulled it up roots and all. We estimated that it would weigh close to fifty pounds.

I can still see that huge head, shaking back and forth, trying to throw the lure. Sure would have made the greatest moving picture ever. Oh well! Those pictures are in my head forever and will never fade!

In the past I have used stories from *Classic Minnesota Fishing Stories* by Joe Fellegy. There is one more story from it I would like to pass on to you. It concerns a 52-pound musky caught by Cass Lake, Minnesota, guide Cliff Riggles:

Cliff's Biggest Musky

The biggest musky I ever caught came from Pike Bay of Cass Lake. It's kind of an odd story. It happened in September, back in the early 1950s when people were less excited about records and weighing big fish.

I took a fellow from Dakota with me. He came through here with a load of fence posts. He had been driving truck most of the night and had to unload right away the next morning. So he was tired, but eager to go fishing.

We were trolling for northerns with Dardevles, along the weeds. The wind came up, blowing from the south. We were kind of on the northwest side and it was getting kind of windy along there. He was in the front of the boat and I was in the back running the motor.

We had caught a couple small northerns, maybe four-pounders, and had a couple more blocks to go when I said, "We'll go up to the end of this point and we'll head 'er on in." It was getting pretty rough. He was tired and was ready to go in, too.

So I just went a few feet — going pretty fast to keep the boat straight —

and man! Something hit hard and I gave 'er a yank. It came out of the water and of course this guy could see it. He said, "My God, you've got a big one now! We'll never get him!"

Well, I told him if the wind didn't blow us into the bulrushes we'd probably be all right. But the wind was blowing us that way and we weren't too far from 'em. Anyway, I got the boat swung the way I wanted it and started the fight. My partner was going to come to the back of the boat to help. But that would have been a mess, with both of us back there, the front of the boat out of the water, and the waves and all. So I told him to stay up there and to get his line in.

Luckily, the fish took off out into the lake, away from the rushes. I was crankin' and trying to handle the boat at the same time. Finally I got out quite a ways and was feeling better because I now had a chance — away from those rushes. Eventually my fish came to the top and boy, he looked big! He was a huge fish. We wrestled him for another ten minutes and finally we got close enough to him and got the gaff hook where it belonged. So I got him into the boat. He thrashed from one end of the boat to the other. But we had him.

We guessed him at 60 pounds. I personally had never been in contact with, or had seen, a fish like that. I was excited and so was he. I got him on a stringer, after he bled all over the place. I had gaffed him pretty good under the gills. He was just about dead when I put him over the side of the boat.

We decided to fish the rest of the way back in hopes of another big fish. So we started trolling again and pretty soon he hit one. And he really had a tough time of it! This time I was free to handle the boat while he cranked away, gaining and losing ground. A number of times I ran up toward the fish. This fish ran away from the rushes, like mine. I'd run up on him and away he'd go. This

C.A. Duke (left) and guide Henry Senecal with five muskies caught by Duke while trolling around Grenedier Island in the St. Lawrence on Nov. 15, 1907. The fish weighed 24, 34, 36, 36 and 39 1/2 pounds.

went on for about 15 minutes before we got a look at his fish.

By this time the guy was getting all in and nervous, even shaky. But he sure got calmed down and was disappointed when he saw his fish. It wasn't a big musky at all. Instead it was about an 18-pound northern, which he snagged in the stomach! We got him, too.

Now that was a fishing trip when the last couple blocks on the way to the dock were interesting. We weighed my fish at home. This guy took it with him and had it mounted. The weight, by the way, was 52 pounds. His name was Mueller — I think that's how you spell it — Bud Mueller from South Dakota. He had a lumberyard.

How about Cliff Riggle's 52-pounder from Cass Lake ... can anyone find a picture?

In August of 1985, I was a guest at Compton's Wilderness Lodge on Upper Manitou Lake, Ontario. In my first visit to the dining room, an old picture on the wall pulled at me like a magnet. It was a very old picture of a huge musky. The "Sherlock" in me took over immediately and I started asking questions about it. Camp owner Bob Compton didn't know its weight or any details about it, but said he would try to find out. I figured it would be some months before I heard the story but Bob took some of his valuable time during the week and came up with some details. From people in the area and ministry personnel, he learned that the man holding the fish was thought to be Lawrence Perkins of Vermilion Bay. The fish, caught in Jackfish Bay, was reported to weigh 52 to 54 pounds and was caught in the mid 1940s.

After returning home I wrote a letter to Jerry Tricomi who had spent 25 years on the Manitou starting in the '40s to see if he knew anything about this fish. His reply:

> There was a guide named George Perkins (same man?) who guided for Lorn MacKenzie on Eagle Lake and who guided for a dude from Chicago in 1945. The dude caught a 61-pound musky and I saw a picture of him at Camp Baribou near Gold Rock holding that fish It was a true monster.

The original "Monster of the Manitou" caught in the 1940s.

Could this be one and the same fish?

Perhaps so, as I believe Compton's was previously Camp Baribou.

From June 21, 1877 *Forest & Stream*:

> A fifty-pound muskelonge — a monster muskelonge (muskinonge), weighing 50 pounds, and measuring 4ft. 8 in., has been sent to John Cummings, of Utica, by Sydney Adams, Gananoque, Ontario. It is one of the

largest ever caught in the St. Lawrence River. It was taken on a hook and line, and occupied the attention of the angler and Charley Lasha, his boatman, for over three hours.

Had records been kept in 1877 that fish could have been the world record until 1916!

And once again, taxidermist Ron Lax of Conover, Wisconsin, comes through. His letter follows:

The 50-pound plus musky found by F.S. Sunderland on Lac Vieux Desert in 1968.

> Dear Larry,
> I've been talking to Mr. Francis Sunderland for the past few years about a 58 1/2-inch, 50-pound-plus musky he found on Lac Vieux Desert in July of 1968 with a Suick lodged in its mouth. He finally dropped off a picture of the fish! So I thought I'd forward it to you. The fish was weighed on a 50-pound maximum scale and it broke the scale. More info on the back of the picture.
> Sincerely, Ron

Here's the story of another Wisconsin giant whose true weight will never be known:

A Possible World's Record Musky?
By John Dettloff

Allison Drake fished and guided in the Chippewa Flowage area since before the Flowage was even formed. He was one of the original pioneer guides along with his son Art Drake, Jess Ross, Harry Lessard and Ken Ackley to name a few. Allison was caretaker of the Moose Lake Dam for many years and in the 1930s caught this gigantic musky below the Moose Lake Dam way up the West Fork of the Chippewa River. The fish bottomed out a 50-pound scale and there were no bigger scales available so they never knew its exact weight — probably over 60 pounds and maybe a world's record at that time. Allison was a big man at about 6-3, according to those who knew him, and from looking at this picture the fish appears to be 60" or more! The world's record musky in 1932 was 58 1/4 pounds. That was the time period when Allison caught this fish. At that time records were scarcely kept on big fish and not many people officially weighed them. Few people mounted muskies then too, Allison just cut up the monster for the meat.

Not many details are known about this fish except one — Allison Drake got one heck of a musky back in those early days. Just look at the picture. Supposedly, the Chicago Tribune wrote all about Allison's fish but that will take

Record Muskies?

more digging to uncover. Allison Drake guided mostly out of the West Fork resorts like Wende's, Willet's, Phil Hall's, and Lessard's and sometimes out of Cammack's Treeland Pines. His last years guiding he would break the day in half and take a nap mid-day but would still get his 8 hours in. He guided till he was in his 80s and was well respected — one of the pioneer guides of the flowage.

Allison Drake's giant from the 1930s bottomed out a 50-pound scale.

From the *Minneapolis Star-Tribune*, by Ron Schara:

A fellow named Isaacson called it "Old Bismarck." Perhaps memory of a big ship by the same name.

But Old Bismarck is a giant fish, a musky to be exact. And it lives near a big boulder called "Elephant Rock," located in Red Gut Bay on Rainy Lake.

By all rights, Old Bismarck should be a myth, taken out of a children's book. The names are too perfect for a fish tale.

And who ever heard of a musky that weighs between 80 and 100 pounds?

Well friends, Larry Hendrickson had heard about it. And Larry Hendrickson also has seen Old Bismarck.

"Sure, I thought it was a myth. But on the third musky fishing trip, I saw Old Bismarck ... right near Elephant Rock," said Hendrickson.

At the time, Hendrickson, of Minneapolis, had just purchased the Silver Musky Lodge from Isaacson. He has since sold the lodge, however, and has nothing to gain by seeing big fish through a resort owner's eyes.

"We were plugging for muskies with a big Rapala when suddenly Old Bismarck appeared," said Hendrickson.

"It followed the plug two or three times and then just lay right beside the boat.

"It was about three-quarters the size of a 14-foot boat. I estimated the weight between 80 and 100 pounds," he said.

Hedrickson said that Old Bismarck has been hooked at least twice, by a Chicago fisherman and a resident of the Rainy Lake region.

"The story goes that the musky just took everything. It ripped off and went. There is nothing in a fishbox that could handle him."

Two years have passed since Hendrickson last saw the mammoth fish. But what does a musky fisherman say when sees such a creature?

"I said some things, but you couldn't print them in a newspaper," he said.

155

Possible? Read what Bob Cary wrote in 1976 in *The Magic of the Muskellunge*:

> Ontario, for sheer surface area of water, has more musky territory than any political entity in North America. Frank Schneider, an official of Muskies, Inc., and a man with musky blood in his veins, considers the northeast segment of Ontario's big Rainy Lake as excellent trophy territory. He and his friends consistently score in the over-20-pound class and swear they had an 80-pounder rip walleyes from their stringers.

In 1966, Arne Juul and I were guiding on Moose Lake at Hayward, Wisconsin, with two couples who were staying at Ghost Lake Lodge. At lunch, Arne related the following story to us:

> The rest of the story: Remember Louis Spray's 69-pound, 11-ounce musky caught on Oct. 20,1949 on the Chippewa Flowage near Hayward, Wisc.?

> One of the great guides of northern Wisconsin was Arne Juul, 80, who lived east of Hayward. Arne has had some 60 years on the water and truly was one of the greats. Arne, told the story about the day before Spray's big catch, Oct. 19, 1949. He was guiding a long-time customer, Fred Osterman, and his wife.

> Arne: He was reluctant to go out on Oct. 19, but I kept telling him, 'Let's go, I've got a feeling.' Remember in those days we could use a pistol to shoot a musky as we got it near the boat. Technically, it wasn't legal, but just a custom, so people and the guides did it. That was until people started shooting too far from the boat and sometimes in the boat, putting a hole or two in them.

> We had to carry our motors down to the boat landing. Think we fished out of Herman's. Well, we did go out. The day was hot as a fall feeding frenzy was on. Osterman nailed a nice 18-pounder. The fish jumped and he lost it. Again, a musky hit— a 30-pounder. And again, it jumped and was gone!

> "I want a musky," Osterman added. "Shoot the ... thing."

> The wily Juul eased near Fleming's bar on the Big Chip and started the casting action again. Blam, something big hit Osterman's line. It was the biggest fish both Juul and he had ever seen. He was offering a tough fight, but was still away from the boat. Juul fired, but missed and the fish broke loose again.

> A disgusted Osterman said, "Let's go home." Juul protested and said let's stay, but Osterman, a bit disgusted, wanted to go. Juul knew that was a special musky and that it would probably hit again and soon. The next day Louis Spray caught his 69-pound, 11-ounce fish near the same bar *(the original report said the fish was caught at Fleming's Bar, but this was later found not to be true—LR)*.

> Juul said Osterman didn't fish with him for two years as he was still steamed. But they were still friends through the years and Juul continued as one of the best guides ever. Juul is truly a jewel of a great guy.

Jim Brabant is one of the top guides on the St. Lawrence River.

Record Muskies?

His article appeared in a publication called *Holiday*, in the summer of 1977:

Musky Fishing: A Guide's View

By James Brabant

Being a native of Clayton, New York — the gateway to the Thousand Islands, St. Lawrence River — raised in this town and having spent most of my life here; I have followed the lure of the great musky like most of the other residents ...

Old timers can tell of 50- to 60-pounders caught and where the large fish are living and have been for years. Once in a while someone hooks onto one of these legendary monsters only to have his or her tackle torn apart ...

Trolling was done in the early 1900s from St. Lawrence River rowing skiffs with linen or cotton lines and Skinner spoons used chiefly for bait. Hand lines were used and later long wooden poles with bells on them. The line was wound around two nails and when the fish was hooked the bell would ring, the line manually fed off to the fish. Some fishermen would throw the wooden rod into the water and follow it until the fish tired ...

Many people have fished a lifetime without so much as a strike.

Roland Garnsey told me that when he was a boy he saw two muskies caught by Joe LaLonde Sr. for Hewitt Morgan, a summer resident at the head of Grindstone Island. The one they caught in the morning weighed 50 pounds and the afternoon catch was 55 pounds — all caught while fishing out of a St. Lawrence River rowing skiff.

More from 1976 and Bob Cary:

Over on Moose Lake there was an old submarine of a fish they dubbed the "Two O'Clock Musky." Resort owners and guides swore that the fish only fed at 1:50 p.m. and that he seldom ventured far from his home territory around Grassy Island. Estimated at 45 pounds, the old warrior had three times defeated Indiana angler Dr. Robert Gibson and ripped a lure off the line of Bill Brown from Riverside, Illinois. One quiet evening my cousin Bill Paull, from Aurora, Illinois, and I were plugging Grassy Island, but with little success. As we moved down the shore, an acquaintance of Bill's, George Perrien, also of Aurora, arrived on the scene with guide Johnny Gates. The first shot out of the box, George let out a yell as his rod doubled sharply and a fish slammed into his lure. Gates rowed for deep water while Bill and I moved over to seats on the 50-yard line ... and the battle was on.

The musky was tough but George was tougher and John handled the boat beautifully. Fifteen minutes elapsed before the fish came headfirst into the net. Only it wasn't the monster, it was a 25-pounder. This was a rare instance where two big fish were in the same territory. Perhaps if Bill and I had made just two more casts we might have scored on one or the other. The last I heard about the Two O'Clock Musky, he was still shredding lines and tearing off hooks.

Cary first wrote about this fish in the *Chicago Daily News* on July 22, 1960:

Husky Musky Too Slippery
Likes A 2 p.m. Lunch

Some muskies get so big, old and mean, they become a tradition.

The "Two O'Clock Musky" of Moose Lake is one of these.

Estimated at 45 pounds, this huge, brown saw-toothed son of perdition has his lair in a hole near Grassy Island. He still is there at this writing.

According to resort owner Mark Smith, this torpedo-sized specimen comes by his name honestly. He hits within 10 minutes of 2 p.m. ... if he hits at all.

Riverside, Illinois, angler Bill Brown tangled with the big boy and came out second best. Dr. Robert Gibson, Columbus, Indiana, hung old "Two O'Clock" three times, but couldn't beat him.

The last time the doctor rammed a black bucktail into the musky's jaw the fish cleared the surface like a stricken porpoise.

This would have been the end of the tradition ... but Two O'Clock gave the lure one last, bone-jarring shake that broke two of the forged hooks and set him free.

For the past few weeks he's been exceedingly coy. He occasionally follows a lure up to the boat, makes a huge swirl in the water and gives some powerful angler a bad case of nerves.

But he's been notoriously hook-shy.

However, an old saw musky the size of Two O'Clock has to eat. He's got a lot of length to keep filled out.

Sooner or later he will mistake a plug or a spoon for one of the dozens of big perch he devours every week ... and he'll wind up a stuffed trophy on someone's office wall.

That is, unless he dies of old age ... the most horrible, ignoble end that could befall such a great fighter.

I fished Moose Lake during the era of Two O'Clock an it was exciting every time we fished Grassy Island.

Record Muskies?

Continuing with Cary:

Ranking at the top for many trophy hunters is Ontario's Eagle Lake, a consistent producer of giants up to 60 pounds. Resort owner Lorne McKenzie steered me into the biggest musky I ever came eye-to-eye with, a trophy Lil and I will never forget. This old tusker had been raised several times in a small rocky bay on the south shore of the lake, but had so far evaded capture. The first time we saw him, we were drifting into the bay with a strong backwind, not using the motor and creating a minimum disturbance with the oars. Several loose logs were being moved around along with other flotsam by the wind and we thought he was just another partially submerged pine bole ... until he moved.

Hastily we cast over and ahead of him as he moved his bulk slowly across the channel outlet of the bay, but he made no move as the baits came whirling past. I let the wind carry us back to open water, then motored up the lake for a couple of hours to let him cool off. About 4 p.m. we eased back into the bay and began casting again. After about a dozen casts, I lifted my bucktail from the water, swished it back and forth, then brought it up for a backcast. Five feet of solid musky fury exploded off the stern as the fish, huge jaws agape, made a desperate grab for the bait. As he crashed down right next to the motor, Lil and I were both hit with a shower of spray. But he didn't get the hooks. A half hour of casting produced no activity.

The next day we were back in the bay at 4 p.m. and after a few casts the big guy rolled up on top, 15 yards from the boat, eyeing us with undisguised hate. But he wouldn't hit. Finally, he dived and vanished from sight. That night, in the lodge, I told Lorne about the big fish and the guests crowded around to listen. It made a great story.

The following afternoon there was a strong wind and we couldn't get back across the main body of the lake to the south shore until almost 5 p.m., but we moved in to the little bay and worked it carefully. Nothing happened. When we got back to the lodge we found out why. At 4 p.m. Chicago angler Ed Klemme had drifted the bay with a guide and busted that big boy on a bucktail. Klemme had his trophy hanging by the ice house. It went an even 50 pounds.

From the *Sawyer County Record* (Wisconsin), 1989:
Man Fights Monster Musky For 10 Hours on Big Chip
By Terrell Boettcher

Otis the musky took Oconomowoc angler Randy Prestash for a 10-hour tour of the Chippewa Flowage last week.

The two engaged in an epic battle from 7 p.m. to 5 a.m. under a full moon Saturday night.

The fish — which Prestash and witnesses believe to be over 60 pounds and more than six feet long — hauled him and his companions about 4 1/2 miles, from Little Pete's Bar to Hay Creek Narrows.

Prestash never let go of the rod, and kept his line taut as Randy Leonard of Deerfoot Lodge maneuvered the 16-foot Tuffy boat and Todd Schultz poised

159

with a big net.

But in the end, the fish won, wrapping Prestash's new, 6-pound test Trilene line around a pine stick in 20 feet of water and breaking the 4-pound leader.

"He did everything right," Leonard said. "He kept good, solid pressure on him. He should have landed it if it hadn't been for that stick."

Dr. Prestash is not exactly an amateur fisherman. The optometrist runs a high tech-tackle store called Fish Doctors, makes "Video Hotspots" to prescribe for fishing success, and has guided for the Lindner brothers of *In-Fisherman* and Camp Fish.

He has fished in the ocean and Lake Michigan, and has had heavy fish of many species on his line before. He has landed a few muskies over 20 pounds.

"There was never one of them I couldn't raise (until this one)," Prestash said. "It's the biggest one I had on in my life."

He had gone walleye fishing Saturday on the Chip and was using a floating jig and nightcrawler when the big fish hit. He had a Mitchell 300 reel with a 5 1/2-foot Abu Garcia light-action rod.

"Once it made a couple of runs, I was certain it was a musky," Prestash said.

He figures it was up feeding on walleyes on the "bump" on Little Pete's, and "I was fortunate enough to be there at the right time," he said. The fish made about 25 runs over 50 yards and many shorter ones. It followed the old river channel, and seemed to sense its depth, keeping one to two feet off the bottom, Prestash said.

"It was a knowledgeable fish," he said. "It made very controlled runs. I didn't tire it. All I did was let it know I was irritating it."

The musky would come up to within six feet of the surface directly below the boat, but no one could get a good look at it, he said. Then it would drop like a stone.

Other boaters witnessed the battle, and at least one stayed all night.

After four hours, one went in and notified Leonard. The anglers transferred themselves and their equipment to Leonard's boat, which offered more space and an open cockpit.

From maneuvering the boat around the fish, they could get an idea of the musky's size, Prestash said.

His hands became numb and cramped with cold, and he could not feel the movements of the fish, he said. A companion held a flashlight on his rod tip. By 5 a.m., they had gone through three trolling-motor batteries and one trolling-motor blade, which broke.

"Even with 20-pound-test line or 30-pound dacron, there was no way I could have turned that fish," Prestash said.

His plan was to tire the fish enough to get it near shore, then jump into the water and gaff it.

"We went toe-to-toe for a long time. I was desperate at the end. It was myself and the fish."

Since then, he has replayed the events many times in his mind, he said, and is "haunted by what-ifs."

But looking back, "I wouldn't have done anything different, except try to speed up the sunrise so I could get it into shallow water," he added.

"It could have been the world's record," he said. Two hours of video and the witnesses document the battle and the size of the fish, he added.

Leonard retrieved the stick on which the fish broke off, and Prestash plans to have it analyzed by the DNR to see if a fish scale or other evidence can be found to discover more about the fish.

He dubbed his musky nemesis "Otis," after the name of the elevator company, "because he went up and down."

As you would have noted in the original chapter, there were several references to large muskies being caught before the season opened. The primary reason these giant fish are caught then is that they are in shallow where the angler can get at them, unlike the main part of the open season. Following are a few more examples:

From John Power's article "Ontario's Top 15 Muskies" in *Ontario Out of Doors*, October, 1989:

> Finally, no collection of 'lunge lore would be complete without mentioning the monster that got away twice — after it was landed! It began near the mouth of the French River in 1947. After observing a fisherman take the musky out of season, game wardens confiscated the fish and charged the fisher. When they finally got around to recording its mind boggling statistics, it still weighed 68 pounds, 14 ounces and measured 62 1/4 inches in length and an astounding 35 3/4 inches in girth (a pre-spawn musky will weigh as much as 20% more at this time and be much larger in girth—LR). It was duly mounted and given a place of honour at Queen's Park from whence it vanished without a trace when the place was refurbished. Moral: Never hire an interior decorator who doesn't fish for musky.

This photo is believed to be of the 62 1/4-inch, 68-pound 14-ounce Ontario musky.

Included herewith is an old photo that is thought to be of the aforementioned musky.

Following is a portion of a letter about a 64-incher caught and released before season on Upper Manitou Lake in northwestern

Ontario:

There are many anglers who feel that it is their privilege to keep exquisite details of their fishing success to themselves. Mike Gambsky of Menasha, Wisconsin, who fished with us last June (1989), is different. He enjoys telling about the super-musky he caught and released on a three-inch Mepps Syclops in Mosher Bay of Upper Manitou on June 7th. And no wonder: it measured 64 inches long, and is probably the longest musky ever released anywhere.

Bob Korzinski
Green Island Lodge, Dryden, Ontario

And from the 1991 *Mepps Fishing Guide*:
Mike Gambsky's Musky Potential World Record

Mike Gambsky, Menasha, WI, may have landed a new world record

musky June 7, 1989, but no one will ever know for sure.

Musky season was not yet open and Gambsky's 64-inch (that's 5 feet 4 inches) fish was released following a brief photo session.

The huge fish was caught in Mosher Bay while Gambsky was vacationing at Green Island Lodge, Lake Manitou, Ontario. He was casting for northern pike with

Dave Korzinski holds Mike Gambsky's musky prior to its release.

a #3 Mepps Syclops when the monster musky slammed his spoon.

His guide, Dave Korzinski, who has fished Lake Manitou for more than 20 years, estimated the weight of the fish at "over 50 pounds." But, there was no scale in the boat and musky season had not yet opened, so the fish never was officially measured or weighed.

For his efforts, Gambsky did receive the Green Island Lodge 1989 Angler of the Year award. He also has received a Mepps Master Angler citation.

Another huge musky was caught from the waters of Georgian Bay in the early 1990s before season. It was caught by an angler from Colorado who was trolling a #5 Mepps for pike when the lunker grabbed hold. An accurate measurement was not obtained, but he stated that it went nearly all the way across the rear floor of his boat which is over five feet. The first photo I obtained was a poor off-angle shot that didn't do the fish justice. When I got to Georgian Bay I was able to obtain a photo that had been taken from another boat. Suffice

it to say that the fish appears huge! Best guesstimate among the experts who have viewed it is in the low to mid 60-pound range. Judge for yourself from the photo.

Let's for a moment refer once again to John Power's article in *Ontario Out of Doors*:

"...how about Frank Eames, who bagged a five-footer near Gananoque in 1938. Eames, who was 85 years of age, never bothered to have his fish officially recognized. Fortunately, Bill McDowell of Burlington, Ont., stumbled across the mount in an antique shop, had it refurbished, and is keeping it safe and sound."

Cameras snap rapidly as the angler strains to hold the giant Georgian Bay musky.

Unfortunately, in addition to the several monsters that have been caught by anglers before (or after) the open season, there are other ways that over the years have brought big muskies into the limelight, as it were. That is the undignified method of the spear, usually through the ice.

The first one comes by way of the National Fresh Water Fishing Hall of Fame. As I visited one day with Hall director Ted Dzialo, he had a great picture to share with me. I later received a letter from Ted with a copy of the picture. His letter stated:

...The fish shown with the kids was speared from the (Chippewa) Flowage in 1938 by Fred Kirk, supposedly the first white man with a farm on the (Lac Courte Oreilles Indian) reservation about 1916. It was 72 pounds.

The next one I learned about from the folks at Mepps. They sent me a picture of a very large musky apparently speared (or shot). The good looking guy in the photo on Page 164 is pointing to a hole in the back of the fish from either a gun shot or spear. The

Did this musky weigh 72 pounds as claimed? No way to know.

fish was taken from a lake north of Antigo, Wisconsin, many years ago.

Next come a monster that was speared

from the Chippewa Flowage, Wisconsin, about 1966. It was legally taken by a Native American, but it is too bad it had to meet its demise in this manner. As far a I know, this fish was never weighed, and estimates of its weight range from 50 to the 64 pounds that was reported to me. It supposedly was 65 1/4 inches long, but photo analysis has determined it to be closer to 55 inches. This would put the weight nearer to the mid 50-pound range, but it could have been as much as 64 with a full complement of eggs! At any rate, it is forever lost to anglers.

A monster musky, but a poor quality photo. Shot? Speared? Over 60 pounds? Who knows?

Now we come to a similar sad story from Minnesota. This musky, had it been sport caught, would have set a new record for Minnesota by 12 ounces. This fish was taken also by spear through the ice, while spearing for pike, which unfortunately is legal in Minnesota (and Michigan). It was taken from one of the lakes of the upper Mississippi

The diminutive Widmer Smith makes this musky appear gargantuan. It was speared in 1966 from the Chippewa Flowage.

A huge Minnesota musky that died via the spear.

River system in 1975. It weighed 54 pounds 14 ounces! The face of the person holding the fish in the photo is blocked out for obvious reasons. My only interest was to preserve the history of big muskies and this was necessary to obtain the photo.

Starting in the late 1940s, Jerry Tricomi built up a musky camp on Lower Manitou Lake and ran it for 25 years. Jerry related to me that in the early days, funds for things like official scales were slim, but huge muskies a not-uncommon occurrence. One such huge fish was caught by Jerry in 1956. After he had placed the approximate 52-pounder in the icehouse, the guides, thinking they were doing Jerry a favor, gilled and gutted the fish while he was away. Jerry was, to say the least, a bit unhappy upon his return. He did however, take the fish to Duluth for mounting and posed for a picture in town.

Jerry Tricomi's gilled and gutted 60-incher still makes an imprsssive photo.

Well known taxidermist and musky angler, Roger Halverson, of Fergus Falls, Minnesota, once told me of an interesting way to judge huge muskies — to measure the length of the head from the tip of the jaw to the end of the gill cover. Ever since that time, I have measured every musky head (real and mounted) that I could get my tape on. He had stated that a 13 1/2-inch head is a whopper. Of the dozens and dozens I have measured, only a few met this length. One however, was even longer! It was massive 14 inches. It is the only one I have ever measured that was over 13 1/2!! This was a mounted head

Andy, with the head of a giant musky. The head alone measured 14 inches.

presented to me by a gentleman named Andy. It was caught from the Turtle Flambeau Flowage in Wisconsin in the 1920s.

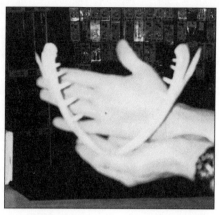

The impressive jaws and huge teeth of the Wabigoon monster.

Throughout this chapter have been references to huge muskies found dead. Well, here comes yet another, thanks to Brian Krau and Steve Kathke. It seems that a huge dead musky washed up on the shore of Wabigoon Lake at Dryden, Ontario, and was found by some kids. They went to the baitshop and told the "old folks" about it, but were ignored for several days. When they persisted, the "old folks" finally went to look. What they found was a decomposing and gull-picked monster of a musky which they measured at 64 inches long! It was too far gone to save, but they did salvage the jaw bone from the fish which was put on display in the baitshop (which is no longer there). Brian and Steve about came unglued when they saw it and after contacting me, made it a point to measure it and get a photo of it the next time they were there. After measuring the jaw spread, they, for comparison, measured the jaw spread of a mounted 50-plus-pounder whose jaw spread was 5 7/16ths of an inch. The Wabigoon jaw dwarfed it by several inches! At 9 1/4 inches wide, it could have made the largest of musky lures disappear! It was rumored that an angler had hooked and lost a huge musky just a couple of days before this one was found dead. Same fish?

While it is unfortunate that the preceding fish wasn't caught by an angler, many other, albeit lesser size ones were caught from Wabigoon Lake. In 1979, in the Canadian Molson fishing contest two names appeared that were to have a monumental and lasting effect on musky fishing in northwestern Ontario. Those names were Craig Dawson and Wabigoon Lake. In that 1979 contest Mr. Dawson entered fish weighing 44-4 and 43-8. This was but a small part of what was to come. In 1980, he made it clear that 1979 was no fluke when he took 1st, 2nd, 3rd, and 9th places in the Molson contest, with fish weighing 49-7; 47-15; 46-10 and 43-2, all from Wabigoon. In addition to the four Dawson fish, two of the others of the top ten also came from Wabigoon!

In 1981, a series of events took place that were to muddy the waters, causing hard feelings and ultimately ending with the death of Mr. Dawson.

In October of 1981, Gary Ishii caught and entered a 55-pound musky from Georgian Bay in the Molson Contest. It was the largest ever entered in the history of the contest. Shortly thereafter came an entry from Craig Dawson, who also entered a 55-pounder that was 56 3/4 inches long. He was awarded 1st place once again, due to the fact that his musky was 1 3/4 inches longer than that of Mr. Ishii's. This decision had been made after Dawson's death. But was it the correct decision? Let's review the facts as I was able to piece them together:

Craig Dawson and his controversial musky, which was claimed to weigh 55 pounds.

1.) Dawson's fish was supposedly caught in July, but it was not entered in the Molson contest until late October.

2.) The Dawson fish was weighed on uncertified bathroom scales, in the boat.

3.) The scales were later checked but not certified, and found to be weighing three pounds "light."

4.) If the scales weighed three pounds "light," why weren't the three pounds added to the original weight?

5.) In the photo of Dawson holding the fish, the fish is being held up by a 50-pound hand spring scale. Why is this, if it was supposedly weighed on a bathroom scale?

6.) When the supposed weight is checked by the "standard formula, it calculates out to 47.95 pounds using the adjusted formula (see *Musky Hunter's Almanac*) and 50.76 pounds without adjusting the formula. Remember, this was a post-spawn July fish, not a late fall fish that was building egg mass.

7.) One of North America's top musky anglers was told by Dawson that the fish had weighed 54 pounds, and that he wanted to get one more than just a few ounces bigger than his 1980 fish, so he released it!

8.) As Dawson was being watched by conservation officers and other resorters, is it possible that he did indeed catch a huge musky, but that it was before season, and therefore had to be released?

9.) Additionally, it was reported that Craig was trying to save his resort from foreclosure and he wanted to convince the world he was the "top" musky guide, and therefore is not likely he would have released a 55-pounder had it been legitimately caught.

10.) A conservation officer supposedly saw Dawson 's fish in a freezer and had no doubt as to its size. Was it the 1980 that he saw? How could he have seen the 1981 fish if it had been released?

So, to my way of thinking as former world record secretary for the National Fresh Water Fishing Hall of Fame and its current fish historian and record adviser, Dawson's fish, while it may well be legit as there is no doubt from the photo that it was huge and Mr. Dawson's past achievements were many, it should not have been accepted in the Molson contest as it was just too questionable. It is for the aforementioned reasons that it will not be found in my 50-Pound Club listing.

As for Wabigoon Lake, it poured out the big muskies in 1981, with seven others over 40 pounds being taken in addition to the Dawson fish, finishing with eight of the top 12 in the Molson Contest. It reached its zenith in 1982, when Don Reed registered a 51-pound 8-ounce monster from there — the largest ever verified. After 1982 I have record of only one additional musky from Wabigoon Lake that exceed 40 pounds. The lake was descended upon by hordes of musky anglers and literally cleaned out, and was subsequently closed to all but release only musky fishing for several years. It was recently re-opened with a 52-inch size limit on muskies.

My conclusion to this chapter is that the mystique is many things in combination, but nothing concrete.

Chapter 3:
Musky Crimes
of the Century

*For this chapter, I have asked John Dettloff to sum up the disqualifi-
cations of several past world record muskies as well as other fish that will
not be found in the chapters on world records and all other muskies over
50 pounds. John's work to clean up this musky mess has, I believe, been a
great service to the musky world and shows how rare muskies over 50
pounds are and always have been.*

By John Dettloff

While the world record musky has been sitting just below the
70-pound mark for nearly the past half century, even the
catching of a musky in excess of 50 pounds has always
been considered to be a rather hallowed angling accomplishment and
those fortunate enough to have made it onto the 50-pound list have
tended to be revered for their angling prowess ... some more than others.

Because they each have reported catching a number of these tackle busters and have made it onto the 50-pound listing for a combined
total of 32 times, the names of Spray, Haver, the Lawtons and the
Hartmans have long been ingrained into the minds of the musky
angling public as being something of musky fishing superstars —
icons in a sport that is both very unpredictable and, at times, even
maddening.

Up until 1992, the historic tally of huge musky catches boasted of
having 21 musky catches over 60 pounds and some 120 fish over 50
pounds. Musky men have long accepted this as being gospel, a belief
which had undoubtedly impacted their perspective on the sport. But
as it turned out, a staggering number of these fish have since proven

to be false claims. In fact, 67% of the largest muskies ever reported caught (14 fish on the 60-pound list) never actually existed, having proven to have been greatly exaggerated in size.

The motivation behind the falsified musky claims was, plain and simple, greed and ego. Many of these musky catches netted the anglers prize money from fishing contests, lucrative endorsements and free tackle, the opportunity to promote their own lure companies, and — let's not forget — bragging rights. It must be said though that times were different back then. Much of this took place during darker times; first, during the tail end of the Great Depression and then, during a time when the "Red Menace" was feared and people were building bomb shelters in their backyards for the fear that Armageddon could come at any moment. So the "fudging" of a mere fishing record probably was not considered something worth losing sleep over.

Amazingly, had it not been for several unconnected twists of fate occurring, most of these falsified musky catches probably never would have been discovered. The ball started rolling when, in 1991, a tongue-in-cheek article printed in a Midwestern newspaper insinuated that Louie Spray's 69-pound 11-ounce record musky may have been a bogus catch. A friend of mine brought this to my attention and, because I was privy to enough information supporting Spray's catch, I decided that it was time the Spray fish be thoroughly researched and, once and for all, either expose any shenanigans that may have occurred and disqualify the fish or kill these irresponsible rumors with the hard facts and support Spray's catch.

As it turned out, Spray's fish passed scrutiny and the publication of my findings on his fish led one reader to send me materials which strongly indicted that the fish which was believed to be the largest musky catch of all time — Art Lawton's 69-pound 15-ounce musky — may have been falsified.

And, after being drawn into an investigation on this fish without ever planning on getting into it — and spending seven months and $2,000 in the process — I discovered musky fishing's crime of the century — that Lawton's fish had indeed been greatly exaggerated in size. On August 6, 1992, Lawton's fish was officially disqualified, jointly, by both the National Fresh Water Fishing Hall of Fame and the International Game Fish Association.

This bombshell revelation turned out to be only the tip of the iceberg and it wasn't long before numerous other record class muskies would fall and a large part of the history of our sport would be revised forever.

The first player in this saga was Percy Haver, a Lake St. Clair, Michigan, musky fisherman who claimed catching four muskies over 56 pound from 1938 through 1940. With two of these fish being listed as official world records (claimed to weigh 58 pounds 14 ounces and 62 1/2 pounds), such a feat would rank Haver as one of the greatest musky men of all time. But this all turned out to be just an illusion. For, in 1995, I discovered all four of Haver's fish to be greatly exaggerated in size and they have since been officially disqualified from the national listing of the National Fresh Water Fishing Hall of Fame and the state record listing of Michigan's Department of Natural Resources.

Upon knowing that Haver stood no more than 69 inches tall and was of slight build, a photo of him holding up his first reported large musky catch (a fish he claimed to be 60 1/2 inches long and 56 pounds 7 ounces) clearly shows the fish to be much shorter than Haver — by at least 18 inches — and serves to immediately invalidate his claim. The very next year, in 1939, Haver caught a musky which was listed as a world record, a fish he claimed to weigh 58 pounds 14 ounces. But after a photo of the mount of this fish revealed it to be no more than 54 inches in length, it became clear that the weight of this fish had been padded as well. Actually, even before the official stamp of approval could be put onto Haver's fish as a world record, Louie Spray ended up catching a larger musky (which proves to be both well documented and legitimate) of 59 1/2 pounds that was accepted as a world record at the time.

And during the following year, in 1940, Haver reported catching two more huge muskies — one of which was reported to be his largest personal musky catch and also held the world record title for a time. This musky, a fish claimed to have been 62 1/2 pounds and 59 inches long, has recently proven to have been a blatant falsification, to the tune of at least 20 to 25 pounds! Amazingly, the key evidence which proves this was always out in the open, but perhaps was too obvious for anyone to ever notice.

For it was in the first edition of this very book, on page 193, that the key to unlocking this mystery was hidden. On that page is a photograph of Haver's niece, standing next to the mount of the musky that Haver identified as being his 62 1/2-pound, 59-inch long world record. On the extreme left hand end of that photo, standing right up alongside the board which the fish is mounted on, is a wooden builder's ruler — with the increments faintly readable!

Upon a careful examination of the photo, it is unmistakable that the mount of Haver's supposed 59-incher was only 53 1/2 inches long (plus or minus one inch). With a length falsification like that, the weight of the fish would also have to correspondingly drop. In fact, because the photos of Haver holding this musky when it was still fresh reveal the fish to have had a rather thin to average build, this musky would have been lucky to make even the 40-pound mark.

For anyone who may be wondering whether it is necessary to be this picky about these musky records, remember that there's no point in keeping records if they're inaccurate. Also, for every falsified musky claim there is a victim — someone whose honest huge musky catch was overshadowed by an exaggerated claim. And in the case of Haver's

The musky next to Haver (top photo) supposedly weighed 56 pounds. At right, this musky was claimed to weigh 58-14 and was accepted as the 1939 world record.

This three-photo sequence shows Haver landing and holding his supposed 62 1/2-pounder. The fish was reported to be nearly five feet long, an obvious exaggeration as Haver was only 5-9. And, can anyone hold a 62 1/2-pounder at arm's length?

This is the "mount" photo. Note the tape measure on the left side of the board.

bogus 62 1/2-pounder, Louie Spray happened to be the victim. For, two months after Haver reported making his catch, Spray registered a catch which tipped the official beam at 61 pounds 13 ounces. But, because it was thought to be 11 ounces smaller, it was never listed as an official world record — not until some 55 years later and Haver's fish finally was disqualified.

The next world record musky to be caught — which later proved to be an exaggerated claim — was a thin 58-inch musky reportedly caught by Alois Hanser on the opening day of the 1947 fishing season, a fish which supposedly weighed a hefty 64 1/2 pounds. While the weight of this fish has been doubted by many a musky man from day one, because this musky only held the title for two years this fish was just kind of quietly ignored by the musky fishing populace. But, when it came time to clean up the record listing during recent years, it was this musky's own documented dimensions which ultimately did the fish in. No thinly built 58-incher with a 24-inch girth could have possibly weighed even 50 pounds — let alone 64 1/2 pounds.

Hanser's reported 64-4 (left) doesn't begin to compare with Myrl McFaul's 53-pound 12-ounce musky, the largest ever from Wisconsin's famed Vilas County.

Enter the Lawtons and the Hartmans: two rival musky fishing couples from New York state's great St. Lawrence River who, during the late 1950s and early 1960s, claimed catching just about more huge musky catches than all of the other musky fishermen of the world combined! With the Lawtons claiming 12 kills in excess of 50 pounds (half of which were reported to be over 60 pounds) and the Hartmans claiming that they bagged 13 themselves over 50 pounds (with six of theirs also breaking the 60-pound mark) these musky anglers seemed to clearly be in a league of their own. But, as someone once said, "the bigger the lie, the more people who will believe it," and the 25 50-pound-plus muskies which these two couples reported catching actually ended up representing the biggest lie in our sport's history.

Perhaps it was because of the unique situation which existed while the St. Lawrence Seaway was being constructed that made this impossible string of super catches seem believable. With all of the dredging and dynamiting of the river which was taking place at that time, it only seemed to make sense that the fish would be herded up in certain stretches of the river and catching them would be like shooting fish in a barrel. Also, because these famous couples were devout motor trollers, many have reasoned that this highly efficient method of straining the water was bound to outproduce any of the casting methods.

As it turned out, not one of the Lawtons' or Hartmans' claimed 50-pound-plus fish can be proven to have existed and, the vast majority of them were actually grossly exaggerated in size. While both couples were competent and dedicated fishermen in their own rights, somewhere along the line they strayed in their fishing and began padding the weights of their musky catches in order to win cash prizes from their regional fishing contest (the Louie A. Wehle Fishing Contest, which awarded both monthly and yearly cash prizes) and *Field & Stream's* national fishing contest, which also awarded cash prizes after the close of each season.

The Lawtons and Hartmans soon found themselves competing against each other and began trying to out-lie each other in the contests. Every time one couple would up the ante a bit further, the other couple would push the envelope even more. They soon both were attaching ridiculous weights and lengths to their fish, turning big musky catches into reportedly huge ones. In the long run, both couples just ended up exposing themselves and this is what eventually brought them all down. Many of their fish were exaggerated as much as 10 inches in length and 15 to 20 pounds in weight. Had they only fudged the sizes of their muskies just a little bit they never would have been found out.

Let's look at Art and Ruth Lawton's two largest reported musky catches — one fish claimed to be the largest musky catch of all time, a fish which held the world record title for some 35 years, and another musky which would have ranked as the fourth largest musky ever caught, as well as the largest ever caught by a woman.

On September 22, 1957, Art Lawton reported catching a musky which was believed to weigh 69 pounds 15 ounces and stretch five feet and four and a half inches in length. After this fish had been registered with *Field & Stream*, the magazine received tips that Lawtons' fish may have been netted by Indians from the St. Regis Reservation.

  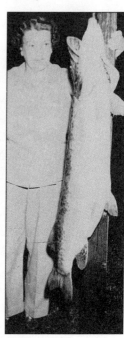

At left, the supposedly "one and only poor photo" that Lawton took of his world record musky. Actually, it may have been the only one taken on September 23, 1957, but one of 29 taken of the same fish. In the middle photo, this is the same fish in the "post photo" referred to by Dettloff. At right, Ruth Lawton claimed this musky weighed 68-5 and measured 61 1/2 inches. Ruth's height was 62 inches.

Field & Stream hired Pinkerton detectives to look into the matter, but were able to learn anything conclusive. While Lawton provided only scant proof backing up his catch, he did satisfy *Field & Stream's* contest criteria and the fish was accepted as the new world record — a title it was to hold for the next 35 years.

Because Lawton allowed his "catch" to be cut up and eaten and not mounted, a segment of the musky fishing world always suspected Lawton's claim to be a bit fishy. But it wasn't until late in 1991, when some very contradictory facts regarding his catch became known to me, that Lawton's "hand" would finally be shown. With my intention being to neither prove nor disprove the Lawton fish, my only goal was to learn all the facts pertinent to his catch with a commitment to the learn the truth.

In summary, Lawton's musky was disqualified because it had been discovered that he submitted false evidence to *Field & Stream* (the record keeping body at the time) supporting his world record claim. It was discovered that the photo he submitted to *Field & Steam* of his 69-pound 15-ounce fish was actually the photo of a much smaller musky of 49 1/2 pounds and 55 inches in length, and, the weigh-in affidavit which Lawton had submitted was false evidence, in that the principle weight witness had recanted his original story.

Among the preponderance of evidence proving the fish to have been falsified, the key piece to the whole affair rested upon newly discovered photos of the same musky, one which showed the fish hanging vertically from a post being supported by Lawton himself. This photo clearly revealed the true size (length) of this fish when compared to the height of Lawton, who was known to be 68 inches tall. The musky turned out to be a foot shorter than Lawton's own height and not the mere 3 1/2 inches shorter as claimed.

After I prepared a 40-page report of my findings and submitted a copy to both the NFWFHF and the IGFA, and both record-keeping bodies reviewed the evidence for several months, the fish was disqualified and the 69-pound 11-ounce musky caught by Louie Spray out of Wisconsin's Chippewa Flowage in 1949 was reinstated as the world record musky. This musky, which was well-documented, stands today as the mark to beat.

Some individuals may wonder if the NFWFHF (a Wisconsin-based record-keeping agency) could have voted to disqualify the Lawton musky in an effort to "bring the record back home." To anyone knowing the facts, this can be easily dispelled. The decision to disqualify the Lawton fish was not made by a handful of Hayward people, but rather by a world board of approximately 40 Advisory Governors made up of people from all over the United States, Canada and abroad.

Another significant catch was reportedly made by Ruth Lawton in 1961 when she claimed catching a 68-pound 5-ounce, 61 1/2-inch long musky. Surely a huge looking musky if one looks at a photo of this fish, but upon closer examination this musky proves to fall far

Art Lawton's Photo Album

Previously you saw the photo that Art Lawton submitted to Field & Stream and a different photo of the same musky. Following are 22 of the additional 27 pictures of Lawton, Lawton and wife, and Lawton's brother Gordon with the same, supposed, world record.

short of its reported size. In fact, of all the Lawton's exaggerated fishing claims, this is clearly the more blatant and gives one a vivid idea of the true scope of their exaggerations.

It is known that Ruth stood only 5 feet 2 inches tall (62 inches) virtually the same exact height as her musky's length. But the photo of this fish reveals it to be far shorter than Ruth's own height — by at least 10 inches and maybe 12 inches! This is hard evidence that this fish could not possibly have been any more than 52 inches in length and run in the mid 40-pound range at most.

As it turns out, the top four largest muskies entered into *Field & Stream's* national contest for that year, 1961, were all fish claimed to be caught by the Lawtons and Hartmans — four fish which were exaggerated. And the poor man who ranked fifth that year, Don Mense, who caught a beautiful 48 1/2-pound musky out of Hayward, Wisconsin's, Round Lake, actually had the world's largest known musky catch for that year but was victimized by deceit.

Len and Betty Hartman probably profited more from their false musky claims than any of their contemporaries. Truly "fishing fools" for most of their lives, the Hartmans found a way to profit from the sport, milking their notoriety for all it was worth. Their repeated wins

Ruth Lawton's musky (left) also falls short of its reported length. Compare the claimed 63-inch length of the fish with Ruth's known height of 62 inches. It was claimed to weigh 60 1/2 pounds. When Larry Ramsell visited with the Lawtons, he measured the mount of this musky at 57 inches. At top, Don Mense's 48 1/2-pounder should have won the Field & Stream contest in 1961.

in the cash-paying fishing contests turned them into nationally known legends, leading to the creation of a devoted guide following which was paying them a combined guiding fee of up to $200 a day. And this was 35 years ago!

Tackle companies endorsed the Hartmans, Len had several of his own lines of lures on the market, and until only recently he was regularly awarded gratis fishing trips all over the musky range. Len's biggest musky claim was 67 pounds 15 ounces and Betty's was 64 1/2 pounds — both fish were later proved to fall far short of their reported sizes. While a careful scrutiny of the Hartmans' reported huge musky catches reveal they all had been exaggerated in size, it also came out that they never caught some of these muskies.

One case in point was a supposed 65-pound musky that Len reported catching in November of 1962. As it turned out, local newspapers some four months earlier ran a photo of a suspiciously similar looking musky which was documented as being 46 1/2 pounds and caught by a local, Edward "Cubby" Kiah. Upon enlargement the photos of both muskies and careful scrutiny, the intricate pattern of complex markings on the sides of both fish proved to be identical in every way.

Because Len was still around to be questioned at this time, Larry Ramsell and I sent Len a copy of his "rap sheet" and gave him a chance to come clean and give us his motivations behind why (and how) he falsified his musky claims. Knowing that he was finally found out, Len

Len Hartman's bogus 67-15 ... actually under 50 pounds. Betty Hartman's claimed 64-4, at somewhat less than her diminutive height, just doesn't add up.

saw this as a good opportunity to finally remove the heavy burden of deceit from his shoulders and promptly contacted Ramsell and agreed to confess on videotape. Thanks to Len's candor, he made great strides to set the record straight, revealing much more about this chapter of musky history than we ever would have learned had it not been for his gutsy admissions.

Candidly admitting, "We always 'padded' them before we took them in for weighing," Len stated that they put water and sand in the bellies of their biggest muskies before they put them on the scales for the witnesses to see. While the Hartmans undoubtedly caught hundreds of muskies and a number of trophy catches in their day, in reality, what they caught was nothing more than what anyone else on the river

Len Hartman (left) holding a musky he claimed catching that supposedly weighed 65 pounds. Hartman later confessed that he added nearly 20 pounds of weight to the fish and that he never caught it. It was caught earlier that year by Cubby Kiah (right), and it weighed 46 pounds.

was catching. Len also stated that he would occasionally pick up walleyes and muskies that were killed during the blasting that took place while the seaway was being built and admitted dealing with the local Indians who were netting the river. Stating that he bought fish from the same Indians who were selling fish to Art Lawton, Len reasoned, "So I figured ... well, if he could do it, so can I."

Commenting that "everybody" was in the fish business up in his area at the time, Len said, "Where you could turn fish into money, you would do it." He sold some of the fish to a buyer from New York City who in turn was supplying the restaurants, and the bigger fish

Len would just add weight to and enter into the fishing contests. Admitting that he didn't want to work a regular job because he liked to fish too much, Len found a way to earn money by living off the land. He reflected, "I feel sorry that I done it, but the point is: the money was there."

So who are the real heroes of the St. Lawrence, the true musky greats of this magnificent stretch of musky water? They are the honest and dedicated musky men whose great angling feats have been overshadowed by yesterday's fakery. They are the James Manning and G. M. Skinners of the past century; Charles Seymour and C. A. Duke, in the early 1900s; Dr. Howeth Pabst, Clay Ferguson, Jim Evans and Brendan Reed of the middle 1900s, and James Brabant, Allen Beans, Ruses Finehout, Clay Ferguson Jr., Norm Seymour, Maurice Lamframboise, Mike Lazarus, Dave Johnson, Dick Garlock and others I am not aware of, of present day. These are the victims of all the fudging of the past and the unsung heroes of the nation's first musky fishing Mecca.

Three huge St. Lawrence muskies weighing a total of 125 pounds, above. Pictured are guide Russ Finehout (40-pounder, at left), Jack Vanio (40-pounder, center) and guide Clay Ferguson Jr. (45-pounder). At right, guide Jim Brabant (center) holds a 39-pounder caught by Philip Dimmick (left) and accompanied by Gerald Dimmick.

So, here we are back on track. World record muskies are out there — even today — but they have always been much rarer than we were first led to believe. The fact that, in all the waters, in all the world, in all the years since records began to be kept, only seven bona fide 60-pound-plus muskies and 93 verified fish in excess of 50 pounds have been known to be caught, tells just how fortunate one really is to connect with one of these phantoms of the deep.

Back to the "Compender," Larry Ramsell:

I would like to add a small bit to the above by John. A Lawton family member, not wishing to believe that his uncle Art could have done what has been attributed to him, has been, since John's original exposé, trying to gather proof that the Lawton 69-pound 15-ounce musky existed. In the years since the Lawton disqualification, he has only been able to come up with a few people who claimed to have seen this fish and even some who say they saw it weighed on a farmer's scale at 70 pounds. One other bit of evidence he claims to have found is actually the picture Lawton submitted to *Field & Stream*. His claim is that the fish in this photo is not the same fish in 28 other pictures. While he is entitled to his opinion, I'm afraid that he is wrong, in fact, an apparent piece of paper stuck to the dorsal fin in the *F&S* picture is also on some the others. That Lawton is wearing a different belt in the *F&S* photo (which I pointed out to him several years ago) can easily be explained, as well as the possibility of his "secret" witnesses who saw the fish weighed at 70 pounds. Quite simply, Lawton removed the subject fish (a 49 1/2-pounder caught the week before his record claim) from the locker plant where he worked, added, I believe, a 20-pound sash weight or some similar weight (I believe a sash weight, as several of the newly uncovered photos of Lawton's big muskies appear to have something very heavy protruding at the center of the fish's stomach, about where the top end of a sash weight would be with the end of it resting at the bottom of the fish's stomach near the tail with the fish hanging), and then presented it to his witnesses for weighing and other friends that day.

Since it is apparent after a phone conservation with him that the Lawton relative does not wish to share any of his supposed new evidence to support Lawton's claim (he considers me the enemy, as after,

and only after, I reviewed Dettloff's overwhelming evidence of fraud, I agreed that the Lawton fish was bogus), I have no choice but to continue to support the disqualification of the Lawton musky. One additional thing I would like to pass along is something I found in Lawton's scrapbook that I found very curious. It was a clipping from an outdoor magazine with the following:

Lawton holds his frozen "65-13" from 1959 (left). This photo was submitted to Field & Stream. In the later photo of the 65-13 (right), the fish is starting to thaw and the top end of a weight in the fish's stomach starts to become visible as the stomach distends.

Estimating Weight of Fish

Question: I do a great deal of surf fishing on Assateague Island and while I fish mainly for channel bass during the fall months, I hook into many big sharks. Some will strip my reel of all the line. The smaller ones, which I can usually land, are approximately five to six feet in length. How can I estimate the weight of these fish?—W.M., Wilmington, Delaware.

Answer: The old formula for estimating the weight of any cylindrical-shaped body is fairly accurate for determining the weight of any fish, except species of the flatfish variety. The formula is to square the girth, multiply by the length, and divide by 800. This will give a very close estimate of the weight. It is suggested that these measurements be taken soon after the fish is removed from the water. There is usually a considerable girth shrinkage, but there is actually very little shortening of the length since the bone shrinking is little or none."

Could this be, with the additional knowledge of the dimensions of Sprays 69-pound 11-ounce musky, how Lawton was able to come up with believable measurements for his bogus record musky?

As John and I have both said, should anyone produce incontrovertible evidence that the Lawton 69-pound 15-ounce musky did in fact exist and was legally caught, we would be happy to reverse the current decision to disqualify and would encourage the same of the current record keeping bodies.

Chapter 4:
A Review of
Muskellunge
World Records

Since there was no official record keeping body prior to the *Field & Stream* magazine contest, I have listed the muskies from Chapter 2 that were published in literature in this chronological listing of muskellunge world records. There were no photographs available of the 49 1/2-pound fish from 1883 and the 55-pounder from 1887, so you will find listed after them a smaller 44-pound 2-ounce fish from 1902 that had photographic proof and documentation of its existence and a rightful world record listing. The 1911, 1916 and 1919 records came from the *F&S* contest. The 1917 listing is based on the existence of the actual mount of the fish and the precise weight of the fish is on the attached plaque. That its weight is expressed to ounces indicates that an accurate type of scale was used but there is no weight verification. The 1923 listing is again only from literature and no picture was available. The 1924 Walker fish is now taking its rightful place in the world record listing. It is verified; a good photo exists and it is still the current Pennsylvania state musky record. The two 1929 *F&S* world records are listed even though they are superseded by the Walker fish. They were considered, for nearly 60 years, as having been world records for a short time.

If you were a reader of any of my earlier works on record muskie you will find several former *Field & Stream* world records missing namely the Haver, Hanser and Lawton fish. These fish, along with several line class world records caught by the Hartmans as well as a of the other Lawton and Hartman 50- and 60-pounders, have bee disqualified due to falsification.

Also, you will find a complete treatise in this chapter of the Malo 70-pound musky, which I have added to my world record list. I hope you will agree after reading that there is no justification for leaving it off.

Larry Ramsell's Chronological Listing of World Records

Date	Angler	Location	Weight	Length	Girth	Lure
8/1883	Annie Lee	St. Lawrence R., NY	36-2	54	na	#3 Gold Spoon (spinner)

From history's archives. Picture exists. No weight verification exists. Listed for information only. See story in Chapter 2.

8/1883	H.K. Greene	Indian River, NY	49-8	54	28	Chapman's #3

From history's archives. No weight verification exists. Listed for information only. See story in Chapter 2.

1887	E.B. Saunders	Planting Ground, WI	55-0	59	28	na

Very limited information available. No weight verification exists. Listed for information only.

1902	A.J. Van Sise	Lake LeBouf, PA	44-2	na	na	na

From history's archives. Picture exists. Documentation exists. See story in Chapter 2.

9/3/11	Dr. F. Whiting	St. Lawrence River	48-0	59	25	#9 Corbett Spoon (spinner)

Field & Stream contest winner.

9/13/16	F.J.Swint	Chief Lake, WI	51-0	55	24	#8 Skinner Spoon (spinner) & frog

Field & Stream contest winner.

1917	William Fulton	French River, ON	57-10	59	30	na

From history's archives. Mount exists. No weight verification exists Listed for information only. See story in Chapter 2.

7/16/19	John Knobla	Lac Vieux Desert, WI	51-3	54	25 1/4	na

Field & Stream contest winner. Listed originally as a world record musky. It is now the hybrid musky world record.

1923	John J. Hoogan	Shishebogama, WI	52-0	na	na	na

From history's archives. No weight verification exists. Listed for information only.

9/30/24	Lewis Walker Jr.	Conneaut Lake, PA	54-3	57	na	8" red chub

Verified but never before listed because it was not entered in the Field & Stream contest. See story in Chapter 2 and the picture and additional story about the catch in this chapter.

7/11/29	E.A. Oberland	Pokegama Lake, WI	52-12	52	29	Pflueger spoon (spinner)

Superseded by the Walker fish but listed here because of its recognition, for nearly 66 years, as having been a world record for a short time. Field & Stream contest winner.

A Review of Muskellunge World Records

Date	Angler	Location	Weight	Length	Girth	Lure
8/25/29	Gordon Curtis	Lake of the Woods, ON	53-12	57	25 1/4	#7 Skinner Spoon (spinner)

Superseded by the Walker fish but listed here because of its recognition, for nearly 66 years, as having been a world record for a short time. Field & Stream contest winner.

7/24/31	J.W. Collins	Lake of the Woods, ON	56-7	55	29 5/8	Pflueger Muskill

Field & Stream contest winner.

9/24/32	George Neimuth	Lake of the Woods, ON	58-4	59	34 1/2	Creek Chub Pikie

Field & Stream contest winner.

7/27/39	Louie Spray	Grindstone Lake, WI	59-8	58 1/4	32 1/2	Marathon Musky Houn

Field & Stream contest winner. Verified beyond any shadow of a doubt.

10/3/39	John J. Coleman	Eagle Lake, ON	60-8	58 1/2	31 1/2	Creek Chub Pikie

Field & Stream contest winner. Verified beyond any shadow of a doubt.

8/19/40	Louie Spray	Lac Courte Oreilles, WI	61-13	59 1/4	32 1/2	True Temper Bass Pop

Field & Stream contest winner. Verified beyond any shadow of a doubt.

7/24/49	Cal Johnson	Lac Courte Oreilles, WI	67-8	60 1/4	33 1/2	South Bend Pike-O-Reno

Field & Stream contest winner. Verified beyond any shadow of a doubt.

10/20/49	Louie Spray	Chippewa Flow., WI	69-11	62 1/2	31 1/4	Spray Sucker Harness/sucker

Field & Stream contest winner. Verified beyond any shadow of a doubt.

6/6/54	Robert Malo	Middle Eau Claire Lake, WI	70-0	55	32	Live sucker

Verified in the author's mind, but not presently accepted by the National Fresh Water Fishing Hall of Fame. See story later in this chapter.

As you will have noted in the above, the stories of the two 1883 fish, the 1902 fish and the 1917 fish can be found in Chapter 2 and will not be repeated here. There are no stories available for the 1887 fish, nor, ironically, the 1919 Knobla fish, although it was referenced in other writings of the day. We will now take the balance of these record breakers and relate known information about them and the anglers' stories of the catch.

1911 ... Naturally, since 1911 was the first year that records were kept and established, the largest musky entered in the contest was destined to be a world record fish, regardless of its size. When the year ended and the contest came to a close, Dr. Frederick L. Whiting emerged from the files as the winner and the recognized world record holder with a 48-pound musky from the St. Lawrence River in New York (second place that year was a 42-pounder from Chautauqua Lake, New York, by Allen A. Thayer). Dr. Whiting's fish was not a case of blind luck as he had caught several large muskies in the past, and again proved his capabilities in 1912 by taking 4th place in the same national contest with a 34-8 from the St. Lawrence River near Lancaster, Ontario.

Annie Lee's 36-pound 2-ouncer starts the chronological world record list.

Following is Dr. Whiting's account of the capture of his record fish:

It has latterly been the practice, therefore, of those of us who are out for the "big fellows" to tow our skiffs down the river by motor boats for a distance of about three miles and then to cast off and begin our day's sport.

A.J. VanSise took this 44-pound 2-ounce dandy from Lake LeBoeuf, PA, in 1902.

Undoubtedly many fine fish dwell in the weed beds thus neglected and probably there are some old granddaddies among them which would well repay a fisherman for any labor expended in their capture, but the average size of the fish below Butternut Island will, I believe, exceed the dimensions of those taken above it.

Within twenty minutes after leaving Stanley Island, Mr. Corbett and I were in our low-backed arm chairs from which the legs had been sawed off, permitting them to sit firmly upon the cross seats of the boat. Louis took the oars and began the gentle dipping stroke, which permits a trolling spoon at the end of eighty feet of line to play at about four feet below the surface of the water. I was using a split bamboo rod, while Mr. Corbett clung to his old and battle-scarred Bristol steel, to the whip like elasticity and lightning-quick recovery of which his unrivaled string of muscallonge killed within the last five years bears eloquent tribute. The lure we were both using was a Corbett spoon, the invention of my companion in the boat, and the most killing bait for big 'lunge of which I have any knowledge. I have tried many varieties, patterns and sizes of spoons: I have trailed them with phantom minnows, and with gangs baited with chub, perch, and bass, with varying degrees of success, and after a fair and impartial trial I cannot too strongly endorse the Corbett spoon as the best tackle to be procured and the ideal lure for large 'lunge.

Having paid out our lines until the little red mark on mine indicated eighty feet, and that of my friend some fifteen feet less, we gazed at one another for a moment in an amiable but unspoken challenge, settled ourselves a little more deeply into the chairs, placed the right thumb firmly upon the reel spool, and were ready for business.

As we paddled slowly along, with Louis casting his small black eyes furtively first upon one and then upon the other side of his boat, and peering down into the depths of the clear stream, in order that he might

Musky fishing on the St. Lawrence River, Thousand Islands, New York, 1890.

more surely hold his course at the correct distance from the edge of the weed beds, my companion, who possesses a positive genius for arousing these phlegmatic guides from their customary lethargy, said: "Well, Louis, what about it? Do you think we will get 'em to-day?" Louis crouched still lower over his oars, cocked his head slowly and cautiously to one side, and glancing up from beneath the brim of his weather-beaten hat, and assuming a look of the most guileful cunning, delivered himself of the longest speech on record. "Yes siree! Dat's de right — get 'em sure! Dis day my eye he wink dat's mean de good de luck! Can't tell, might be get de big de 'lunge!"

Louis' enthusiasm became contagious, and almost unconsciously we took a firmer grasp upon our rods, and tightened the pressure upon the reel spools, with a fisherman's superstitious hope that so unusual and oracular an utterance might indeed have been inspired. Scoff not, ye doubting Thomases, lest your derision recoil upon your own heads, for never was a prophecy more speedily and literally fulfilled.

We had crept along the upper edge of the weed beds below Butternut and were approaching a stake known as Martin's buoy — so called because an Indian, Dave Martin by name, had stuck a pole in the mud at that point and decorated its top with an empty tomato can — when suddenly I had a strike, the force of which for a moment suggested that I had hooked fast to a trolley car going at a thirty-mile clip in the opposite direction. My answering strike was instantaneous and vicious, and was accompanied by as piercing a whir, as the line was stripped from the firmly held reel spool, as ever gladdened the heart and thrilled the pulse of a sportsman. I took a firmer grip upon the rod, raised its tip at a sharper angle, drew my feet firmly beneath me, and the fight was on. Three titanic, sagging heaves or rushes there were, following one another in lightning quick succession, each ripping off a few yards of my reluctant line and each compelling my good rod to bow its admiring acknowledgments until, bent in a quivering arch, its tip disappeared beneath the water. Three contemptuous messages of defiance from the fiercest and most courageous fish that swims the water were thus flashed up the line, before the gallant foe, his fury at being restrained fully aroused, consented to show himself. But having thus identified himself — for the short sagging rushes at the beginning of the fight, instantly announce to a 'lunge fisherman the character and size of the game he has encountered — he disdained to fight longer under cover, and came to the surface with a mad, swirling rush that carried his great body entirely out of the water. Such a sight as this magnificent fish presented at the moment when, trying to throw the hook, he projected himself into the air, I cannot describe, but shall never forget.

In the excitement of the moment, he looked as big as a motor boat, and as he remained poised for an instant in the air, his full length clear of the water, with his great jaws yawning wide, his blood red gills distended. and his fierce eyes rolling wildly, he certainly appeared the incarnation of Satan escaped from the infernal regions. Louis gazed spellbound in open-mouthed admiration, and then, as the leviathan plunged back into his native element with a tremendous splash, gave vent to the exclamation, "By gar, dat's de big feller!" He then seized his oars and began turning his boat in a wide circle around the fish as a center. Mr. Corbett, while this preliminary skirmish was in process of completion, had rapidly reeled in his tackle in order that I might have a free field in which to operate during the ensuing encounter, and having placed his rod in the boat, he turned to me and remarked casually as he settled back to enjoy the scrap, "You seem to have connected with a small pike, Doctor!" I was too busily engaged with affairs of moment just then to frame an appropriate response to this bit of sarcasm on the part of my host, but I did manage to spare enough breath to reply, "If that's a pike, he's a corker," and thereafter I had sufficient entertainment to occupy my attention with the business on hand.

When the 'lunge first disappeared in that mad dive of his, he went straight to the bottom, and began to surge or heave on my line with such weight and force as to leave me no choice but to play it slowly out in order to relieve the great strain on the rod. This maneuver I was obliged to repeat frequently during the next few minutes, in order to save my tackle, and the snitch of the reel click, as yard after yard was reluctantly yielded, became an anxious and worrisome sound, for, as all fishermen know, every yard of line that a game fish, especially a big one, gets beyond forty, increases the hazard and danger of losing him by a distressing percentage, and increases the likelihood of his pulling off some successful stunt to the angler's undoing.

Louis was working valiantly at the oars in an ever-widening circle, and exhorting me to hold him, for to Louis every snitch of the reel as the drag of the 'lunge pulled the line from beneath my thumb, was like a stab in the vitals. He thought I was tempting fate, and ejaculated between strokes — "You loose — you loose sure!" — but I knew how much the rod would stand, and I did not dare hold any harder. I also knew that no fish could endure such a strain for any length of time, and expected every moment to see the rod straighten as the 'lunge began to tire. But he was an 18 karat fighter and a foxy fellow to boot, and his next little piece of strategy nearly caused me heart failure, for I thought I had seen the last of him.

Just before he broke for the second time, I was still holding firmly against his brutal and obstinate drag, when suddenly the rod tip leaped upward, the strain upon my wrist was relaxed like an automatic cut-off from an electric switch, and my line hung slack and dangling in the water. The consternation depicted upon Louis' countenance at this junction would have been a most comical sight to a disinterested spectator — but there was no such person in the gallery — his oar blades hung motionless in the water, his jaw dropped, and a sigh as long as your arm escaped him, together with a despairing cry of "By Gar, he gone!"

My fellow fisherman said nothing, for the same idea had occurred to each of us simultaneously, and I reeled in with all possible speed, in the hope that the 'lunge had suddenly taken it into his head to stop fighting the rod, and to rush the boat instead. As good fortune would have it, my idea was correct, and immediately I had recovered the slack line and raised my rod tip with a snap, I received a jerking tug that was joyfully reassuring. "Pull, Louis," I yelled, "he's on!" The oars lashed furiously into the water in a frantic effort to regain our lost headway, and so fierce was the stress of Louis' excitement and so sudden his physical exertion, that at that precise moment he swallowed a large and juicy quid of tobacco which he had previously been holding between his clenched teeth.

The fight was now at shorter range, and I became conscious of a growing feeling of mastery of the situation. My wily foe had played two of his high trumps, but the control was still in my hand, so I proceeded to put on the screws. As I increased the strain upon the rod, he refused to yield an inch, and there was telegraphed up the tense line to my tiring wrist a feeling of grinding and grating caused by the crunching force of his iron jaws and hound-like teeth upon the spoon and gang of hooks which he was trying to crush. The sensation thus conveyed to the fisherman is like nothing in the world so much as the feeling of broken bones grating upon one another, and is characterized by the doctors as "bony crepitus." Of all the sensations which a captive fish at the end of the line affords to the angler, there is none, I believe, that imparts such a sense of keen gratification and delight as this rasping, grating vibration, for it signifies that you have met a foeman worthy of your steel, an antagonist who still has enough fight in him to grind his teeth with fierce determination, and to whom the prick of the hook, so far from being an inducement to quit, is rather a spur to more furious resistance.

But while the courage of the muscallounge is boundless, and although he possesses an unconquerable spirit, there is still a limit beyond which the power of flesh and blood may not endure. The lessening strain on rod and line told only too plainly that the terrific struggle which the fish had so gallantly sustained was telling on him and was rapidly reducing his strength. Therefore, I determined not to allow him any time for a breathing spell, appreciating full well that such a rest would surely contribute to his capacity for making mischief. Up to the present moment the angler had been entirely on the defensive, but now he determined that the psychological moment had arrived to push home the attack.

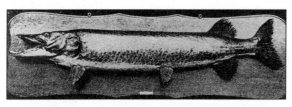

"Grandfather 'lunge" by Dr. Whiting at Stanley Island, 1911.

I raised my tip sharply, and obedient to the steady upward pull of the rod, the fish again shot to the surface, coming up straight out of the water for about half his length he supported himself momentarily in this position, and shook his head until the spoon protruding from his yawning jaws rattled like a dinner bell, thus serving notice upon us that, although growing tired, he was by no means "all in." A sharp pull at the oars by the vigilant Louis, and a quick backward snap of the rod, prevented the fish from gaining any slack line during this maneuver, and as he plunged again into the depths, I realized with a grim sense of satisfaction that his speed was much reduced, that he seemed to swim down with an effort, and took but little line from us, whereas, on his first plunge, he had gone down with the speed of an express train and to the high pitched accompaniment of a singing reel.

Four successive times, under the steady strain of the relentless rod, he came to the surface, still battling as fiercely as his rapidly waning strength permitted, until at length, completely exhausted and unable to overcome the spring of the rod, he turned upon his side, his great gill covers spread wide, his chest heaving deeply, and his fierce eyes proclaiming his unspeakable and impotent rage.

As he lay thus, feebly waving his fins, but a few feet from the boat, he was a picture to arouse the unqualified admiration of a sportsman. Never have I seen so grand a fish, and I gazed at him almost loath to administer the coup de grace. Not so Louis, who was fairly exhaling the spirit of primeval savagery, to whom stern experience had taught the truth of the oft-told adage, "there's many a slip' twixt the cup and the lip."

"Shoot him! Shoot him!" he shouted, reaching forward for his gaff. Mr. Corbett pushed up the safety clip of our little .22 rifle, and said quietly: "Bring him around a little to the side, Doctor, and I'll shoot him."

But the momentary rest which our prospective victim had enjoyed while enduring our admiring scrutiny, had somewhat restored his strength and afforded him an opportunity for one last display of his indomitable courage. With a swish of his tail and a boring, wriggling motion, he lunged downward under the stern of the boat, in a last despairing effort to foul or break the tackle. But, though the spirit was willing, the flesh was weak, and exhausted nature was unequal to the task. A good sharp pull on the right oar, and a quick jerk of the rod to the left, brought him promptly to the surface again, where a shot through the spine mercifully dispatched him.

As we brought him unresisting alongside the boat, preparatory to taking him aboard, Louis, still greatly excited, called out, "Take de gaff! Take de gaff I 'fraid you lose!" — at the same time pushing that instrument toward my companion. But the boss 'lunge fisherman disdaining this cautious injunction, reached out his hand and quickly eye-holed him into the boat, notwithstanding his great size and weight. Louis, now wreathed in smiles, promptly clutched the fallen monarch and thrusting him forcibly under a seat amidships, covered him with a rug upon the sides of which he firmly planted his feet, for such an unbounded respect has he for the ability of a muscallonge to get away, that he never feels quite at ease regarding his quarry until he sees him hanging safely on a hook in the icebox at Stanley Island.

It was a gallant struggle, and an experience in which one lives a year's duration in the short space of half an hour. It was also a fair fight, in which the angler matched his skill against the fish's strength and courage, and the exultant thrill which the fisherman experiences in such a victory, serves to mitigate the mortification and diminish the sting of many a previous defeat.

As Butternut Island was near at hand, we decided to go ashore in order to cool off a bit and to scrutinize our capture more carefully and leisurely. When stretched upon the grass, he measured fifty-nine inches in length, and about twenty-five inches in girth. his weight upon a standard scale when we returned to Stanley Island was an even forty eight pounds.

This fish had been hooked at the base of the tongue, and was therefore at a great disadvantage in fighting for his life. Had he been hooked in his hard and bony jaw, I believe he would have tested my tackle and skill far more severely, and might even have had the better of the argument.

As I gazed upon the beautiful fish and thought of the magnificent sport his splendid courage had afforded me in our recent encounter, I could but wonder that any person in whose veins circulates good red blood, instead of ice-water, could fail of an enthusiastic appreciation for the matchless fighting spirit of the 'lunge.

As for me, I have long been thoroughly inoculated with the bacillus of muscallongitis, a germ not commonly mentioned in standard works on bacteriology, and lest some inquisitive reader should desire to learn the definition of the term, and should not have access to the latest edition of the medical dictionary, I hereby gladly furnish the desired information:

"Muscallongitis is a progressive malady, characterized by certain bilious and unappreciative observers as a harmless form of mania, for the taxaemia of which there is no known antidote. It terminates only with life, and but one single remedy has ever been found effectual in temporarily arresting its most violent manifestation, and that is for the victim of the disease to take as often as opportunity permits a hair of the dog that bit him."

Muscallonge caught on September 3, 1911, on St. Lawrence River, below Stanley Island.

Weight, 48 pounds; length, 59 inches: girth, about 25 inches.

Tackle used: Split bamboo rod, made by Von Lengerke and Detmold: weight, 12 ounces: length. 7 feet 6 inches.

Line, 300 feet of braided linen. No. 4, Vom Hofe reel.

Large brass swivel and three-foot copper leader. No. 9 Corbett spoon, with feathered gang of three large hooks.

Note that the term "spoon" was actually an inline spinner, what anglers today usually refer to as a bucktail.

Although Dr. Whiting's 48-pounder was not large by the standards we observed in later years, it proved a worthy record as it held the title of world's record for five years until September 13, 1916, when F.J. Swint landed a 51-pound fish from Chief Lake, Wisconsin.

1916 ... A Fremont, Ohio, fishing club had for years been making annual trips to northern Wisconsin lakes in search of the superb game fishing that the area offered, in particular, the muskellunge. The second week of September 1916, found a party of several Fremonters making a journey to Sawyer County, Wisconsin, near Hayward. Among the travelers was Harry Waggoner, a newcomer to the group, and F.J. Swint, a veteran of many such trips. Swint and Waggoner teamed up (Swint had a hunch that the "rookie" would bring him luck) and chose Chief Lake to start their "hunt" for the elusive musky.

Chief Lake was one of the 10 original lakes that are now part of the vast Chippewa Flowage. The "Big Chip" was created when the Northern States Power Company constructed a dam on the Chippewa River just below the confluence of the East and West Forks. Dam construction took three years and was completed in 1923, and the flowage was filled in 1924.

That Great Musky Moment
By F.J. Swint

Great soldiers, statesmen and financiers have spoken about the great moments of their eventful lives. Great sportsmen, football men and diamond

A Review of Muskellunge World Records

heroes have related of how one moment's "punch" that stirred a nation, came about. Now, speaking for myself, I, the champion rod and line fisherman of the great northwest, can, in the following lines, relate the most stirring event of my long career as a fisherman. Wednesday, September 13, 1916, is the day of all days in my memory, for it was on this occasion that I landed with rod and line a "musky" that measured 55 inches in length, 24 inches in girth and weighed exactly 51 pounds.

A fishing club composed of Fremonters has for a number of years been making annual trips to the lakes of northern Wisconsin, in search of the savage fighting musky or any other gamy fish that swims the waters of the clear cool lakes and streams that abound in that section.

The second week of September, 1916, saw the party, myself included, for I have fished most every lake in Sawyer County, Wis. numbered among the party. Harry Waggoner was a man that was making his first trip as an adventurer with rod and reel, and I, being a veteran, sort of took the "rookie" in tow. Having a sort of a hunch that this same Mr. Waggoner would bring me good luck, I decided to take him to Chief Lake, located about twelve and one half miles from Winter. Chas Miles,one of my former guides, who by the way, has advanced a notch in the progress of human events, and is now driving an auto between a trading post and Winter, took myself, my companion and outfit to the scene of our coming great adventure, as they portray in the movies.

It was a perfect fall day. There was a slight tinge of the cold, that was soon to come, while the vegetation along the route was a riot of varied hues. Chief Lake, a glasslike-appearing body of water, two miles in length and a mile in breadth, was the mecca that drew me, like the Turk to his shrine, or the former woodsman to his "call of the wild."

We spent the greater portion of the first day, the 12th, in giving the newcomer a couple of degrees in the "big out of doors lodge." He was an apt candidate. Willie, Belelle, a half-breed Chippewa, was our guide on this occasion. What this swarthy son of the open does not know about boating, fishing, etc., has never been found in Isaac Walton. We spent several hours on the lake, during the first day, with varied success. Mr. Waggoner caught the prize on his initial trip, a 13-pound musky, while I was satisfied with several smaller specimens of the same variety. When we called it a day, the guide rowed us to shore, and in gathering gloaming we made our way to the backwoods shack of a French-Canadian where we took supper and spent the night. After a few hours spent on beds the models of which were brought into the great woods by men of the breed and stamp of Father Marquette, LaSalle and Joliet, we arose at the first flash of dawn and made ready for one big day's drive on the deep, cool retreat of the musky.

The Indian manned the big rowboat and armed with the necessary bait and tackle we shoved off and made for the haunts of the big fish, a location of which I had considerable knowledge, thanks to my previous visits. A backwoods breakfast, composed of bacon, corn bread, baked potatoes and coffee had put us in splendid trim. I placed a 10-inch perch on a No. 8 Skinner trolling spoon, and with this securely tied to a kingfisher line (35-pound test), and with the latter attached to a 4 1/2' Bristol steel musky rod, I was prepared for all emergencies.

We carefully followed the west shore line and journeyed to the south end of the lake. No success. Before we turned about to continue the trolling tactics, I ordered the Indian to catch a few frogs. My bait of perch did not seem to appeal to the appetite of the big fellows in the deep.

The Indian guide followed my instructions and after securing a frog a bit larger than the ordinary, I re-baited the No. 8 spoon. We skirted a weed bed,

F.J. Swint's 51-pounder from Chief Lake, 1916.

located 600 feet from shore and being unsuccessful, we started for a sand bar located directly across the lake. The sinewy arms of the Indian had propelled the boat, perhaps 400 feet from the weed bed, when the curtain went up on the event of my career as a fisherman. Waggoner and myself were talking, I don't remember the subject. It must have been on matters pertaining to the coming world's series or the world's war. We were in deep confab when it happened.

Zing! and the blow had fallen. Zang! Zang! and the battle was on. It was a fight to the death. I had no idea of the size of my strike until he came to the surface a few moments after taking the bait. I had 125 feet of line out when the fish struck, and as he lay on his side panting and swinging, he for all the world looked like a miniature model of a U-boat, Mr. Waggoner and even the stoical Indian, used to musky ways, were immediate victims of "buck fever."

Speaking for myself, dear reader, I must honestly confess that there were single moments in life when I have felt more calm and collected. When the finny monster turned his head toward the boat and showed that big ugly mouth, Waggoner cried: "For the love of Mike! He'll swallow the whole outfit. Heaven's sake. keep him off." He probably remembered his biblical teaching regarding Jonah and the whale.

The big fish, a regular Jesse Willard, of his class, suddenly dove and went clean to the bottom. He battled as only a musky can, and leave it to me, the vivid scene and action of the duel will never be obliterated from my memory. The fighting fish threw water like the rush of a speeding torpedo boat, and the bloody spray dashed high whenever he came to the surface. Belelle wanted to pull ashore and beach the fish, but I insisted on having a fight to the finish on the lake. The boat was rowed fast, then slow, according to my direction for my dander was up, and I wanted to win that fight. I had visions of that ugly head, mounted and placed with my trophies of the rod and reel.

A Review of Muskellunge World Records

After about 50 minutes of strenuous battle the fish came up, and as they would say in ring parlance, he appeared to be quite groggy. It was high time to end the battle with a gun shot. I asked Mr. Waggoner to take out Colt's .38 and finish off the fish. Mr. Waggoner replied that he couldn't hit the inside of a cistern. Belelle, credited with being a high class marksman, fired two shots and missed each time at a distance of 125 feet. I reeled in and brought my big fellow to within 10 feet of the boat, and I'll be danged if the Indian didn't miss again. It was the last cartridge we had, too. On any other occasion the poor shooting would have been as funny as "The Three Twins," but at this time and place it was very tragic indeed. The last shot caused the big fellow to use his last ounce of energy and he dove again. When I pulled him up for the last time, Belelle hooked him under one gill with the gaffhook, and getting a good hold on the opposite gill with his hand, he hoisted the beauty into the boat.

It took the combined efforts of Waggoner and the Indian to hold the fish in the boat and never did Frank Gotch in his prime slip out of deadly holds like this husky musky. He was finally conquered when about one-third of his length was shoved under my seat in the rear of the boat, and I assisted by holding the fish with my knees. When the K.O. had been administered we, as they say in that song of the ancient mariner "Pulled for the Shore."

It was some time, some place, and also some fish. By actual measurement my muscallonge (*Esox estor*), a specimen of the pike family, is the largest fish ever known to be caught with the rod and reel in the great northwest. While happy over the fact that that day's work made me a champion, I was completely fagged and my left wrist was so sore from the plunging of the fish, that I felt the effects for two weeks after.

It is needless to say that when we pulled into camp with the big fellow, all the Fremonters gave the newly crowned " champ" a great ovation.

Fremonters have made Sawyer County, Wis., famous by the many big catches they have made on their many trips to that section.

Hanging on the scales, the musky pushed the needle to 51 pounds 0 ounces, and measured 55 inches in length with a 24-inch girth The fish broke the previous record from 1911 by three pounds, and was to hold the recognition of being the world's record for almost three years, when in July of 1919, it was beaten by another Wisconsin musky by only three ounces! Swint made another attempt at regaining the record but fell far short of the mark, as his name again appeared in the 1927 *Field & Stream* contest lists. He only finished fourth that year, even though his October 11 fish from Big Twin Lake weighed 45 pounds 0 ounces.

1919 ... F.J. Swint's world record was not as long lived as Whiting's, for when Wednesday, July 16, 1919, dawned, the musky world was only a few hours away from crowning a new king! It was on this day that John A. Knobla caught a 51-pound 3 ounce, 54-inch (25 1/4-inch girth) musky out of Lac Vieux Desert, Wisconsin, and

eclipsed the previous record by only 3 ounces! For John Knobla, this fish was a well deserved trophy as he had been an area guide for many years, and probably one of the best and most well known in the state of Wisconsin. He was a friendly person and very talkative when he was around people, not to mention his expertise on musky fishing. In fact, well known outdoor writer of the times, Fred Bradford Ellsworth, frequently wrote about Knobla, and always with the utmost of praise.

John Knobla and his 1919 world record which is currently the hybrid musky world record.

An interesting abstract to John Knobla's world record is that in many stories written about his fish, it was described as a "beautifully marked Wisconsin tiger musky." This and stories I have heard in Eastern Wisconsin from various people, indicated that Knobla's musky was possibly a hybrid musky. Through research by Rod Ramsell, a documented and authentic picture of this fish was found, which revealed that the stories and tales were in fact correct. John Knobla' s 1919 world record musky was in fact a "tiger" or hybrid musky!

It was not realized by fisheries biologists and scientists until the late 1930s that these "well marked tiger muskies," which occurred occasionally throughout musky country, were actually a muskellunge and northern pike cross. And until that time, the hybrids that were caught were believed to be, and promoted as just well marked "true" muskies.

Even today, many anglers mistake the hybrid for the genuine musky, and probably will for years to come. But, as history and lack of knowledge of the times would have it, John A. Knobla's 1919 world record will always be noted as a muskellunge.

1924 ... As you will have noted in Chapter 2, there was a monster musky caught in Pennsylvania in 1924 that was never listed as the world's record. The only reason for this for this I could find is that it is because it was never entered in the *Field & Stream* contest. I have done considerable research on this fish and find no reason why it should not take its rightful place in history and in the world record listing. I have now placed it in the list and here in its proper chronological place in this chapter, I present to you the story of the catch by the angler himself:

Mr. Walker's story:

On the morning of September 30, 1924, I left the dock at Conneaut Lake Park, on the upper end of the Lake, about 6:30 a.m. It had been raining very hard for several days, and the lake was at least two feet higher than usual. There was a slight north wind, but not enough to make more than a ripple. About one-half mile down the lake from where I started is a point extending into the lake, which has always been a favorite fishing ground of mine. In fact, about three days before I had caught a musky there that weighed twenty-eight pounds.

As I was in a hurry to reach this place. I rowed rather faster than usual, until I got nearly there, when I stood up and cast over a favorite patch of weeds. Getting no rises, I started to row to the point itself, and after going a little way, stopped to light a cigarette. Of course, my boat was moving along a little, but the bait must have sunk, as I did not see the strike. It was not a usual strike, as my reel turned over only once or twice, and the usual musky strike is very vicious and takes out from six to fifteen feet of line. Of course, I stopped the boat at once, thinking perhaps I had hooked a weed, but as I backed up, the line continued to go out very slowly, so I knew I had a fish. For some reason it did not settle at once, as a pike or 'lunge usually does, but kept moving along. For this reason I began to think I had picked up a pike perch [walleye], which are very plentiful in the lake. I have caught them up to nine pounds in weight. Finally, however, it stopped for a moment and then moved off rather slowly. Of course I struck at once and immediately knew it was not a small fish that I had hold of. Even after the strike this fish did not make the usual first run, nor did it come to the top of the water as usual.

My method of fishing for muskies is somewhat different from that of other fishermen. The only bait I ever have is live bait, or rather dead, as I always kill the chub, sucker, or shiner. I do this because I hook the bait crosswise in order to make it spin, and it will not do this when alive. Of course, I sometimes cast over likely patches of weeds and use a very short line; in fact, not more than the length of the pole, as I have found these fish are not at all afraid of the boat. My greatest success, however, has come when I was dragging the bait about thirty feet behind my boat and moving along at a rate that would keep the bait in sight and probably only six inches under water. In this manner I find it possible to work over weed beds where I know the fish are to be found, and also generally have the pleasure of seeing him when he strikes.

But to go on — fortunately, I was near the edge of the weeds, and the wind was right, so that I very shortly found myself over one of the deepest holes in Conneaut Lake. The fish kept going deeper and deeper until at one time it had over a hundred feet of my line, and I was beginning to get worried. It was fighting savagely with short quick runs, and I was very careful not to give

Lewis Walker's 54-pound 3-ounce musky, which remains the Pennsylvania state record.

it a chance to put its weight on my outfit. I succeeded, however, in gradually getting my line in; and finally, a half-hour or more after I had hooked the fish, it came to the top of the water for the first time about sixty feet away from the boat. I will have to admit frankly that when I saw what I had on the end of the line, I did have a few moments of buck fever, even after all my years of experience catching muskies. It looked as big as the boat! It took about an hour and a half to boat this fish.

After being on the top of the water for about a minute, down he went again, and carried on the battle for at least twenty or twenty five minutes more forty or fifty feet under the water. Finally, I worked him up to the top of the water again, this time about fifteen feet from the boat, and again I pretty nearly had a fit when I discovered that instead of being hooked in the stomach, as is usual when using live bait, the musky was hooked only in the corner of the mouth, but fortunately in the gristle, which is hard to tear. The hook was not even through this gristle, but was sticking in about a half-inch. Fortunately, I always use a stiff hook, though not a particularly large one.

As soon as I discovered this fact, I knew that I must get him the first time I tried to net him or all would be lost. I always net a fish and have never shot or stunned one with a club, as I believe netting gives the fish a better chance; it also adds considerably to my fun in fishing. After coming to the top the second time, the fish proceeded to perform all kinds of gymnastic exercises on top of the water, but he was too big to jump. My heart was in my mouth all the time, as I expected every second the hook would tear out, though I was putting as little pressure as possible on the line, but of course keeping it tight. Finally, I worked the musky in close to the boat. He was now on his side, but still going pretty strong; yet on account of the way he was hooked I took a chance, and by great good fortune got him in the net, head first. I use an extra deep net, probably thirty-six inches deep. It is however, rather narrow at the top, as I do not like to have a netted fish double up in the net; a big one will break his way through in pretty near every case. The tail of this fish stuck out of my net at least two feet. This, however, was really a piece of good luck, as it enabled me to clamp my knee on the tail in getting the fish over the edge of the boat; and by getting hold of the ring at the top of the net I was able to slide it into the boat. I could hardly believe my eyes when I looked at this specimen. As I usually do, I put the head of the fish under the seat at the end of the boat and the tail under the seat I was rowing on. All the time I was fighting the fish, we had been working down the lake, but I had been careful to keep out in the middle, where it was deep, by taking a few dips of the oars, though in truth, the fish had pulled me most of the way. I at once started back to the upper end of the lake, but after about a minute's rowing the musky decided that it didn't like its position, and I certainly had a battle for three or four minutes in order to make it understand it couldn't get back into the water. Here came one of the most ridiculous performances I have ever indulged in while fishing; after getting Mrs. Musky (the fish proved to be a female) quieted down, I discovered that in the fracas I had lost both my oars, and that they were being carried down the lake by a slight wind. Here I was in the middle of the lake with no other boat in sight, and at the rate I was going would not reach the foot of the lake for an hour or two. After some thought I decided to see if by paddling with my hands while sitting on the musky I could make some progress towards the oars. Fortunately I could, and after one or two miscalculations I was able to hook in one of the oars with my pole.

After that it was easy going to procure the other and get back to the dock. To say that this fish caused some commotion is putting it very mildly.

The musky was immediately put in a live-box, but we found unfortunately that in the battle I had with the fish in the boat, I must have injured its back in some way. I brought it into Meadville the next day to have it mounted.

This musky officially weighed fifty-four pounds thirty-six hours after being caught though I understand that it was weighed on other scales without my knowledge and weighed fifty six pounds. It was fifty-seven inches long. Incidentally it is unfortunate that the girth of the musky I caught was not taken for it was the thickest and fattest muskalonge I have ever seen. I was using a long canepole with a forty-two pound test Cuttyhunk line. The hook was a large size very stiff Cincinnati hook which I buy two for five cents. The leader was picture wire about three feet in length with of course a strong swivel. The bait was an eight-inch red chub. I make this outfit myself as I find it much better than any I can buy for this kind of fishing

Since catching this whopper I have been fishing for two others I know of; which I believe will go to sixty or sixty five pounds. I have seen them both but have never been fortunate enough to have them strike my bait.

I have a hunch that if I continue this wonderful sport I will sometime get hold of another great big musky — and it certainly makes up for all the hard work and the other days of fishing when I never see a scale.

In his 1931 book, *Let's Go Fishing*, Charles Reitell speaks of Mr. Walker's fish:

> On September 30, 1924 he (Walker) won the great honor of catching a musky fifty-seven inches long with a weight of fifty four pounds. From all I can gather this is the largest musky ever caught by rod and line.

So, there you have it, the story behind the Walker musky. I have inserted it here in this chapter because this is where it belongs. However, as you read on, it will read as if the Walker fish had never existed, as that is the way it was written and accepted at the time.

1929 dawned a year in which many world fishing records were to fall, including the 10 year old record for muskies, In fact, John Knobla's 51-pound 3-ounce world record from 1919 was to be beaten twice in the same year, the first time in recorded musky fishing history that such an occurrence was to happen. The first man to dethrone Knobla as world musky King was E.A. Oberland, who caught a 52-pound, 12-ounce 'lunge from Lake Pokegama, Wisconsin (near Lac du Flambeau), on Monday, July 1. Although few details are available on Oberland's fish because his record was short lived and little publicized, this fisherman was no stranger to big fish. There are several references to large fish that Mr. Oberland caught during his angling

E.A. Oberland, 1929 world record holder.

years. In fact, his first claim to national recognition was in 1925 when he finished fourth in the *Field & Stream* contest with a 42-pounder from the same Lake Pokegama. His career peaked in 1929 when he broke the existing record by 25 ounces, but as mentioned earlier, his reign as king was short lived.

After considerable searching we now have, from Mr. Oberland's son, a picture and a brief story of his record catch:

> I have finally located a picture of my father, the late E.A. Oberland ... I was working in Chicago at the time he caught the record fish, so was not too familiar with the

details. I believe he was fishing with a Harold Frazier of Manitowoc, Wisconsin, and that it was caught by trolling with a Skinner spoon with a feather cluster (actually it was a Pfleuger spoon—LR). My father was understandably reticent about his musky catches since he did not wish to encourage an influx of anglers to Lake Pokegama ... At Lac du Flambeau my father was considered both an expert and a lucky fisherman. Professional guides would try to observe where he fished, and how. Actually his success was due to two things — fishing almost daily during the long twilight hours, and knowing the precise location of the weed beds. Practically all his good fish were caught trolling at the edge of weed beds, in water ranging from six to twelve feet in depth. He used ordinary tackle of the type generally used for bait casting, and most of the larger fish were caught with Pfleuger or Skinner spoons with either a bucktail or feather cluster. A few were caught on large plugs of his own carving. Most of the fish were released, keeping only those for friends or institutions which wanted one for mounting ... I fished many hours with my father, during high school and college vacations and it is interesting to note that we never raised a large musky by casting — all the large ones were caught by trolling. Perhaps we never developed the proper casting techniques to entice them. We never fished with live bait, because a deeply swallowed bait could seriously injure a fish we would not wish to keep ..."

It was late August of 1929 when Bill Miles, Jr. and Gordon M. Curtis put their heads together and decided to head for Sabaskong Bay on Lake of the Woods, Ontario, to angle for the trophy muskies that the area was famous for.

Battling A Record Breaker
By Gordon M. Curtis

It has been our custom each summer to spend all the time possible in fishing throughout the northern states. Mrs. Curtis is about as enthusiastic over the sport as I am, and our boys — Gordon Jr., and Edward — seven and six years respectively, have also been bitten by the "fishing bug." On many winter evenings they plan with great detail how to outdo one another during the summer to come.

Last summer, Bill Miles, Jr., my old fishing partner, met us at our familiar haunts in Minnesota. After a powwow, it was decided that he and I would start at once for Sabaskong Bay, Lake of the Woods, Ontario, which place, we heard, was famous for its musky fishing. The rest of my family was to join us in about a week.

The morning after we arrived at Sabaskong Bay, we headed for Height O' Land Lake. about twenty miles to the north. Ernie, the guide assigned to me, was a splendid chap. He proved to be a woodsman par excellence, a good fisherman and, above all, a good sport. To him goes much of the credit for the pleasure of our trip.

The next morning we started out, on the big lake. I fairly tingled with excitement. At last I was to try my luck in the waters I had heard so much about! As we were working along the shore we came to a narrow inlet entering a bay. I saw Bill and his guide, Chuck, working toward us; so we waited for them to catch up. Bill was letting his line run out behind him. They had nearly come abreast of us when Bill had a terrific smash on his line. A big swirl, a leap — and a musky weighing about 30 pounds shot out of the water.

A big flat rock and a reef just under the surface made a V-shaped pocket, where the fish had been lying. Bill's tight line and the speed of their canoe had carried the fish into that pocket so it couldn't turn. That musky jumped clear over the reef! I have never seen anything like it in all my fishing experience. Chuck pulled for deep water and Bill fought hard, but the hook had been loosened in the jump and the fish got away. We left Bill and Chuck telling each other in no uncertain terms what each should have done.

Gordon Curtis and his 1929 world record of 53 pounds 12 ounces.

Across the bay was another inlet — a long stretch of water strewn with big boulders that just showed on the surface. I began trolling down through the middle. About half-way, I felt a sharp tug, a big splash and — nothing! He had missed. I didn't know whether I had stung him or not: so we paddled back. Right in the same spot he struck my lure again. This time there was a good swirl: but no splash. I quickly set the hook. and the party was on.

He put up a good scrap, but we finally flipped him over the gunwale. He was 45 inches long and weighed 24 pounds. After admiring the fish to our heart's content, Ernie put him back over the side, held him til he revived and then patted him on the back as he dove for the bottom. Chuck spoke up and said: "By golly, I've lived all my life in musky territory, and that's the first time I ever saw a 24-pounder thrown back. What kind of a prize are you looking for anyway?"

That remained to be seen.

The next day we had practically no luck. The following morning Chuck and I went out. It was hot, and the lake was very calm. As we were paddling near the end of an island we passed three trees that had fallen into the lake. When my spoon reached the second tree, it struck something. As a matter of fact, it stopped the canoe. Chuck leaned hard on the paddle, but I was afraid my 18-pound line would snap: so I paid out several yards.

There had not been a sign of life on the end of my line — only the feeling of a dead weight. Then the line started going down, but I couldn't budge the weight on the end of it. For several minutes the contest was a draw. Then, in a series of wicked side swipes, the weight on the end of my line started coming up. Now, for the first time, I was certain I had hooked into a fish and not a log. Out went my line, faster and faster — 10, 20, 30, 40 feet. I thought he would never stop. Thumbing my reel as hard as I dared, I burned the skin off my thumb.

Now the fish slowed down, turned and started toward us. Then he swung around in back of us and came up near the surface. I had a look at him. I was not much impressed — in fact, I was downright disappointed. Chuck sat spellbound and uttered in an amazed whisper, "Just look at that fish!"

Suddenly my musky made a lunge sideways, and I opened my eyes. At the distance and from the angle at which I had first seen him, only that portion from his head to just beyond the middle of his back was visible. When he turned sideways, however, I saw his full length. My blood pressure soared to new heights. After this, the fish woke up. Except for one more dive, all the rest of his fight was on the surface. He was everywhere! I nearly lost him once.

The thing that finally helped me most to come off victorious was the insatiable curiosity of that fish. Time and again he would swim alongside of the canoe, glaring at us. Each time Chuck would make a pass at him with the gaff, and finally managed to get a good hold on his gills. With a strong heave Chuck got the fish's head over the gunwale, and then, with a big flop, he came over the side. Chuck sat on the big fellow's head and pulled for shore, where we measured and weighed our catch. My musky was 57 inches long, and weighed 53 pounds and 12 ounces. My tackle comprised a Von Lengerke and Antoine rod, a Meek reel, an Invincible line and a No. 7 Skinner spoon.

1931 ... After almost two years on top, 1931 proved to be the year of Curtis' undoing as world record holder, and a Baudette, Minnesota, native named J.W. "Jack" Collins emerged with a larger musky to claim the title. It was late July when Harry Johnson, Barber Kane, and Collins drove to Nestor Falls, Ontario, and set out on Sabaskong Bay for trophy muskies.

J. W. Collins' 1931 world record musky of 56 pounds 7 ounces.

A Compendium of Musky Angling History

World's Record Musky

By J. W. Collins

... Our little party consisted of Harry Johnson, Barber Kane and myself. We hied ourselves away from Baudette. Minnesota, on July 23rd and drove by car to Nestor Falls. From there we went by boat to our camps. a distance of about two miles.

The following morning we started out early for the fishing grounds. We cranked up the old outboard and went sailing among the islands. Presently our guide shut off the motor and we paddled over to a reef. In the meantime we had assembled our tackle and were ready.

I began operations by casting over toward a reef among some boulders, where there was a sort of pool which looked as though it might harbor a musky. On my second cast I hooked one. This caused considerable excitement. Even Billy, our guide, jumped to his feet and began to instruct me how to land this monster. But alas, we were doomed to disappointment! Mr. Musky took a sudden notion to go south, and believe me, he went there! He steered a course directly amidships. and our musky was gone, The line parted just above the leader.

Putting on a different lure, I started in all over again, but our luck had apparently ebbed. We tried another and still another lure, but in spite of what we offered them we had no better luck.

The following morning we were again casting on the reef. My hook caught on a weed. Billy began to paddle back to release me, while I made every effort to get the hook to slip off the weed. The line parted. Why? Simply because I was fishing with a rotten line. Then I took off the remainder of the old line and put on a new U. S. line of 30 pound test, which I took along in case of emergency. I began all over again to try to conquer the fresh-water tiger in his lair. And lo and behold, within an hour I had hooked my big 56 1/2 pounder.

Jimminy Christopher! Everybody was excited now! My host and guide, Friend Billy, indulged in some very swift and mysterious movements and exclamations. He put out to deep water, and for the longest time the musky and I kept battling back and forth. Then, as the fish began to show signs of tiring out, we headed for a sandy beach. This was a distance of a mile or more, and it was some job with a rip snorting musky at the other end of my line! Four men and our equipment in an 18 footer with 5-foot beam! Billy called it "The Ark." Still the line held, the Pflueger Muskill lure held, the Heddon Waltonian reel held, and the True Temper rod held — and best of all, Billy held. But boy, it was some fight!

By the time we arrived at the beach. I was leading along about the tamest musky in the world. It slid out of the water on its belly without a scratch. A perfect specimen — a beauty!

Well, that's that. Do you wonder that I'm feeling happy about it? A world's record breaker isn't caught every day.

A Review of Muskellunge World Records

A short time later, the 55-inch musky held the scales down at 56 pounds 8 ounces, and measured up with an impressive 29 5/8-inch girth. A new world record by 2 3/4 pounds! Although this fish existed as the world record for 14 months until it was beaten by another Lake of the Woods fish in 1932, it was recognized as the Minnesota State Record up until 1976. Now, everybody who knows the Lake of the Woods, knows that Sabaskong Bay lies entirely within Ontario, Canada, and no matter how you cut the pie, Minnesota just doesn't come up with a piece! Well, in late 1976 this was finally brought to the attention of the Minnesota DNR and they proceeded to set the record books straight and gave credit for the state record to a 54-pounder caught by Art Lyons of Bena, Minnesota, in Lake Winnibigoshish on August 28, 1957.

1932 ... The early Thirties were a dim light on this great nation's history, and millions of Americans suffered through the hardships that those years brought. Among those that were hit hard was a Chicago man named George E. Neimuth.

World's Record Musky
By George E. Neimuth

It is every fisherman's heartfelt desire to catch a real trophy. He is always in hopes, even though his efforts avail him little in actual accomplishment. He will suffer many privations, deprive himself of many pleasures which he could otherwise afford, in order to bring it to realization.

On my last trip I believe I caught the mastodon of the fresh waters — a musky weighing 58 1/4 pounds, at Nestor Falls, in Lake of the Woods, Canada. This fish measured 59 inches in length and 34 1/2 inches in girth.

It has been my custom for the past five years to arrive at Lake of the Woods on July 1st. Like many others, I was hit hard by the depression and intended to defer my 1932 trip. When vacation time approached, my friends were constantly reminding me by asking, "Well, how's the fishing this year?" My power to resist finally broke down.

When the camp proprietor wrote me that the muskies had not hit well all summer but were showing some signs of life since the first good frost, he wrote at the psychological time. I had been brooding over the fact that the season was rapidly coming to a close and I had nothing new to divert my mind when troubles incident to the regular routine of life were causing sleepless nights. This letter was the deciding factor, and I decided to go at once.

On September 18th my son and I started out. From that instant I forgot that there were taxes and interest on the mortgage to be paid, that the insurance had run out, and that there were a lot of other irons in the fire. They could all burn as far as I was concerned. I calculated that Jack Frost comes early in the

Lake of the Woods, that few fishermen would be there, that the fish would have had a period of rest, and that there would be more wind than earlier in the season — all of which are favorable factors. My equipment is always ready and the tackle box loaded with a generous assortment of plugs and spoons.

We left Chicago at 5:40 p.m. and arrived at Nestor Falls the following night. After a hearty dinner, we did not waste much time in getting under the blankets. The following morning we punched the breakfast clock right on the dot. We were not the only ones — three little bear cubs waited patiently for their bread, and a dozen or more partridge seemed to recognize the breakfast bell too.

George Neimuth's 1932 world record musky weighed 58 pounds 4 ounces.

As we left the dining room after a feast of culinary inventiveness known only in the far reaches of the North Woods, we met our guide Jack, who, we afterward learned, was a trapper, lumberjack, moose hunter and culinary genius. He possessed remarkable aptitude for his chosen occupation, and as he was preparing our boat he frequently cast a glance toward our cabin. Needless to say, it spurred us on.

We were all set to try again for the ones that had got away in previous years. It was only a few minutes until the outboard sputtered rapidly, anxious to lend us a helping hand. There was a strong wind blowing, and the lake was rough. I knew we were flirting with an unwelcome bath when we crossed the big stretch. En route I again tested my line and placed a Pikie minnow on the snap. As soon as Jack shut off the motor I started to cast. My son's tackle was a duplicate of mine. We cast alternately, so as to keep at least one bait in the water all the time. This routine was continued for about an hour, but only a few walleyes were hooked.

Then I suggested a spot close by which had long been in my memory, for I had visited it in previous trips and either had a strike or a follow up from a mighty musky. So Jack rowed the boat toward the big stretch, where the strong autumn wind was lashing the water. As we neared the favored spot I began to cast my plug again. After several casts which landed just behind a protruding rock, I suddenly had a violent strike. A moment later I could see the musky, with his mouth wide open, nearly on the surface — a sight that would strike awe in the most blase fisherman. I believe a quart cup could have been thrown into this muskie' s mouth.

He immediately sounded, and there seemed to be no bottom to this particular place as he reeled yard after yard from my reel. If ever I appreciated a level winder, it was then. I at once put on the click and drag to prevent backlashes from the short but violent jerks. Jack, without being told, was heading the boat away from shore, and I worked the fish up again, this time within ten feet of the boat.

The wind was buffeting the boat about so that it was difficult for Jack to manage. I began to despair of success. The musky would sound and sulk, but short, quick jerks would put him into action again. I kept a compelling strain on him, and the increasing arc of the rod warned me to be cautious. I must keep him in deep water. His runs continued for more than an hour, but he was growing perceptibly weaker and the rushes were not so long. His direction could then be controlled, although he still had plenty of fight in him, for as soon as I would get him close to the boat he would muster all his strength and rush away again. My part was to coax him back and keep him working at all hazards, I was out to win, and so was he. These tactics were continued until I pulled him alongside.

Then we looked around for a good landing place, which fortunately was close by. It consisted of a rock gradually tapering into the water — an ideal spot for the purpose. Jack stood in about a foot of water and instructed me to draw the fish to him, which was not an easy matter. He placed both of his hands in the lower gill and pulled the mastodon ashore. Thus ended my most successful musky day.

The tackle which stood up so eloquently throughout this ordeal consisted of a True Temper rod, a Pflueger reel, and Ashway line.

Upon weigh-in, the musky tipped the scales at 58 pounds 4 ounces and stretched the tapes to 59 inches in length, and 34 1/2 inches in girth. To George E. Neimuth, it was a dream come true, as he had always hoped to someday catch a musky that was a real trophy. And what a trophy it was, as he set a new world record that would stand until 1939 at which time it was broken two times in one season.

1939 ... The year 1939 dawned over musky country and little did anyone know that this was the year that would rewrite the history of musky fishing. The world's record 'lunge had stood for almost seven years now, that being the fish caught in Lake of the Woods, Ontario, by George E. Neimuth of 58 pounds 4 ounces, on September 24, 1932. On July 27, Louis Spray broke the record with a 59-pound 8-ounce musky from Grindstone Lake, near Hayward, Wisconsin. Following is Louie's story:

... We had moved the cafe in 1938, while still in Hayward, to an adjoining building, and in its stead, put in casino equipment. Tom Campbell, one of the best dice men in the business, took care of the crap table, and Stew Dorsey, a fine wheel dealer, operated the roulette wheel. We had a late crowd this one particular night and I did not get to bed until around 6:00 a.m., was dog tired but for some reason could not sleep, so decided to get up and go fishing a few hours. I stopped at the lunch counter and there was Tom, also unable to sleep. I invited him to go fishing with me and we went out to Red Harmon's place on Grindstone Lake to get a boat. Red and his gang had been in the evening before and stayed late, so there were no signs of life out there. I left a note, took a boat and went out. I was casting a Musky Houn when the big one hit and broke water immediately. I could see at a glance it was unusually big and I worried about the light line, 20 pound test and wondered how well he was hooked. Everything else was favorable. There was no wind to speak of and what there was, was in our favor. My .22-caliber pistol was on the seat between Tom and me and I reached over and put it by my side on the seat. When Tom saw this,

Alton Van Camp holding Louis Spray's 1939 world record of 59 pounds 8 ounces.

he grabbed a .45-Colt that I had taken along, thinking that I might get in some target practice with it, because I never did very well with the .45. It immediately dawned on me that an accident could easily happen, not knowing what Tom knew about guns. So I reached and asked him to give it to me. I took a glance at his face to get his reaction at my taking the gun from him, and he had a frightening look of terror on his face, had dropped the oars and was hanging on the side of the boat with each hand. Then I had nothing to worry about but the fish. I had the fish up several times but was unable to shoot from the particular angle so I let him do his thing and waited.

Finally, almost out of nowhere, up he came head out of water a little ways and was just an ideal target. I quickly grabbed what I thought was my .22 and shot. But it was not the .22, it was the .45 which I had laid beside it. It almost scared the wits out of me when that .45 roared, but I hit him exactly as planned, about four inches in back of the eyes right where the spine connects to the head. That baby never moved, for the moment at least. Then he shuffled off a ways. I led him back and reached down to get a hold of his gills, and Tom hollered, "Look out, you dummy, he'll bite your hand off." When I pulled the fish into the boat, I noticed it was different from most muskies. It was very chubby, with a small head, but otherwise, a very beautiful specimen.

A Review of Muskellunge World Records

The musky crown hardly had time to settle on the "King's" head when the unbelievable happened. The world's musky record fell for the second time in the same year, this time by a fish caught in Ontario, Canada. Louis Spray fished only for records and one of such short duration didn't satisfy him, especially after dedicating most of his life to the sport. He again pounded the waters of Northern Wisconsin as soon as the news had reached him, fishing only where he had raised potential record fish in the past, but 1939 ended with John J. Coleman as "King."

The following is Mr. John J. Coleman's own story of catching this biggest of all muskies:

To an experienced member of the Izaak Walton fraternity, there would undoubtedly have been nothing unusual in the morning of October 3. It was gray and a trifle chilly, and the rain pocked the surface of the lake in little craters as far out as the eye could see. As our two boats pushed away from the pier there was absolutely nothing in the air or in our minds to forewarn us that this day was to hold the greatest thrill of our fishing lives.

I'm not much of a fisherman. Bud, a real angler, had invited me to join his party for a few days of musky fishing at big Eagle Lake, some six miles from Eagle River, Ontario. I had accepted more with the expectation of good company and good food around the camp fire than from any very great desire to catch a fish. In fact, I didn't even have any equipment.

We had driven hard all the day before, and pulled into the camp past midnight. After breakfast in the main lodge the next morning our party assembled at the pier. George and Art, the guides, had two boats ready. They were 16-footers with 8 hp outboard motors, each big enough to accommodate two anglers and a guide.

It was decided that Art would go along with Bud and Kay, while George shepherded the two tyros, Ray and me. Bud had lent me one of his rods and a reel and his favorite bait — a Pikie Minnow, somewhat dulled in color from much use and many fish caught.

We pushed off after promising to meet for lunch on a nearby island. The boats kept fairly close together, with George expertly

John J. Coleman with his 1939 world record of 60 pounds 8 ounces.

213

keeping us near the rocks and shallows, where the muskies were likely to be lurking.

A fairly uneventful morning passed, with the rain dripping steadily down and dampening our spirits, as hour after hour slipped by with no catch. I had had only one good follow — a musky that decided against my bait at the last moment — and it was pleasant to find ourselves in the vicinity of the island just before noon. A good lunch would restore our spirits and send us into the afternoon with our optimism renewed.

Bud's guide had already started his outboard and was heading for the island and Ray was suggesting that we follow him when George motioned me to make one last cast. I did, and nothing happened. Well, I'd try just one more.

Scarcely had the bait plopped on the surface near the rocks when whang the granddaddy of all muskies struck like a thunderbolt and streaked away. George quickly got the boat into deeper water, shouting encouragement and instructions as I clumsily played the fish. Bud noticed that we had hooked something interesting and his boat soon came alongside.

The big musky hauled and veered as far out as the line would take him, and charged under the boats several times. After what seemed to be hours, George decided our catch was ready for landing, and I brought him up to the side. As he lay flopping in the bottom of the boat the usual guessing went on, with our estimates as to his length and weight varying with our inexperience. I guessed around 40 pounds while Art was inclined to believe the big fish would go over 50. Bud, with years of salt-water fishing to back him up, ventured that he wouldn't be surprised to see the scales go to 55.

Of course, there was no more thought of lunch on my part. With the party's congratulations ringing in my ears, George and I pushed off for camp immediately to get our fish weighed. Ray stayed on the island with Bud, Kay and the guide to lunch on walleyes, eggs, bacon and coffee.

As soon as we landed back in camp my prize was weighed and measured. You can imagine the thrill when we learned that I had caught the largest musky ever taken from the water on a line! He weighed 60 pounds 8 ounces, and measured 58 1/2 inches in length and 31 1/2 inches in girth.

The usual pictures were taken and the big fish sent off to be iced and prepared for shipment to the taxidermist.

The fruits of victory are sometimes not so sweet as they seem. Take my case, for instance. Overnight I have been converted from a lukewarm angler to a red hot fisherman — all through the accidental and unforeseen circumstance of catching a record fish. Now I'll probably be a fisherman until I die. But my future is already behind me. Instead of working onward toward an inviting and possibly unattainable goal, which is one of the great thrills of fishing, or any other sport, I have blundered in at the top, and from now on every victory will seem paltry compared with one already achieved in the distant past.

The result was the first musky ever caught exceeding 60 pounds and the second new world's record for 1939! Anyway, the whole story behind Coleman's fish proves that novice musky fishermen have just as good a chance to catch a record fish as do the experts. In one well placed cast, he had shown the best in Wisconsin that beginners could be kings too, but his reign was short lived as 1940 produced two fish larger than his.

1940 ... The year dawned after one of the wildest seasons (1939) in the history of musky fishing in which two world record fish were caught, including the first musky ever recorded in excess of 60 pounds. Musky country had seen more excitement and records broken in one year than had been seen in the last ten years. But 1939 was just the calm before the 1940 storm!

It all started with Louie Spray again, the same man who got things going in 1939. Yes, Spray had done it for the second time in his life, and again ruled as king of musky country a little over one year from the day of his first record (July 27, 1939).

On August 19, 1940, Louis Spray hung a fish on the scales weighing 61 pounds 13 ounces, and right away, Hayward again laid claim to the title.

From the time he was dethroned in 1939, Louis Spray pounded the

Louis Spray with his 61-pound 13-ounce world record, caught in 1940.

waters of northern Wisconsin, concentrating on the hang-outs of big muskies he had seen in the past. He was unhappy with a record that was broken and forgotten shortly after being caught. Finally on Monday morning, August 19, Spray reclaimed honors by bringing to gaff a musky caught in Stoogy Bay, of Lac Courte Oreilles, that weighed 61 pounds, 13 ounces.

Louis' partner for the day was Tom Campbell, a Hayward resident and employee of Spray's tavern (oddly enough, Campbell was also his partner in 1939 when Spray caught his 59 1/2-pound world record musky on 20-pound test line). The two men had been splashing the lair of a large musky that Spray had spotted several times in the past with all the lures they had, having no success. Finally, Spray let up and sought some relief from the monotony of casting with heavy gear. He changed to lighter tacker (his heavy line snarled easier and he couldn't get the distance casting lighter lures that he could with a lighter line) and decided to try for a few bass in the same area.

Louis tied on a True Temper Bass Pop, a dishpan like lure about two inches in diameter with a single hook dressed with pork chunk frog. The ancient Bass Pop was not effective in hooking the few bass hits he got, and the action wasn't to Spray's liking. He then tried attaching a small treble hook, with feathers on it, to the lure. This combination was even worse, for now the bait skimmed the surface with no action whatsoever. Louis started to retrieve the "crippled" lure with considerable disgust when the big fellow hit! The 18-pound test Ashway nylon line and the flexible True Temper Bass Rod equipped with a Coxe reel met the musky's every challenge and finally brought the old warrior to boatside. A well placed shot with a .22 pistol dispatched the fish when the first good chance presented itself. The fish was then lifted into the boat with a gaff and the battle was over only 55 minutes after the misfit lure found its mark.

Immediately the fish was taken to Karl Kahmann's taxidermy shop where there was an inspected and certified scale. The fish ended up hanging on the scale in Pufahl's Hardware where a city clerk, a local insurance agent, and a hardware store employee witnessed the weighing. The fish was then displayed in Spray's Bar before being returned to the taxidermist so that everyone in town could see the monster. In the meantime, the town of Hayward let the world know about their newly caught record.

Ontario also made a bid of its own to regain the record in 1940. In fact, it was almost one year to the day, making Eagle Lake the first body of water in the world to produce a second musky in excess of 60 pounds. The Eagle Lake monster weighed at 61 pounds 9 ounces, and for 48 years stood as the Ontario record, and also the record for all of Canada.

The lucky angler was Edward Walden, who, like Spray, was an

experienced muskellunge fisherman. Walden was casting a #12 Pflueger muskill in Vermilion Bay on Tuesday, October 8, when he buried the hooks in the huge fish. Walden had battled the fish for exactly 56 minutes before he managed to bring it aboard and subdue it. His Gladding 30-pound test Invincible line, Gephart rod and Coxe reel stood to the test of the record proportioned 'lunge. What a disappointment it must have been for him to realize that his fish was only the second largest ever caught of all time!

1949 ... Nearly nine years passed when suddenly, on Sunday, July 24, 1949, a record cry was heard from the Hayward area once again. This time the lucky fisherman on the receiving end was noted outdoor writer, Cal Johnson. In the original story of the capture, Cal was accompanied by his

Though not a world record, Ed Walden's 61-pound 9-ounce musky stood as the Canadian record for 48 years.

son Phillip and Jack Conner, outdoor editor of the Minneapolis *Star & Tribune*. But shortly after, Conner denied being in the same boat as he supposedly took another boat that morning and went bass fishing instead. Nevertheless, he was staying with Cal and Phil at Moccasin Lodge on Lac Courte Oreilles. (More on this later.)

Following is the story of the catch of Cal Johnson's fish as told by his son Phil in the *Ashland Daily Press*:

How The Record Musky Was Landed
By Phil Johnson

It was 4 a.m. (July 24, 1949).

There's a little background to it, but we'll start there.

After sleeping through a terrific thunderstorm at Moccasin Lodge on the Lake Courte Oreilles, 10 miles southeast of Hayward, our alarm clock woke us up at 4 o' clock.

In our party was Jack Connor, outdoor editor of the *Minneapolis Star and Sunday Tribune*, and Dad (Cal Johnson, noted outdoor writer formerly of Ashland) and myself.

The clock went off. Jack Connor got up and turned the clock off. Dad was already awake and almost ready to go fishing. At this time it was still thundering and lightning and the rain was still coming down. We sat around on the porch impatiently waiting for the storm to stop.

The rain slowed up about 5 o'clock. There was still just a little rain, but we decided to go out.

Lake Courte Oreilles is the second largest natural lake in Wisconsin. It is not an artificial flowage, but a natural lake. It is about 10 miles east to west, and from north to south it varies from about a mile to 4 miles in the widest place.

There is over 86 feet of water in some of the deep holes.

We knew there were some big muskies in there and we had been working on one ever since the season opened.

We think we raised this same fish three or four times. A big one, maybe this one, followed into the boat three or four times, then turned around without striking.

We have been fishing there since the season opened May 25. In the meantime we have caught some muskies, the largest one 21 1/2 pounds caught about a month ago.

The lake has been known as a lake of extremely large muskies. This year we saw this big fish follow in toward the boat — the biggest fish we had ever seen. It would get within 6 feet of the boat but not strike the bait.

The fish was caught on a Pike-Oreno. This is the same kind of bait it followed up to the boat. We also used the large bucktail made from natural buck with a large spinner, but it was the Pike-Oreno that the musky finally struck on.

We used a two and a half outboard motor and one of Mike Solo's 16-foot round bottom boats. It was still raining just a little bit. We could hear just a slight rumble of thunder as we left the dock.

The lake is bordered by spruce and balsam, maple and birch.

We started trolling right from the dock. We went straight out to a drop off, and then southwest to what is known as Moccasin bar, a weed bar of sand. Over the bar is about 5 or 6 feet of water, and it drops off to 12 or 15 feet and then down.

We hadn't been on the water more than 15 minutes when "Wham!"

Cal Johnson's 67-pound 8-ounce musky held the record briefly in 1949.

Dad's reel started singing and he hollered. "We have a big one." The fish took a run of about 60 feet, and then went straight to the bottom. It was in about 15 or 20 feet of water.

218

A Review of Muskellunge World Records

I don't remember just what Dad said, except to repeat, "We have a big one." We couldn't tell how big, because the fish stayed right down for about half an hour. Dad said, "The only thing we can do now is let him try and land me, and after we tire him out, then land him."

Dad was smart enough not to try to yank him loose and lose him. He knew better than to try to "horse" in a fish like that. With the terrific muscle power that a fish that size possesses it would be impossible to bring that fish alongside the boat before it was tired.

The bottom is rock bottom, quite clear of sunken debris. If this had been in a flowage with many trees under water, we never would have got him.

Fifteen minutes went by, we just sat. We worked the boat to about 40 feet of the fish, but no closer, for fear he would cut under the boat.

Then we waited some more. Dad knew he had a fish — at no time did he think it was a dead head.

Dad could sense that the fish was chewing and mauling the bait, he could actually feel it through the line. He could watch the rod tip work when the fish would shake its head.

Another fifteen minutes went by. Finally the fish started to move. Dad worked him closer to the boat, which was the first time we saw the fish.

The first time we saw it there was a huge shadow about 10 feet from the boat and about 6 feet below the surface. He came in slow and easy, not tired a bit. It was then that we had an inkling of what he had tied into.

Dad worked him alongside the boat. The fish was right alongside the boat. I made my first and last attempt to gaff it.

The fish rolled and went out into deep water again. Oh, man, that was a heartbreaker.

Dad said, "The only chance we have is to beach this fish."

So we started to work in toward the shore. By this time about 45 minutes had gone by.

When we got about 35 feet from shore, about a quarter of a mile from Moccasin Lodge, the water was only about three feet deep, so I went right over the side, carrying my gaff and a small club.

Dad worked the fish close to me. I slipped the gaff under his gills and headed for the woods with the fish in tow.

The fish didn't start acting up till probably when the fish's belly touched the sand.

Then he nearly tore the gaff right out of my hand. I kept right on. I hauled him behind me at least 30 feet up on shore before I stopped.

The fish was flopping around to beat heck.

Finally I subdued him with the club, hitting him right on the seam between the head and body, what would be the neck. That did the business.

By this time Dad and Jack were out on the shore, telling me what to do, advice that I sorely needed. We never, never carry a gun. Dad feels this is bad sportsmanship, and that if a fish is clever enough to get away before you can gaff him or beach him, more power to him.

The fish was then taken to Moccasin Lodge where everyone woke up to see what the excitement was all about. Little did they know that it was angling history in the making. Mike Solo and Serge Bagny, proprietors of the lodge, got a scale and weighed and measured the big fish. Johnson had no idea it was a world record till then. The musky tipped the scales at 67 pounds 8 ounces, and measured 60 1/4 inches long and 33 1/2-inch girth. The fish was then taken to Karl Kahmann, a Hayward taxidermist, who investigated the fish and found no sign of disease, no spear marks, and no cuts or abrasions other than those caused by the hooks of the Pike-Oreno. No spawn or natural food was found in the fish when it was skinned for mounting. The affidavit of the catch was witnessed by Oscar A. Paul of Farrisville, Kentucky; Karl W. Kahmann, Hayward; M. Solo and S. Bagny of Moccasin Lodge, Hayward; and John O. Moreland of Hayward, who notarized the document. To this day, Cal's musky remains on public display in Hayward, Wisconsin.

Well, Cal Johnson was busy celebrating and displaying his world record musky mount when word reached him of a larger one being caught. Yes, the ink was scarcely dry in the record books again when Louis Spray hung one on the scales (less than three months later) that eclipsed Johnson's short-lived stay at the top.

The date was Thursday, October 20, 1949, and the place was the Chippewa Flowage. The reason Louis Spray was there was obvious, he was after record proportion fish. He had been relatively inactive in musky fishing for several years, content to live on his past reputation, but when Johnson recorded his musky, Spray viewed this as a new challenge. He held steadfast to his old tactics and fished the places where he knew big fish existed in the past. He chose the "Big Chip" as he thought it would contain the best chance for setting a new record. Spray had remembered an overgrown fish he had seen there on occasion, and decided to concentrate his efforts on that particular fish. Spray "camped" on the old giants' lair, determined that this particular fish would again make him the king of musky country. Spray kept after the elusive monster for 19 straight days without a sign of the fish's interest. Day after day, from sunrise to sunset, the anglers pounded the brute's home territory to no avail. Finally, on October 20, a miserably cold, damp (occasional drizzle), and windy day at about

5:00 p.m., Spray connected with the fish he was after. He was just about to give up due to the poor and chilly weather, when the guide insisted that Spray try a short time longer.

Let's go back and let Louis tell the story:

I have mentioned in a previous article that I was now in Rice Lake, 49 years old and was taking a good hard look at my financial future, and to heck with my fishing. But I could not get it out of my head completely. I knew of a monster in the north fork of the Flambeau, and one in the Chippewa Flowage. So in the fall of 1949 I decided to have one last fling at these two fish and then forget about it, win, lose or draw.

But, now who do I fish with? Good old Tommy Campbell was in Florida and while I learned later that there were some excellent musky fishermen in Rice Lake, I had not met them. Ted Hagg, who operated a night spot in Sarona, Wisconsin, came into the bar one day and I approached the subject to him. Ted was the kind of individual whom everybody wanted to be around, with always a witty crack on the end of his tongue. He wise-cracked something about. "How much do the Indians charge per 100 pounds?" but he said it would be good for him to get away from the place for awhile, and I had myself a partner. I told him I wanted to fish the entire month of October and he was agreeable. So October 1st, we took off for Herman's Landing on the Chippewa Flowage and did so each day until the 20th, when we finally hooked and landed old "Chin Whiskered Charlie," as I had named him. He was a granddaddy, 69 pounds, 11 ounces. 5 feet 3 1/2 inches long, and a girth of 31 3/4 inches.

On that particular day, George Quentmeyer, a guide who was off duty, joined Ted and myself for a fishing expedition. Ted could never understand why I always kept going to one particular spot, off and on, during the days we fished the flowage, but George caught on but fast. He knew I had one spotted. Mostly it was chilly and damp, sometimes a slow drizzle and generally nasty weather. About 3:30 p.m., I

Lou Spray's 69-pound 11-ounce musky is officially recognized as the world record.

knew Ted was freezing because he was not dressed for the cold so I suggested we go in and have some hot drinks and get warm. He was all for it. George, who was no novice at handing out the old malarkey jazz himself chided us with such remarks as "tenderfoot, pansies and city slickers." When we left the tavern, George took over the motor and ran us right back into the same old spot. Ted said, "What again ... well, that beats me," and just sat there huddled up. I myself hated to get down into that cold water in the minnow bucket for a sucker, but I did, and rigged my own make-up of a harness on the sucker and laid him in the water. George was rowing around in that spot, sort of trolling like. The sucker was really too large to cast and besides the trolling was by far the better percentage.

Well, believe me, or you don't have to, but it seemed no time until old "Chin Whiskers" hit the sucker and about a half dozen little treble hooks were set into his jaw, that I had placed on the harness. "Chin Whiskers" asserted himself in the usual way, breaking water and splashing and Ted stood up in the boat (an unpardonable sin in the ethics of musky fishing). George immediately directed him to sit down or get clouted with an oar. Ted was stone deaf. His eyes were glued on the fish battling away out there. So I said, "Ted, will you help me a second?" He agreed. I said, "Sit down and don't stand up again." Ted countered by asking George if he would do something for him, like take him to shore. So now in the next few lines you will see who was responsible for landing a world record musky. George was an artist in handling a boat. There was a wind blowing us toward a log jam along the shore which would have been fatal had "Chin Whiskers" successfully reached there. But good old George worked the boat away from shore and as best I could, I got the fish out in the lake and then there was nothing to do but wait for the opportunity to plug him. I had the fish up a few times, but there was always a wave or something to prevent a good shot. One time George commented asking, "Why don't you shoot?" I told him why and he understood.

Finally "Chin Whiskers" came up again, this time back by George. My back was to George so I did not know what he was up to but I heard bing-bing and I saw the fish stiffen up. I could have kissed George on the spot. He had stuck two deadly shots right on target. After old "Chin Whiskers" took his last little swim in a sort of semi-circle, George grabbed a fish stringer laying there and put it through his gills, saying, "We ain't going to take no chance on this baby getting away now." We got him into the boat and I straddled him for awhile. The game was all over for poor old Charlie. So now, it boils down to this. If it hadn't been for George, we wouldn't have gone back to that spot. Had not it been for George, the boat would probably have drifted into the log jam and the fish would have gotten off. Had it not been for George shooting the fish, it might have gotten off, as anything can happen when fighting a large fish like that, although I did have on a really heavy line this time. So in reality, I got the credit for the catch, while George was 99% responsible for it.

The battle was over only 40 minutes after it started and Spray had in his hand his third world record.

Spray's Union Hardware rod and Cycloid reel, equipped with Gladding line, held to the test and Louis wasted no time in making his catch known. The three anglers took the monster into Herman Ceranske's Landing, where a short celebration was held in the bar, then headed to Hayward to weigh the fish in.

The stores were closed in Hayward, and Pastika's Bait Shop had no scales, so they then went to Stroner's Store, but his grocery scales didn't have the capacity to weigh it. They then stopped at Kahmann's Taxidermy to weigh the musky there. But Karl refused them due to the fact that he did not want to contend with the mob of people that would follow the story of a world record again. From there they went to Stone Lake and stopped at R.A. Schmock's Tavern to show off the fish at 8:30 p.m. Mention was made that Jack Reinke, the postmaster for Stone Lake, might come down to the post office and weigh it. Reinke arrived in a few minutes and the fish was hung on the scales. The musky weighed in at 69 pounds 11 ounces, was 63 1/2 inches long with a 31 1/4-inch girth. Witnesses were RA. Schmock, Louis Spray, Ted Hagg, and Jack Reinke, the postmaster. Spray took his fish the next day to Schofield, Wisconsin, where a taxidermist named Hugh Lackey lived. Lackey agreed to mount the fish provided Spray told no one where the fish was to avoid the curious mob again.

World record muskies seem to catch doubt from all sides as to their authenticity, and Johnson' s and Spray's fish were no exceptions. But in spite of all claims to discredit their catches,1949 ended and in March of 1950, *Field & Stream* magazine announced the acceptance of Spray's musky as the official new world's record for the species. (More about the doubts later.)

With the record in his hands once again, Louis Spray chose to fade out of the musky fishing scene, only picking up the ol' rod and reel on occasion.

1954 ... Almost five years had gone by and Louis Spray was still the holder of the world record for muskellunge. His record stood through a few tense moments in June of 1954 when Robert Malo caught his 70-pound 4-ounce fish in Wisconsin, but failed to qualify for an entry in the *Field & Stream* contest and thus was denied record recognition. More about this musky later.

Now that we have the stories on all of the world records, let us backtrack and review all of the doubts and controversies. We will review all known accusations and in most cases will rebut them with facts, affidavits, etc.

For the past 30 years I have heard and read various versions of how this or that record was not on the "up and up." I believe you will find sufficient data here to finally set the records straight (at least all the facts are here for you!)

The only gray areas for the first seven world record fish were Knobla's fish, which was in fact a hybrid and not a purebred musky; and J.W. Collins' fish, and the question of where it was caught. For many years, it was listed as the Minnesota state record, caught in Lake of the Woods, Minnesota. But in fact, it was caught in Sabaskong Bay of Lake of the Woods, which is in Ontario. Minor details at best. But, from there one, the water got quite muddy; I assume due to A.) jealousy; B.) poor communications; and C.) journalistic sensationalism. As is the case with any rumor, each person retelling it colors it as they hear or see it, and often several retellings down the line the story barely resembles the original rumor. So, keeping this in mind, let us start.

Perhaps most controversial of all record holders and/or contenders was Louie Spray. Not that I believe that there was any wrongdoing, but Louie did things his way, and because of that it caused controversy. Most of the controversy took place in Wisconsin. Most of it that reached print nationally was through prominent outdoor writer Mel Ellis. In his article, "Throw Those Muskies Back Boys," in *True* magazine, Ellis wrote:

> Fifteen years ago the record musky taken on a rod and reel weighed 52 pounds. It was a Wisconsin fish, but in 1938 the record went to Michigan with the capture of a 56 pounder. (This is in error, as were several outdoor articles of the time — see the world record list.)
>
> The next year, however, Louis Spray, a former musky-hunting hero from Hayward and now a Rice Lake tavern keeper, came up with a 59 pound 8 ounce musky and it turned out to be the fish that was the first in a series that has been characterized in the press as not-so-nice smelling muskies.
>
> But Louie the indomitable came right back the next year with a whopper that went 61 pounds 13 ounces, and this was another fish some people insisted smelled as though it might not be strictly fresh.
>
> Nevertheless, he claimed a world record (in 1939) and during the time that

this fact was in considerable doubt, he announced that he would soon produce the necessary statistical proof ...

Eventually along came notarized statements that the fish had existed, and had been caught by Mr. Spray. There were the pictures and further detailed evidence revealed that it had been weighed at a creamery station and a tavern, and that it tipped the scales at 59 1/2 pounds and measured 58 inches.

Spray's 1939 fish was beaten by John J. Coleman, which Ellis missed completely! We previously reported the story of the capture of Louie's 1939 fish; so let's pick up Louie's story from there:

We headed for Red Harmons but still no one was up. Well, we got them up but quick. The door was not locked so we walked right in and hollered "musky" and I wish you could have seen the goings on. It was in July and everybody was only half dressed, women and all, milling around.

I believe there was more booze at Harmon's place than there was in Spray's bar. Everybody had a bottle in his hand of all makes and description and everybody was bound we should have one on them. So, on an empty stomach, well, you can guess the consequences. Finally, Tom and I broke away and started

The mount of Louis Spray's 1939 musky, which weighed 59 1/2 pounds.

for home. However, when we hit the main highway I figured I would like to go over to Draper-Loretta way and show the boys over there how I do it now. There was no scale there that would weigh the fish, so someone came up with a bathroom scale. We put a board on the scale, weighed it, put on the fish, weighed it, subtracted the weight of the board and it came to between 59 and 60 pounds. A young man running a filling station, Widmer Smith, told me that he thought it might be a world record, but that it should be weighed on an official scale to be authentic. Somebody took it into Winter, Wisconsin, a distance of ten miles, and brought back the weigh slip of 59 1/2 pounds. The old record was 58 1/4 pounds.

So right now, the multitude gathered there, pronounced me the musky king of the world, which naturally called for some whoopee, including some beverage gargling. While the gang was at it, Tom and I ate a lunch, then, headed for Park Falls to show off our catch over there. We did that all right, but in the ensuing hours, some of the gang, all my friends, stole my fish and proclaimed they would give it back only after they had run my tab up to about where they wanted it. To expedite, they finally gave it back to us and we started for home via Glidden and Clam Lake, on Highway 77. We passed up not one tavern. The next day I awoke about 3:00 p.m., and could not, for the moment, remember what had happened but knew it was something big. Did we win a lot of money, lose a lot in our business, or why did I get so plastered? It finally came to me and I hustled down to the tavern, unshaved and half undressed, to see if the fish had been properly cared for. My wife had had the porter put ice on it in the basement and covered it. I went upstairs into the tavern and the place was full.

There were reporters there with cameras, all asking questions of all natures, but mostly, "Where's the fish?" In my stupor, and from my experience the day before, in having my fish stolen, gave some weird answers such as "I gave it away, I can't find it, and give me time to get sober, will you?" All I knew was that I was not going to come up with that all

Lou Spray poling a supply-laden boat in his early days, before resorts were readily available.

important fish until after I had contacted Karl Kahmann, the taxidermist. He wasn't in when I called his place. About that time I met my wife again and she exclaimed in no uncertain terms, "You get up to bed and stay there until you are presentable." Which I was glad to do to get away from that mob and especially those reporters, who were half drunk and with that "you got to show me" attitude. I had just reached the apartment when up came Karl and was I glad to see him. My wife had shown him the fish and he said as long as it was kept iced it was okay. After the usual congratulations from Karl. I spent the balance of the afternoon in the house.

About 8:00 p.m., I went down to the tavern. The mob had left, just the usual crowd was around. I inspected the fish and found it well iced, so I went out and built a box to display the fish. The next morning I put the fish on display with a glass over the box, kept it well iced and offered a cash prize to the one who could come the nearest to guessing its weight and length, and put a book there for them to register their name and address. By then, for the first time in a couple of days, I was once again myself.

After 36 years, I am looking at that book right now. Pop Adams, who represented a bait company, was the first to register and Ray Noggles, a guide from Hayward, was second. There were 620 entries and after their guesses were all added up and divided by the said 620, the average guess was within a pound of the actual weight of 59 1/2 pounds and there were nine ties. Some amusing guesses, mostly by women were weight 90 pounds, length 29 inches (it had to be 30 inches to be legal). Another was 75 pounds and six feet two inches long. The lowest weight guessed by a man was 46 pounds. The sports writers made much of the bathroom scales that had been used, with full knowledge that it had been officially weighed. Others claimed it was never displayed as I had given it away and others had their own ways of discrediting my catch. Mostly, sports writers in general ran down the facts first and then came up with a favorable story on it. Many of those writers later saw the book that I am looking at right now, and thought some day it was going to be a very prized possession.

In addition to the above story from Louie's book, *My Muskie Days*, I have gathered additional fact and information to add to this story from a series of affidavits that were prepared at the time. First an affidavit stating the following:

> We the undersigned wish to state and declare that we witnessed and saw a fish belonging to Louie Spray of Hayward, Wisconsin, on the 27th of July 1939, that the fish was a musky, that we have seen several large muskies before and that this was the largest musky we have ever seen.

This statement was signed by 18 people. Next is the official statement of the happening released by Louis Spray on July 31, 1939:

> The musky was caught by Louie Spray, Hayward, Wisconsin, between ten and eleven A.M. July 27th, in Grindstone Lake, near Hayward.
>
> The musky was weighed at a cream station operated by W.J. Zecherle, Winter, Wisconsin. Also, at John Geschel's Tavern, Loretta, Wisconsin and on each scale weighed 59 1/2 pounds. The length was 58 inches.
>
> Several people witnessed the weighing and measuring and affidavits of same are on record in the Court House in Hayward, Wisconsin.
>
> The man holding the fish is Alton Van Camp of Loretta, Wisconsin, a licensed guide and life long friend of Spray.
>
> The musky is being mounted and will be on display at Spray's Cafe & Bar, Hayward, Wisconsin, as soon as completed.
>
> Signed, Louie Spray, Hayward, Wisconsin

On October 17, 1979, Louie sent me a note of clarification on the above statement:

> **To Whom It May Concern:**
> For purposes of clarification and with reference to the attached "Release,"

after the fish was weighed at the Cream Station, myself and my fishing pal, Tom Campbell, drove to Park Falls where I was raised to show off the catch. Some of my old buddies whom I was wining and dining, stole the fish, as a joke of course, and wouldn't come up with it until I had bought their fill of grog.

When they finally gave the fish back, Tom and I finished celebrating on the way home via Glidden, Clam Lake, and every Joint on Hy-Way #77, and naturally got home very late like Two Bells in the morning, and was pretty stiff from the consumption of all the grog.

After the fish had been displayed at Spray's Bar for a few days, Karl Kahmann picked up and skinned it out in preparation for mounting. And when I started to look for my camera which had a full spool of film in it, I couldn't find it and never did. I recalled that Alton Van Camp had taken a few shots of the critter with his camera, but there was not a photo of me on it. There was a good picture of Van holding the fish, and this is the picture we used in Officially Registering the catch with the American Museum of Natural History, New York.

The attached "Release" was left at the Bar so the reporters would have the correct dope with which to draft their Story. But as it turned out, some of them did not follow the script to the extent they saw that the fish was weighed on a Bath Room Scale, which it was, but not for official purposes and they knew it.

I've said it before and I say it here now, that if you ever catch a world record musky. Reporters will delight in kicking you in the teeth, and their publishers are of no help in straightening out the wrong they did you.

Additionally on July 31, 1939, comes the following affidavit:

We the undersigned wish to state and declare that we witnessed and saw a musky belonging to Louie Spray of Hayward, Wisconsin, weighed and measured in John Geschel's Tavern, Loretta, Wisconsin, on the 27th day of July, 1939. The weight was 59 1/2 pounds and length was 58 inches.

This was signed by Alton Van Camp, Widmer Smith and John Geschel. Again comes clarification from Louie:

The above mentioned fish was officially weighed at the Winter, Wisconsin, Creamery, Winter, Wisconsin, and was officially recognized as a world record by the American Museum of Natural History, in 1939. And Widmer Smith, one of the affiants above, was the one who knew that the scales should be official in order to have the fish acceptable.

On August 2, 1939, the following affidavit was signed by a Mr. Wm. Harmon:

I, William Harmon, of Hayward, Wisconsin wish to state and declare that on the 27th day of July, 1939, I rented a boat to one Louie Spray of Hayward, Wisconsin and that he returned to my boat landing on Grindstone Lake about nine thirty or ten o'clock the same morning with a musky that measured 58 inches in length This fish would not weigh on a fifty pound scale that we had at the resort.

The final affidavit regarding the 1939 fish comes from a Mr. W.J. Zecherle:

I, W.J. Zecherle of Winter, Wisconsin wish to state and declare that on the 27th day of July 1939, I weighed a musky belonging to Louie Spray, of Hayward, Wisconsin. The weight was 59 1/2 pounds.

In an August 1, 1939 letter to Mr. R.G. Lynch, sports editor of *The Milwaukee Journal*, Louie had the following statement:

Dear Mr. Lynch:

Gordon [MacQuarrie] was here Sunday and found me in none too good a shape Re: the fish. Since Thursday I had taken on a lot of that refreshment that comes in that Black and White package. However, it was a good thing he came along because he woke me up to the fact that Wisconsin as well as myself, had something and since Sunday I have straightened out everything.

I now have the fish back and absolutely under control. He will be in my place of business as soon as the mounting is completed. This however was no small job and naturally took a little time.

There is still one more affidavit to file and I will send you a copy as soon as I get it executed.

Re: these affidavits, they are recorded, but I would like them back if possible.

The only decent photograph I salvaged was one with Alton Van Camp holding the fish. Therefore I am sending a snap of myself, (still full of that stuff) if you care to run it along with the other picture. I still haven't found my Camera containing the best pictures of the thing.

As far as this being a Record Fish. I don't know anything about that, but I guarantee you that the fish is everything we claim it is and it will be here to be looked at by anyone who might be interested.

If there is any further information you might desire I will be only too glad to give it to you.

So, that takes care of Louie's 1939 fish. In as much as Mr. Ellis completely missed Coleman's world record from 1939, let us pause here to review the only discrepancy I have uncovered regarding that fish. The following letter was written to the American Museum of Natural History (then record keepers) on March 18, 1940, by Karl W. Kahmann, a noted Hayward, Wisconsin, taxidermist:

Dear Miss LaMonte:

A Compendium of Musky Angling History

Purely as a matter of putting your institution on its guard as regards the recording of the largest fish caught on hook and line, I will try to point out several things I have noticed in my many years of mounting fish and particularly in the two large muskellunge recorded for the year 1939.

You have all data on length, weight and girth of the fish caught in Grindstone Lake, Wis. by Louis Spray and the one taken in Eagle Lake, Ontario, by J.J. Coleman, so we need not go into this except to call your attention to the fact that the girth of the Spray fish exceeds that of Mr. Coleman's by several inches — and — girth enters very largely into what a fish will weigh.

I have mounted roughly 3000 muskellunge in the past 35 years and naturally can guess the weight of a fish fairly closely, unless it has been filled with sand and gravel, rocks, steel shafting, sash weights, or just plain water, which is too often the case.

In the case of the large muskellunge, a pound or two difference may depend on whether the fish was "drowned" in landing. or whether it was weighed immediately after landing or hours or days afterwards, even where the "filling" referred to above is not done.

I saw the Coleman fish at Marshall Fields Sporting Goods Dept. in Chicago and mounted the Spray fish. I am satisfied that the Coleman fish does not come up to weight or measurements, although it is a fine specimen, certainly a large one, and well mounted.

The mount of Louis Spray's 61-pound 13-ounce musky from 1940.

I am afraid that there is too much commercialization, and too much of "Fisherman's Liberty" in these "Records" for any scientific institution to safely vouch for them. On the other hand. I cannot see how you can do more than to rely on affidavits and

The mount of John Coleman's world record, the first 60-pounder ever recorded.

scaler's record stubs, but these do not show whether the specimen was "filled" before weighing.

It really makes very little difference whether the record musky was caught in Wisconsin, Canada or elsewhere, but it evidently does make a lot of difference to the bait and tackle manufacturers and fishing resort owners.

All my life I have been interested in exact data in bird study and have belonged to just about every ornithological club including the A.O.U. — at present I am Treasurer of the Wisconsin Society of Ornithology — and — I do not envy your position in regards to attempting to vouch for "Fishermen's Record Catches."

Although Kahmann's letter indicated that the girth of Spray's fish exceeded Coleman's by "several inches," the records indicate that Coleman's fish was only one inch less in girth!

Back to Ellis' persecution of Spray:

Louie's record fish became a second best shortly thereafter when Lake St.Claire in Michigan produced a larger 'lunge. (Actually it was the Coleman fish that bested Louie!) But Louie was back out there pitching again in 1940, and sure enough he came up with a musky that weighed 61 pounds 13 ounces.

Wisconsin didn't know whether to be happy or apprehensive about Louie's new claims. It wanted the world-record musky to come from Wisconsin, but it didn't like the stories then making the rounds.

Louie said at the time that he had caught the fish on August 19 in Rice Lake. The night previous a man named Jens Jorgensen of Hayward was in Spray's tavern with a musky that draped from his chin to the floor. He said he had caught the fish in Lac Courte Oreilles. No one ever heard of, nor did anyone ever see, the Jorgensen musky after that night.

Russ Lynch, sports editor of the Milwaukee Journal, and as honest a newspaper man as can be found despite the fact that he flicks his left out front plenty, duly reported the new developments and Louie's answer, which was published follows in part "the old saying is, Once a fisherman always a liar, and a few friendly and harmless jests are welcomed by any sportsman, but that cheap, chippy, chiseling bunch of lousy white lies, insinuations and intimations you wrote in your article could hardly be tolerated by anyone."

Louie continued to maintain he had caught a world-record fish and in some circles he made his claims stick.

It finished second in the *F&S* contest in 1940. Let us now get Louie's story:

When we got him in the boat we put on the tape and it appeared to be around five feet long. We headed straight for Karl Kahmann's taxidermist shop. He had a fairly accurate scale that showed the fish over 60 pounds, but he advised me to go where there was an inspected, sanctioned scale and weigh in.

It was weighed at the Pufahl Hardware with Johnnie Moreland, insurance man, Herb Simminson, city clerk, and Ray Ingersol, Pufahl Hardware employee, as the weighing committee. By now I had learned, no more bathroom scales! The weight was 61 pounds 13 ounces, which was a record. That fish was also placed on display in Spray's Bar and again a prize offered for the nearest weight, length and girth with the weight being the major factor. Here once again, I have the book before me. There were 607 guesses, and six ties. The local Hayward people who tied were: Sigure Tonstad, Henry A. Larsen, manager of the trout pond, Bill Marquardt, golf pro at the Hayward course, Nester Gaden, blacksmith, Gail W. Davis, plumber, and Earnest F. Rice. No one guessed the exact weight, but were within an ounce of it. Nester Gaden, the blacksmith guessed 61 7/8 pounds.

Louie, who had been through it all the previous year, expected the onslaught, and prepared himself with many affidavits of the circumstances surrounding the fish. Following are those affidavits:

August 23, 1940
An Affidavit To Whom It May Concern:

We the undersigned Committee representing the Chamber of Commerce of the City of Hayward, Wisconsin, hereby state and declare under oath that we weighed and measured a muskellunge caught by Louie Spray of the City of Hayward, Wisconsin, at the Pufahl Hardware. That the weight was Sixty One Pounds and Thirteen Ounces (61 lbs. 13 oz.) That the Length was Fifty Nine and One Quarter inches (59 1/4 in.) That the Girth was Thirty Two and One Half inches (32 1/2 in.).

Signed by Committee,
John O. Moreland
Herbert Simonson
Karl W. Kahmann

August 26, 1940
To Whom It May Concern:

I, Louie Spray of the City of Hayward, Wisconsin, herein depose, state and declare under oath, that on the 19th day of August 1940, I, in company with Mr. T.W. Campbell of West Palm Beach, Florida, caught and landed a huge muskellunge in Couderay Lake near Hayward, Wisconsin.

That said muskellunge was weighed and measured in public by a Committee representing the Hayward Chamber of Commerce of the City of Hayward, Wisconsin, and that said muskellunge weighed Sixty One Pounds and Thirteen Ounces (61 lbs. 13 oz.), was Fifty Nine and One Quarter inches in length, (59 1/4 in.) and had a Girth of Thirty Two and One Half inches, (32 1/2 in.).

Further, that said muskellunge was on display in the City of Hayward, Wisconsin, for a period of three days during which time a guessing contest as to weight was conducted. That 607 persons registered their guess and that the total average guess was 62 1/4 pounds.

Further, that said muskellunge is being Mounted by Karl W. Kahmann of the City of Hayward, Wisconsin, and will be on display as soon as completed. That said weights and measurements are Recorded in the Court House in the City of Hayward, Wisconsin.

September 5, 1940
An Affidavit To Whom It May Concern:

This Affidavit concerns two Newspaper articles, namely, the *Rice Lake Chronotype* of Rice Lake, Wisconsin, in their issue of August 21st, 1940, and the *Milwaukee Journal* of Milwaukee, Wisconsin, in their issue of Sunday September 1st, 1940.

In each of the two mentioned issues of the two mentioned Newspapers, my name, Jens Jorgensen, was used and mentioned in connection with a Sixty One Pound Thirteen Ounce, (61 lbs. 13 oz.) muskellunge caught August 19th,1940, by Louis Spray, of Hayward, Wisconsin, intimating and insinuating that there might be something irregular or fictitious concerning and regarding the muskellunge in question in the Newspaper articles mentioned above.

Therefore, I, Jens Jorgensen, of the City of Hayward, Wisconsin, first being duly sworn on Oath, depose, say, state and declare, that I know nothing about the Spray 61-pound 13 -ounce muskellunge, except that I saw it on display at Spray's Cafe & Bar, Hayward, Wisconsin. Further, that I had nothing to do with catching or helping to catch the muskellunge herein mentioned.

Signed Jens Jorgenson

September 7, 1940
An Affidavit To Whom It May Concern:

I, Ray Ingersoll of the City of Hayward, Wisconsin, being first duly sworn on oath, depose, say, state and declare, that I am employed at the Pufahl Hardware Co. of the City of Hayward.

That on the 22nd day of August 1940, a muskellunge was brought into the Pufahl Hardware Store to be weighed by John O. Moreland, Herbert Simonson and Karl W. Kahmann, a Committee in charge and Louie Spray, the owner, all of Hayward, Wisconsin.

That I weighed and measured the muskellunge in the usual manner. That the Weight was Sixty One Pounds Thirteen Ounces, (61 lbs. 13 oz.). That the Length was Fifty Nine and One Quarters inches (59 1/4). That the Girth was Thirty Two and One Half inches (32 1/2 in.).

Signed Ray Ingersoll

In addition to these affidavits I have had in my possession and now have a photocopy of the book Louie mentioned with the guesses of weight for the fish. It is exactly as he stated.

Again quoting Ellis:

The resort business on the musky lakes boomed right after the war, and then business began to fall off, until by summer of 1949 it was labeled as far from good in many areas. There was no doubt that the resort business needed a shot in the arm.

Another world-record musky would be nice and it might do the job, so on July 24th of that summer Cal Johnson of Teal Lake accommodated by beaching a 67 1/2 pound fish. It was caught in Lac Courte Oreilles, Johnson said.

In the beginning, everybody was pretty happy about that musky. Cal Johnson is a professional fisherman and an outdoor writer of many year's standing. It was fine to have a man who had taken thousands of muskies to be catching a world record fish.

The mount of Cal Johnson's 1949 world record 67-pound 8-ounce musky remains on display in Hayward, Wisconsin.

Johnson told how he and his son, Phil, and Jack Connor, an outdoor writer for a Minneapolis paper, got out on the lake just as a thunderstorm was grumbling its way off into the distance. He told this story:

"It was still raining a little and there were some lightning flashes in the east and the thunder was still rumbling. But it was a musky morning, I said, "You can smell muskies. If we don't connect this morning, we never will.

"I took the stern position in the boat. Connor went to the bow and Phil, who was guiding, stayed at the oars."

Johnson tells of how they trolled and how the big fish latched on and how it felt as if he was tied to a log.

"For thirty minutes he stayed right down just bulldogging and then he started to tire. I knew it would be impossible to lift him on a gaff into the boat, so I told Phil to row slowly to shore. It took us another thirty minutes to coax him to shore.

"Phil jumped over the side then, raincoat and all, into waist-deep water. The big fish was rolling by this time, so Phil set the gaff beneath the gill cover and began running. The head of the fish was under his fanned-out coat, and the big tail was churning. Phil didn't stop running until he was thirty feet back on dry land."

Johnson then told how the fish was weighed and the witnesses' statements notarized, and Wisconsin and especially resort owners around Hayward celebrated and almost everybody was dandy about the whole thing until — wham! bang! blooey! — like some of that lightning that had been playing around on the morning of the big catch — Connor suddenly announced that he had not been in the boat with Johnson and did not see the fish caught.

So another world record 'lunge became just a little tainted, because both Johnson and Connor stuck by their stories. Later, however, Johnson admitted that Connor had not been in the boat nor did he see the fish landed.

Johnson's enemies immediately said, "He had it tied out in the woods fattening it." His friends said "Johnson knew no one would believe he had caught a world record musky, so he said Connor was with him just to bolster his story. You can't blame him, the way things have been in Wisconsin lately."

Johnson's musky was first recognized as legitimate by *Outdoors*, a magazine which has since been combined with *Outdoorsman* (in turn combined with *Hunting and Fishing*), and the prize of a new automobile was awarded to Mr. Johnson.

The Milwaukee Sentinel had a vital interest in the Cal Johnson fish, and went to great lengths to clear the mess up as is evidenced in *Sentinel* Outdoor Editor Lew Morrison's column:

What's the Lowdown on the Big Musky?

What's back of certain rumors that are bringing discredit to the state and to the Hayward area in particular?

Yes, what is really behind all this fuss and what does it really amount to?

The Sentinel is vitally interested in this world's record musky, because it represents a most valuable asset to the state's recreational interests. Any shenanigans should be exposed.

But likewise, if the catch was on the up and up, as the real facts reveal it to be, unwarranted rumors can bring irreparable harm to the entire state.

In view of what transpired lately, the Sentinel moved into action, determined to get to the bottom of things.

As a result of a very careful and thorough investigation, here are hard, cold facts that cannot be denied.

Facts Prove Legality of Big Catch

All of the facts, without a single exception, clearly and conclusively prove beyond the slightest shadow of doubt that the world's record musky taken by Cal Johnson in Lac Courte Oreilles on the morning of July 24, was legally caught, accurately weighed and measured, witnessed by reputable citizens and the papers officially certified by notary John Moreland, well known member of the Wisconsin Conservation Commission, who inspected the fish personally.

It might clarify several things if it is pointed out here that the *Sentinel* made an agreement with Cal Johnson on the Monday forenoon following the catch whereby the *Sentinel* obtained the exclusive rights to exhibit the fish in Wisconsin.

The first showing of this world's record musky in Wisconsin therefore, will be at the *Sentinel* Sports and Vacation show next April, except for the Hayward celebration referred to later in the story.

In the interests of clarity, let's start at the beginning of this memorable fishing trip.

On the evening of July 23, Cal Johnson, his son Phillip and Jack Connor, outdoor editor of the *Minneapolis Star*, drove to Moccasin Lodge on Lac Courte Oreilles to do some fishing the next day.

But when the morning alarm called them it was raining and Connor, at the last moment decided to try for bass in another boat.

Cal and his son started to troll immediately after leaving the dock. In less than half an hour the big fish hit.

The battle lasted about an hour and ended when the fish was beached.

Before returning, Cal moved out to where Connor could see him and waved him in, both boats arriving a few minutes apart.

Word Flashed of Record Musky

The hour (6 o'clock) was early for most Sunday morning vacationists, but as word of the world's record musky spread, the place was soon overrun with people.

The first story out of Hayward, said Connor, Cal and his son were fishing together. Another had it that Connor had caught the fish. In this, all three are equally responsible for allowing this impression to remain. But before passing judgment, it might be well to consider that in the excitement, "toasts" certainly were in order for an event of this kind. They might have been coming pretty fast and things might have been said in the spirit of the moment without giving much thought to them.

And even if it might have been agreed at the moment that Connor was to share in the glory of the catch, what of it? Any way you look at it, it is trivial. But let's give Cal credit for standing by Connor when the latter later reversed his position.

Facts Available for All to Verify

Really the only pertinent factors in this affair are whether the fish was legally taken, and whether weights and measurements were accurate and properly witnessed.

The facts are available for anyone to verify.

Here is one clinching fact that proves the legality of the record catch:

The fish was immediately turned over to Karl Kahmann, Hayward taxidermist, who is not only an expert on muskies, but is a man who bears a most enviable reputation.

Before coming to Wisconsin, Kahmann practiced taxidermy in Chicago for some 25 years. He has done work for leading museums, as well as individuals, during which time he and his staff handled close to 5,000 muskies. He, therefore, speaks with more than passing authority.

We asked Karl if, in his examination of the fish prior to preparing it for mounting, he had found any evidence of disease. His reply was "no."

That disposes of the question of whether the fish was "found" as some rumors had it.

Fish Not Penned, Netted or Trapped

We next asked him whether there were any abrasions on the nose or tail that would definitely show up if the fish had been penned, netted or trapped?

His answer was "no."

Asked whether any marks on the jaw might show that the hooks had been freshly removed, he replied "yes."

When asked how he was sure the fish was freshly caught, he answered:

"It certainly was a freshly caught fish because rigor mortis had not set in when the fish was delivered to me about 6:30 on the morning of July 24."

Karl further stated that the weights were double checked and that two scales gave exactly the same reading ... 67 pounds, 8 ounces. Both scales are now being state inspected. Measurements, he said, were taken with a steel tape.

Now forgetting for the moment that Cal Johnson is a sportsman of national reputation, and that his writings over the years portray his character better than anything we can say about him. Karl Kahmann's statements definitely eliminate all possibility that the fish might have been speared, netted or trapped.

The fish didn't die of disease or old age. It did not carry so much as a bullet mark because the fish was gaffed. The fish was still limp when weighed and measured. With all this evidence clear and above board, just where, we ask, can there be any deception?

In his column in the *Minneapolis Star*, July 25, Connor writes: "So it's no wonder Cal Johnson is wearing that ear to ear smile for his world record muskellunge — 67 pounds, 8 ounces of it.

"His feat climaxes two years of effort to nail this particular fish, which measures 60 1/4 inches long, 33 1/2 inches in girth."

And Charles Johnson, sports editor of the *Minneapolis Star*, had this to say:

... "Today comes an official looking affidavit from Cal Johnson

Noted Hayward taxidermist Karl Kahmann at work on Cal Johnson's musky.

with the signature of a member of the Wisconsin conservation commission along with others as proof of the catch.

"More power to you, Cal. We never had any doubts. The only thing that makes us mad is that we weren't on the receiving end ..."

There is only one exception to the *Sentinel's* exclusive Wisconsin showing of Cal Johnson's world's record musky. This exception will be at Hayward when a celebration befitting the occasion is planned for around Labor Day, depending on how soon the fish can be mounted. The musky's permanent home will be in Hayward.

It is planned to have Gov. Rennebohm to do the honors, assisted by Conservation Commissioner John Moreland and other conservation and civic leaders.

Cal will make his first Wisconsin appearance at the *Sentinel* Sports and Vacation Show next April in his famous bait casting act. Sports Show director, Charles D. Collins, plans also to have Cal show how he lands a world's record musky in the big tank in the main arena of the auditorium.

The world's record musky will be on display in a special booth at the *Sentinel* Show and Cal will be on hand every day and evening to give anglers the benefit of his rich experience.

And here's something else about Cal I want to clarify. He is not the "poor" boy some have pictured. Neither does he run a resort. Instead, he has a lodge and one guest cottage for his friends on Teal Lake. He writes for a number of magazines and manufacturers of outing equipment and was recently retained by the Chicago International Sports and Outdoor Show in Chicago to handle its public relations.

His musky will be exclusively shown in Chicago at the Amphitheater Show.

You don't hire a brass band to accompany you on a musky trip. Neither do you set up a standard to check your movements. And you don't just snag into a world record musky every day either.

The result is that in taking a record fish there is always a doubter. But Cal Johnson's record breaking musky has been documented by the most reputable men in Wisconsin's north country. We' re completely satisfied that everything is on the level.

Finally, Ellis attacks Spray's 1949 World Record:

Spray said he caught his new record fish on October 20 between 5:30 and 6 p. m. with an 18-inch sucker off Fleming's bar in the Chippewa Flowage. He said that in the boat with him were Ted Hagg, a tavern keeper from Sarona, Wisconsin, and a Hayward guide, George Quentmeyer. There was the usual story of how the fish was finally boated, but then shortly after the news got around, along comes one Tony Burmek, another Hayward guide, who said: "I was fishing on Fleming's bar and Pete's bar, right near it, from three o'clock until dark on October twentieth, and Spray was not there. Nobody else was there. Spray wasn't on Fleming's bar the day before either. Fleming's bar is only two blocks long, and I don't see how I could have overlooked another boat, especially if it spent forty-five minutes landing a fish as big as that one."

Right away Nathan W. Heller of the Lie Detector Laboratories in Milwaukee announced through The Milwaukee Journal that he would examine free of charge any musky fisherman who might want to prove his stories. His offer still stands, but he has received no takers.

Burmek came in for considerable criticism from resort owners who wanted to know whether he was for or against Hayward. "You are one of Hayward's leading guides," they said, "and you should be proud of Hayward."

Burmek, in a long letter to the press, explained that he was proud of Hayward, but added that he certainly would like to see this musky mess cleaned up.

And so would a lot of people in Wisconsin, and in some other states that claim the 'lunge as a head-liner in their resort advertising.

But what is done is done, and both Johnson's fish and the one Spray said he caught have been recog-nized in some cir-

Ted Haag (left) and Louis Spray with the mount of the 69-pound 11-ounce world record.

cles as world record catches. Considering the notarized statements these men submitted, the judges had no other choice.

Could Ellis' article be considered sensational journalism? The "cir-cles" he refers to are the official' record sources; his article is not with-standing! Let us return now to Louie Spray's story after the catch:

We headed for Herman's Landing where the grog flowed freely for a few minutes — then to Hayward to weigh it, but the stores were closed.

We stopped at Charlie Pastika's Bait Shop, but he had no scales. We stopped at Stroner's Store, but his grocery scales would not weigh it either, so we went down Highway 27 and on out to Karl Kahmann's, the taxidermist, whose scale I thought would weigh it, but Karl had had his fill of world record muskies, with the Cal Johnson catch that had beaten me not too long before. He showed us how they had to get a bulldozer in to make a road from his shop back to the main road, because the narrow road into his place from the Town Road had become so plugged with cars when the word got around that Cal's fish was out there, that they, nor anyone else, could get out of the yard. They tore up his lawn: they backed over his shrubbery and did untold damage to his grounds. Karl said, "Get it out of here and don't come back." I reasoned with him that due to our long and continued friendship that I was quite perturbed by his attitude toward me. He calmed down and said that he was not angry with me or anyone else but just did not want to be bothered with the mob again. I was sure down in the dumps because, who could I get to mount such an important fish, should it be a Record? When we got to Stone Lake, Ted said he was thirsty for a drink of water. (Imagine Ted drinking water!) So we stopped at Smock's Tavern to get it and show off the fish. We were asking about scales and someone mentioned that Jack Reinke, the postmaster, might come down and weigh it. The post office was alongside of Smock's Tavern and Jack did come down to weigh it. It was 69 pounds 11 ounces ... a new world record. We set up some whoopee then and there, and Ted had had enough "water" (on the side), we headed on for home but I was very worried about who would mount that fish.

It was late when I got home so I carefully packed the fish in ice in the basement and got busy on the phone looking for a good qualified taxidermist. Les Fossum, a bait and tackle salesman, told me about a man in Wausau, Wisconsin, whom I called. He said he wanted to look at it before making any decision, so early the next morning I was on my way over there. His store and shop was located out of Wausau a ways, at Schofield. He asked me why I did not have Karl Kahmann mount it and I told him why. Then he was afraid of a mob busting into the place and informed me that he was not equipped to handle a multitude of curiosity seekers. However, after some coffee and get-acquainted talk, he promised to do the job, providing I kept it strictly confidential. I left the fish with him and didn't even tell my wife where it was. Because of this, the fish was not placed on display before it was mounted, as had the other two record muskies I had caught. All in all, I was very disappointed because I could not display it or even tell where it was, so naturally, once again I got some very unfavorable publicity from sports writers and such, but good old Hugh Lackey, the taxidermist, went right to work and I soon had the fish on display, and the gossip, rumors, and "you gotta show me" attitude, narrowed down to the fact that someone must have caught the critter because there it was. I finally got the gang off my back.

Now that we have Louie's story, let's back it up with proof. The first bit of proof was obtained immediately after the weighing of the fish on a United States postal scale. On United States Post Office stationary is the following:

10/20/49 69 pound 11 ounce musky weighed, above date. 63 1/2 inches in length 31 1/4 inches in girth, Witnessed by J.C. Reinke, George Quentmeyer, T.A. Hagg, Louis Spray.

A short time later, Louis got busy and obtained affidavits from everyone involved, from the people with him right on through the taxidermist(s). Following are those affidavits:

Ted Hagg, of Sarona, Wisconsin, being first duly sworn, on oath says that he accompanied Louis Spray of Rice Lake, Wis. on October 20th, 1949, on a fishing trip, and was present in the boat with him and George Quentmeyer, licensed guide of Hayward, Wisconsin. That the three of them fished together from the same boat near Herman's Landing on the Chippewa Flowage near Hayward, Wisconsin. That at about 4:00 p.m. on that date he saw Mr. Louis Spray hook and land on rod, reel and line, a muskellunge weighing 69 pounds 11 ounces and measuring 5 feet 3 1/2 inches long. That although he did not time the actual fight he would estimate that to the best of his knowledge, it took approximately 45 minutes to land said fish. That Mr. Spray fought and landed the fish without any assistance except that the guide George Quentmeyer shot the fish twice. That to the best of his recollection the fish was landed at approximately 4:00 p.m. That he went with the said Louis Spray and George Quentmeyer from Herman's Landing on the Chippewa Flowage where they got the boat and where they landed with the fish, to Pastika's Bait and Tackle Shop to obtain ice, thence to Stroner's Store at Hayward, Wisconsin to have the musky weighed. That the scales at Stroner's store were not large enough to weigh the fish so they proceeded to the Stone Lake, Wisconsin post office where the fish was weighed in my presence by Jack Heinke, local postmaster, on the governmental post office scales. That the said fish weighed 69 pounds 11 ounces. That I was present when Mr. Reinke measured the fish with a steel tape and that it measured 63 1/2 inches in length and 31 1/2 inches in girth. That the said fish was weighed at the Stone Lake post office at approximately 6:45 p.m. on that date. That thereafter they proceeded to the shop of Karl Kahmann, taxidermist at Hayward, Wisconsin, and inquired whether or not he would mount the fish. That Mr. Kahmann said it would be impossible for him to get at the job for from 60 to 90 days so it was taken to another taxidermist.

Signed, Ted Hagg

George Quentmeyer, of Hayward, Wisconsin, being first duly sworn, on oath says that he is a licensed guide and that on the 20th of October, 1949, he was employed by Louis Spray of Rice Lake, Wisconsin. That he accompanied Mr. Spray together with Ted Hagg of Sarona, Wisconsin on a fishing expedition on the Chippewa Flowage near Hayward, Wisconsin. That they put out from Herman's Landing and fished for several hours. That while accompanying Mr. Spray on this occasion Louis Spray did hook and land with rod, reel and line a muskellunge weighing 69 pounds 11 ounces and measuring 63 1/2 inches long. That your affiant shot the fish twice but that otherwise the fish was hooked, played and landed by Mr. Louis Spray without any assistance, except that this affiant also helped lift the fish into the boat. That he was present in the boat with Mr. Spray as was Mr. Hagg at all times above described. That he would estimate that it took Mr. Spray approximately 50 minutes to land the fish. That the bait used was a sucker minnow, and that the fish was finally landed at about 4:00 p.m. of that date. That they then proceeded to Herman's Landing where they showed the fish to the proprietor and his wife. That from there they proceeded to Pastika's Bait and Tackle Shop to obtain ice. Then to Stroner's store at Hayward to have the fish weighed. That when it was discovered that Stroner's scales were not large enough to weigh said fish they proceeded to the Stone Lake post office where the fish was weighed in the presence of this affiant and in the presence of Mr. Spray and Mr. Hagg by Jack Reinke, Stone Lake postmaster. That the fish was weighed on the official post office scales and that it weighed 69 pounds 11 ounces. That after the fish was weighed Mr. Reinke measured the same with a steel tape. That from the tip of the tail to the tip of the snout the fish measured 63 1/2 inches and around the girth that the said fish was 31 1/4 inches. That the said fish was so measured in my presence.

Signed, George Quentmeyer

Herman Ceranske and Edna E. Ceranske, his wife, being first duly sworn, on oath do each for themselves say that they are the proprietors of a resort known as Herman's Landing located on the Chippewa Flowage near Hayward, Wisconsin. That they were present at their resort on the 20th of October, 1949. That they, of their own personal knowledge, know that Mr. Louis Spray and Mr. Ted Hagg fished the Chippewa Flowage in a boat rented from them in the company of each other and in the company of Mr. George Quentmeyer, licensed guide, of Hayward, Wisconsin. That at about 4:15 p.m. of said day, they were present when the above named parties landed at Herman's Landing with the same boat they had rented from them and that Mr. Spray had in his possession the largest muskellunge that either of them had ever seen. That the musky had been freshly caught and the parties told them Mr. Spray had just caught it. That present with them at the time that Spray, Hagg and Quentmeyer landed was one Mr. Nixon Barnes, a carpenter of Hayward, Wisconsin. That Mr. Barnes measured the fish in the presence of all the above named people and claimed it measured 5'4" long. That this is by far the largest muskellunge that we or any of us had ever seen. That we did not have a scale at our resort strong enough to weigh said fish and it was not weighed in our presence.

Signed, Edna E. Ceranske
Herman Ceranske

Nixon Barnes, being first duly sworn, on oath says that he is by occupation a carpenter and that he was at Herman's Landing on the Chippewa Flowage on the 20th day of October, 1949 at about 4:15 p.m., when Louis Spray, Ted Hagg and George Quentmeyer landed at said resort and had with them a muskellunge which they all said Mr. Spray had caught in the Chippewa Flowage. That it was by far the largest muskellunge I had ever seen. That I measured the same and found it measured 5'4" long. That there was no scale at Herman's Landing sufficient to weigh the fish so it was not weighed there. The fish was undoubtedly freshly caught at the time we had seen it.

Signed, Nixon Barnes

Charles Pastika, being first duly sworn, on oath says that he is the owner of Pastika's Bait and Tackle Shop near Hayward, Wisconsin. That he was present in said shop at approximately 6:00 p.m. on October 20th, 1949 when Mr. Louis Spray, Mr. Ted Hagg, and Mr. George Quentmeyer came to said shop to obtain ice with which to pack a large musky. That I saw said musky and that it was undoubtedly the largest musky I had ever seen. That I did not weigh or measure said musky. That I did observe that it was freshly caught and that Hagg, Spray and Quentmeyer all said that Mr. Spray had just caught it from Herman's Landing on the Chippewa Flowage. That the parties did not stay at my shop very long as they were in a hurry to have the fish weighed and measured.

Signed, Charles Pastika

Jake Jordan of Hayward, Wisconsin, being first duly sworn, says that he was at Pastika's Boat & Tackle Shop at about 6:00 p.m. on October 20, 1949, when Mr. Louis Spray, Mr. Ted Hagg and Mr. George Quentmeyer came in said shop for ice. That Mr. Spray displayed a large muskellunge which he had just caught in the Chippewa Flowage. That the musky was undoubtedly the largest that he had ever seen and that it was obviously freshly caught. Mr. Spray stated in the presence of myself and Mr. Pastika and the others that he had caught the fish on Fleming's Bar in the Chippewa Flowage on a large sucker minnow.

Signed, Jake Jordan

Milton Stroner, says, being first duly sworn on oath, that he is the proprietor of Stroner's Store at Hayward, Wisconsin. That on Thursday, October 20, 1949, while we were having our evening meal, Mr. Louis Spray, Mr. Ted Hagg and Mr. George Quentmeyer called at the store and showed us the largest musky that I have ever seen. Mr. Spray had just caught the same in the Chippewa Flowage near here and wanted to have it weighed and measured. However, the scale I had in my store would not weight anything over 35 pounds so it was impossible to weigh the fish. Mr. Spray then brought some gas at my store and the three of them again departed with the fish.

Signed, Milton Stroner

Jack Reinke, of Stone Lake. Wisconsin, being first duly sworn on oath, says that he is the postmaster of the Stone Lake, Wisconsin post office. That about 6:45 p.m. on October 20, 1949, he was called upon by Mr. Louis Spray, George Quentmeyer and Ted Hagg. who had in their possession the largest muskellunge that he had ever seen. That all of the parties said that Mr. Spray had caught it that afternoon in the Chippewa Flowage near Hayward. That at their request we proceeded to the post office where I personally weighed the fish on the post office scales. That the fish weighed 69 pounds 11 ounces. That thereupon I measured the fish with a steel tape and it measured 63 1/2 inches long. That I measured the girth of the fish and that the same measured 31 1/4 inches. That Louis Spray. George Quentmeyer and Ted Hagg were present when I weighed and measured said fish.

Signed, Jack Reinke

Karl W. Kahmann, being first duly sworn, on oath says that he is a taxidermist at Hayward, Wisconsin, and that in the evening of October 20, 1949, Mr. Louis Spray called at his shop with a muskellunge which Spray claimed weighed 69 pounds 11 ounces and was a new world's record. That I personally saw said musky although had not measured or weighed it. That I saw the same was freshly caught and was undoubtedly one of the largest muskies I had ever seen. That Mr. Spray requested me to mount said musky but that I advised Mr. Spray it could not be done by me within the next 60 to 90 days and that I advised Mr. Spray that if he wished the musky mounted sooner he should attempt to get some other taxidermist to do the same.

Signed, Karl W. Kahmann

I, Hugh A. Lackey, being first duly sworn on oath, says that he is a taxidermist at Schofield, Wisconsin, and that on Saturday, October 22nd, 1949, Mr. Louis Spray of Rice Lake, Wisconsin, delivered to him a very large musky to mount. That Spray told him it was a world record musky. That a price was agreed upon and that he would mount the musky, provided such information was kept from the press and public until after the mounting was completed. That examination of the musky disclosed that there was nothing inside or out to add artificial weight. That I am mounting the musky and it will be ready for delivery about November 20th, 1949.

Signed, Hugh A. Lackey

Now for a moment let us review the statement and subsequent newspaper articles surrounding the Burmek allegations. First, here are the newspaper articles as written by R.G. Lynch, sports editor, the first dated November 12, 1949, followed later by the second one:

Where Was Louie on the Afternoon of Oct. 20?

Louis Spray, Rice Lake tavern keeper, says his latest world record musky was caught about 5:30 or 6 o'clock on the afternoon of Oct. 20 off Fleming's bar in the Chippewa Flowage. Now comes Tony Burmek, a Hayward guide, who says: "I was fishing on Fleming's bar and Pete's bar, right near it, from 3 o'clock until dark on Oct. 20, and Spray was not there. Nobody else was there." Spray has two witnesses to his catch — another tavern keeper, Ted Hagg of Sarona, and a Hayward guide, George Quentmeyer, who say that they were in the boat with him.

Quentmeyer has said: "Several of us knew there was a big fish on Fleming's bar. Spray and Hagg had been after it for three weeks. I worked with them the last three days. Thursday, we worked from noon until 5:30 or 6. There was quite a fuss when Louie hooked the big one, then it went down and Louie gave him plenty of time before he brought it in and I shot it. About 45 minutes, I think."

Now Burmek says: "Spray wasn't on Fleming's bar the day before, either. He was hanging around the Dun-Rovin resort. That was Wednesday. On Thursday, I didn't see him at all. Fleming's bar is only two blocks long and I don't see how I could have overlooked another boat, especially if it spent 45 minutes landing a fish as big as that one."

Suggests Lie Test

Spray's musky weighed 69 pounds, 11 ounces. It surpassed a record fish of 67 pounds 8 ounces brought in July 24 on Lac Courte Oreilles by Cal Johnson, a Hayward outdoor writer. Spray had told Johnson that he would beat Johnson's fish before the season ended.

"Cal was cussing Spray all over Hayward," reports Burmek, who has returned home to 4173 N. 15th St. for the winter." I told him it was up to him to challenge Spray's fish. I said, 'Challenge him to a lie detector test, Cal. Tell him you'll take the test if he will.' Cal thought that was a good idea, but the next time I saw him he didn't think so much of it."

The sports editor can understand why Johnson might not think the lie detector test such a good idea, in view of the fact that he first said that Jack Conner, Minneapolis newspaperman, was in the boat when he landed the fish, next called Conner a liar after Jack denied having been with him, and finally admitted that Conner had not been along.

The lie detector test is a good idea. We pass Burmek's suggestion along to *Field & Stream* and the American Museum of Natural History. Before they authenticate the muskies of either Johnson or Spray as world record rod and reel catches, why not, in view of the conflicting stories, ask these men to submit to the lie detector?

Wouldn't that be something? A lie detector test for fishermen!

The following letters were received after Lynch's column appeared:
Free Lie Detector Tests Offered Musky Men

Mr. Lynch: I read your column which contained Mr. Burmek's suggestion of lie detector tests for the men who caught the record musky. To my knowledge, the polygraph (lie detector) has never been used to test the veracity of a fisherman. The idea is novel and in this instance meritorious, considering that a world record is involved. I have never engaged in fishing, nor do I know of any of the individuals named in your article, and therefore I can have no personal bias in the dispute. In the interest of good sportsmanship, I offer to examine free of charge as many of the individuals involved as will submit willingly to a lie detector test.

Respectfully submitted,
Nathan W. Heller,
Lie Detection Laboratories
632 N. 2nd St.

P.S. And *The Journal* will pay the expenses of Louis Spray and Cal Johnson, who caught the controversial muskies, if they will come to Milwaukee for such tests. This would get Hayward more national publicity than it ever has had before.

Burmek Explains

Mr. Lynch: Since you printed in your column my statement that I was on Fleming's bar in the Chippewa Flowage Oct. 20 from 3 p.m. to dark and did not see Louis Spray who claims he caught his world record musky there late that afternoon and my suggestion of lie detector tests for both Spray and Cal Johnson, who caught a record musky some weeks before, I have received many letters from resort owners and friends in Hayward, who ask, "Are you for or against Hayward?" They add, "You are one of Hayward's leading guides and should be proud of Hayward."

Certainly, I am proud of Hayward, but I am also a sportsman and will answer honestly and to the best of my knowledge any question put to me about these fish. Since I returned to Milwaukee, many persons have said, "You're a Hayward guide. What's the dope on those record fish?" How many of those Hayward folks can honestly say that they have not been asked the same questions?

Everyone knows there have been some things, confusing to the public, about how and where these fish were caught If, through my suggestion to you, pressure is brought to bring out the true stories about these fish, then I will be of service to Hayward.

Nobody doubts that the record belongs to Hayward. Cal Johnson is a personal friend of mine and I honestly believe he caught his musky. But I was on Fleming's bar at the time Spray claimed he caught his fish there and I did not see him. Because of that, and because many doubted Cal also, I suggested the lie detector test.

Julien Gingras, editor of the Hayward newspaper, suggested on the same page that Spray's record fish was announced, that the conservation commission should set a time limit for a full report of a record catch to a game warden, county official or licensed taxidermist. He said:

"In any other sports field, the requisite for a world record is very rigid and I believe fishing records should be given the same standards by which to qualify for a world record."

Boosts Hayward

Hayward enjoys a reputation as one of this country's finest fishing areas. I have chosen to guide there for that reason, having fished all over northern Wisconsin.

A Review of Muskellunge World Records

Hayward shipped more fish out of the state in 1947 than any other city in Wisconsin. The conservation department reported that of a total of 3,348 shipments, 432 went from Hayward. Woodruff was second with 287. In 1948, more than 670 muskies with a combined weight of over six tons were taken from the Chippewa Flowage, according to an article in the Wisconsin Conservation bulletin.

More muskies are caught in the Hayward area, I believe, than anywhere else. Such lakes as the Chippewa, Couderay, Grindstone. Callahan, upper and lower Twin, Tigercat, Spider, Teal, Lost Land, Round and others are very productive musky waters. Nelson Lake (Totogatic flowage) is famous for fine pike fishing. The area also abounds with good trout streams.

Yes. I am proud of Hayward and will sing its praises. but always honestly, because I believe as a guide that one of the major requisites is to teach our fellow fishermen good honest sportsmanship.

Yours sincerely,
Tony Burmek
4173 N. 15th St.

The foregoing articles were sent to me by Tony Burmek in the late 1970s, and had the following note:

I was the only one who showed up for the lie detector test. Neither Spray or Cal showed up.

I then wrote to Louie Spray to get his version. On January 14, 1980, I received the following comment:

On the matter of the Burmek thing, that he said I wasn't on Fleming's bar at all that day, see pages 4 and 5 (of affidavits) or there about.

And to this day I have never met either of these fine gentlemen. And they even paid the attorney fees to make the affidavits.

These affidavits are from anglers who disagree with Burmek. The affidavits referred to are as follows:

Elmer Germanson, being first duly sworn, on oath does depose and say that he is a resident of Hayward, Wisconsin, and that on the 20th day of October, 1949, he was fishing on the Chippewa Flowage with Carl Haag, also of Hayward, Wis. That he and Mr. Haag were fishing at Pine Point which is located about 3/4th of a mile from Treeland Pines Resort, and approximately four miles north of Fleming's Bar on the Chippewa Flowage. That they commenced fishing at about 8:00 in the morning and that they fished at this location all day until sundown. That they did not leave the water to eat but just pulled their boat over to shore and ate the lunch they brought with them. That while they were so fishing and after they had started fishing, one Tony Burmek. Milwaukee, Wisconsin, was fishing near them in an aluminum boat from the

Dun-Rovin Lodge. That he is personally acquainted with Tony Burmek. That he knows that Tony Burmek is a licensed guide. That on October 20, 1949, Tony Burmek was guiding a fishing party fishing crappies and sunfish. That Burmek fished in the same vicinity with your affiant and that they carried on conversations back and forth during the afternoon. That Burmek did not leave the spot where they all were fishing near Pine Point until he quit fishing in the evening. That Burmek quit fishing before Carl Haag and this affiant did: and when he quit, he proceeded in an easterly direction directly toward the Dun Rovin Lodge from which he had brought his boat.

That he knows of his own personal knowledge that the said Tony Burmek couldn't have been anywhere near Fleming's Bar on the Chippewa Flowage during the afternoon of October 20th, as he was always within our sight and was always near Pine Point, which is at least four miles from Fleming's Bar by water. That it has recently come to the attention of your affiant that said Burmek has since made statements to the effect that on the 20th day of October, 1949, the said Burmek was fishing on Fleming's Bar. and that he had fished there all afternoon. That he had not seen Louis Spray there, and therefore inferred that Louis Spray could not have caught the world's record musky on that date.

That your affiant specifically remembers that he was fishing near Burmek on the 20th of October because of personal conversations had with Burmek and with Carl Haag on that date, and because he remembers specifically that he heard on the next day about Louis Spray having caught the world's record musky. That both dates stick firmly in his mind and he knows there is no confusion about them.

That your affiant has no personal interest in making this affidavit. That he is not a personal friend of Mr. Louis Spray, and that he is making this affidavit for the sole purpose of bringing the truth to the public.

Signed, Elmer Germanson

Carl Haag, being first duly sworn on oath says that he is a resident of Hayward, Wisconsin. That he was fishing on the Chippewa Flowage with Mr. Elmer Germanson on the 20th day of October, 1949, at a place known as Pine Point which is located near the Treeland Pines Resort. That he knows of his own personal knowledge that said Pine Point is at least four miles from Fleming's Bar on the Chippewa Flowage, which is the spot where Louis Spray caught the world's record musky on October 20th, 1949.

That he and Mr. Germanson commenced fishing near Pine Point at about 8:00 in the morning and that they fished continuously at that spot until sundown. That they did not leave the water even to eat lunch but ate their lunch from the boat. That in the afternoon of said day while they were fishing, he saw another boat fishing near them. That Elmer Germanson and one of the occupants of the other boat carried on a great deal of conversation during the afternoon. That he asked Elmer Germanson who the other man was, and that Germanson told him he was Tony Burmek of Milwaukee. That this was the first time that your affiant had ever seen Tony Burmek to his own knowledge and that he recalls specifically the man and his characteristics. That he knows that said Tony Burmek fished near Germanson and himself until just before sundown. and that when Burmek left, he proceeded directly east back to the location of the Dun-Rovin Lodge from where he had gotten his boat.

That thereafter he saw in the Milwaukee papers an article written by Lynch in his column known as "Maybe I'm Wrong" in which one Tony Burmek claims to have been fishing on Fleming's Bar on October 20, 1949, and also claimed that he did not see Louis Spray in the neighborhood of Fleming's Bar on that date. That immediately upon seeing the article he remembered that this was the same Burmek from Milwaukee that Germanson had talked to on the 20th of October, 1949. That this was the first time he had ever met Tony Burmek and that he recalls the day specifically because the next day he heard about Louis Spray having caught the world's record musky at Fleming's Bar and had commented to many people that he was only four miles from the spot when it was caught and remarked about the fact that they had been fishing in the wrong place. That he immediately brought this article to the attention of Elmer Germanson and that Mr. Germanson suggested that the two of them make affidavits of the true circumstances.

That your affiant has no personal interest in the affair other than the establishing of the truth. That he is not a personal friend of Louis Spray. That he makes this affidavit of his own free volition and not at the request of any other person than Elmer Germanson.

Signed, Carl Haag

SPRAY'S COMMENT: On the matter of the affidavits, pages 4 and 5 of this Album, some of the news media splashed all over the front page, that Tony Burmek claimed that he had fished all day on Fleming's Bar, where I caught the fish, and that I was never on that Bar, that day. But George Quentmeyer, a guide, who was with I and Ted Hagg when I caught the fish, jumped Burmek about the matter, and Tony denied saying it. The above has to do with the 69-pound 1- ounce musky I caught on Fleming's Bar, October 20, 1949, in the Chippewa Flowage, Sawyer County, Wisconsin.

And so it went! Let us one last time return to Mr. Ellis, who in the July/August 1980 issue of *Wisconsin Sportsman*, saw fit to dust off his earlier story, rename it, "The Great Musky Hustle," and start things over, with the same inaccuracies as before. In addition, he added a couple of statements that had not been in his earlier article, even though they would seem to have had great importance if in fact that is the way it had happened. Those statements were:

I was on the scene two hours after Johnson's announcement. He would not see me, nor would anyone permit me to see the fish.

And this in regard to Spray's catch:

This writer was on the spot within hours after the announcement. Again no interview. When told the fish was at the taxidermist's I went there. The road was barricaded to the house. I walked in. I was turned away at the door. Well, it is no wonder he was turned away, as Karl Kahmann had refused to mount the fish and didn't even have it!

At any rate, Louis Spray received a copy of Ellis' 1980 article and responded in a letter to the editor of the January/February 1981 issue of *Wisconsin Sportsman*. I believe his comments sum up nicely:

A Voice From The Past

This letter is in answer to an article written by Mel Ellis and appearing in this magazine in the July/August issue of 1980.

First, I cannot see for the life of me, why a writer of Mr.Ellis' ability could not have covered the same ground he did without tearing someone apart. Second, he went off half cocked in many places that are actually of public record, should he have cared to avail himself of the facts.

Referring to my catch of 59 1/2 pound musky in 1939 he said. "Spray at the time said he caught the fish in Rice Lake August 19." Ellis had to know better than that, or else his memory is not very good at going back 41 years. Actually, the fish was recorded with the American Museum of Natural History, New York, as being caught July 27, 1939, in Grindstone Lake, Sawyer County, Wisconsin.

Then he goes goofing-off about a Jens Jorgensen who caught a large musky about the same time and used phraseology such that he asked his readers to believe that I, somehow, used Jorgensen's fish to record my catch.

With reference to my catch of a 69 pound 11 ounce musky caught in 1949, Ellis claims that I was not at the spot where I said I had caught the fish at all that day, because a Tony Burmek said that he was fishing at that particular spot all that day, and that I was not there, which was October 20, 1949.

It just so happens that Burmek on October 20, was fishing all day in the Chippewa Flowage, at a place known as Pine Point, and a Carl Haag and Elmer Germanson also fished there all day October 20. Burmek never left the area that day, and Haag and Germanson talked with Burmek many times during the day. And further, that evening Burmek left in the direction of Dunn-Rovin Lodge. so that it was impossible for him to have been at Fleming's Bar, where I caught the fish at any time on October 20. Fleming's Bar is some four miles south of Pine Point.

The above is not just hearsay, as the facts are documented in affidavit form by Mr. Haag and Mr. Germanson. Mr. Petrie, publisher of this magazine, has in his possession said affidavits.

Since I am now nearing 81 years of age, and won't be around too much longer, I ask one favor of publishers and writers. All of my record muskies are recorded in the Recorder's Office, Hayward, Wisconsin: some 24 affidavits. For a very small fee, he will supply you with a photostat copy of those affidavits. Be sure to mention the facts on which fish you want and enclose a stamped and self addressed envelope so he can reply, stating his fee for same. And one other request, pick on someone else for a while, I've had 41 years of it, and I believe I have served my time.

Lou Spray, Morristown, AZ

Perhaps the Ellis articles aren't sensational journalism, but rather a retaliation for not being given the scoop as he seemingly inferred in his 1980 article. I don't know ... you be the judge!

While the dispute over where Louie actually caught his fish was never satisfactory settled in 1949-50, the puzzle was to be solved in 1991. It appears that Louie, like most musky anglers of then and today, was trying to protect his hotspot. In 1991, a new claim was made about Louie's fish. This caused John Dettloff, director of the Sawyer County (Wisconsin) Historical Society and historical editor of *Musky Hunter* magazine, to undertake the task of proving once and for all if Spray's 1949 catch was legitimate or not. To put it to bed, I will, with John's permission, reprint his two-part article on this matter that appeared in the December/January 1991 and February/March 1992 issues of *Musky Hunter* magazine:

In Defense of Louie Spray
By John Dettloff

Last summer [1991], several newspapers including the *Chicago Tribune* ran articles impugning the credibility of the late Louie Spray. The articles not only maligned his character but also made claims that his 69-pound 11-ounce world record was a sham and not a legal catch. The article grew out of a tall tale spun by an old timer, an alleged head of a Chicago crime syndicate, claiming he caught the musky while illegally fishing below the Winter Dam at night. He said he sold the musky to Spray for $50, and Spray went on to claim it was his fish.

In an effort to document the truth, I undertook one of the most intense investigations of any big musky ever attempted.

My investigation of Spray's catch was both exhaustive and thorough, gathering every attainable tidbit of information and piece of evidence possible. In an effort not to hold anything back, all pertinent information is presented in this article. As much as I would like to believe in his fish, my primary concern — as an officer of Sawyer County Historical Society and fishing historian — was to separate fact from fiction and to document the truth. Constantly acting as my own devil's advocate trying to disprove Spray's catch, I looked for any inconsistencies or damaging evidence. However, deeper probing only unearthed additional evidence to substantiate the fact that Louie Spray did indeed catch his world record musky legally in the Chippewa Flowage.

We will start with the key question raised during Larry Ramsell's investigation of Louie Spray's musky in his book, *A Compendium of Muskie Angling History.* Where was Louie on the afternoon of Oct. 20? This was the only loose end left hanging after his investigation. Mine takes up where Larry's investigation leaves off. The following article, as well as many other pieces of evidence, were given to me by Larry Ramsell. This article was written on November 12, 1949 by R.G. Lynch, sports editor, for the *Milwaukee Journal*:

(This article was the same that has already appeared on Page 244 of this book. Please refer to it.—Ed.)

After Burmek made the suggestion that both Spray and Johnson take the lie detector tests on their record catches, both men declined to show up — even though the Milwaukee Journal offered to pay the expenses of taking the test. The only man who did show up to take the test was Tony Burmek. Apparently he had full confidence in his account of the afternoon and was willing to back it up by taking the test. Why Johnson declined I am not sure; but why Spray declined will become clear as you read on.

Spray's collage of photos showing his big muskies, including the head shot of his 69-11 while still fresh.

Larry Ramsell also supplied me with two affidavits negating Burmek's claim that he was actually near Fleming's Bar at the time in question. The affidavits were made out by Elmer Germanson and Carl Hagg of Hayward and are printed fully in Ramsell's book. Basically, they both state that Germanson and Hagg were fishing together at a location known as Pine Point, which is located about 4 miles from Fleming's Bar, and they observed Tony Burmek fishing near them on the afternoon of October 20, at the time when Louie caught his musky. They said Burmek couldn't have been near Fleming's because he was actually at another location, Pine Point.

Well, obviously someone is lying or, to be more kind, is grossly mistaken. Both Germanson and Hagg are deceased so I couldn't question them but, after contacting people who knew them and had knowledge of the incident, several pertinent things were learned. First, Hagg didn't know Burmek at the time and went on Germanson's word that the boat nearby did contain one Tony Burmek. So in essence it's Germanson's word against Burmek's word. Secondly, one source told me that Germanson was given an outboard motor by Spray in exchange for making affidavits negating Tony Burmek's statement, thus leaving Fleming's Bar location uncontested. This certainly is very plausible because Spray did receive two Martin outboard motors in consideration for appearing in a Martin motor advertisement with his 69-pound 11-ounce musky.

Before Tony Burmek passed away, I talked with him at length about fishing as well as what he knew about Louie Spray's musky. Tony reiterated everything he said in the Milwaukee Journal article and, when I asked him if he had any reason to suspect Spray didn't catch his musky, he said, "No, not at all. I just know he didn't catch it on Fleming's Bar because I was there at the time he caught the fish." Tony further told me, "Herman Ceranske, the owner of Herman's Landing at the time, and I were friends and one

Document 1

AFFIDAVIT

Jess Ross says he has been guiding for around 65 years and resides east of Hayward near the West Fork of the Chippewa River. That he has been an avid fisherman and hunter during his life and is very familiar with the Chippewa Flowage. That on the day that Louie Spray caught the 69# 11 oz. muskie out of the flowage, I was duck hunting from afternoon till sundown on Horseshoe Island - which is located close by just to the east of Fleming's Bar - and I never saw Spray's boat or any other boat fishing Fleming's Bar that day. Therefore, if Spray did catch the fish, I know he didn't catch it on Fleming's Bar because I was nearby and would have certainly seen his boat and heard the excitement from where I was located. I remember that day well and present this information with the idea of making all facts pertinent to Louie Spray's 69# 11 oz. muskie catch known and recorded.

Sincerely, Jess Ross

night when we were alone and Herman was closing up, he told me that Spray never caught his fish where they claimed and that they just said Fleming's to promote his business." The way in which Tony told me these things coupled with the fact that Tony showed up for the lie detector test to substantiate his story is pretty convincing evidence that Tony was the one telling the truth.

To further substantiate the fact that Spray's musky wasn't caught on Fleming's Bar, I discovered additional testimony from two reliable and well respected long time Hayward area residents — Milt Dieckman and Jess Ross. Milt, a retired game warden, remembers that on the day that Louie Spray caught his 69-pound musky, he was duck hunting with friends late in the afternoon in the Pocketbook area, a location just east of Fleming's Bar. With all the commotion, and the two gunshots that were fired at the fish, Milt finds it very unlikely that it could have taken place in the Fleming's Bar vicinity since he was close by and noticed nothing. Jess Ross also was nearby that afternoon and signed an affidavit documenting what he saw. (See Document 1)

With such well known local area sportsmen coming forward and revealing something was "fishy" about the location of Spray's catch, a shadow of doubt was immediately cast upon Spray's catch among the local populace. This was the first strike against his catch. Many people reasoned that maybe Spray didn't catch his fish at all and the *Milwaukee Journal* added more fuel to the fire by reprinting some unfavorable press concerning Spray's two previous large musky catches — 59 1/2-pound and 61-pound 13-ounce muskies. This bad press was the second strike against his catch. Spray has had unfavorable press written about him since the late 1920s concerning game violations. It should be noted that it was proven he didn't commit the biggest one with which he was charged.

AFFIDAVIT

Tom Jandrt says that he now resides in Rice Lake, Wis. and was a good friend of Louie Spray's for years starting in around 1957. That Louie, at the time, was building and selling houses and I was a driver-salesman for Walter Bros. hauling siding and lumber to Louie. Louie was a pretty good craftsman and was always good about paying his bills. We eventually became friends and would often talk about fishing.

When I asked Louie Spray where in the Chippewa Flowage he caught the 69# 11 oz muskie, he told me he caught it 3 or 4 miles from Herman's Landing in a place he called the "Kitchen". Louie told me he caught it on a sand point and talked about a sand bar too. The point is what he said; I can remember that clearly.

Louie didn't pinpoint the spot to me but this is his description of the spot. In the years I've known Louie, he has always been honest in all of our business dealings and with me in general. He was a good man and I have no reason to disbelieve him as to what he has told me.

Sincerely, Tom Jandrt

Tom Jandrt

Eric Thoreson
ERIC THORESON
7-11-91
Notary Public-State of Wisconsin
My Commission Expires June 27, 1993

Document 2

AFFIDAVIT

Bruce Tasker says that he is a licensed fishing guide, having been guiding since 1946, and resides in Rice Lake, Wis. That he was a close friend of George Quentmeyer at the time of Louie Spray's record muskie catch and they would frequently talk fishing and compare notes. Quentmeyer was, of course, accompanying Spray when the 69# 11 oz. muskie was caught. When I asked George if they really got the muskie off Fleming's Bar, George hesitated and said with a grin, "Well....., not really. We caught it a little further south." One thing about the experience that George relayed to me that I'll never forget is when the fish first broke water, George thought the fish looked 80#! You know, he wasn't that far off. What a sight he must have beheld.

After talking to John Bennett, of New Post, Wis., he filled in the gaps and told me he watched Louie catch the fish on Graveyard Point near the old Indian cemetary. I have no reason to doubt the word of either George or John as I knew them both well and can vouch for their honesty. I truely believe Louie Spray caught the 69# 11 oz muskie legally and caught it on Graveyard Point because of what both George Quentmeyer and John Bennett told me.

Signed, Bruce Tasker

STATE OF WISCONSIN
Sawyer County
Subscribed and sworn to
before me this 5th day
of July, 1991.
Ruth M. Skinner
Ruth M. Skinner
Notary Public
My commission expires 11-24-91

Document 3

Without proof of his guilt, newspapers did a smear campaign branding Spray as a violator, a reputation that stuck with Spray all his life. As a result, many wild rumors were spawned concerning his record musky catches.

Levi Packard, a long-time game warden, summed up Louie this way, "Louie did things that were illegal but never immoral. He bent and broke the same kind of rules like everyone else during those early years was breaking in order to survive." Many of these fish and game rules were new and wardens were trying to regulate people who were raised with no rules. Times were different and were tough then and rules were just a guideline. Fishing and hunting was not as much of a sport; rather it was a way of life and means of support and sustenance.

Louie Spray, like most everyone else, was by definition a violator, especially during those early years. Louie did what he thought he had to do in order to

A Review of Muskellunge World Records

survive. What you can't take away from Louie is the fact that he was a diehard musky fisherman, a real musky addict. After listening to a one-hour taped interview with Louie, as well as reading things he has written on the sport, it is obvious that he was no phony because the tips and advice he gave only could have come from a real musky fisherman.

The third strike against Spray's musky involved a comment he made following Cal Johnson's 67 1/2-pound world record musky catch. Cal was a frequent Hayward area visitor, sportswriter, and well liked by the area residents who greatly accepted and embraced his record catch. Now enters Louie Spray, and at a celebration thrown to honor Cal Johnson's catch a gag telegram sent by Spray was read to the crowd:

DON'T GIVE AWARD YET. I WILL CATCH A NEW WORLD RECORD MUSKY THIS SEASON. SIGNED LOUIE SPRAY.

Low and behold if Spray didn't come up with a bigger musky like he said! Cal was upstaged by Louie's catch and many people couldn't believe it. Not wanting to see Johnson's fish dethroned so quickly, they were very receptive to believing and spreading rumors discrediting Spray's catch. Spray's comment is not surprising though, for he had known about and spotted a record-class musky during the past several seasons on the Chippewa Flowage. His comment

Document 4

AFFIDAVIT

Tim DeBrot says he is a police officer for Sawyer County, the grandson of the late Chick DeBrot, and resides in New Post, Wis. That many years ago, when I was a young boy, my grandfather, Chick, took me out in the boat to the area just past Graveyard Point - just north of the point - and told me that this was the exact spot where Louie Spray caught his world record 69# 11 oz. muskie. That my grandfather, Chick, told me he saw Louie Spray fishing in that area on and off for the whole month of October, prior to the catch; and, that he saw Louie fishing in that area on the very day that Louie caught his world record 69# 11 oz. muskie.

My grandfather was ill most of my life and could hardly speak so he couldn't go into detail on the catching of the fish. It is very possible my grandfather witnessed the actual catching of the fish but the above information is as much as he was able to tell me at the time, because of his ill health. I truely believe Louie Spray's 69# 11 oz muskie was caught legally and was caught exactly where my grandfather said it was caught - on Graveyard point. My grandfather was an honest and reliable man and I would never doubt his word.

Signed, Tim DeBrot

Document 5

AFFIDAVIT

Arnold Hendee says he was a policeman for the city of Hayward, long time area resident now residing in Delavan, Wis., and the brother of Don Hendee, owner of Indian Trail Resort from 1944 to 1952. That Don told him that he knew something was going on over near the Graveyard Point area because for weeks he saw Louie Spray working the whole area, across the lake from the resort. On the day Louie caught his 69# 11 oz muskie, October 20th, just behind the point - just out of sight - northeast of the point, Don heard an awful commotion - shouts and 2 or 3 gunshots. He saw Spray's boat go racing out from behind the point and off into the distance towards Herman's Landing. Don said Spray did stop in at his resort (Indian Trail) sometime that day.

The details listed above are what my late brother, Don Hendee, told me and I truely believe these things to be true as my brother would have no reason to lie to me.

Sincerely, Arnold Hendee

255

was probably half jest and half very serious, knowing that he did have a chance to better Johnson's catch.

It is very possible that without Cal Johnson's world record catch, Louie Spray's world record catch wouldn't have happened either. The catching of Johnson's musky within Spray's own stomping grounds seemed to rekindle the

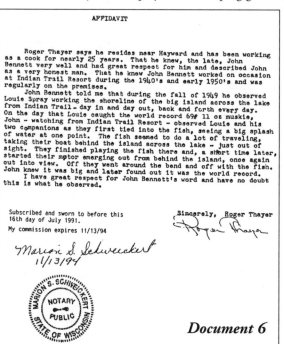

AFFIDAVIT

Roger Thayer says he resides near Hayward and has been working as a cook for nearly 25 years. That he knew, the late, John Bennett very well and had great respect for him and described John as a very honest man. That he knew John Bennett worked on occasion at Indian Trail Resort during the 1940's and early 1950's and was regularly on the premises.

John Bennett told me that during the fall of 1949 he observed Louie Spray working the shoreline of the big island across the lake from Indian Trail - day in and day out, back and forth every day. On the day that Louie caught the world record 69# 11 oz muskie, John - watching from Indian Trail Resort - observed Louie and his two companions as they first tied into the fish, seeing a big splash of water at one point. The fish seemed to do a lot of traveling, taking their boat behind the island across the lake - just out of sight. They finished playing the fish there and, a short time later, started their motor emerging out from behind the island, once again out into view. Off they went around the bend and off with the fish. John knew it was big and later found out it was the world record.

I have great respect for John Bennett's word and have no doubt this is what he observed.

Subscribed and sworn to before this 16th day of July 1991.

My commission expires 11/13/94

Sincerely, Roger Thayer

Marion S. Schweickert
11/13/94

NOTARY PUBLIC
MARION S. SCHWEICKERT
STATE OF WISCONSIN

Document 6

competitive spirit in Spray, motivating him to embark on one of the most serious fishing marathons of his life. Spray seemed to be on a quest. That October of 1949 was to be Spray's last hurrah; he put his all into it and, through persistence and drive, won the gamble and the greatest jackpot in Wisconsin fishing history.

Back to the Investigation:

Two other people were in the boat with Spray on that fateful day — George Quentmeyer, the guide, and Ted Hagg, a Sarona restaurateur. Since both are deceased, I contacted the offspring of both men hoping they could shed additional light on the catch. Upon asking Ted Hagg's daughter, Ann Amour, if she remembered much about Louie Spray's musky or if she knew where it was caught, she responded:

"My dad was very proud to be involved with the catching of the fish and had saved lots of newspaper clippings and photos. I was a young girl at the time of the catch and don't remember much about the fish. I don't know where it was caught but do remember hearing that the spot that they gave out to the public wasn't the spot where they caught the fish. They wanted to throw everyone off track as to where it was caught so they could keep the real spot secret and to themselves."

Hoping to learn something from the Quentmeyer clan, I contacted George Quentmeyer's son-in-law, Harry Tyler, who confirmed what Ted Hagg's daughter had told me. Harry also didn't know many details of the catch either, but did tell me:

"My father-in-law, George, took me right to the spot where they had caught the world record musky just a short time before. We were driving by, on the way to a walleye spot, and he pointed it out."

When asked if he remembered where on the flowage it was, he said he wasn't real familiar with the flowage and it would be hard to say. I told him Louie had reported it was caught on Fleming's, which is within a half-mile from Herman's Landing, and asked him if that could have been the spot. He replied:

"Oh no, it wasn't near Herman's Landing. At the time, we were heading south and the bar was on our right. The land around there was desolate and wild. Also, to our left was a lot of open water."

After contacting a totally different source, a Tom Jandrt, he documented a notarized statement regarding Spray's 69-pounder. (See Document 2)

Now this doesn't prove that Spray caught his musky, but it is certainly substantial evidence that the 69-pounder was not caught on Fleming's Bar as Spray reported.

Then where was it caught? Enter Bruce Tasker, a close friend of George Quentmeyer's, who documented what he knows about Spray's catch in his notarized statement. (See Document 3)

AFFIDAVIT

Elsie Hornewer says she was owner of Indian Trail Resort from 1952 to 1963 and now resides in Altoona, Wis. That John Bennett worked for us at the resort on occasion and helped teach us the ropes when we first bought the resort. That John was reliable and a good worker and lived in New Post, Wis. That when we first bought the resort John, his close friend Chick DeBrot, and Don Hendee, former owner of Indian Trail Resort from 1944 to 1952, told us they knew Louie Spray caught his world record right across the lake from our resort, behind the island. They knew he had something spotted in the general area, out in front of our resort, Don said that for several weeks, almost every single day, he spotted Spray fishing the area. On the afternoon of October 20, 1949 John, Chick, and Don heard the commotion of shouts and gunshots coming from Spray's boat, which was just behind the island across the lake. Their boat was just out of view because it was just around the corner on the other side of Graveyard Point. They knew it was Spray because after they boated the fish, they could see Spray's boat come tearing out from behind the point, out into view, and off in the direction of Herman's Landing. John, Chick, and Don knew they had a big fish from all the yelling and commotion but didn't know exactly how big. Sometime later they heard it was a world record muskie that Spray had caught but reportedly on Fleming's Bar.

This was exactly what the three of them had told me shortly after I purchased the resort and I have no reason to doubt their word.

Signed, Elsie Hornewer

State of Wisconsin
County of Eau Claire

Elsie Hornewer personally came before me on July 15, 1991 and has sworn to the above statement in my presence.

Susan M. Beelman, notary public
My commission expirese 2-2-92

Elsie Hornewer

Document 7

Paul Albrecht, a close friend and confidante of Louie Spray's for many years and publisher of Spray's book, *Looking Back At That Phase Of My Musky Days*, said Louie had told him that the 69-pounder was caught in the area of the old Trading Post. That just happens to be where Graveyard Point is located and it just happens to be 3 to 4 miles from Herman's Landing.

New Witnesses

My research recently produced three additional witnesses to Spray's record musky catch. Besides Quent-meyer and Hagg, three other individuals witnessed Spray not only catching the 69-pounder, but also observed him fishing the area around Graveyard Point during the whole month of October of that year, 1949. The three witnesses, Don Hendee, John Bennett, and Chick DeBrot, are all deceased now but did pass down to close relatives what they had seen. These relatives are all upstanding, reliable people and documented these notarized statements as to exactly what they were told by each individual witness. (See Documents 4, 5 and 6).

DeBrot also passed on this in formation about Spray's musky to an Elsie Hornewer, the next owner of Indian Trail Resort after Don Hendee. Indian Trail Resort is located within a quarter-mile of Graveyard Point. The reason the three witnesses were able to observe Spray fishing this area so often and catching his musky was because they were on the resort premises nearly at all times that fall. A boat such as Spray's, spending every single day in the same area, quickly drew attention. Mrs. Hornewer documented and had her statement notarized as to what she was told as well. (See Document 7)

In Defense of Louie Spray — Part II: Louie Speaks for Himself

By John Dettloff

The Martin motor photo that Spray disliked. Martin gave Spray two motors for the use of his 69-11 in promotions. Spray insisted this photo not be used as the superimposed image of Spray standing on the dock was out of proportion to the actual size of the record musky.

My next witness is Louie Spray himself. Inadvertently, he had stated in his book detailing the account of his 69-pound catch, his one-hour taped interview, and his correspondence with me, certain clues that point to Graveyard Point as the location where he caught his 69-pounder. Louie made this quote about his record musky in the taped interview:

"Even George Quentmeyer, as much as he guided the Chippewa Flowage, didn't know what I was there for. He must have surmised that there was a big fish lookin' around there. But he use to kid me about going back to the log jam, he called it. And there was a lot of logs there. A pretty wicked place to try to land a big musky."

In other words, Spray is telling us that Quentmeyer had no prior knowledge of the musky Spray was working and eventually caught. Conversely, in a *Milwaukee Journal* interview shortly after the catch, George Quentmeyer was quoted as saying: "Several of us had known there was a real big fish on Fleming's Bar. I raised the big fellow twice this summer and he was really big."

Quentmeyer knew about a huge

musky active on Fleming's, but didn't know about the musky Spray was work-ing, because Spray's musky was not the Fleming's Bar fish. The Fleming's fish was just a convenient alibi, and, since everyone knew about it, they would fig-ure that was the one that Louie caught. The Fleming's musky was hooked and lost by Arne Juul's party the day before Louie caught his musky, according to a detailed account of the fight given by, the now late Arne Juul on the Tony Dean Outdoors TV show aired early in 1991. Roy Risberg was another angler who dealt with the Fleming's musky earlier in 1949. After he lost the fish he told Louie about the musky and, upon hearing that Louie caught his world record, and it came off Fleming's, stopped in at Spray's bar in Rice Lake and said, "Louie, you owe me the best quart of whiskey in the house. I told you where that fish was." Louie, being in no position to argue, gladly handed Risberg one of his best bottles of whiskey.

In Spray's book he further elaborates on the catching of his musky and reveals additional clues. In it Louie stated:

"George was an artist in handling a boat. There was a wind blowing us toward a log jam along the shore which would have been fatal had "Chin Whiskers" successfully reached there. But, good old George worked the boat away from shore and as best I could, I got the fish out in the lake and then there was nothing to do but wait for the opportunity to plug him. Had it not been for George, the boat would probably have drifted into the log jam and the fish would have gotten off."

The words "log jam" are a big key to the location. After checking with two of Herman's Landing's most diehard musky fishermen of the late 1940s, Bruce Tasker and John Zeug, they both told me that there were no log jams on or near Fleming's Bar at that time. They said the closet log jam was three-fourths of a mile north of Fleming's. Furthermore, upon going to the precise location that the three witnesses said Spray's boat was in when he caught his 69-pounder, I noticed, even today, a pocket along the shoreline with a small log jam of about 15 logs. Twenty years ago this log jam was noticeably larger, according to my own memory, and 40 years ago it must have been substantial.

Since Spray's boat was blowing toward the log jam during the fight, the wind direction is an important detail. After checking with the Hayward Ranger Station, I discovered that at 5 p.m. that afternoon the wind was out of the northeast. A northeast wind was the only wind that could have blown Spray's boat into the log jam from where the three witnesses said Spray's boat was!

Don Hendee, the owner of Indian Trail Resort at the time and one of the three witnesses to Spray's catch, said Spray and his two companions stopped in at his resort for drinks on the afternoon that Spray caught the controversial fish and, after they left, they went right back out to the same area that they'd been working, Graveyard Point. Spray confirmed this in his book and in a letter he wrote to me. In his book, Louie stated his partner, Ted Hagg, was not proper-ly dressed for the weather and was cold and hungry so they stopped at a tavern for some hot drinks and to get warm. Louie wrote, "When we left the tavern, George took over the motor and ran us back to the same old spot." And in a letter Louie wrote to me on April 29, 1982 he wrote, "The 69-pounder was caught on Fleming's Bar. And we did stop in to Hendee's place in early afternoon for a few refreshments on the evening I caught the fish."

Well, Spray stuck with Fleming's Bar, but did confirm he was at Hendee's resort on the afternoon of October 20, 1949. Question — What is he doing having drinks at Hendee's resort, Indian Trail, if he was fishing Fleming's Bar — Herman's Landing had food and drinks available and was only a half-mile from Fleming's. It's easy to understand why Louie was so determined to stick with Fleming's Bar and go to such great lengths to keep the real spot secret. It was one of his best spots. "The Kitchen," as Louie referred to the spot where he caught his famous fish to his friend Tom Jandrt, "was the best water for big muskies on the Chippewa Flowage." Louie said, "For some reason that's where the big, female muskies hung the most and where the biggest fish were."

Because Spray stuck with Fleming's Bar until the day he died, it helped prove that what the three witnesses observed during the month of October of 1949 was real and not staged. If Spray could have taken his fish by other means at an earlier date and brought the fish out with him to stage what the three witnesses had seen, it would be logical for Louie to publicly say Graveyard Point was his spot, to take advantage of the elaborate 20-day staging he went through. Saying Fleming's Bar indicates it wasn't staged.

It's important to note the assemblage of evidence proving Spray's fish was freshly caught. Spray caught his musky around 4 p.m., according to notarized affidavits sworn and signed by George Quentmeyer and Ted Hagg. These two men swore under oath that they were present in the boat with Louie when he caught his 69-pounder and that he caught it legally. The three men then brought the musky into Herman's Landing around 4:15 p.m., according to notarized affidavits sworn and signed by Herman and Edna Ceranske and Nixon Barnes. They testified to the fact that they saw Louie's 69-pounder, that

Guide George Quentmeyer waits for Spray (center) and Haag to load their tackle aboard.

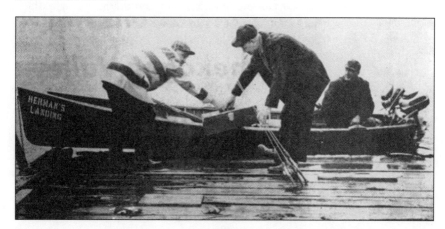

it was freshly caught, and that Barnes measured the musky at 64 inches.

After doing some digging on my own, I discovered two other witnesses present at Herman's Landing who saw Louie's musky — Leonard Dorazio and Lester Heath. Leonard Dorazio, in a telephone interview, stated: "I was about 14 years old and heard about the fish by phone. Everyone in the area was on a party line and, evidently, someone from Herman's put out a call on the emergency ring in order to inform everyone at once. I got to Herman's as quickly as possible and remember seeing Spray and his two friends and Herman. The musky was outside near the old dock (where the baithouse is now) hanging from a pole or an oar. The musky was as long as I was tall. Its tail wasn't much off the ground but I still had to look up at it. People were taking pictures. The fish obviously hadn't been frozen and looked like it had just been caught within the last couple hours."

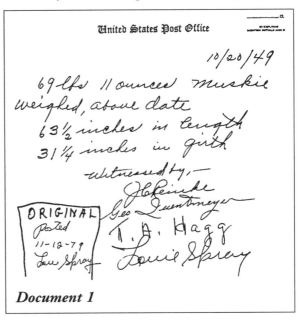

Document 1

Another person who was there was Les Heath, a well known area guide. According to fellow guide Ray Blank, Les said, "I had just returned to Herman's Landing with my guide party when Louie came in with his musky. It was so huge and fresh and shiny, like it hadn't been out of the water long. I was sure it was just caught."

From Herman's, the three men took the musky to Hayward looking for a place to weigh it. They first stopped at Pastika's Bait Shop to obtain some ice to pack around the fish. The proprietor, Charlie Pastika, and a Jake Jordan were present and signed affidavits, swearing on oath that the fish brought in around 6 p.m. was the largest musky they had ever seen, and observed it was freshly caught.

Louie's party then took the musky to Stroner's Store in Hayward, thinking they could weigh the fish there. Unfortunately, the scale was inadequate. Milton Stroner, the owner, also signed an affidavit, swearing under oath that Spray had brought the big musky to his store to weigh what was the largest musky he had ever seen, and that Mr. Spray bought some gas. The three men then departed with the fish. They then took the musky to Stone Lake, where the fish was officially weighed at the Stone Lake Post Office by postmaster Jack Reinke. Reinke signed an affidavit, swearing under oath that he had weighed and measured Spray's musky at around 6:45 p.m. Reinke testified that he weighed the fish on the post office scale in a 69 pounds 11 ounces, measured the length of the fish at 63 1/2 inches, and the girth at 31 1/4 inches. Larry Ramsell sent me proof documenting the weigh-in of the fish on United States Post Office stationary. (See Document 1)

I tried to contact Jack Reinke but he had passed away so instead I contacted his successor, Postmaster Francis Mattis. Mattis remembered that, when he first took over his position, the post office equipment — including the scale — was the same as it was when Reinke was postmaster. Mattis assured me of the accuracy of the scale and that Reinke was a precise individual when it came to his job. Mattis had no doubt that the fish was accurately weighed .

Spray then took the musky to Karl Kahmann's taxidermy studio that evening hoping Karl would mount his fish. Karl declined. Karl did sign an affidavit, swearing under oath that Louie's musky was a freshly-caught fish and was one of the largest muskies he had ever seen. Why did Kahmann refuse to mount Louie's musky? This interesting story is best told by Louie himself in this excerpt from my one-hour taped radio interview: "When we came from the flowage I went right into Kahmann's to show him what I had, to let him know he had a job on his hands. He told me he wouldn't take the job for $5,000. It was Cal Johnson's fish that wrecked the joint. He took me out and showed me where the multitude of cars had pulled into his yard, without any chance of ever getting out of there. (They all had come to get a look at Cal Johnson's fish when Kahmann was working on it, just three months earlier.) They had to get a bulldozer in and make a road up around the field to get the cars out of there. It was an awful mess, they tore down his shrubbery. He just wouldn't have nothing to do with it (my fish) which put me on the spot. Normally, we always took these record muskies and put them on display and even had people guess the weight and put up a small prize. I didn't know just what to do then. Karl was very uncooperative. He congratulated me. When I asked him where I could take it, he said he didn't know. Now the thing was to protect it, so I took it home (to Rice Lake) and put it in my basement. And, due to the influx of people, and human nature being what it is, I didn't tell anybody where it was. Until I found out about this man in Wausau who was an excellent taxidermist, Mr. Hugh Lackey. I made a trip over there and talked with him and he didn't want no part of it on account of the publicity. He said all I'll have is people over here to look and, he said, I won't sell nothing. So we made a deal to keep it confidential and that's how it worked out. He finally mounted the fish for me."

While Louie had his musky under wraps at home, I discovered he did show the fish to his close friends. Paul and Joe Jachim were two such people. Paul Jachim remembered, "I was at my late brother's house, Joe's house, when Louie pulled up to the side of the road. He opened the trunk and showed us this monster musky. It filled the whole trunk! It was unbelievable! It was huge. I also remember Louie showing it to a couple of other people. He seemed like he didn't want to draw a crowd, he just gave them a little look and shut the trunk."

Incidentally, Hugh Lackey signed an affidavit, swearing under oath that on Saturday, October 22, 1949 Louie Spray delivered the 69-pound 11-ounce musky to his studio for him to mount and, after an examination of the musky, disclosed that there was nothing inside or out to add artificial weight to the fish. The mount was to be completed for pick up by November 20th of that year. Harold Brunette, a photographer from Rice Lake, and Ted Hagg accompanied Louie Spray when he went over to pick up the mounted fish.

Summary

The evidence in this article shows that practically every aspect of Spray's catch was well documented. From the two people who were present in the boat with Spray when he caught the 69-pounder, to the three witnesses who saw Spray working the Graveyard Point area and finally catching his fish, to all the people present at Herman's Landing when Spray first brought the fish in, to the witnesses in Hayward who saw the fish, and, finally, to the weighing of the fish by Jack Reinke; Spray's 69-pound 11-ounce world record musky is perhaps the best documented of all the world record muskies. This documentation should dispel all of the wild rumors and innuendo that has followed Spray's catch for so many years. Louie Spray's 69-pound 11-ounce musky is obviously no sham and stands as Wisconsin's all time champion musky catch and is still the current world record musky caught by conventional means.

During my investigation, I was unable to uncover a single hard fact showing Spray's musky was illegally taken, falsely weighed or tampered with. Louie Spray's story, in his own words: "I was living in Rice Lake, Wisconsin, was 49 years old, and taking a good hard look at my financial future — to heck with fishing. But I could not get it out of my head completely. I knew of a monster in the north fork of the Flambeau and one in the Chippewa Flowage. So in the fall of 1949 I decided to have one last fling at these two fish and then forget about it — win, lose, or draw.

"But, now who do I fish with? Ted Hagg, who operated a night spot in Sarona, Wisconsin, came into the bar one day and I approached him on the subject. Ted was the kind of individual whom everybody wanted to be around, always had a witty crack on the end of his tongue. He said it would be good for him to get away from the place for a while; I had myself a partner. I told him I wanted to fish the entire month of October and he was agreeable. So on October 1st, we took off for Herman's Landing on the Chippewa Flowage and did so each day until the 20th, when we finally hooked and landed old 'Chin Whiskered Charlie,' as I had named him. He was a granddaddy, 69 pounds 11 ounces, 5 feet 3 1/2 inches long, and a girth of 31 1/4 inches.

"On that particular day, George Quentmeyer, a guide who was off duty, joined Ted and myself for a fishing expedition. During the preceding five days, it was very warm with temperatures in the 60s and winds from a southerly direction. Upon waking up on that Thursday of October 20th it was still warm, but the weather made a sudden change and a major cold front had moved in. Mostly it was chilly and damp with temperatures in the 40s, sometimes a slow drizzle, and a strong N.E. wind had blown up — generally nasty weather. Ted was sitting in the front of the boat, I was in the middle, and George was in the rear on the oars. My Union Hardware rod, Cycloid reel, and 42-pound test Gladding line provided me with the good gear I needed because he was laying in a pretty bad place. George was an excellent man to handle the boat and I knew he would be a great help if we ever did catch him.

"Ted couldn't understand why I always kept going to one particular spot. Off and on, we'd fish there for an hour or so, and then go away and fish some-place else — but we'd always come back to it several times a day. Even George Quentmeyer, as much as he guided the Chippewa Flowage, didn't know what I was there for; but he caught on fast. He must have surmised that there was a big fish lookin' around there. By mid afternoon, I knew Ted was freezing because he was not dressed for the cold so I suggested we go in and have some hot drinks and get warm. He was all for it but George chided us with such remarks as "tenderfoot, pansies, and city slickers." When we left the tavern, George took over the motor and ran us right back into the same old spot. Ted, bored with that spot, said, "What again ... well, that beats me"... and just sat there huddled up. I myself hated to get down into that cold water in the min-now bucket for a sucker, but I did, and rigged my own make-up of a harness on the 14-inch sucker and laid him in the water. George was rowing around in that spot and I would let the sucker troll out and then bring it in with a series of jerks. The sucker was really too large to cast.

"It seemed no time until old 'Chin Whiskers' hit the sucker and about a half a dozen little treble hooks, that I had placed on the harness, were set into his jaw. There was quite a fuss for a minute or two, as 'Chin Whiskers' assert-ed himself in the usual way by breaking and splashing the water. When the fish broke water for the first time, we all thought it weighed 80 pounds! He was heavier to handle than my other fish and I had to use a certain amount of horse sense. The only difficulty we had was with Ted Hagg when he stood up in the boat, an unpardonable sin in the ethics of musky fishing. George got to using a little swear words, telling him to sit down or he was going to clout him with an oar. Ted was stone deaf, as his eyes were glued on the fish battling away out there. So I said, 'Ted, will you help me a second, sit down and don't stand up again?' Ted countered by asking George if he would do something for him, like take him to shore.

"George was an artist in handling a boat. There was a wind blowing us toward a log jam along the shore which would have been fatal had 'Chin Whiskers' successfully reached there. The musky leaped out of the water three times, just high enough for us to get a glimpse of it. I had my .22 pistol, at many times, ready to shoot, but couldn't do it. The wind was quite high, George was busy with the boat working it away from shore, and, as best I could, I got the fish out in the lake and then there was nothing to do but wait for the opportunity to plug him. I had the fish up a few times, but there was always a wave or something to prevent a good shot. George was quite perturbed, at least once, when he thought I should have shot and I didn't, but he couldn't see exactly my predicament. George asked, 'Why don't you shoot?' I told him why and he understood. Finally, 'Chin Whiskers' came up again, this time back by George. My back was to George so I did not know what he was up to and, as it went past, I heard BING-BING and saw the fish stiffen up. I could have kissed George on the spot. He shot the fish twice, right on target, in rapid succession in a very vital spot and he killed it. After old 'Chin Whiskers' took his last little swim in sort of a semi circle, George grabbed a fish stringer laying there and put it through his gills, saying, 'We ain't going to take no chance on this baby getting away.' We got him into the boat and I straddled him for a while. The game was all over for poor old Charlie. The battle had lasted about 40 minutes and we finally landed the fish at around 4:00 p.m.

"So now, it boils down to this. If it hadn't been for George, we wouldn't have gone back to that spot. Had it not been for George, the boat would probably have drifted into the log jam and the fish would have gotten off. Had it not been for George shooting the fish, it might have gotten off, as anything can happen when fighting a large fish like that. So in reality, I got credit for the catch, while George was 99% responsible for it. We headed for Herman's Landing where the grog flowed freely for a few minutes ... then on to Hayward to weigh it, only to find we had to weigh the fish in Stone Lake."

Are there still record breakers out there these days? Yes, Louie certainly thought so. But what does it take to get one? According to Louie, it takes a lot of luck combined with a lot of time on the water. Louie once said to his good friend, Tom Jandrt, "If you want to catch a world record musky, you have to fish every day of the legal season, each year, for five years and you'll have a world record."

As I mentioned at the beginning of this chapter, I would be including a complete treatise of the 70-pound Malo musky, which is now found on my world record list. After I had done a complete re-investigation of this fish, I published a booklet of my findings in 1987. It is from that which you will read here. Again, I feel that after you read it (hopefully with an open mind) that you too, will feel that the Malo musky belongs on the list.

Is This The World Record Muskellunge?
The Malo Musky Investigation
By Larry Ramsell

Foreword

When I began the Malo musky investigation, I had no idea of what I was getting into. I must confess that this project of investigation, and particularly this write-up which alone took nearly 80 hours, has been the most difficult, exhaustive, expensive, time consuming and complicated that I (or I suspect anyone else) have ever undertaken in the matter of a record fish.

Introduction

In June of 1954 a sad series of events took place. Robert Malo, of Port Arthur (now Thunder Bay), Ontario, caught a very large musky. It was a short, fat fish. Its stomach contained several pounds of eggs and partly digested northern pike flesh.

The scale used to weigh the fish was not certified at the time of the weighing. Although subsequent testing of that scale was done, that scale and several other circumstances combined to get Malo's fish disqualified.

Before you read this bizarre story, I would like to make two recommendations should you ever be fortunate enough to catch a record size fish:

One, if you catch a record class fish that has substantial stomach contents, I suggest that you leave them in the fish, and immediately contact one or both record-keeping organizations and ask that a representative be sent as soon as possible.

Two, when you weigh your fish in front of several witnesses, do it on a certified scale if at all possible. Then, in order to prove true and exact weight after weighing your fish, immediately call in an official tester/certifier. If one is unable to come immediately, quarantine the scale until arrival of the tester. Then have the tester place weights on the scale until all witnesses agree that the scale is reading exactly as it did when the fish was weighed Then, by adding the total of the weights on the scale, exact weight will be known and it will be beyond reproach!

And now, on to the story ...

Malo Musky Investigation — 1987

In the spring of 1986, the mount of a big musky caught June 6, 1954, by Robert Malo of Thunder Bay, Ontario, from Middle Eau Claire Lake, Bayfield County, Wisconsin, was again made available for public viewing after being kept private for over 25 years. The controversial weight of this fish, and the weight used to apply for world record recognition at the time it was caught, was 70 pounds 4 ounces.

The resurfacing of this fish has stirred a great amount of interest — and controversy — among the musky fraternity.

In 1977 I was involved in a search of the facts surrounding this fish, and from that search drew a conclusion which went into my book, *A Compendium of Muskie Angling History*. In looking back at my review, I think that perhaps I was guilty of being in sympathy with the then-recognized world record holder, the late Art Lawton, who at that time was a friend and excellent musky angler, vs. Robert Malo, who in my opinion, hardly knew what a musky was. I feel also, that rather than attack that review on the basis of trying to get the Malo fish recognized (if indeed it was justifiable), I instead tried to salve conscience by fitting a very large, legitimate and forgotten musky into, at least, a prominent place in musky history. This I was able to justify and placed it third on the all-time list of big muskies at 69 pounds 8 ounces.

A Review of Muskellunge World Records

Since publication of my book, I have become privy to all correspondence between key persons involved at the time and *Field & Stream* magazine editor, Hugh Grey. The *Field & Stream* contest was viewed at the time as the source and authority for world records, and thus, *Field & Stream* the official record keeping body.

During the past decade and a half there have been a couple of major changes in fresh water world record keeping from private to public organizations. The National Fresh Water Fishing Hall of Fame (NFWFHF) became involved in record keeping and a few years later, *Field & Stream* turned over all of its fresh water records to the International Game Fish

George Cruise and Robert Malo with the giant musky.

Association (IGFA), salt water record keepers since 1939.

This spring (1987), as I was reviewing the various 1986 write ups about the Malo fish, I realized how shallow my previous search had been, and, as a musky historian, a representative of IGFA, and chairman of the World Record Board of Review for the NFWFHF, I felt perhaps I had an obligation to re-open the Malo investigation; to do an intense and thorough job and come to a complete and final finding.

In reopening this investigation, my sole intent was to determine if in fact the Malo musky received its just dues. Let us remember that records are fish not people — they are only caught by people.

My thanks to [the late] J. Peter Haupt of the Muskellunge Club of Wisconsin and the Boone and Crockett Club for taking time from his busy schedule as an official measurer for the Boone and Crockett Club, to work with me during this investigation. Peter and I spent several evenings burning the midnight oil as we carefully went over every aspect of the case. In all, over 225 man hours and several hundred dollars were spent on the investigation. Also, several thousands of miles were driven and all available key persons were interviewed.

Peter echoed my sentiments, when he said, "We must address the matter of Malo's fish now in 1987 and not turn our backs on it as did the keepers of records 33 years ago."

My approach to the investigation was to first review the vast amount of data I had accumulated, list all discrepancies, and from this, develop literally dozens of questions on all aspects surrounding the catch and subsequent events, ie., transporting the fish to the taxidermist, measuring, weighing, skinning the fish, weighing stomach contents and having the scale checked. There were nearly as many versions of the above facts as there were reporters covering the story. This situation repeated itself in the many stories of 1986.

Once these questions were developed I set about resolving them. This was done in two ways. The first was to cross reference the discrepancies with the affidavit facts. The second was to interview the appropriate people involved and get their story.

Perhaps the best way to bring everyone up to speed (especially those of you who know nothing or very little about this fish), is to retell the story and interject all of the misinformation vs. the facts.

Malo's World Record, Muddled, Muffed, Wrongway, State's Record, Giant, Just Huge, Big, World Beater, And It Didn't Get Away, Musky!

That title alone (some of the many used at the time) should give you some idea of what is to follow:

Robert Malo was not a musky fisherman. Middle Eau Claire Lake was not a known musky lake. Malo, from Port Arthur (now Thunder Bay) Ontario, came to Sportsman's Lodge on Middle Eau Claire Lake, where he had been vacationing since 1950, on that June, 1954, weekend to visit friends and to party. In fact, party clothes were all that he brought along. While partying with his friends, Art and George Cruise, George convinced Robert to borrow clothes and fishing gear from resort owner Hank Boroo, and join him for a few hours early the following morning to try for some big northern pike. Almost all accounts agree that 4 a.m. Sunday morning, June 6, was the time the two anglers started out from Sportsman's Lodge to begin fishing (one account said crack of dawn). The method of fishing was row-trolling and still fishing live suckers. It is here that the "facts" became variable in the press. Depending on which account you read, the length of the sucker the big musky was caught on was: "medium"; "nine inches"; "thirteen inches"; or simply, "big."

FACT: According to the affidavit of George Cruise, the sucker was nine inches long. When I interviewed Malo, his recollection was "seven to nine inches."

The two anglers rowed to one of Cruise's favorite spots in a nearby bay and fished there awhile until another boat came in. At that point, they row-trolled to another bay. After they fished there awhile they noticed the other boat had left, so they returned, row-trolling, to the original spot.

Here again accounts vary. One account said that when the fish took the sucker being trolled by Malo, "It just hit and then started to move."

Another account said that after they arrived back at the bay, Cruise instructed Malo to drop the anchor, "But I urged him to row a few feet further, Bob went on. Then it happened The musky struck viciously and raced out with my line. Never had I felt such a tremendous surge of power!"

The two previous accounts were printed in 1954 and 1955.

Now for a couple of accounts printed in 1986:

"I was cursing it for a snag and then it started to move."

And, "After an hour's worth of drowning sucker minnows something big took a hold of Malo's offering."

So here we see fair consistency shortly after the catch, but slightly different views in 1986.

FACT: I referred to Malo's 1954 affidavit and got this account: "When approaching the bay with George Cruise rowing the boat, I got a strike from what seemed to be a fish of tremendous power."

When I interviewed Malo, I inquired about the snag that appeared in the 1986 account. He stated that they had been catching up in the weeds during the morning and he, "Thought at first it was again snagged up and then it started to move."

Before continuing the story we will review confusion over tackle; how the sucker was hooked; whether a bobber was used; time the fish was hooked and length of battle.

None of the accounts mentioned the rod or reel manufacturer other than it was a "musky rod," or a "five-foot split bamboo rod."

FACT: The rod was a Montague and the reel a Shakespeare.

All accounts listed the line as 40-pound test.

FACT: The brand of line was Higgins.

Accounts differed on the hook and leader. One account said, "Big hook on 18-inch wire leader," and another said, "Musky hook and 30-inch wire leader."

FACT: When I interviewed Malo, his recollection was, "A big square hook and a 6- to 8-inch wire leader."

My opinion is that it was probably a standard Weller type musky hook/leader combination, with an 8/0 or 10/0 square shanked hook and a 12- to 18-inch wire leader.

One 1955 account had them, "Using bobbers to keep the bait down about ten feet." This referred to "Still fishing."

FACT: When I talked to Malo he said that at the time the fish hit, he had no bobber on and was free-lining.

Accounts of how the sucker was hooked were, "Through the mouth and under the jaw," and, "Through the lip."

FACT: In asking Malo for clarification he stated, "I put the single hook through the sucker's mouth and out through the gills. The leader was then fed under the belly of the sucker and the hook placed through the meat of the suck-ers tail. I had used this method in pike fishing for years."

At what time was the fish hooked? Most accounts said either 5 a.m. or an hour after starting out, which is essentially the same. One account said 4: 30 a.m.

A Compendium of Musky Angling History

FACT: The affidavited time of hook-up was, "Approximately 5 a.m."

How long did the battle last? All printed accounts said either one-half hour or about 30 minutes.

FACT: In a letter from Malo to *Field & Stream* on July 4, 1954, he stated that it took "... about 25 minutes to land."

Now back to the battle. From a 1954 newspaper account: "When Malo realized he had something big, the fishermen started moving the boat towards shore. 'We moved towards a short sand beach and when I got the fish in shallow water, it slapped the boat once,' Malo said. 'Then I jumped out of the boat and kept nosing the fish into the beach. George got out. He had the pistol in his jacket and let fly with two shots. The fish quit fighting and started to quiver. We just stood there and sweated for awhile'."

Three other brief 1954 newspaper reports had the fish being landed in a "swampy area."

A 1955 magazine article had it this way: "I let him take as much (line) as I dared, then I managed to turn him. Our boat was only about 200 yards out, and I yelled to George to pull for shore! As he rowed, I gained some line on the big fella. But I wasn't prepared for his next move. Suddenly he raced toward us — and, in that moment, we experienced an awesome sensation as if we were whalers feeling the charge of a maddened bull! Water sprayed over us as the monster crashed head on into the boat. And for the next few moments he was the hunter. We were the hunted! Then, slowly but steadily, I gained back line. George got the boat into shallow water and I leaped in. I figured it would be safer to try to beach the fish, rather than risk a tangled or broken line if he made another rush for the boat. George jumped in behind me, and gave the boat a shove toward shore. With gaff hook in one hand and his .32 revolver in the other, he entered the fray. As I got the musky in close, he surfaced and George aimed a fast shot."

"Just as I shot," George picked up the story, "the fish spun like a halfback. I thought I missed him completely, but, later found that the shot had nicked his spine near the tail. I thought my second shot missed too ... but I got the fish through the head. He dove swiftly away. Then, in a moment, he surfaced, quivered, then lay still."

In a 1986 newspaper account, the writer, after interviewing Malo, wrote it this way: "As the monster fish neared the boat, things got hectic for the two fishermen. There was some shouting, a holler or two, a little gunfire. One shot went astray, but the other plugged the big fish right between the eyes.

"That slowed the beast down a trifle, and the men grabbed it by the gill covers and hoisted it into the rowboat." Further on in the article, the story was as follows: "'Oh, boy. We just couldn't believe it,' he (Malo) said recalling his first glimpse of the fish. Cruise happened to keep a pistol in his tackle box and this seemed like a good time to put it to use. In those days it was common practice to shoot a musky before bringing it into the boat ... After shooting and landing the musky, the men rowed back to the lodge."

When I interviewed Malo in 1987, I asked about the shooting discrepancy in the 1986 story. He stated that memory after 33 years may be a little foggy and that things certainly were hectic at the time. He recalled that, "As they neared the shallows and after the fish slapped against the side of the boat, George thought maybe he'd better shoot now. As I was half in and half out, he fired a wild shot. I told him to calm down. His second shot hit the fish in the eye."

FACT: I then referred back to Malo's 1954 affidavit. "Immediately after the strike, I gave George Cruise orders to try to hit the shore of this bay, where there was a clean sandy shore line. Having gotten to a point where the water was shallow enough, I jumped out of the boat and George Cruise followed me by jumping out of the boat, and shoved the boat out of reach of the musky, and during the beaching of his fish, the said fish, while in shallower waters, by this time, became more violent in his actions and was shot by George Cruise at this time with two shots, one lodging into the spine near the tail, and one bullet landing in the head. After beaching this fish, we marveled at our achievement and inspected the fish. After we calmed down from the catch and the beaching of this fish we loaded the fish into the boat and proceeded to the landing, directly in front of Sportsman's Lodge."

Additional things intrigued me. One was a reference in a 1954 news article: "Malo said the sucker was in the fish's stomach when he inspected it on the beach after the fish had been shot"; and a statement in Malo's letter to *Field & Stream*: "To my statement, I might add that the musky was hooked deep in the vitals, and ruptured internally during the fight."

FACTS: I asked Malo about these statements. His reply: "As I inspected that fish on the beach and attempted to unhook it, I discovered that the fish was hooked in the stomach and that during the fight, the hook had pulled the guts up through the fish's throat and that the hook was nearly straightened out from the fight. I later wondered about blood on my hands and discovered I had cut them in the musky's mouth while unhooking the fish on the beach."

A 1954 news account: "The fishermen then returned to the lodge and aroused Hank Boroo, operator and several other guests."

A 1955 magazine account: "The two happy fishermen lugged their huge prize to the lodge and banged on the door."

"'I couldn't believe my eyes when I opened the door and saw that tremendous fish draped across the porch,' Hank Boroo exclaimed. 'Never had I seen such a fish and we've had some big ones.'

"'How much gas is in your car?' Bob blurted out. 'I want to take this one to the taxidermist in Duluth right away.'

"'Better get out of those wet clothes first,' Hank suggested. (While Bob was changing, Hank awakened all the guests in camp.) 'Guess I was as excited as Bob and George,' he admitted later. 'Gosh! It was only 5 a.m. but none of them minded being routed out early, when they saw what the ruckus was about.'

"'Everyone crowded about the huge musky, and peppered the two fishermen with questions. 'Good thing it took Bob's sucker instead of mine,' George said. 'That musky rod of Hank's was stout enough to handle him. Mine would-n't have held up.'"

FACT: From Malo's affidavit: "... then tying up the boat, we took the fish and carried it to a spot directly in front of the door, leading to the barroom. We kicked on the door until Henry Boroo came and opened it. At this time, he viewed the fish with great alarm, and ordered all the guests to be awakened in the lodge to view this fish that we caught."

The time that the anglers returned to the lodge was pretty stable, as all news accounts and six affidavits from people who saw the fish placed the time at 5:30 a.m. One magazine account had the time at 5 a.m., writing "The exciting struggle consumed but about 30 minutes. Although neither Bob nor George had time to look at a watch. Actually, less than an hour elapsed from the time they left the dock."

FACT: George Cruise, in his affidavit, stated then: "... at approximately 5 o'clock I was handling the 16 foot round bottomed row boat, with outboard motor, and rowing with oars when a giant musky hit the nine-inch live sucker bait on the line of one Robert Malo."

Add the 25-minute fight and time to return to the lodge, and 5:30 a.m. bears out. Now begins a series of events that caused even more confusion.

A 1954 news account "Later they took the fish to Duluth where it was weighed at the Thomas Storey taxidermy firm and then skinned for mounting."

The 1955 magazine article: "... Impatient with the delay, Bob finally broke things up, got George and Hank to help load the fish into the car trunk, and drive to Duluth. It was 8 o'clock that Sunday morning when they arrived at the Storey taxidermy shop only to find it closed. But they phoned taxidermist George Flaim at his home, and he rushed over. The fish was carefully removed from the car trunk and placed on the shop scales."

A 1986 newspaper account: "Within a few hours, Malo, Cruise, and Hank Boroo, the resort owner, headed off for Duluth to take the musky to a taxidermist."

A 1986 magazine account: "... after a few hours' wait for the taxidermist to open, the fish was weighed."

Various other articles had the time of arrival at the taxidermist as 7:30 a.m. and as much as 12 hours later.

If these seemingly unimportant facts get screwed up, it is understandable that the important ones would too. It is no wonder that doubt is cast upon record fish!

FACT: It is very easy to resolve this one by referring to taxidermist George Flaim's affidavit "I, George Flaim ... a taxidermist, received at 7:30 a.m., Sunday, June 6, a muskellunge of mammoth size."

From Robert Malo's affidavit, a continuation of his story: "After having shown the fish to all the guests and others in the lodge, we immediately proceeded to a taxidermist, known as George Flaim of the Storey Taxidermy Company in Duluth, Minnesota. Upon arrival there, we went first to the taxidermy shop. From there to his residence and got George Flaim to admit us into his shop. Henry Boroo and I carried the said fish from the trunk of his car and placed it on the work table."

From the previous scenario, two questions came to my mind:

1.) Why wasn't the fish weighed before going to the taxidermist?

FACT: Malo's reply: "Good Question. There was no scale around the lodge or the immediate area that could weigh the fish."

2.) Why were you in such a hurry to get the fish to the taxidermist?

FACT: Malo's reply: "I had to go to work on Monday; I had yet to pack, and had a 300-mile drive home. A friend of mine had used Storey Taxidermy previously to get a pair of brook trout mounted, and I knew he was a good taxidermist."

And now, the most serious points in the whole episode — the measuring and particularly the weighing of Malo's fish. This part is enough to make a researcher crazy! There were so many variations of length, girth, weight, and weight of the stomach contents, that it was enough to make me pull the rest of my hair out!

I shall not attempt to reproduce here all of the written accounts, rather, shall stay with two primary stories of those we have used thus far and list the other differing stats from many other write-ups.

As for stomach contents, there were three different versions of the weight of the spawn (eggs) present, and five versions of the weight of the northern pike that the musky had eaten. They were:

SPAWN/EGGS	NORTHERN PIKE
8 1/4 pounds	3 pounds masticated flesh
8 1/2 pounds	3 1/2 pounds half digested
10-12 pounds	5 1/2 pounds partly digested
	5 1/2 pounds half devoured
	5 1/2 pounds

FACTS: Again, this is easily resolved by referring to taxidermist Flaim's affidavit "I, in the presence of these three people (Malo, Cruise and Boroo), first weighed, then measured and then cut the musky open. Found in the fish was eight and a quarter pounds of spawn and about three pounds masticated flesh of a northern pike in the stomach."

The 1955 magazine article: "... The indicator climbed up ward, stopping at 69 pounds 12 ounces! Flaim measured its length at 52 1/2 inches from the fork of the tail over the curvature of the body to the tip of the lower jaw. It has a tremendous 32-inch girth."

From a 1986 newspaper account: "The taxidermist, George Flaim, did not have an official scale, and his scale only had markings for each pound — no markings for quarter pounds or ounces. When they put the musky on Flaim's scale, the needle quivered somewhere between the 69-pound mark and the 70-pound mark. The men agreed the needle was at least halfway and probably three-fourths of the way to the 70-pound mark, which would make it 69 pounds,12 ounces. The musky was 55 1/2 inches long and had a 33-inch girth that stretched almost to the tail."

So, here in just two accounts, we have:

WEIGHT: 69 pounds 12 ounces; and, somewhere between the 69-pound mark and the 70-pound mark, with the men agreeing that the needle was at least halfway and probably three fourths of the way to the 70-pound mark, which would make it 69 pounds 12 ounces.

LENGTH: 52 1 /2 inches from the fork of the tail to the tip of the lower jaw, and, 55 1/2 inches long.

GIRTH: A tremendous 32-inch girth; and, a 33-inch girth that stretched almost to the tail.

In addition to the above, I found 23 other accounts of length, girth and weight, resulting in a total of nine different reported length measurements and four different reported girth measurements; and 19 different reported weights!

They were as follows:

WEIGHT
Between 69 and 70 pounds originally
About 69 1/2 pounds
69 pounds 8 ounces
At first 69 1/2 pounds to 69 3/4 pounds
69 1/2 pounds to 69 3/4 pounds originally
69 pounds 12 ounces
69 pounds 12 ounces originally
69 pounds 12 ounces originally plus 1/2-pound correction
About 70 pounds
70 pounds, possibly 70 pounds 4 ounces
70 pounds minimus
70 pounds 1/2 ounce
70 pounds to 70 1/4 pounds
70 pounds to 70 1/4 pounds after scale check
70 pounds 4 ounces
70 pounds 4 ounces corrected weight
70 1/4 pounds after scale correction
70 pounds plus 6 ounces error correction
70 1/2 pounds before scale correction

LENGTH
51 inches
51 inches unofficially
51 inches with a yardstick
52 1/2 inches
52 1/2 inches fork length
52 1/2 inches total length
52 1/2 inches remeasured length
55 inches total length
57 1/2 inches from tip of tail to tip of lower jaw — under belly

GIRTH

32 inches
32 inches with a tape
33 inches
33 1/4 inches unofficially

Several of the newspaper reports account for the 51-inch length as an original measurement "with a yardstick." No mentions are made where the 33-inch girth measurements came from.

FACTS: One need only to refer to taxidermist George Flaim's affidavit for the correct numbers: "Length of the musky, measuring with a tape from the fork of the tail over the curvature of the body to the tip of the lower jaw was 52 1/2 inches; girth measurement was 32 inches."

In addition to Flaim's affidavit, a letter from Clarence A. Wistrom, of the Wisconsin DNR, to Hugh Grey, *Field & Stream* editor, contained the following:

"The 52 1/2 measurement was fork length (customary for Canada). My own total length measurement was 55 inches."

I asked George Flaim why he used a fork length measurement, instead of a total length measurement. He stated that that was how he based his mounting charges to allow for normal shrinkage in mounted fish.

My own measurement of the mount in 1987, showed a total length of 54 inches from the tip of the tail to the tip of the lower jaw. This would, based on Wistrom's measurement of 55 inches, show a shrinkage of one inch.

I must point out that, although there were 19 different weight variations reported, the actual number of reporting sources were less, as, in follow-up articles after the scales were checked for accuracy and found to be weighing light or, "slow," reporters attempted to determine actual weight.

FACTS: Here again we will refer to Flaim's affidavit:

"The scales, marking pounds, tipped the needle to near the 70-pound mark, with our (Malo, Cruise, Boroo, and Flaim) estimate being 69 3/4 pounds. Weights and measures tester from Minnesota at Duluth on Wednesday (June 9, 1954) attested that the scales were one-half pound slow at 70, leaving the weight of the musky to be 70 and a quarter pounds."

It is here that the controversy centered — the accuracy of the scale. It was so stated in a rejection letter from *Field & Stream* editor Hugh Grey to Robert Malo, on July 28, 1954: "... In view of this inaccuracy, involving a most critical matter, we regret that we have no recourse but to refuse acceptance of your entry. As you undoubtedly realize, any other course would immediately involve us in endless controversies."

Apparently though, they did reconsider, as a report in a newspaper on January 12, 1955, reported "Grey (*F&S* editor) told the *Journal* that no final decision had been made by the board of judges which oversees the contest, that the final decision was up to the judges, and that the Malo fish is still being considered."

We will return to that decision, but for now we will move on to additional controversies surrounding the scale.

The type of scale used and its accuracy, created the major problems. This is evidenced by the many different reported weights in the press and *Field & Stream's* early rejection. So, what is the story about the scale and the subsequent check and re-checks of it?

First, the scale type. Various reports gave four options: 1) Utility (300-pound capacity); 2) Flat commercial; 3) Grocery; and 4) Bathroom.

FACT: In reviewing pictures of the scale and talking with retired Minnesota Weights and Measures Tester Marlowe Axell, there is no doubt that the scale was a flat bathroom-type. According to Axell, it had a 250-pound capacity.

After it was determined that perhaps Malo's fish was a contender for the world's record, and due to the fact that the scale the fish had been weighed on was not a certified scale, Hank Boroo, acting as Malo's "official United States representative" to look after his interest in regards to his musky, set out to have the scale officially checked by making arrangements with Minnesota's Department of Weights and Measures.

On Wednesday, June 9,1954, Hank Boroo, George Cruise and several representatives of the press took the scale to the Duluth Board of Trades building, where the scale was officially examined by Marlowe Axell, state weights and measurements inspector.

FACTS: Here we must refer to Inspector Axell's affidavit dated June 9, 1954: "I Marlowe Axell, Minnesota State Weights and Measures inspector, being duly sworn, do hereby certify that I inspected scale of George Flaim of the Storey Taxidermist Company, Duluth, Minnesota, on which the world record musky, caught by Bob Malo of Port Arthur, Canada on June 6, 1954 at 5 a.m. was weighed. I found the said scale to register one-half pound slow, which would make the actual weight of the fish seventy and one-quarter pounds."

I asked Mr. Axell how he tested the scale. He stated that he first tested it at the 250-pound capacity of the scale, and then checked it at 70 pounds, which was near the weight of the fish. (Originally, the fish was weighed on a board on the scale. The scale was re-zeroed after the board was placed on it. Axell said he re-zeroed the scale before checking it without the board.)

I then asked him how he knew it was a world record, and that the "actual weight of the fish seventy and one-quarter pounds," was so, as stated in his affidavit. He said that he based that part of his statement on what he had been told.

After the July 28 rejection letter from *Field & Stream* to Malo, Boroo again had the scale tested. For the results of the second round of testing, we go to the second affidavit from Axell, dated August 5, 1954: "To whom it may concern. I, Marlowe Axell, have been in the employ of the Weights and Measures Department of the State of Minnesota for seven (7) years. During this period I have tested scales of all makes and sizes. During my experience with this Department, there has never risen any doubt as to the accuracy of my work.

"On June 8, 1954 (actually 9th) I tested a scale upon which a musky was weighed that was caught by Robert Malo of Port Arthur, Canada, and at the time of this testing the scale definitely was one-half pound slow at 70 pounds. Today, August 5, 1954, I have tested this same scale fifteen (15) times and each time the scale registered exactly the same as it did June 8 (9th), 1954, one-half pound slow at 70 pounds."

When I talked to Malo about the scale he said that when it was re-tested, they "jiggled it and jumped on it."

I then asked Axell about the "jiggling and jumping" on the scale during re-test, to see if it would test the same. He said that he did that with the weights as he put them on and took them off of the scale. He also stated, that in his estimate, it was surprisingly accurate (meaning repeatability accurate) for that type of scale!

So, the testing and subsequent re-testing of the scale proved that it was consistent and was "surprisingly accurate," even though it was weighing one-half pound slow at 70 pounds.

This fact, though, did not change the minds at *Field & Stream*. In a letter to Mr. Boroo on January 12, 1955, Editor Hugh Grey said, "... in accordance with our original decision, the catch has not been recognized because of the discrepancy in the scales."

I will deal with this more in my conclusion, but for now I would like to head off in a couple of different directions.

As I was reviewing my mountain of data, I became aware of an undertone; no, make that several undertones, of negativity, surrounding the Malo musky. So, I set about developing a list of possible negative influencing factors that I thought might have had some bearing on the final outcome. After I developed that list, I attempted to develop a logical reply, if possible. From that evolved several mini-stories and, I believe, the underlying reasons why Malo's fish was rejected and seemingly forgotten.

Possible Negative Influencing Factors

1.) It was reported as a tiger (hybrid) or possible hybrid cross between a musky and a northern pike.

REPLY: I won't dwell on this point. It came directly from reporters' conjecture. George Flaim, taxidermist, who had handled thousands of muskies and musky hybrids, stated in his June 9th affidavit that, "This was definitely no tiger musky." Also, the fish was checked by the Wisconsin DNR biologists.

2.) Due to controversies that had surrounded previous record muskies there was "standard" doubt about Malo's musky.

REPLY: With any record fish there is always natural apprehension and negativity. With muskies, especially in light of past record claims and counter-claims, this one became an immediate target.

3.) Malo was indifferent about the record

REPLY: Because Malo was not a musky fisherman and didn't realize the significance of what he had done, he left the pursuit of the record up to resort owner Boroo. This led to accusations that he didn't catch the fish.

4.) Malo was not a musky fisherman.

REPLY: No, he was not a musky fisherman, but he was a northern pike fisherman and had caught them up to 15 pounds. This helped to contribute to his indifference.

5.) Malo gave the fish away.

REPLY: Yes, he gave the meat to Boroo to be eaten by the guests at the lodge, and, as I learned in my 1987 interview with him, he made an agreement with Boroo to keep the mount if he (Boroo) would pay for the mounting ($300, which was a lot of money in 1954), and give him (Malo) free American Plan lodging for the rest of his life.

6.) The musky had 11 1/4 pounds of eggs and pike in its stomach.

REPLY: If we subtract the weight of the stomach contents from the total weight, we end up with an actual body weight around 59 pounds.

7.) The musky "actually" weighed only 59 pounds.

REPLY: As Wisconsin DNR Aquatic Biologist Leon Johnson stated in his article "And It Didn't Get Away," in the August 1954, *Wisconsin Conservation Bulletin*, "If caught a few days later it might have weighed less. The 8 1/4 pounds of eggs might have been spawned out and the partly digested 5 1/2-pound northern pike in the musky's stomach might have been fully digested. But these are fine points in establishing the record breakers."

NOTE: Legitimate stomach contents are considered part of a fish's weight.

8.) How could a musky of that length weigh 70 pounds?

REPLY: In addition to the stomach contents, the fish had rolls of fat, indicating that it had indeed been eating well. However, most of this type of statement came before the stomach contents weight became a known fact, and when the 51-inch length was being reported, rather than the actual total length of 55 inches. To anyone knowing muskies and having seen the picture and the mount, there should be no question that it was indeed a 70-pound-class fish, as the huge girth extends from head to dorsal fin. In Wisconsin DNR Coordinator Wistrom's letter to *Field & Stream* regarding that very questioned fact, he stated "The Malo musky could have weighed 70 pounds," and, "There are great variations in weight in this size muskellunge so it is believed the Malo musky could have weighed 70 1/4 pounds."

9.) The musky was skinned right away.

REPLY: As you read previously, Malo was in a hurry to get back and pack and head home. Since they wanted the fish to eat, it was skinned right away.

10.) The fish was eaten.

REPLY: Yes, after being weighed. It was not destroyed — stomach contents were examined and weighed and dozens of people saw the carcass before it was cooked.

11.) The musky was shot.

REPLY: In those days in Wisconsin, it was practically tradition to shoot a musky, especially a big one, before landing it. Also, it was perfectly legal to do so, in fact, the record in place at the time, Louis Spray's 69-pound 11-ouncer, had also been shot prior to landing.

12.) The fish could have been shot spawning in shallow water.

REPLY: While possible, it would have required tremendous amounts of luck. They had only a small caliber pistol; water refraction would cause aiming problems; water impedes bullet penetration — especially small caliber; unless killed instantly, the fish would dash to deep water and be lost, as dead muskies sink rapidly; and this fish was/had been feeding, and was not likely spawning.

13.) Indians in the area were shooting big muskies.

REPLY: A common story with no basis of fact.

14.) The musky was brought down from Canada by car.

REPLY: This is one of my favorites. Malo told me that as he was packing the car that Sunday afternoon to leave, a group of people came over. One fellow leaned into the trunk and smelled it. He then said to Malo, "Boy, you sure got that smell out of there quick," to which Malo replied, "We didn't take the musky to Duluth in this car, we used Hank Boroo's." The man then said, "No, I mean the smell from bringing the fish down from Canada."

15.) The musky was flown in from Canada.

REPLY: A game warden caused this one. He still to this day smiles as he refers to the float plane sitting at the dock. However, no one ever said anything about having heard a plane land that morning, and most pilots would not attempt to land a small float plane in the dark. Since the musky still had life in it when it was brought in, this factor is very unlikely.

16.) Middle Eau Claire Lake was not a known musky lake.

REPLY: Since this lake was north of the Hayward area's hotbed of musky lakes, and hardly anyone knew it had muskies in it, it was doubted that the Malo musky had come from it.

17.) Muskies were first stocked in Mid Eau Claire in 1937.

REPLY: This is only true as far as the records go. I talked to Wisconsin DNR Biologist Frank Pratt and learned several things: A.) Pre-1933 stocking records are not accurate or are lost; B.) Haphazard fry planting was common in those days; C.) Fish taken in Mississippi River winter rescue projects were sent to Hayward by train tank car and stocked wherever; D.) from 1900 to 1933 there were a lot of field transfers and stocking done with no records; E.) When he referred to a book entitled, Fishes of Wisconsin by Becker, he found that the first Wisconsin fish survey done by Greene in 1935 showed muskies present in the entire Eau Claire chain of lakes!

When we discussed this further, it was his feeling that due to the watershed's connection with the Mississippi River, that muskies had always been present and that northern pike was probably the introduced species!

18.) The scale used was not certified

REPLY: As we have already learned, that is true. However, subsequent testing proved repeatability.

19.) The scale was in error.

REPLY: Yes, it was but the exact amount of error was certified and re-certified as "one-half pound slow."

20.) Perhaps, as one article suggested, Field & Stream suspected some after-the-fact scale tampering.

REPLY: If they did, it was never mentioned. There is no way to tamper with repeatability of a scale.

21.) The musky was caught on live bait.

REPLY: This is negative only in the respect that since it was not caught on a commercial lure, there was no support from that quarter to help try to get the fish recognized.

Now, we start getting into the real nitty-gritty of the undertones.

22.) There were personal and professional jealousies in the area.

The finished mount of Robert Malo's 70-pound musky.

REPLY: There were many people in the area who made it known that they didn't like or trust Hank Boroo.

23.) Cal Johnson, a former world record holder, popular outdoor writer for *Sports Afield* magazine, and Hayward resident, was a big promoter for Hayward and was outspoken against Malo's fish.

REPLY: Johnson publicly accused taxidermist Flaim of cutting Malo's fish in four pieces and dropping the flanks to give the fish the appearance of extreme girth. What Johnson was unaware of at the time was that in excess of 60 people watched Flaim mount the fish. It would have been impossible for him to cut it as Johnson claimed.

24.) Louis Spray, world record holder at the time, wrote *Field & Stream* to complain about Malo's fish.

REPLY: Louie's main complaint was about a 51-inch musky weighing 70 pounds. He also wondered why they didn't claim his reward (which we will cover shortly).

25.) The Malo fish was ugly.

REPLY: Well, perhaps it was (if any 70-pound musky could be considered ugly!). Talk heard at the time in Hayward was something like: the last two world records were both well proportioned fish, from area lakes known to be musky lakes, by well known musky anglers. Why should we help get this ugly fish recognized?

26.) *Field & Stream* did not wish to become involved: "... in endless controversies."

REPLY: Controversies cost money. *Field & Stream* was/is a for profit organization. Even though *Field & Stream* was looked upon as the official record keepers, it did not even send a representative to the area to check the catch out. The magazine relied strictly on letters (and possibly phone calls — although there is no record of any) to base the decision.

27.) A record would be worth $25,000 in promotional and advertising value to the area where the fish was caught.

REPLY: This could certainly have had an impact on decision makers as well as people who could have helped support the record claim.

28.) Cash was involved. Louie Spray was offering a $2,500 reward to anyone who could beat his 69-pound 11-ounce record; and, *Field & Stream* contest winners received a $100 bond.

REPLY: Again, this could have had an influence on the decision makers. In fact, it was rumored that Louis Spray told *Field & Stream* that if they accepted the Malo fish as a record then they could pay the $2,500 reward, or he would sue them.

I found nothing in this regard in writing, however, neither did I find any evidence that Malo attempted to claim the reward.

Fact is that Spray's rules required that he weigh and measure the fish before he would pay out the reward. The fact that Malo's fish was skinned right away put him out of the running even had his fish weighed 75 pounds!

29.) We now come to what I found that I feel put *Field & Stream* on a negative footing right from the start. It was a mid-June, 1954, letter from *Milwaukee Journal* outdoor writer Gordon MacQuarrie, who also wrote from time to time for *Field & Stream*. (Gordon MacQuarrie was always a highly respected Wisconsin outdoor writer. I do not believe he had any intent to dissuade *F&S* from accepting Malo's fish as a record. In fact, the intent of his letter was to inform *F&S* what he knew about the Malo musky. In his newspaper article of June 13, 1954, he wrote: "A new world record will be asked for this fish and from the evidence at hand it would not be surprising if it were allowed.") However, many of his statements to *F&S* could have been interpreted differently by them. Judge for yourself.

REPLY: From MacQuarrie's letter to Hugh Grey, *F&S* editor: "... The Middle Eau Claire Lake is MY lake. I have known it since 1914, own a home on it ... the Eau Claire chain is NOT typical musky water, by any means. I would not think of trying for a musky there if I knew I HAD to catch one. The fact that the middle lake has got all this publicity does not sit well with me at all but I can do nothing about it ... It has never been developed on a big league resort basis ... Could be this fish will end all that, or at least put enough angler pressure on it to make the days horrible with outboard music?"

"... Because it happened on MY OWN lake I deplore the whole damned situation, wish Malo had never caught the fish, and fear what the invading musky madmen will do to the relative peace and quiet of this lovely little 700-acre lake."

A June 17, 1954, reply to MacQuarrie from Hugh Grey included the following: "... I sympathize with you and your horror at the thought of your favorite lake being turned to a froth this summer by intrepid musky fishermen."

Again, I do not believe MacQuarrie had any intent to dissuade *Field & Stream* by the above, rather he was venting his frustrations. I do believe, however, that it could have had an impact on them.

In addition to the negative quotes from MacQuarrie's letter, he also mentioned the hybrid possibility and suggested that the men guessed at the "plus" over the 69-pound mark on the scale.

The MacQuarrie letter also contained several positive statements. I will cover them in the next segment on positive factors.

When I concluded my review of the data for negative factors, I then decided to go through the data again and pull out what should have been possible positive influencing factors and develop a reply for them if necessary. My thinking was that although there were many negatives against the Malo fish that surely there had to be several positive factors also. There were indeed!

Possible Positive Influencing Factors

Since the MacQuarrie letter was the first knowledge *Field & Stream* had regarding Malo's musky we will start there.

From the MacQuarrie to *Field & Stream* letter of mid-June, 1954: 1-6.) "In the course of telephone conversations with newspapermen in Superior and Duluth who covered the story up there, I got the impression from them that Malo was naive, that his catch was a legitimate big fish, and there had been no frame up. Circumstances tend to support that — the fish was not caught on a commercial plug but on a sucker. They didn't start hollering world record until the taxidermist weighed the fish, AND they ate the fish after leaving the skin and head with Flaim — where it is now almost completely mounted."

7.) "I know those newspaper boys up there, all sound men ... They all are inclined to think this Port Arthur guy is legit."

8.) "My inclination now is to accept the Malo-Boroo story as gospel."

9.) "Some 10 years ago (circa 1944) state test nets on the Upper Eau Claire turned up one around 50 pounds. The state's records show that musky planting was not started there until 1937."

REPLY: This 50-pound class fish further proves that muskies were in the Eau Claire Chain prior to 1937. It would not have been possible for a fish stocked in 1937 to attain a weight of 50 pounds in only seven years. A recent age study (Casselman and Crossman, 1979-1983) indicated a maximum weight of a 7- or 8-year-old musky to be 27 pounds.

In his June 13,1954, *Milwaukee Journal* column, MacQuarrie made the following positive statements in addition to those in the *F&S* letter:

10.) "A new world record will be asked for this fish and from the evidence at hand it would not be surprising if it were allowed."

11.) "The people involved in its capture did not know they had a record or near record, until a taxidermist weighed it."

REPLY: Actually it was later than that as I will cover in my conclusion.

12.) "There is no question that it is a giant musky."

And now on to the other positive factors.

13.) Both Clarence Wistrom and Leon Johnson of the Wisconsin DNR felt Malo's musky could have weighed 70 or more pounds as learned from Wistrom's letter (see negative factor number 8).

14.) The Wisconsin DNR's Johnson checked the fish and aged it at 30-35 years old.

REPLY: This supports the fact that it was not a hybrid and puts Malo's fish at or over the age of the 65-pound O'Brien musky. There are no records of any muskies older than that.

15.) Middle Eau Claire Lake was not a known musky lake.

REPLY: We have already proven that there were muskies present prior to known stocking record indications. Mid Lake is north of Hayward's hotbed of musky lakes and therefore relatively unknown for muskies. One possible reason could have been due to a low population density and the proliferation of northern pike.

16.) Taxidermist Flaim, who mounted several world record fish, believed the fish should have been accepted as the world record.

REPLY: From a 1986 newspaper article, "Today, Flaim still believes the musky was a record."

In a taped interview Flaim made the following statements: "(Malo' s musky is the) biggest ever caught"; and that he felt *Field & Stream* didn't give Malo the world record, "Because Spray would have sued them."; "No question it was a world record"; and that he was, "Convinced it was a 70-pound fish."

17.) There were 11 affidavits prepared within six days of the catch that certified all pertinent facts.

18.) An area guide of 30 years, Wilbur Smith was in Madison the day of the catch and didn't see the fish. For some time he doubted a musky that size came from Middle Eau Claire. However, in a subsequent year (circa 1955-1958), he saw one in the early spring before season in Mid Lake that he felt was even bigger (estimated 80 pounds) than Malo's fish.

19.) Malo was/is not a "musky nut."

20.) Malo had been going to Middle Eau Claire Lake and Sportsman's Lodge since 1950.

REPLY: He was not "imported" to "catch" the fish.

21.) When witnesses first saw the fish it still had life in it.

REPLY: In his August 27, 1954, letter to *Field & Stream*, Hank Boroo said: "... When I saw the fish it still had life in it." This was backed up by a former Hayward PR person who was on the scene shortly after the fish was caught. That person said to me in a confidential interview, "When I first saw the fish lying there on the grass its gill covers were still moving."

22.) Many people saw the fish "fresh."

REPLY: In addition to the former Hayward PR person, Malo, Cruise, Boroo and Flaim, there were six other people who signed affidavits attesting to the fact they saw the fish at 5:30 am. that Sunday morning, June 6, 1954.

I asked taxidermist Flaim about the fish's freshness when I interviewed him. He related that he was upset with the men for the way they had handled the fish. It had not been kept moist and was starting to dry out and was creased from being in the car trunk. He did indicate, however, that he was sure it was a freshly caught fish.

23.) *Field & Stream* did not send a representative to investigate the claim.

REPLY: I feel that an important sport fish, such as this one was, deserved more than it got. Should a 70-plus-pound musky be caught today, I'm confident that both fresh water record keeping organizations, NFWFHF & IGFA, would check it out thoroughly!

Conclusion

As you are aware, hindsight is always 20-20. It is always easier to look back on a subject, especially with a large quantity of relative data at hand and make a decision that may be contrary to previous decisions. It is done every day in the court system. Robert Malo had no appeals court to turn to. He had to accept the *Field & Stream* decision, like it or not. I feel that *Field & Stream* did not do a good job in handling the Malo record claim and that they were, possibly, sympathetic with the perceived plight of Gordon MacQuarrie and "his" lake. In a confidential interview, I was told by a person in Wisconsin who was trying to help Malo and was in a position to do so, that that person's superiors had told them to "leave it alone."

I believe, also, that much of the confusion in the press was due to deadlines and reporter desire to get the scoop, as well as slightly different versions related by the key persons being interviewed at different times by different reporters.

Always logical questions were: Why didn't they do it right? Why were things, especially the critical weighing, botched up? Why was only one picture taken?

The answer to these questions is really simple. The men did not realize at that time that Malo's musky was a potential world record. In Malo's June 12, 1954, affidavit, we find the following: "After this (finishing up at the taxidermist), we immediately proceeded back to the Lodge, made a stop at a tavern known as Bismarck Gossell's place, and informed him of our huge catch. On the way to the Lodge, we stopped at a place known as The Cabin, operated by Babe Desrosiers, and also informed him of my catch. We arrived at the Lodge and Henry Boroo called a number of the resorts around the lakes and informed them of the catch. Up to this moment, we did not realize that we had a world record fish. We were under the impression that the world record was over 71 pounds, and it was not until a few hours after we arrived at the Lodge, that someone found a book published by the Wisconsin Indianhead Country, Incorporated, giving the dimensions and weight of the world record musky. After having this information, we immediately started to establish proof of our catch."

Malo related to me that he couldn't understand what all the commotion and hollering was about. All he wanted to do was get rid of his headache and head for home. From Henry Boroo's June 9, 1954, affidavit we learn: "At that time (at the taxidermist's), we were more interested in a big fish rather than that of one having a world record because we were all under the impression that the record musky was 72 pounds or over."

In a September 1, 1954, letter to Hugh Grey at *Field & Stream*, Boroo said, "True, Bob Malo fouled things by having the musky weighed on improper scales. This was all done before anyone thought of the fish being of world record size. Whatever Bob did was done in innocence and without any fraudulent intent."

AP (Associated Press) writer Dion Henderson, who reported on the catch at the time, said that the fish "nearly escaped attention altogether."

From *the Superior Evening Telegram* of June 11, 1954, came: "It wasn't until *Evening Telegram* State Editor Lucille Horn informed the Eau Claire lakes anglers what their fish's weight meant, that all-out contention for official recognition began."

1.) In light of the way things were botched up, there is no way that anything had been "planned." Had they been planning to fake a new world record the three men would have taken the fish to a certified scale and would have come up with a higher weight.

2.) Due to the fact that the scale was found to be slow, the weight of Malo's musky definitely exceeded the weight of Louie Spray's 69-pound 11-ounce world record.

3.) Although the scale used to weigh Malo' s musky was not certified at the time of the weighing, it was promptly checked by an official weights and measurers tester.

4.) The scale was re-tested two months later, 15 times, and found to be testing exactly the same as it did during the first test.

5.) The testing and re-testing conclusively proved the repeatability and exact amount of error of the scale.

6.) Of the 15 listed world record muskies, I have no record of any of the scales having been re-checked or re-certified after the original weighing. One record musky had been weighed on two different scales, both showing the same weight, and a reference was made about having them re-tested by the state, but I find no record of its having been done, although it probably was.

7.) My records indicate that of the listed world record muskies, there are references for only five of them having been weighed on a certified scale. There were many controversies over record muskies starting in 1939. In all cases, however, the controversies were over facts and circumstances rather than the scale used. In one, Spray's 1939 fish, part of the controversy was that the fish had first been weighed on a bathroom scale, but it was later weighed on a certified scale. Apparently little thought was given to what should have been the most critical fact, the scales.

8.) The standard formula for calculating fish weight bears out for Malo's musky. Taxidermist Flaim used a formula, that he said was also used by *Field & Stream*, to determine if the reported weight of a fish was correct. *Sports*

Afield also uses this formula. It is: Girth X girth X length, divided by 800 = weight. Flaim indicated that 70% of a fish's weight is water, so the formula is extremely accurate. When we apply the formula to Malo's fish we get: 32-inch girth x 32-inch girth = 1024; x 55-inch total length = 56,320 divided by 800 = 70.4 pounds; 16 ounces per pound x .4 pounds = 6.4 ounces (or 70 pounds 6 ounces).

As you can see, 70 pounds 6 1/2 ounces is very close to the claimed weight of Malo's musky! One variation that *Sports Afield* had was to divide by 1,000 for pike-shaped fish (long and skinny — which Malo's fish wasn't).

If we divide by 1,000 instead of 800 we get the following result:

56,320 divided by 1,000 = 56.32 pounds

16 ounces per pound x .32 pounds = 5.12 ounces (or 56 pounds 5 ounces).

If we return to the approximate 59-pound actual body weight of Malo's fish, without the eggs and pike contained in the stomach, we again are very close.

It is very apparent from the use of the formula that the stomach contents were indeed the key to a 55-inch musky weighing 70 pounds. Again, legitimate stomach contents are considered part of the fishes' weight.

9.) Six of the record muskies had references to stomach contents. Two of them had substantial weight in them. One had 12 pounds of eggs (spawn) and one had a 14-inch walleye and an 11-inch sucker in it.

10.) The circumstances of the entire story were too wild, too bizarre, and too consistent to have been fabricated.

11.) Official recognition of Malo's fish, if granted at this late date, would change little in Robert Malo's life.

12.) Malo does not currently own the mount of his fish and there would be no monetary gain to him even if it is officially recognized as a world record.

Resolution

That taxidermist George Flaim was not personally involved with the catch had no stake in the fish being recognized as a world record and had made a statement to the press before the scale was tested that: "... his organization cannot take any responsibility on the official weight of the fish," is a FACT.

That the only affidavited statement regarding the weighing, "The scales, marking pounds, tipped the needle to near the 70-pound mark with our estimate being 69 and 3/4 pounds," made by taxidermist George Flaim should be the only considered FACT.

That from my investigation of the scale involved and others of a similar type, I found that the white space between the pound marks on the scale used would have been sufficient to determine only if the scale indicator needle was in the lower one-half pound area or the upper one-half pound area. Therefore, the acceptable scale reading should be only that the needle was in the upper one-half pound area of the white space.

That the scale was one-half pound slow every time it was tested, 16 times at the fish's weight of 70 pounds, and that it repeated exactly the same with each test, are FACTS. Therefore, the scale used, with a weight adjustment of plus one-half pound, should be accepted.

That although current world record acceptance procedures do not allow visual fractionalizing of weight and allow only weights indicated by the graduations on the scale, and that any weights that fall between two graduations on a scale must be rounded down to the lower of the two, the extenuating circumstances of the scale reading one-half pound light at 70 pounds should be considered. If the scale had been reading exact, it would have put the needle over the 70-pound mark and would therefore put the acceptable record weight, based on that reading, at 70 pounds even.

Therefore, it is the finding of this investigator that the official recognized weight of Robert Malo's musky should be 70 pounds even.

Epilogue

What I attempted to do in the above was to show how facts and stories can be misinterpreted, confused, misquoted and just plain changed. What I did not do was to review all of the many dozens of questions that I developed from researching the data unless they were directly applicable. The questions were developed using investigative techniques that I developed many years ago to use in verifying and clarifying facts when interviewing key people. Usually, the majority of seemingly important questions have a simple and very logical answer. They are the many smaller points that if left unanswered become a source for insinuation and rumor that develop into major negative thoughts and comments against a particular fish.

I must state here, that all of these types of questions that arose regarding the Malo musky, were satisfactorily resolved.

Whether either of the two fresh water record keepers choose to accept Malo's musky and list it as the record as I have recommended, will be up to them. As far as this investigator is concerned, Robert Malo's musky is one of the two largest ever caught, by weight, and I believe the largest!

Bibliography
Books
Musky Fishing as Told by the Three Old Guides to the Author by J.W. Jackson, self-published, 1958.

Muskie Fever by Bob Pinkowski, A.S. Barnes, 1961

How To Fish From Top To Bottom by Sid Gordon, Stackpole Books, 1955

A Compendium of Muskie Angling History by Larry A. Ramsell, Echo Printing, 1982

Fishes of Wisconsin by Becker, G.C., The University of Wisconsin Press, 1983

Managing Muskies, American Fisheries Society Special Publication 15, 1986

Magazines
Wisconsin Conservation Bulletin, August, 1954 ("And It Didn't Get Away" by Leon Johnson)

A Compendium of Musky Angling History

Sports and Recreation, January-February, 1955 ("70 1/4 lb. Musky Landed" by Rollie Nystrom)

Fishing Ontario, Fall, 1986 ("World Record Muskie?" by Geoff Coleman)

Newspapers

The Duluth News Tribune (Duluth, Minnesota) June 8; 9; 10, 1954; June 13, 1954 (Bud Lomoe); January 12, 1955

The Evening Telegram (Superior, Wisconsin) June 8; 10, 1954 ; June 11, 1954 (Lucille Horn); August (circa) 6, 1954; (Lucille Horn) January 11, 1955

The Sawyer County Record (Hayward, Wisconsin) June 17, 1954; July 1, 1954; August 12, 1954; January 13, 1955; May 18. 21, 1986 (Terrell Boettcher); July 16, 1986 (RBK)

The Minneapolis Star (Minneapolis, Minnesota), June 14, 1954

4 Seasons News (Hayward, Wisconsin), May 19, 1986 (Jim Bailey)

St. Paul Pioneer Press and Dispatch (St. Paul Minnesota), July 13, 1986 (Bill Gardner)

The Milwaukee Journal (Milwaukee, Wisconsin), June 13, 1954 (Gordon MacQuarrie)

North Country Vacation Guide (Hayward, Wisconsin), August, 1977

Montreal Gazette (Montreal Canada), August 25, 1954

The (Chicago Sun?) *Times* (Chicago, Illinois?), June (circa) 13, 1954 (Elmer Bernard)

plus several unidentified clippings.

Letters

Gordon MacQuarrie to Hugh Grey, circa June 15, 1954

Gordon MacQuarrie to Hugh Grey, circa September 17,1954

Hugh Grey to Gordon MacQuarrie, June 17, 1954

Hugh Grey to Gordon MacQuarrie, July 29, 1954

Robert Malo to Hugh Grey, June 15, 1954

Robert Malo to Hugh Grey, July 4, 1954

Hugh Grey to Robert Malo, July 28, 1954

Henry Boroo to Hugh Grey, August 27, 1954

Henry Boroo to Hugh Grey, September 28, 1954

Hugh Grey to Henry Boroo, September 21, 1954

Hugh Grey to Henry Boroo, January 12, 1955

Hugh Grey to Wisconsin DNR, September 12, 1954

Clarence Wistrom to Hugh Grey, October 5, 1954

Clarence Wistrom to Hugh Grey, October 29, 1954

Hugh Grey to Clarence Wistrom, October 29, 1954

Louis Spray to *Field & Stream*, June 30, 1954

Louis Spray to *Field & Stream*, November 4, 1954

Hugh Grey to Louis Spray, July 29, 1954

Louis Spray to Hugh Grey, January 19, 1955

C.J. Mickelson to Louis Spray, June 11, 1954

A Review of Muskellunge World Records

Hugh Grey to Hayward, Wisconsin Mayor, October 7,1954
J.E. Wesslen to Hugh Grey, November 10, 1954
Antony Wise to Hugh Grey, November 11, 1954

Note:

Gordon McQuarrie — Outdoor writer for the *Milwaukee Journal*
Hugh Grey — Editor for *Field & Stream*
Robert Malo — Angler who caught the 70-pound musky
Henry Boroo — Then owner of Sportsman's Lodge
Clarence Wistrom — Area Coordinator, Wisconsin DNR
Louis Spray — Musky world record holder
C.J. Mickelson — A Duluth, Minnesota taxidermist
J.E. Wesslen — Secretary/Treasurer, Hayward, Wisconsin Chamber of Commerce
Antony Wise — Mayor, City of Hayward, Wisconsin

Affidavits

George Flaim, taxidermist, June 9, 1954; Henry L. Boroo, lodge owner, June 9, 1954; Marlowe C. Axell, scale tester, June 9, 1954; George Cruise, with Malo, June 9, 1954; John Tarkka, lodge guest, June 10, 1954; Selma Malo, Malo's wife, June 10, 1954; Elmer Tarkka, lodge guest, June 10, 1954; Barbara Walsh, lodge employee, June 12, 1954; Hilda Boroo, lodge owner, June 12, 1954; Arthur Cruise, lodge guest, June 12, 1954; Robert G. Malo, Angler, June 12, 1954; Marlowe G. Axell, scale tester, August 5, 1954

In addition to the above written references, there were personal interviews with George Flaim, taxidermist; Robert Malo, angler; Marlow Axell, scale tester; Frank Pratt, Wisconsin DNR Biologist; Confidential, Hayward, Wisconsin; Wilbur Smith, area guide.

Malo Musky Fact Sheet

MUSKELLUNGE; MASKINONGE (Canada) MUSKIE; MUSKY: *Esox masquinongy*, Caught June 6, 1954 (Sunday) by Robert Malo, Thunder Bay, Ontario, Canada, at 5 a.m. (landed at 5:25 a.m.) Fish was landed by beaching and shooting.

Record weight: 70 pounds 0 ounces
Length: (total) 55 inches
Length: (fork) 52 1/2 inches
Girth: 32 inches
Stomach contents: 8 1/4 pounds of eggs (spawn), 3 pounds of masticated northern pike flesh
Rod: Montague
Reel: Shakespeare
Line: Higgins, 40-pound test
Bait: A nine-inch live sucker

Chapter 5:
Tiger (Hybrid) Muskies
(Esox masquinongy x esox lucius)

In an effort to properly introduce a multitude of anglers and fisheries scientists to the complete history of the hybrid muskellunge, this research has been done referencing both scientific and popular angling literature dating back to 1890. All references are identified. The quotes were used as they pertain to the subject. Care was taken to prevent using these quotes out of context. It is the intent to provide known scientific literature as it existed, as the hybrid musky was a relative unknown, even in scientific circles, for many years. This chapter will also help to explain how the term "tiger musky" originated and was applied to the true musky, when in fact it was usually the well-marked hybrid musky that was the subject of the descriptive term "tiger" in popular angling literature. Also brought to light is the fact that even though the subject fish is a musky x northern pike cross and biologically not a viable species, it has always been highly regarded and considered as a musky in the eyes of the angler as well as the fisheries scientist.

What's in a Name?
By Peter Haupt

Muskellunge and northern pike hybrid is the proper name for the fish we address. I do not care for the vernacular "tiger musky" for several reasons. Often mistakenly used to describe any musky with stripes, it ignores one half of the parentage. Sometimes it is used with a flair of bravado to describe all muskellunge.

With tongue-in-cheek I announced to the editor that we call them hybrid northerns or tiger pike. He answered by reminding me of the powers of editorship! We will be using the simple word "hybrid" to talk about the *Esox* cross breed.

I recall being part of a musky fishing gang working the Fence Lake chain about 30 years ago. There was a prize for the largest musky. As the four-day outing drew to a close one of the guys who caught a northern pike larger than any of the muskies bagged came forward to claim the reward, "After all," he said, "this fish is 50% tiger musky."

From *Forest & Stream*, July 3, 1890, by E. Hough:
This was a regular wild zebra of a fish and a beauty if ever there was one.

From *Pike, Pickerel And Maskalonge*, by Alfred C. Weed, Assistant Curator of Fishes, Field Museum of Natural History, Chicago, IL, 1927, Zoology leaflet 9, Hybrids:
There has been much discussion of the possibility of hybrids between the various species of pikes and pickerels. Largely on theoretical grounds, many have denied the possibility of such specimens in nature. Lately, however, there has accumulated a large body of evidence showing hybridization is not only possible but comparatively common among wild animals. Several years ago two specimens were caught in the Dead River at Beach, Illinois, a short distance north of Chicago. It is known that muskalonge have been planted in that stream. The two specimens are like ordinary pickerel except that the scaling on the head is like that of the muskalonge. It is quite possible that they are hybrids. One specimen of Chautauqua muskalonge sent to Field Museum from Bemus Point, NY, had a distinct patch of scales on the cheeks. It is possible that this may have been a hybrid.

From "The Tiger In Its Lair," by Ben C. Robinson, *Outdoor Life*, August, 1928:
We find a variety of bewildering and vividly marked specimens of the *Esox masquinongy*. I have seen Wisconsin and Minnesota specimens of this fish that, unless one knew the unfailing characteris-

A super fish and a super picture — Delores Ott Lapp and her 50-pound 4-ounce hybrid, the No. 2 tiger musky of all time.

tics that distinguish the species whereby they could be indisputably classified, would have caused even the closest student of musky classification to pronounce them of some other variety. Banded, tiger-striped, vermiculated and criss-crossed with checkerings of black brown, bronze and olive green colorings, presenting a dizzy contrast to another specimen taken from an adjoining lake that might be silvery green in color, with a few faint brownish spots marking its powerful body.

From "A Prize musky of Lac Vieux Desert," By Fred B. Ellsworth, *Field & Stream*, September, 1915 ... Reference a musky Mr. Ellsworth was fighting:

It was fully sixty inches long or over, and must have weighed sixty or seventy pounds. It had an enormous head and tail." (I used this reference because as the following references will point out, Lac Vieux Desert is now well known for large hybrid muskies, which exhibit an oversize head and tail — Particularly in the large specimens — and the fact that Mr. Ellsworth's guide at the time was John Knobla who in 1919 caught a world record musky from Lac Vieux Desert, which has since been identified as a hybrid.)

George C. Pfifer and his 31 1/2-pound hybrid from the St. Lawrence.

From "*Masquinongy* The Great," by Robert Page Lincoln, *Sports Afield*, March, 1932 — editor's note:

Mr. Lincoln will reveal for the first time the results of his life-long study of this huge fish ... Mr. Lincoln is acknowledged to be the world's foremost authority on the muskellunge ... Without a doubt the muskellunge, *Esox masquinongy* or *Esox nobilor*, whichever you will, is one of the most eagerly sought after of the fishes that are native to the waters of North America. The muskellunge is a great game fish. It is not the greatest of finny scrappers, but it is a fish that wins the respect of every fisherman who lays on line and lure for him. I will not say that the muskellunge is a consistent top notch performer in all waters at all times, for he is not. I have taken muskellunge that have been landed with great ease and in short duration after setting the hook in the jaw of the splendid fellow. I have even made the statement that many times the common great northern pike will "walk rings" around *masquinongy*; hard as it has been for me to make this assertion; for the great grey warrior means a lot to me in every sense of the word. But facts are facts.

Lincoln captions a picture in the article: "very unusual specimen of the tiger musky from Northern Ontario." — which was in fact a hybrid. More:

> Were Gerrard and Jordan and other scientists who have passed on, to go into the Lake of the Woods region today, they would find the unspotted muskellunge hobnobbing in those waters along with at least two or three other variously colored and marked fish of this species, including the so-called "tiger" or zebra striped musky which some have said is found in certain lakes in Wisconsin only. (Again a direct reference to the hybrid.)

From "Old Man Muskie," by Arthur Hawthorne Carhart, *Field & Stream*, September, 1935. Caption under a picture of a hybrid:

> Note the markings of this fish. They are the reason that some muskies are called tiger muskies.

This hybrid weighed 48 pounds 8 ounces three days after capture. It was caught from Pickeral Lake, Wisconsin.

Additional misconceptions from "Old *Esox masquinongy*," by Bert Claflin (a top musky expert of his day), *Field & Stream*, July, 1936:

> With this article I show a picture of a musky which is typical of the old specimens. Picture quote: "A 49 pound 'tiger' musky from Wisconsin. This is not a different species but a particular type of marking." (The fish is in fact a 49-pound hybrid taken from Pelican Lake, Wisconsin.)

From "What Is A 'Tiger' Muskie?" by Cal Johnson, *Sports Afield*, February 1938:

> We often hear anglers refer to certain territories or lakes as places where the famous 'tiger' muskellunge can be caught. Is he a separate species of the pike family — or just another musky dressed in different clothes? As a matter of fact, there is no difference in so far as the actual species goes, for the fish we know as the muskellunge is the same species regardless of its colorations or where caught. But we will always call the striped variety of the "tiger" 'lunge, I suppose, if for no other reason than to let our fellow fisherman know that our fish is of the finest and most beautiful coloration.

From "68 Muskies in 69 Days," by Ray Perry, *Sports Afield*, May, 1940:

Another misapprehension of "who is who" — on the musky register "from which we all seem to suffer," is our inability to identify a true "tiger" musky from the wholesale run of green or silver species. Despite the fact that a "tiger" is horribly overrated as a superior battler, he is, nevertheless, definitely a blood relation of the often-scorned northern pike, or so-called pickerel, with whom he is crossed and interbred. "Tigers" are found only in lakes and streams in which these pickerel abound. As a positive means of his quick detection, he has well rounded tail, identical in contour with that of his cousin, snake-pickerel. In contrast to this, the tail of the common green or silver musky is sharply pointed. So — by their tails you shall know them!

From "Northern Pike-Pickerel-Muskie," by Walter J. Wilwerding, *Sports Afield*, June, 1940:

... they are now catching numbers of so called tiger muskellunge, to which the species name of *immaculatus* certainly does not fit, for it is anything but immaculate, being barred with fused spots and lines of spots until it looks like a finned jaguar. It is perhaps a very dark variety of the northern muskellunge

with perhaps some mixture of the spotted muskellunge. The bars also have a striking resemblance to the bars on the Lake Chautauqua muskellunge, though darker. The abundance of these tigers in recent years causes me to believe it to be a hybrid. Whatever the cause that has produced it, this tiger is a finned beauty without a flaw. Species distinctions in these various forms are but local variations of a type species, which would result in interbreeding where one form is introduced into waters inhabited by another. (This author failed to consider hybridization of muskies with northern pike.)

From "Muskies Pay Taxes," by Gordon MacQuarrie, *Field & Stream*, September, 1940:

Not long ago I was at the Minocqua hatchery. There's a yarn developing up there for musky maniacs. Last spring, Wendell Anderson, hatchery superintendent, and Lyman Williamson, state biolo-

George Barber with his 49-pound Pelican Lake, Wisconsin, hybrid musky.

gist, went over to nearby Tomahawk Lake and seined out a female musky and a male northern. Each fish weighed about 12 pounds. Both were ripe. They fertilized the musky eggs with northern pike milt. They got about 500 active little fish from this mating, and every one of them looked like tiger muskies! Anderson says: "It's strictly an experiment. So far we do know those hybrid fish look like tigers, reputedly the gamest of muskies. We know too, they are the liveliest, fastest-growing members of the pike family we ever had in a rearing pond. They seem better able to shift for themselves than

Gary Caskey with the mount of his 38-pound tiger from Lac Vieux Desert.

Delores Ott Lapp with the mount of her 50-pound 4-ounce hybrid. Photo courtesy Ron Lax

true bred baby northerns or muskies. I may be shot for saying it, but my hunch is, our famous tiger musky is a hybrid northern pike — musky!" You'll hear more about that; and if you are a bona fide muskymaniac, your hackles may rise when the tiger is described as half northern. But hear Superintendent Anderson: "I've spawn netted muskies for twenty years. Never in that time have I taken a tiger musky on a spawning bed. Wouldn't that seem to indicate they are hybrids, which probably means they lack the power of procreation, like mules? In a couple of years we'll know more about it. We think now they won't reproduce, Williamson will find out. For the present I'm satisfied we've stumbled on the explanation of what a tiger musky is!"

Continued misconceptions from "The Musky Hangs High," by Bert Claflin, *Field & Stream*, July, 1943. The first page of this article features a one column by full page length picture of a hybrid musky:

> In the parlance of fishermen there are several varieties, but that means
> nothing scientifically ... certain waters produce muskalonge bearing dark spots;
> others, specimens having well-defined vertical stripes which make them "tiger"
> muskies; and still others have fish marked with both stripes and spots.

From "Artificial Hybrids Between Muskellunge and Northern
Pike," by John D. Black and Lyman O. Williamson, Wisconsin DNR
Wisconsin Academy of Sciences, Arts and Letters, 1947:

*A northern pike/amur pike hybrid caught in
Pennsylvania. It was a result of an experimental
crossing by the Pennsylvania Fish Commission.*

The problem of hybridization between these two species and the relationship of the so-called "tiger" muskellunge to the hybrids in Wisconsin, arose in 1937 when Dr. Edw. Schneberger (unpublished data) observed a small northern pike taking part in the spawning act of a pair of muskellunge in Island Lake, Rusk County, Wisconsin. Early in June of that year he obtained a specimen about 20 inches long from Island Lake that displayed both muskellunge and northern pike characteristics and had some of the vertical bars of the "tiger" muskellunge. Dr. Schneberger

*A "Russian Musky" — an amur pike from
Glendale Lake, Pennsylvania. Actually, it's a
cousin of the musky and northern pike of North
America brought to the U.S. from Russia by the
Pennsylvania Fish Commission.*

identified the fish as a northern pike x muskellunge hybrid. This identification was confirmed by Dr. Carl Hubbs, then Curator of Fishes at the Museum of Zoology, University of Michigan. Experienced muskellunge fishermen who have examined the large adult hybrids, declare them to be the same as the highly prized "tiger" of the northern waters.

From "An Unusual Maskinonge From Little Vermillion Lake, Ontario," by G. S. Cameron, *Canadian Journal of Research*, October, 1948:

So keen are anglers to exhibit their catch of a rare "true tiger" that every specimen of this variant taken during the time of the study was in progress was photographed and examined. The fact that of the 69 specimens examined only six were of the "true tiger" type indicates that this type is comparatively rare. This rarity, together with the striking beauty of the fish, makes it a prize eagerly sought after.

Taxidermist Ron Lax of Conover, Wisconsin, who has remounted both the Knobla and Ott Lapp giant hybrids. The fish he is holding is the Knobla world record. Photo courtesy Ron Lax

From "The Food and Growth of The Maskinonge *(Esox masquinongy, mitchell)* In Canadian Waters," by Alan S. Hurston, Royal Ontario Museum of Zoology and Dept. of Zoology, University of Toronto, 1951:

Specimens of a *E. masquinongy x E. Iucius hybrid* appeared to be infertile. They did not differ from the maskinonge specimens in their length-weight relationships but make faster growth than did the maskinonge from the same region.

From "Maskinonge," by the Department of Lands & Forests, Ontario (undated), reprinted from *Fishes of Ontario*, by H. H. MacKay, M.A., Ph.D.:

The characteristics of the hybrid fish appear to be superior to either the maskinonge or the pike.

From "How Wisconsin Saved The Musky," by Gordon MacQuarrie, *Science Digest*, 1953:

The musky researchers turned up an extra dividend ... an elegant hybrid, known as a tiger musky ... this "cross" ... comes into the world with what the biologists describe as "hybrid vigor." It eats like a pig and it grows like a weed. It attains the legal size of 30 inches much sooner than either of its progenitors ... the many tigers reared and released at Woodruff were wondrous creatures (A picture display of the first hybrid experiment at the Woodruff hatchery is on display at the National Fresh Water Fishing Hall of Fame). For the man who wants something like a bolt of lightning on the end of his line, the tiger fills the bill as well (some say better) as the true musky ... One tiger musky, weighing 50 pounds (4 ounces) taken from Lac Vieux Desert in 1951 by Mrs. Delores Lapp ... deserves special mention. Dr. Schneberger and others have described this fish as the handsomest member of the musky tribe they ever saw. It placed in a national contest not first, but had the rating been on looks as well as size there are those who have said it would have been the musky of the year.

This young lad struggles to hold up a dandy hybrid from days gone by.

From "The Lure of Musky Fishing," by Gordon MacQuarrie, *Sports Afield*, July 1956:

"The handsomest musky I ever saw was a 50 pound (4 ounce) tiger from Wisconsin's Vieux Desert Lake, caught three years ago by Mrs. Delores Lapp, wife of a guide. There wasn't a marking on that fish, or a line of its body that was out of place. Big, beautiful, symmetrical, and brutal, was he.

From *The Northern Pike*, by Keen Buss, Pennsylvania Fish Commission, 1961:

Muskellunge x northern pike crosses and the reciprocal hybrids were heavily barred fish and there was no evidence of the characteristic color markings of the northern pike.

From the book, *Muskie Fever*, by Bob Pinkowski, copyright 1961:

There is the hybrid musky, a cross between a true musky and a northern pike. This is the most abundant of the three and is a beautiful looking

298

specimen, with contrasting olive-mottled stripes running down across a silvery-bronze body. "Tiger of the North," it is called in Wisconsin, where state conservation department biologists created the fish artificially after many years of cross breeding. Here is truly the most vigorous freshwater battler around. The stripes give him a bold, dashing, debonair look, which he lives up to supremely.

From Thermal Resistance of Pike *(Esox lucius L.)*, Muskellunge *(E. masquinongy, mitchell)*, and Their F1 Hybrid, by D.P. Scott, *Fisheries Research Board of Canada*, 1964:

There appears to be some hybrid vigor in that hybrids tend to be more resistant to thermal stress at the average acclimation and test temperatures encountered in the experiments ... At the average acclimation and test temperatures, the three groups are highly different, the hybrid being most resistant, the muskellunge least so, and the pike intermediate ... This may indicate hybrid vigor in that the differences are to benefit of the hybrid.

"Muskellunge Management in Wisconsin," by Arthur A. Oehmcke, *Wisconsin DNR Report* #19, 1969:

For the practical fish manager, one of the best indicators of fishing success is the satisfied fisherman ... We estimate that 40 to 50% of the "muskellunge" caught annually from Lac Vieux Desert are natural hybrids.

Evidence that this hybridization has been taking place for some time is indicated by the 50-pound 4-ounce, 56-incher caught by Delores Ott Lapp from Lac Vieux Desert in 1951. It has also been learned from Mr. Fred Aman, a former taxidermist near Lac Vieux Desert, who has undoubtedly handled more large hybrids than anyone, that the fish that is mounted and said to be the 1919 world record of 51 pounds 3 ounces caught by John Knobla from Lac Vieux Desert was a hybrid; as was a 60-inch full-bodied specimen that had been hooked, shot (when legal) and lost in Lac Vieux Desert and later found dead — measured and verified by Mr. Aman.

Back to Oehmcke:

Big tiger musky caught from Werner's Resort, Sayner, Wisconsin, circa 1930.

This cross breeding of a native species is of definite management concern and presently begs for research attention.

It would appear from angler catch records that the hybridization taking place in Lac Vieux Desert is having no ill-effect on the natural muskellunge population. In an area that encompasses over 200 top musky lakes, Lac Vieux Desert has, since 1967, produced 19 muskies (2 of them hybrids) in the top 10 (3 in 1976) in the Vilas County (Wisconsin) Annual Musky Marathon. This is 12 more than its nearest competitor during that time. Ironically, of the only 3 registered sport caught muskies from Lac Vieux Desert to weigh over 50 pounds, 2 have been hybrids — as was the 60-incher that was found dead!!

From *Muskellunge Management in Michigan*, by John D. Schrouder, Inland Fisheries Specialist, Michigan DNR (undated):

More than 17% (13,765 acres) of the state's inland musky water is now under tiger management. Tiger musky growth data, although limited, indicates

that the hybrid grows faster than either of the pure-breds. Hybrids have reached 32 inches in just two growing seasons (age 1 plus) in the southern portion of the state (personal communication — James Copeland, 1972) ... Harvest: Approximately one-half (7,520) of the state's total harvest came from Lake St. Clair. The remainder of the catch was comprised of about 80% hybrids and 20% northern muskellunge. The figures point out two important points in Michigan's muskellunge program. First, the muskellunge spawning area in Lake St. Clair and St. Clair River is important to the entire program. Second, the hybrid musky is contributing about 40% of the statewide annual harvest of muskellunge. This is significant in the light of the fact that legal-size tiger muskies have only been available to fishermen in Michigan since 1969 ... Musky lakes are currently managed to provide a trophy fishery ... The fact that tigers generate fewer angler days per creeled fish is probably related to their relatively high vulnerability to fishing, a favorable characteristic from the fisherman's standpoint. They are also suited to a wider range of waters than purebreds ... Because of these factors, Michigan will continue to stress hatchery propagation of tiger muskellunge for production stocking in selected waters.

LaMont Roth with a beautiful 24-pound 5-ounce hybrid from Eagle Lake, Ontario.

1948 was the same year Red DeGroot caught a stocky 49-inch hybrid from Round Lake near Hayward. It weighed 43 pounds 11 ounces. Several years later George Tally took a 42-pounder from Round. Fence Lake, at Lac du Flambeau, produced a 42-pound hybrid during the same era.

George Tally with his 13th-ranked, 42-pound-plus hybrid from Big Round Lake near Hayward, Wisconsin.

Although Round and Fence are 80 miles apart they are both drained by the Chippewa-Flambeau watershed. Maps of today will show the Bear River, which drains the extensive Fence Lake chain, to conflue with the Manitowish and Turtle Rivers to form the Flambeau Flowage. Downriver those names disappear as the north fork of the Flambeau takes the water to the Chippewa. To picture this system in pre-flowage days it is evident that the Manitowish and the Flambeau is one continuous river rising in Vilas County's High Lake. An early (1848) map drawn by surveyors shows a long river rising in Trout Lake and joining the Chippewa below Ladysmith called the Manadowish. A portion of the south fork was called the Doré Flambeau.

Interpretations varied when the French tried to write the spoken-but-unwritten Ojibwe language. Spelling was inconsistent. For example, the Wisconsin River, after which the state was named, was originally called "Ouisconsin." History reveals strange truths.

From "A Report To Little Green Lake (Wis.) Muskellunge Fishermen On The Results of The 1971 Fishing Season," *Wisconsin DNR Report*:

> During 1970, Little Green Lake received a bonus plant of hybrid muskellunge in addition to the regular stocking of true muskellunge. The growth and survival of the hybrid muskellunge has been so spectacular to date that we anticipate that many hybrids will be caught during 1972, shortly after they reach 2 years of age!

A Compendium of Musky Angling History

From "The Results of a Ten Year Voluntary Creel Census at Little Green Lake, Green Lake Co., Wisconsin, 1963-1972," in the May 1973, *Wisconsin DNR Report*:

> The creel census records show the first legal hybrid was caught on May 15, 1972, when it was 2 years of age. Two hybrids were registered during May, two in June,13 in July, 38 in August, 39 in September, 38 in October and 15 in November, for a total of 147 (7.93% of the total stocked in 1970). Hybrid muskellunge comprised 39.8% of all fish registered during 1972. Analysis of the hybrids registered shows that they averaged 30.9 inches, with a range from 30.0 to 33.0 inches in length. (Average. weight 6.7 pounds — range 5.5 to 9.5 pounds). Hybrid muskellunge taken in seine hauls made in 1971 and in 1972 showed that almost every fish checked appeared to have eaten a bluegill or sunfish. True muskellunge, similarly sampled rarely, if ever, appeared to feed on sunfish shaped fish ... The 10 year voluntary creel census at Lt. Green Lake has supplied a great deal of information helpful to fish managers, some of it unavailable or only rarely recorded in fisheries literature.

Len Kubicki with a 40-pound hybrid from the St. Lawrence River.

From "Comparative Growth, Survival, and Vulnerability To Angling of Northern Pike, Muskellunge and The Hybrid Tiger Muskellunge Stocked In a Small Lake," by George B. Beyerle, Michigan DNR, Fisheries Division, *Fisheries Research Report # 1799*, July 11, 1973:

> The naturally occurring hybrid between muskellunge, (*Esox masquinongy*) and northern pike (*Esox lucius*), called the "tiger" musky, was the first reported in Illinois in 1927, according to Crossman and Buss (1965). — Ref. to Weed 1927 — tiger musky eggs often showed greater viability than muskellunge eggs; young tiger musky grow faster and are hardier than either parent. Scott (1964) found increased thermal resistance in tiger musky compared to the parent species. Field observations and angling reports have indicated that, generally, tiger musky have survived at higher rates. The tiger musky is considered to be more exciting to catch than pike.

From "Pennsylvania Pikes," by James W. Meade III, May 17,1974:

> The new and increasingly popular hybrid, the tiger musky, which is being stocked extensively ...

Tiger (Hybrid) Muskies

Much information was taken from works by Dr. E.J. Crossman of the Royal Ontario Museum. Other authors whose works were used included Samuel Eddy (Minnesota) and Keen Buss (Pennsylvania) ... tiger muskellunge ... Rare in nature ... Growth — Among hatcherymen the tiger musky is known for its superior growth rate and hardiness. Survival from egg to fry is high. Relation to Man: This "artificial" or "man-made" variety of pike is becoming popular with anglers. High survival rate and susceptibility to angling yields a high rate of return to the fisherman. Not only is this fish a bit less expensive to propagate but due to the return rate the sportsman gets much more for his fishing dollar.

Head like a musky, fins and tails like a pike, body black and silver. Not a hybrid, but actually a mutant northern pike caught by the author's father from Ealge Lake, Ontario. In the lower photo, it is shown next to two northern pike.

From "Smashing The Musky Myth!," May/June 1974, *Wisconsin Sportsman*:

The lake (Little Green) was stocked with several species of game fish, including both true and hybrid muskies, very little was known about musky fishing other than ancestral lore and legend. (The article was concluded with the results of the 10 years' study; including date, lure and hours of capture. Because hybrids are thought of as muskies, the data on all musky captures includes hybrids. This study was conducted by the Wisconsin DNR!).

From the Sixth Interstate Muskellunge Workshop, September 25-26, 1974. Artificial Diets For Esocids And Walleye Culture, by Charles H. Sanderson, Fisheries Technician II, Pennsylvania:

The results of the 1973 diet testing program indicated that we could expect good results with tiger muskellunge on dry feed. The results with pure muskellunge revealed limited success ... Advantages Rearing Predator Fish on Artificial Diets — The results of a full scale production program on artificial diets have conclusively substantiated that tiger muskellunge can be produced in large numbers on dry feed ... Question from Bob Miles, West Virginia: "Using the same cost, could you rear more on a dry diet than on minnows?" Answer by Sanderson: "Definitely ... Sheyrl Hood, Pennsylvania: "Labor savings is significant. For example, you eliminate the labor in harvesting minnows." ... Sanderson: "At one time in 1974, one man was caring for 70,000 fish on dry feed." General discussion period: Dick Colesante, New York: "A questionnaire was sent to several states and Canada regarding the naming of the 'hybrid muskellunge' (male northern pike x female muskellunge) and the majority opinion was that it should be called the tiger muskellunge. This name will be recommended to the Naming Committee of the American Fisheries Society."

A good comparison: left — Chan "Doc" Cotton with a large northern pike; center — Roger Halvorson with a 25-pound hybrid; right — Al Skaar with a 31-pound-plus purebred musky.

From *Northern Outdoor News*, April, 1975, "Tiger Musky":

Interest in the hybrid, or tiger musky, by midwest fishermen has increased rapidly in recent years due to its spectacular markings and fighting ability. The hybrid seems to take the better qualities from each parent. It has oversized fins and tail, which might account for its strong fighting tactics.

From "State Anglers Take Aim at New Hybrid Musky Mark," by Jim Lee, *The Wausau Herald*, Friday, June 27, 1975, page 4:

Wisconsin anglers have a new mark to shoot for as a result of a recent decision by the state to recognize the hybrid musky as a separate, distinct species (category). The world record hybrid, or so-called "tiger musky" was caught in Wisconsin waters. The hybrid musky is coveted by fishermen for its outstanding fighting qualities and its strikingly beautiful markings. The first artificial breeding attempts were the results of fishery experts trying to combine the size of a musky with the catchability of northern pike. Their efforts worked as the

Tiger (Hybrid) Muskies

crossbreed has been a fast growing fish and packs on weight easily as the record shows. But, where the experts had hoped for a fish with a greater willingness to take an angler's lure, they were foiled. The hybrid has remained a real trophy fish and it has been protected by the same size limits that relate to muskies. They were originally intended to serve as a predator fish in lakes with stunted panfish populations. The DNR chose to stock hybrids in many of these cases because they will not reproduce and their numbers could be controlled.

From "Muskies Move South," by Tom Wendelburg, *Wisconsin Sportsman*, May-June 1975:

Arm weary musky fishermen tell it takes on the average, thousands of casts to tie into one of the brutes. Don Jung had hardly unlimbered his arm when he said with the assurance of a veteran musky hooker, "There's one" ... The nearly 20 pounder (46 inches) would have been a good catch anywhere, though Don, a resident of the southern part of Wisconsin, had fished Pewaukee for muskies only a couple weeks. Don knew the DNR had been stocking muskies and catches had been reported. After many years of musky fishing, he knew how to start out on a lake which had this new, larger fish. The musky had moved south. From reading the annual growth rings on the scales, biologists determined the fish was only in its seventh year. It had been one of the muskies of the 1967 stock, planted in the lake when it was not much longer than a 12 inch ruler.

Picture caption: At right Don Jung's 46 inch tiger musky taken from Pewaukee Lake on a yellow bucktail. These hybrids have taken hold in southern waters where natural muskies failed.

Most or all of the muskies being stocked in these waters are hybrids ... the growth rates and qualities as a sport fish make hybrids a desirable stock. Hybrids have taken hold in southern waters where natural muskies haven't provided steady angling. Decades ago, natural muskies were stocked in Pewaukee, but this was discontinued ... I caught my first legal musky (hybrid) another day.

From "The Great Outdoors," by Steve Henry, *Outdoor News*, June 27,1975 :

The hybrid musky has come in for a share of publicity in recent months. This cross between the northern and musky is a beautifully marked fish and has stirred the hearts of many an angler when caught.

July 30, 1975, letter from Donald Zumwalt, Curator of Fishes, Shedd Aquarium, Chicago:

Regarding ... the hybrid cross between a male northern pike and a female muskellunge ... This hybrid can be distinguished from either a northern pike or muskellunge and therefore, could be established as a distinct records category.

From a letter dated 8-7-75 from C.W. Thereinen, Acting Chief, Fish Management Section, Wisconsin DNR, to Delores Ott Lapp:

> Up to now Wisconsin has not included the hybrid in our state record listing. However, in the future we will recognize the hybrid and thus we have noted your catch as the state record. (Of course, Mrs. Lapp's fish was later displaced by the 51-pound 3-ounce Knobla fish.)

From a 1975 letter by Peter Haupt, then-chairman of the Hybrid Committee, The Muskellunge Club of Wisconsin:

> The next time you catch a musky with unusually bright markings, look for a large rounded tail (caudal fin tips). You might have a hybrid musky. Be it 30 pounds or 30 inches, it is a rare trophy and one of nature's most beautiful creatures.

From a letter by Steve Statland, then-president of the Illinois Chapter of Muskies Inc., to Pete Hadley, president of Muskies Inc., September 28, 1976:

> The tiger musky has always been a most sought after prize by musky fishermen and traditionally never been considered anything but a musky. We (the board of directors of the M.I. Illinois Chapter) think only in the most purist sense could it not be looked upon as a musky.

From November, 1976, *Northern Outdoor News*, "Hybrid muskellunge Project is Completed":

> An experimental introduction of 3500, 12 inch fingerling hybrid muskellunge ... has been carried out in Fish Lake, Burnett County according to local DNR fish manager, Stan Johannes. The hybrids were stocked on August 26,1975. The purpose of this experiment is two-fold, reports Johannes: 1. To control an overabundant, slow growing panfish population. 2. Provide a fishery of trophy status in a lake where none now exists ... Fishermen are reminded that the hybrid muskellunge is considered to be a muskellunge from a regulations standpoint.

From a December 15, 1976 letter from Mepps to Leonard Grunow, Rockford, Illinois:

> I heard from one of my fishin' friends ... that you caught a whoppin' big 30 pound 8 ounce hybrid musky on a Mepps spinner. A 30 pound musky is a trophy in anybody's book, and a tiger musky that size is record class. (It was, in fact, a line class world record.)

From the December 1976, West Virginia Husky Musky Club

newsletter, an interview with Bob Miles, fish management supervisor, Department of Natural Resources, West Virginia. Roane County Lake "A Blessing for West Virginia":

> In June of 1974 ... the W.Va. DNR began stocking 690 tiger muskies ... We knew this hybrid was a hardy fish ... the area was opened to fishing just this year, and on opening day a 38-inch tiger musky was caught. A growth rate of about 16 inches per year! The tiger musky is hardier, faster growing ... states such as Ohio, New York and Illinois are complementing their already established pure musky fisheries with the tiger because they're cheaper to raise, easier to raise, and provide a quicker return to the fisherman ... The tiger musky program in W. VA. was initiated for the smaller type reservoirs in order to relieve some of the pressure off the stream (pure) musky ... the tiger will open up a new state record classification ... This is a tremendous opportunity for the W.VA. musky fisherman and a blessing for West Virginia! ...

West Virginia recognizes tiger muskies and has established a new state record category for it; Ohio recognizes tiger muskies; Pennsylvania recognizes tiger muskies; The Iowa Great Lakes (musky) Fishing Club recognizes Iowa hybrids as muskies as evidenced by the 1974 tournament winning musky and the largest caught for 1974 — in State — were both hybrids; as was a 1975 tournament fish-picture captioned in the newsletter, "It was his first legal musky," and the Iowa size limit on hybrids is the same as it is for muskies, 30 inches; Michigan recognizes tigers, has a state record tiger and the size limit the same as it is for muskies; Wisconsin recognizes tigers, has a state record tiger and the size limit the same as it is for muskies; Illinois recognizes tigers and the size limit is the same as it is for muskies; North Dakota recognizes tigers, has a state record tiger; Minnesota recognizes tigers, and the size limit is the same as it is for muskies; Bill's Musky Club recognizes tigers; the Muskellunge Club of Wisconsin recognizes tigers and has a yearly trophy category for them; The Vilas County Musky Marathon (Wisconsin) considers tigers as muskies in the yearly contest; The National Fresh Water Fishing Hall of Fame and IGFA maintain world record categories for tigers.

Let us at this point review the establishment of world record status for the hybrid. In June of 1975, the Fishing Hall of Fame put out the following release:

> Through the efforts of the hybrid committee of the Muskellunge Club of Wisconsin, absolute verification has been obtained for a 50 pound 4 ounce

muskellunge hybrid (*Esox masquinongy x Esox lucius*), 56 inches long, with a girth of 26 inches, that was caught June 28, 1951, by Delores Ott Lapp of Land O Lakes, Wisconsin, from Lac Vieux Desert, Wisconsin.

Due also to the efforts of the hybrid committee, the Department of Natural Resources of the State of Wisconsin, is establishing a separate category for muskellunge hybrids, and will undoubtedly recognize Mrs. Lapp's fish as the Wisconsin state record.

In keeping with the goals of the National Fresh Water Fishing Hall of Fame, new world record categories have been established for the muskellunge hybrid. In addition, because of the absolute verification of the hybrid caught by Delores Ott Lapp, it is now officially recognized as the All Tackle World Record Hybrid Musky!

This Ott Lapp musky was, of course, later replaced by the Knobla musky. From Peter Haupt:

"Katikitigon" was the name the Ojibwe people used for the water that Frenchmen call Lac Vieux Desert. The natives resided on the northeast shore and thrived on wild rice and other lake-related bounty. French traders made a settlement on one of the islands. The logging industry used its strong influence to put a dam across the outlet, the source of the Wisconsin River, and impounded the lake about three feet. They needed a head of water to flush pine logs downriver to mills at Eagle River and Rhinelander. Resorts began to spring up along the south and west shores. A fisherman could board a train at Chicago or Milwaukee and ride all the way to Stateline (now called Land O' Lakes) or get off at Conover's Stop and take the logging spur to Hackley (now Phelps).

Writings that predate the turn of the century told of catching a "pickerel or maskinonge with stripes like a tiger." Then thought to be a separate species it would be another 30 years before hybridization was considered.

Now we are at mid-century. Ott's Resort and Lapp's Resort are side-by-side and when an Ott daughter married a Lapp son the teamwork was formed to catch one of the most reknown fish in Wisconsin angling history. On a June morning in 1951, with husband and wife fishing well off the south shore, Delores Lapp caught the 50 pound 4 ounce fish that would eventually be recognized as the world record for the northern pike and muskellunge hybrid.

Later in the 1950s Dick Lapp (brother-in-law to Delores) caught a 43 pound hybrid from Vieux Desert. The mounted fish is displayed at the Minnow Bucket bait and tackle shop located just southwest of the lake. Also displayed is the Knobla ranking world record hybrid of 51 pounds 3 ounces.

Vieux Desert produced hybrids of 38 and 39 pounds in the 1960s while Big Sand yielded a 38 pound hybrid. Plum Lake in Vilas County and Riley Lake in Forest County produced 40 pound hybrids in the 1960s also. Other area lakes had catches up to 35 pounds and this trend continues today. Clearly, the golden age of all musky fishing was fading and, along with it, the catch of giant hybrids.

Tiger (Hybrid) Muskies

As pressure increased and equipment improved the 40 pounders were thinning out. This is not to say that record class hybrids no longer exist. In 1988 guide Duane Horstman found a freshly dead 54 incher floating in a Lac du Flambeau area lake and in 1983, one year after catching a 47 pound musky from Round Lake, I had a follow from a larger musky that appeared to be a hybrid (also in Round Lake).

Why do the majority of the known hybrids over 40 lbs. come from a concentrated area? These are natural hybrids, incidentally, not planted from hatchery stock. Rule out watershed as three separate major systems are involved.

One guess is that it is the weather that hits this area. This is Lake Superior snow country and late winters give way to sudden thaws causing an overlap of spawning periods for the two species involved. The high headwater lakes warm rapidly and some years find the muskies moving in to spawn before the northern pike have left. Conditions are then ripe for hybridization.

June and July have been the best time for big hybrids. Any musky lure will attract them used around weed cover. If a new record is to be caught I would look for it in either Lac Vieux Desert or Eagle Lake, Ontario.

As additional research was pursued and completed, the following release was sent out in May of 1979:

New All Tackle World Records
Muskellunge hybrid or tiger musky
(Esox masquinongy x Esox lucius)

In June of 1975 the National Fresh Water Fishing Hall of Fame established a category of world record recognition for muskellunge hybrid. Through the efforts of the Hybrid Committee of the Muskellunge Club of Wisconsin, absolute verification was obtained for a 50 pound 4 ounce muskellunge hybrid caught June 28, 1951 by Delores Ott Lapp from Lac Vieux Desert, Wisconsin/Michigan and it was accepted as both the Wisconsin state and the world record. At the time the Lapp hybrid was being investigated, another fish was also checked out. That fish was a 51 pound 3 ounce musky, also caught from Lac Vieux Desert in 1919. Although that fish was the world

John Knobla with his 51-pound 3-ounce record hybrid from Lac Vieux Desert on the Wisconsin-Michigan border.

record muskellunge from 1919 to 1929, the Hybrid Committee had reason to believe that it may have, in fact, been a hybrid, as the mounted fish reported to be the 1919 fish was repainted by expert taxidermist Fred Aman of Conover, Wisconsin, who verified that the mount was indeed a hybrid (Mr. Aman handled over a hundred hybrids). Although the weight and date on the plaque of this mounted fish corresponded with the 1919 world record, the angler's name was omitted, preventing a conclusive tie in. More importantly, there were no available pictures of the 1919 fish at the time, therefore precluding absolute verification. Since 1975, the Hall has continued the investigation of the 1919 fish and subsequently verified that it was, in fact, a hybrid. After extensive perusal of the archives, the final tie in was made when a very good photograph of the angler and his fish was located in the November, 1920 issue of Outdoor Life magazine (page 312).

Since the world record musky of 51 pounds 3 ounces caught by John A. Knobla on July 16,1919, was in fact a hybrid, it will therefore assume the position of All Tackle World Record Muskellunge Hybrid.

New Record Data
51 pounds 3 ounces
54-inch length
26 1/2-inch girth
Caught July 16, 1919,
Lac Vieux Desert, Wisconsin/Michigan
By John A. Knobla

Mr. Knobla was a well known and highly respected guide fishing out of the Thomas Resort on Lac Vieux Desert. See: "A Prize Musky of Lac Vieux Desert" by Fred Bradford Ellsworth in the September 1915, issue of *Field & Stream*; "A Bass Bug Fly Angler Asks About Muskies," by Mr. Ellsworth in the June 1918 issue of *Outdoor Life* and "Tigers Of The Fresh Waters," by Mr. Ellsworth in the November 1920 issue of *Outdoor Life*. Mr. Knobla's fish was the *Field & Stream* contest winner in 1919 and was listed as the world record musky until August 25th,1929. See: "Tale of Record Fish," by Seth Briggs in the May 1930 and April 1933, issues of *Field & Stream*.

In addition to the world record change, the state of Wisconsin, when presented with the above information, also placed the Knobla fish in their record book as the state record hybrid.

Just how big do hybrids usually get, other than the Lapp and Knobla fish? How common are big hybrids? The answer to both questions is that hybrids in the 40-pound and over class are very rare! It is hard to reconstruct actual possible large hybrid catches from the past, since hybrids have only been known for about 35 years and still today, many anglers catch them and do not know what they have. I have, however, with the help of the late Peter Haupt, put together a list of large known hybrids. I cannot, however, say that all of these weights are verified.

The 40-Pound Hybrid Club
Compiled by Larry Ramsell as of March 5, 1997

The hybrid cross between a true muskellunge and a (northern) pike, is one of nature's beautiful creatures. Hybrids over 40 pounds are extremely rare and only two have ever exceeded 50 pounds officially, with one other near 50 that wasn't weighed for three days. The list of hybrids over 40 pounds is relatively short compared to the length of recorded musky history. I'm sure there are others I do not know about and readers are encouraged to advise me of any they may know about. Interestingly, nearly, all fish on the list were natural hybrids, rather than hatchery hybrids.

One huge hybrid caught in 1996 was released by Pete Meronek of Stevens Point, Wisconsin, on July 28, 1996. To prevent injuring the fish, Pete took only a quick girth measurement just behind his 52-incher's head. As you are aware, in most cases, a musky's largest girth is in the middle. Because he failed to get a full girth measurement, we are unable to apply the formula to ascertain an approximate weight. From the looks of the video, pictures, and the estimates of his fishing partners, the fish was in the 40-pound range. Based on these factors, I am placing it in the list as an Honorable Mention.

No.	Weight	Angler	Date	Length	Girth	Lure	Water
1.	51-3	John Knobla	7/16/19	54	25 1/4	Skinner Spinner	Lac Vieux Desert, WI/MI
2.	50-4	Delores Lapp	6/28/51	56	26 1/2	Marathon Musky Houn	Lac Vieux Desert, WI/MI
3.	49-0	George Barber	1928	NA	NA	Heddon Vamp	Pelican Lake, WI
4.	48-8	Unknown	1943	52 3/4	NA	NA	Pickerel L., WI
5.	47-0	Elmer Caskey	1947	NA	NA	NA	Lac Vieux Desert, WI/MI
6.	44-9 1/2	Thomas Isaac	10/1/94	52 3/4	23 5/8	12" Rapala	Georgian Bay, ONT
7.	44-6	Wally Heinrich	7/11/46	NA	NA	Heddon Jtd. Vamp	Planting Ground Lake, WI

40-Pound Hybrid Club continued on Page 312

A Compendium of Musky Angling History

No.	Weight	Angler	Date	Length	Girth	Lure	Water
8.	43-11	Red Degroot	1948	49 1/4	25 1/2	NA	Round Lake, WI
9.*	43-8 1/4	John Novak	6/9/96	51 1/2	26	Bucher Baby ShallowRaider	Lac Vieux Desert, WI/MI
10.	43-0	Tony Kerscher	late '40s	NA	NA	NA	Lac Vieux Desert, WI/MI
11.	43-0	Dick Lapp	1950s	NA	NA	NA	Lac Vieux Desert, WI/MI
12.	42-6	Allen F. Praefke	6/17/48	54	26	8" Sucker	Palmer Lake, WI
13.	42-0	George Tally	1950s	NA	NA	NA	B. Round L., WI
14.	41-0	Charles Casey	July 1920	51 3/4	NA	So. Bend Bucktail	Kawaguesaga Lake, WI
15.	40-2	Jason Potter	7/24/94	53	23 7/8	Burt Jerk	Quincy Reservoir, CO
16.	40-0	Dr. C.I. Pershbacker	1945	54	NA	NA	Big Sand Lake, WI
17.	40-0	M. Haroldson	1966	51	NA	NA	Riley Lake, WI
18.	40-0	Marvin Lee	1975	NA	NA	NA	Gravel Lake, ND
19.	40-0	Len Kubicki	NA	NA	NA	NA	St. Lawrence R.
Honorable Mention							
1.	40-0?	Pete Meronek	7/28/96	52	?	Moore's Flap-tail	Lac Seul, ONT

* "Formula weighted" as the fish was released.

Since I wrote the chapter on hybrids in the original edition of this book, things have changed slightly — some new fish have been added and some deleted. The above list is current. Since 1981, I have received additional information and photographs of most of the old (and still valid) "list" fish, and of course, information and pictures on most of the new list fish too.

Wally Henrich of Eagle River, Wisconsin, caught the prize fish of 1946 when he went south a few miles to take a 44 1/2-pound hybrid from Planting Ground Lake, a part of the Three Lakes chain which drains to the Wisconsin.

Could this be the largest fish to ever come from the Three Lakes chain? Is it mounted and on display? Comments from readers are invited.

Throughout the chapter you have seen the photos of list fish that were not available for that first

printing. Many thanks to all who have been helpful in providing me with additional photographs and information. Of most help was the late Peter Haupt and where applicable, I will use the information from his article, "The Golden Age of Hybrids," that

This beautiful hybrid, the No. 8 fish on the list, was taken in 1948 by Red DeGroot from Round Lake near Hayward, Wisconsin. It weighed 43 pounds 11 ounces. Photo courtesy of Mike Brandt.

appeared in the December 1992/January 1993 issue of *Musky Hunter* magazine. Let us now take a look at the rest, including one additional big hybrid that was found dead that would have made the list had it been angler-caught, and a supposed 56-pounder from 1916, as reported by Dean Bortz in the February/March 1991 issue of *Musky Hunter* magazine.

From the August/September 1996 issue of *Musky Hunter* magazine, by Steve Heiting:

Giant Tiger Musky Ranks No. 9 Of Top 20 Ever Caught

An Illinois angler who extended his vacation by a day because the weather was bad back home ended up catching — and releasing — a 51 1/2-inch, 40-pound plus hybrid musky on his "extra" day.

John Novak of Savanna, IL, boated the monster on June 9, 1996, while fishing Lac Vieux Desert in Vilas County, Wisconsin. The giant tiger ranks among the top 20 hybrids ever caught and will officially tie for the longest of its kind ever released.

Novak's musky, though a half-inch longer than the all-tackle world record released hybrid musky in records maintained by the National Fresh Water

John Novak with his giant hybrid, which he released.

This huge hybrid was found dead by John Hirschfeld and Bob McSweeney in 1949 on Big Round Lake, near Hayward, Wisconsin. It was 47 1/2 pounds and 56 inches long when found. The late Peter Haupt said: "Note the big 'chest' and sharp drop at the dorsal fin, then note the withdrawn stomach. I'll put the live healthy weight at 55 to 57 pounds." It was Peter who did the detective work on this one.

Fishing Hall of Fame in Hayward, Wisconsin, will be listed as a tie for the all-tackle record. According to NFWFHF release division rules, "all fractions in length are dropped to even inches." Currently, 51-inch hybrids released by Marie Blanchet in Colorado's Quincy Reservoir and by Tom Brill in Georgian Bay, Ontario, both in 1995, are the longest ever released.

The kept division's world record hybrid is a 51-pound 3-ounce fish caught by John A. Knobla from Lac Vieux Desert in 1919.

Novak's fish takes a solid early lead in the prestigious Vilas County Musky Marathon's released division. WIth a measured 26-inch girth, Novak's musky would have weighed more than 43 pounds, according to the Length X Girth X Girth/800 formula, which is generally accepted by musky anglers when estimating the weight of their released fish.

"I was supposed to go back yesterday and I heard it was raining down there, so I decided to extend my trip another day and I'm really glad I did," Novak told *Musky Hunter* less than 12 hours after he caught the hybrid.

Novak had raised the musky the day before and thought it was a tiger. The next day he said he "did the *Musky Hunter*-type thing and went back after it at sundown. I twitched the bait because that's what Joe (Bucher) had said to do in the early season. I just twitched the bait a couple of times and blam, it hit."

Novak was fishing alone and has no idea how long he fought the musky outside of that "there were stars out" when he got back to the dock. "It seemed like forever. It was pretty much a miracle that I got him in. He would pull and I couldn't gain on him for a long time.

"I finally got him in the net in the water and I tried to take a picture but my camera was rattling. I was in a small boat with no livewell, so I used the trolling motor on its lowest setting to go back to the dock. There I was able to find some other people who had cameras that didn't rattle."

Seven people witnessed the release. For the

Tiger (Hybrid) Muskies

record, the big tiger hit a perch-colored Bucher Baby ShallowRaider. Novak was using a Shimano spinning reel and Garcia rod loaded with either 14- or 17-pound test Berkley Trilene XL.

Novak's giant tiger is enough of a story by itself. However, there's more.

Novak's brother is Mike Novak of Hinsdale, IL, who on Sept. 1, 1994, caught a 55-inch, 46-pound 10-ounce purebred musky, which also had a 26-inch girth. Mike Novak's musky went on to win the Vilas County Musky Marathon's kept division that year.

Again by Peter Haupt in *Musky Hunter*:

Perhaps the center of the universe for hybrids is Lac Vieux Desert. Astride the Michigan-Wisconsin border, the shallow weed-filled lake is all habitat.

One gets the feeling that each of its 4,300 acres holds a musky or two. A countless number of hybrids have been caught there over the years including a few 40- and 50-pounders.

Chicago restaurateur Tony Kerscher caught a nice, thick, 43-pound hybrid fishing out of his summer home in the late 1940s. Having caught two more muskies over 40 lbs. he was already a leg-

Tony Kerscher with his 43-pound, No. 10 hybrid.

end when the author began fishing there in the mid 1950s. A big man with a thick European accent, it was delightful to talk fishing with him. Although he had ample craft in his boathouse he preferred to fish out of his old cedar strip guide boat with a small "kicker" clamped on the transom. Often fishing alone, his small boat seemed to have no more than six inches of freeboard amidships.

One lasting lesson I learned from Mr. Kerscher was that a musky fisherman need not stand to be successful. Sit down, relax, and catch more than the stander.

High in the forested table lands along the Michigan-Wisconsin border the woods and marshes give rise to Palmer Lake whose waters

Allen Praefke's 42 1/2-pound hybrid ranks No. 12.

315

flow north to Tenderfoot Lake. It flows through miles of Michigan forest, via the Tenderfoot Creek, joining the Ontonagon River downstream from the border straddling the Cisco chain. The Ontonagon flows northward to Lake Superior dropping hundreds of feet in elevation prior to reaching the Great Lake. Muskellunge inhabiting headwater lakes in the Lake Superior watershed make an interesting story. We will cover that subject at another time. The matter at hand is Allen Praefke's 42 1/2 lb. hybrid taken from Palmer in 1948. The 54 inch fish took a live sucker on June 17th. It survives as a nice mount and is displayed in the Land O' Lakes area.

In addition to the above copy regarding this No. 12 fish, I received the following information from Mr. Prafke's son Skip:

It was "... caught at 12:45 p.m., on June 17, 1948 (Thursday) ... using an eight-inch sucker. The fish was weighed at the Trails End Resort by Roy Grober and at a bait shop and grocery store in Land O'Lakes — 42 lbs, 6 oz, (a slight correction of Peter) 54 inches long, with a 26-inch girth.

"... initially after he reeled the musky near the boat, he could not get the fish off the bottom so he 'strummed' the tight line and the vibrations brought the fish to the surface — an 'old Indian trick.' ... after failing to net and gaff the musky, he ended up having his mother, Meta, row the boat towards shore. He exited the boat in three feet of water and walked it in towards shore, drowning the fish in the process."

The No. 14 hybrid was caught by a Mr. Charles Casey of Cambridge, Ohio, from Kawaguesaga Lake, Minocqua, Wisconsin, in July of 1920. It weighed 41 pounds and was caught on a South Bend bucktail gang.

From the October/November 1994 issue of *Musky Hunter*:

Whoever thought that in eight short years anyone would be hearing about the largest contemporary hybrid tiger muskies coming from a well known trout state like Colorado? Well there are believers like Paul Framsted and Jason Potter who are convinced that it is possible that in a couple of more years the new world record tiger musky could be caught in Colorado.

Jason Potter of Denver, Colorado, eclipsed the two-week-old Colorado state record with his catch at Quincy Reservoir. Jason's fish tipped the scales at

40 pounds 2 ounces with a length of 53 inches and a girth of 23 7/8 inches. The previous record caught by Paul Framsted was 50 3/4 inches long and weighed 35 pounds 10 1/2 ounces.

Jason caught his monster fish casting a 9 1/2-inch jerkbait. He hooked the fish around 8 p.m. Sunday, July 24, 1994. His fish was witnessed by Quincy Reservoir rangers, Milt Hunholz and Garland

Jason Potter of Denver, Colorado, holds his state record hybrid, a 40-pound 2-ounce, 53-inch fish from Quincy Reservoir.

Lessley. The state record was verified by Division of Wildlife Officer Liza Moore. This fish will no doubt qualify for a new world line class record in the 45-pound line class. The current record for hybrid musky conventional angling subdivision is 27 pounds 11 ounces.

This tiger musky now becomes Colorado's largest gamefish of record. Until Sunday the largest fish recorded in the state was a mackinaw caught in 1949 in Deep Lake, Garfield County, Colorado. That fish weighed 36 pounds. Jason has been a familiar face at Quincy Reservoir and has tallied numerous legal muskies over the past few years. His most recent catch and release was a 45-inch musky on June 8.

Dr. C.I. Pershbacher took this 40-pounder from Big Sand Lake in 1945.

From Peter Haupt in *Musky Hunter*:

Big Sand Lake located east of Phelps, Wisconsin, and a few miles south of Lac Vieux Desert is the headwaters of the Deerskin River which takes an indirect route to the Wisconsin.

In the summer of 1945, Dr. C.I. Pershbacher of Appleton, Wisconsin, and son John headed out from the historic Sand Lake Club fishing resort in a rowboat pushed by a six horsepower Neptune outboard. Young

John was on the oars as they worked a spot called "The Pike Hole." Casting a straight Pikie Minnow with a Heddon Pal steel rod Dr. Pershbacher hooked into a big hybrid. A spectacular fight ensued and with no means to boat the 54" fish, John carefully rowed to a nearby shore and their trophy was beached.

Later the 40 pound fish was packed in ice in the trunk of an old Buick coupe and driven back to Appleton where it fed 45 people at a community dinner.

We thank Dr. Pershbacher, now 91 years old, for the elements of this story.

Our "Honorable Mention" fish was taken and then released by Pete Meronek of Stevens Point, Wisconsin. This one though didn't come from Wisconsin, as have most of the others. It was caught in Lac Seul, Ontario, Canada. This fish led a troubled life for a while, as lake biologists and conservation officers had never seen a Lac Seul hybrid and were reluctant to pronounce it one. After I saw the picture and had other biologists who had done work with hybrids look at it, the fish obtained its rightful designation and took its place in hybrid musky history.

Pete Meronek's 52-inch hybrid receives an honorable mention — a likely 40-pound hybrid, but without an accurate girth measurement it is uncertain whether it indeed was a 40.

Perhaps, if this next hybrid would have been properly weighed and verified, it would be the current world record!

From the February/March 1991 issue of *Musky Hunter* magazine:

56-Pound Tiger Musky Taken in 1916

When 26 year old Art Jackson caught a big tiger musky on a hot July day in 1916, he did not know it would be the biggest musky he would ever catch, nor did he know it could have been a world record.

Jackson did what any fisherman did with his catch in those days, he ate it. All 56 pounds of it. The world record hybrid muskellunge, or tiger musky, recognized by the National Fresh Water Fishing Hall of Fame is a 51 pound 3 ounce fish caught by John Knobla in August of 1919 from a Wisconsin-

Michigan boundary water, the fabled Lac Vieux Desert.

A second 50 pound tiger came from Lac Vieux Desert in 1951 when Delores Ott-Lapp caught a 50 pound 4 ouncer.

Those two fish could have ranked second and third had Jackson realized what he pulled out of Little St. Germain Lake that day nearly 74 years ago.

The resort owner's grandson, Ken Jackson of St. Germain, investigated the catch this past year and tried to have the fish verified as a record, but photographs were not enough.

Jackson said he heard about the fish as a young boy whenever resort guests asked his father how big the biggest musky was that ever came out of Little St. Germain. His father then retold the tale of Art Jackson's monster tiger.

Ken Jackson then forgot about the story, but was reminded of it when he found two pictures of the fish while cleaning out an old desk in the resort last year.

Art Jackson's 56-pound hybrid, pictured with a smaller purebred musky.

"When I found the pictures I remembered dad telling guests that it was the biggest musky to ever come out of Little Saint Germain," Jackson said.

"It measured somewhere between 54 and 58 inches and it weighed 56 pounds."

He said his grandfather was fishing a seven foot deep weed flat near the north tip of the large island in Little Saint's lower east bay. The big tiger grabbed a No. 8 Skinner Spoon.

"He didn't mount the fish; he couldn't afford to. They ate it. I'm sure that when he caught the musky, he thought that he would catch bigger ones."

Legend has it that Little Saint Germain fishermen of that era, including Jackson, saw muskies larger than the 56 pound tiger musky.

Jackson did catch two more big muskies, but neither of them approached the size of the 1916 hybrid. One weighed 44 pounds and the other was more than 40.

Ken Jackson said he tried to have his grandfather's catch recognized as a world record, but said there was no way to verify the musky's weight.

Art Jackson's big tiger will just go down as the biggest musky ever caught from Little Saint Germain Lake. That in itself says a lot.

Following is information that should be helpful to anglers in deciding whether or not the fish they have caught is a hybrid or true musky:

Definition of Terms

CHEEK: The cheek is that part of the side of the head which is just behind and below the eye. It is part of the movable structure which makes up the side of the mouth and gill cover.

OPERCLE: The opercle is the true gill cover. It is that part of the side of the head which is behind the cheek and is usually marked off from it by a distinct groove.

BRANCHIOSTEGAL RAYS: The branchiostegal rays, more commonly called branchiostegals, strengthen and support the gill membranes below the cheek and opercles.

MANDIBULAR PORES: The mandibular pores are the pores on the underside of the lower jaws.

Taxonomic Descriptions of Muskellunge, Northern Pike and Tiger Muskellunge
Esox masquinongy (Muskellunge)

Body long and oval with light bars on sides, fading to green or brown dorsally. Some individuals may be all green or brown on sides with no bars. Cheeks and opercles scaled no more than 5/10 laterally. Mandibular pores usually 12 to 18. Branchiostegal rays usually 34 to 36 (total both sides). Tail tips pointed.

Esox lucius (Northern Pike)

Body long and oval with light golden or yellow spots on darker background. Cheeks fully scaled. Opercles scaled 5/10 laterally. Mandibular pores 9 to 10 total. Branchiostegal rays 26 to 32 (total both sides). Tail tips rounded. Always spotted sides, even in older specimens (Except for the mutant silver pike which is gray and silver).

Esox masquinongy x Esox lucius
(Tiger Muskellunge, or hybrid)

Body long and more oval than muskellunge or northern pike, particularly muskellunge less than 30 inches in length. Body of larger hybrids and muskellunge is a laterally-compressed oval. The body of a hybrid is deeper for any given length than that of a northern pike or muskellunge. Body characterized by dark bars, spots and broken

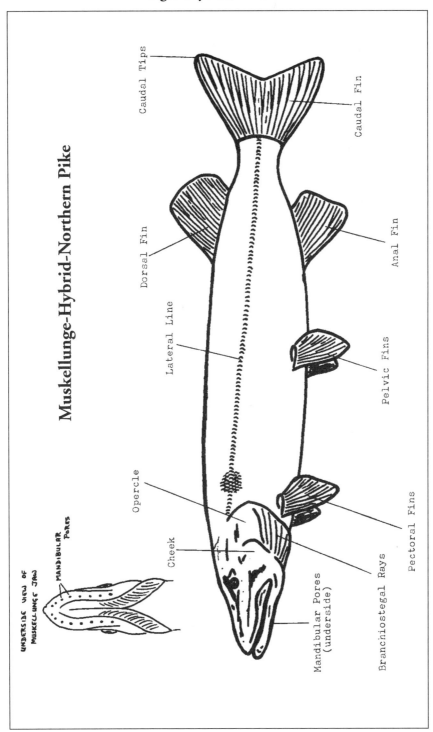

Muskellunge-Hybrid-Northern Pike

Caudal Tips

Caudal Fin

Dorsal Fin

Anal Fin

Lateral Line

Pelvic Fins

Opercle

Cheek

Pectoral Fins

Mandibular Pores (underside)

Branchiostegal Rays

UNDERSIDE VIEW OF MUSKELLUNGE JAW

MANDIBULAR PORES

stripes on a lighter background. Cheeks and jaws usually spotted. Cheeks 8/10 to 10/10 scaled. Opercles usually scaled 5/10, but never fully. Mandibular pores 10 to 16. Branchiostegal rays usually 34 to 38 (total both sides), but individuals can be from 32 to 42 total. Tail tips more rounded than muskellunge. Fins contain distinct spots. The head is unusually massive compared to either species (northern pike or muskellunge), the fins larger for any length, and the caudal peduncle (V in the tail fin) deeper, eyes — yellow.

NOTE: It is thought by some anglers that the oversize fins and tail (very obvious in the larger specimens) accounts in part for the claim that the hybrid is a more powerful fighter than either northern pike or muskellunge of similar size.

The No. 18 hybrid caught by Marvin Lee from Gravel Lake, ND in 1975. It weighed 40 pounds.

The No. 17 hybrid, caught by M. Haroldson from Riley Lake, Wisconsin, was 51 inches and 40 pounds. The author has no additional information on this fish. Taxidermist Neal Long, whose shop is near Plum Lake, Wisconsin, provided this photo and thought it possibly was of a 40-pounder rumored to have come from Plum. Peter Haupt thought this photo was the Haroldson fish. Were there two 40s, or is this indeed the Haroldson fish? Anyone with information is asked to contact the author.

Chapter 6:
Musky
Happenings

We can best set the stage for this chapter by referring back to a quote in Chapter One from Wynn Davis: "It takes a lot of know-how and a lot of fishing time to land a legal musky. This goes even for the experts fishing the best waters. There are exceptions, of course — times when the big fish seems to go on reckless feeding sprees- but such occasions are so rare they make newspaper headlines. In musky fishing, perhaps more than in any other fresh water angling, the odds favor the patient expert who thoroughly knows the water he's fishing.

"Muskies grow big, and the average angler who goes musky fishing, especially the beginner, has a trophy fish in mind. I'd say the odds against a beginner landing a lunker are even greater than the odds against his winning the daily double at any race track in the country."

That quote covers not just one, but both of the 1955 "happenings" that follow. In order to report these instances as accurately as possible, we will quote extensively from the stories of two top writers of the time. Jack Connor wrote "Five Crazy Days," which was published in the November 1955 issue of *Outdoor Life* magazine. His story follows:

Experts Baffled as 105 Muskies Are Caught in Minnesota Lake Splurge

No one suspected that musky-catching records would be shattered — or even challenged — on that still, steamy Friday morning, last July 15. By 6 a.m. that Friday, the mercury had already vaulted to the upper 70s, and Warren Bridge, fishing launch operator at Federal Dam, Minnesota, was wondering why any angler would want to be taken walleye fishing on such a day. Waste of time, he reflected. It certainly would be 90° by noon.

He was dripping sweat by the time his passengers boarded, but he took them out — to Leech Lake, via two miles of winding river. The 20-mile stretch of Portage Bay lay open to him on a southwest bearing, and he cruised up to Sawmill Bay at Two Points.

There, off the rushes, his fares tried in vain for walleyes with minnow and spinner rigs. Suddenly Warren's roving eye caught the flash of a rolling musky. Why not try it?

"I figured this was better weather for muskies than walleyes," he said later. "They like it hot and still."

From the bow he dredged up an eight-inch minnow-shaped plug, hooked it onto a 12-inch, 45-pound test cable leader, and heaved the contraption at the musky's eddy. He was using a two handed surf-casting rod and 40-pound line.

The fish struck like a flesh starved tiger. It followed through with a leap that cleared the surface four feet.

"Only weighed 30 pounds," Warren commented " But the taxidermist at Nevis figured it would have weighed 45; its stomach was empty."

That afternoon Warren was back at Sawmill Bay with his brother Delbert. They picked up a 20-pounder and a 17-pounder.

The same a.m. Mr. and Mrs. Al Storer, who have a cabin on nearby Boy Lake, were walleye fishing in Boy River near the point where it flows into Leech Lake. Mrs. Storer got a terrific hit on her minnow and spinner. She worked the fish close enough to see it was a big musky, then lost control in the shock of the discovery. Off went the fish with all her terminal tackle.

In the evening the Storers drove to Federal Dam and got a boat from Merle Wescott, another launch operator. News of the hot musky strikes had preceded them and Merle, his father, and son, were about to take off for Sawmill Bay and Two Points. By dusk, the Storers were back at the landing with two big muskies. The three Wescotts pulled in later with five more.

The word passed like a prairie fire whipped by a high wind. Before dawn the next day, Saturday, the little town of Federal Dam, population 200 plus, was jammed with cars. People were pounding on the doors of the five launch operators — Bridge, Wescott, Bob and Garry Neururer, Warner Stillman, and Al Bader- whose 15 launches could only accommodate 105 people. Ten extra rowboats could handle 30 more.

"Saturday was like a dream," Mrs. Storer said later. "Boats were everywhere. Those big muskies were right on the surface and leaping all over the place. In nearly every boat somebody was landing or playing a fish."

Nineteen of them scaling from 18 to 40 pounds were brought to the boat landings before dusk — certainly some kind of a record. The 40-pounder was boated by Ralph Hewitt of Des Moines, Iowa, who was vacationing in the area.

Now the word spread to radio and television stations in the Twin Cities. Sunday dawned upon complete bedlam in Federal Dam. The caretaker at the dam counted 180 cars parked in the 200 yards from the dam to the five landings. The town' s two cafes ran out of food before sunup. People came with duckboats, rowboats, prams and scows. By midmorning there were 89 boats at the hotspot on Sawmill Bay, and one seaplane — with four men fishing from its pontoons.

Musky Happenings

"Well" said Warren, "that Sunday was a record-breaker, even though it was calm, hot and muggy again. By 10 o'clock several launches were flying musky flags — hand towels tied to the handle of a landing net. Eleven muskies were brought in that morning."

In the afternoon 15 more were caught. Some boats had two on at the same time. Guides were warning other boats to stay clear when a musky was hooked. It meant nothing. Musky plugs and spoons were at a premium, and there were no favorites. The fish were hitting anything that moved. A few of the launch operators even rented musky plugs.

And so the great day of the Leech Lake musky rampage came to its climax. No one knew how or why the fish had gone berserk. Crowds kept coming for a week, until the winds turned north, cooled the water, and Leech Lake's muskies stopped their striking spree and took to sulking.

Now that there was time to think local operators tallied things up and found that 105 muskies had been checked in at the landings from Friday through Tuesday. Walter Kreutner of Shellsburg, Iowa, appears to have wound up with the heftiest fish of the lot — 42 pounds, 6 ounces. No one could guess how many muskies were caught and not reported by anglers who brought their own boats.

The big question was: What had caused this concerted fury among the muskies of Leech Lake. I called Dr. John Moyle, supervisor of the Minnesota Department of Conservation's Fisheries Research, to see if he had any ideas.

"I haven't the faintest," he said "We just don't know. It isn't like muskies."

L.G. Hiller of St. Louis, Missouri, who was among the successful anglers,

For reasons unknown, the muskies of Leech Lake went on a rampage in 1955. As was the custom then, the fish were killed and hung for display.

said he had fished the bay about 200 times in the past 30 years and never hooked any large muskies.

Newspaper headlines in Chicago blamed the heat. Stories of the rampage were carried in papers and on the air from coast to coast. There seemed nothing to do but make a trip to Leech Lake and start probing. Somewhere there was bound to be an answer.

But it was early August before I could get up to Walker, Minnesota, on the west shore of Leech. I bivouacked with Clem Plattner, local publisher. Certainly he'd know the explanation.

"Look, we've always known we had muskies here," he told me. "Used to catch 'em 20 years ago. Every year 30 or 40 turn up in the sporting-goods store window."

"But this flurry — 105 in five days?" I asked.

"In an ordinary season we have maybe a half a dozen people fishing for muskies," Clem said. "All of a sudden two or three hundred are fishing 'em. They're bound to catch more."

It wasn't quite satisfying. So we went over to the locker plant to see Paul Kreuger, whose hobby is taxidermy. He had 35 muskies in the plant, stacked up like cordwood for mounting.

"Doesn't surprise me. Leech has got a lot of muskies," Paul said. "It's fed by the whole Woman Lake chain, and every lake in the line has muskies. There's Mann, Baby, Boy, Girl and Woman Lakes, and there's Wabedo, Inguadona, and Long Lakes. All musky water."

That wasn't it, either. What had caused this sudden musky madness?

"Well I don't know," Paul admitted. "But if it'll help I can tell you one thing. When I opened those 35 muskies for mounting there wasn't one of 'em had any food in its stomach. And all but one were females."

A wheelbarrow load of muskies from the Leech Lake rampage. One angler, Roger Halverson of Fergus Falls, Minnesota, was said to have boated 22 muskies during the spree.

Musky Happenings

That, of course, could mean anything — or nothing. The smartest thing to do was to find the best musky guide on Leech Lake and go fishing with him. Somewhere along the line he might drop a hint.

Clem assured me Dick Pence was top dog. Hadn't he caught seven already this season and 16 last year?

Two hours of trolling and casting produced nothing more than a roll from one musky.

But still the big fish didn't cooperate. We saw five more musky rolls. One bruiser leaped clear of the surface as he lunged but missed some wary whitefish.

"Might as well go home," Dick said "They just won't hit in rough waters. Besides, the water's cooler now and they're getting over their sore mouths. I figure that's what made 'em hit during that hot spell — sore mouths. They were just plain mad."

That was another opinion. But I couldn't buy it, for the biologists claim muskies are more or less always shedding teeth and getting new ones, which contradicts the idea of a sore mouth period.

Next day Clem and I drove to Federal Dam to chat with Warren Bridge. Maybe he'd have the solution.

"Hasn't been much action since that splurge," he said " Only four brought in this week; that's more like normal."

Could Bridge crack the mystery?

"No," he said. "I've never seen anything like it. I know it wasn't sore mouth, because none of the fish we brought in showed evidence of it. And it wasn't lack of food because the lake is full of whitefish, which rate high on their diet. There must have been some chemical or something in the water that attracted all those females. Maybe they were allergic to something in the water."

What puzzled Warren was the fact that so many big muskies were concentrated in such a small area, in violation of all known musky lore. They are "loners," solitary fish for the most part.

"A musky needs an area 100 to 200 feet square to get enough to eat," Warren said. "But I saw 25 caught in an area less than 100 feet square. And they didn't put up the fight they usually do. Ninety percent of them were boated in less than 10 minutes. It stumps me.

"There was a woman from Shennandoah, Iowa, who hooked a 25-pounder on a big spoon. It came in easy, but when she got the fish near the boat she took one look and, scared to death, handed the rod to her husband."

When we got back to Walker we learned from Les Reed that this very day Dr. G.E. Montgomery of Washington, Iowa, had caught a musky weighing 39 1/2 pounds out of Walker Bay, practically on the town's front doorstep. It was his seventh big musky from Walker Bay in 10 days. And there went the theory that muskies only hit during hot, muggy, calm weather, for Dr. Montgomery's exploits occurred when it was cool and windy."

Why try to fit a musky into any pattern? It's enough to catch one in a lifetime, without asking how, when or why they bite.

In Jim Peterson's *Outdoor News*, July 16, 1976, we have this editorial comment:

Will there ever be another "Musky Rampage" at Leech Lake or any other lake?

While checking on recent musky catches with Jeff Arnold of Reed's Tackle Shop in Walker, Minn., and with the Walker Chamber of Commerce, we got to talking about the big explosion of musky action back in 1955. That's when 51 muskies from 18 to 42 pounds were caught in two days, July 16 &17, 1955, and before the week was out more than 100 fish were caught.

So, this weekend is the 21st anniversary of that big Leech Lake rampage — and are conditions ripe for another one?

"Yes," said Arnold. "It's been sticky hot again, the same as it was in 1955. But, if I were to predict another rampage, I would be crazy. Nobody can do that. However, the lake level is fairly low, like it was in '55 — and there has been a lot of musky activity. We had 17 muskies weighed in here last week — and that doesn't count the big number that are being released every day."

Arnold said the one big difference between 1955 and 1976 as far as the muskies are concerned is that right now (Wednesday, July 14) they are still in fairly deep water off the weed beds and rocky dropoffs. They are not up in the shallows like in '55.

One theory is that the super hot, calm weather of July 16-17, 1955, produced a quick summer kill of tullibees, and the musky hordes were in the shallows feeding on them. However, Leech Lake, as well as Mille Lacs and other large lakes, hasn't had a big summer kill of tullibees since.

"The tullibees apparently were trapped in the shallow eastern part of Leech Lake by weed growth in the channel to the western, deep, part of the lake in 1955," Arnold explained " They were in the shallows and just couldn't get back through the weedy channel — which was low — before they died. I don't think we'll ever get exactly those same conditions again."

However, if the weather does stay sticky hot and the wind which has plagued anglers for the past several days ever does calm down — and if the tullibees are there in the eastern lobe ready to die — there might, just MIGHT be another musky rampage at Leech Lake.

Following Mr. Connor's article was "The Twelve Days," by Gordon MacQuarrie in the September, 1956, issue of *Outdoor Life*. Gordon saw it this way:

The Twelve Days
By Gordon MacQuarrie

A few minutes before midnight of October 29, 1955, Tony Burmek and his brother Fred set out from Milwaukee, Wisconsin, on a trip that produced one of the most incredible catches of muskellunge in the history of this unpredictable sport.

Musky Happenings

At the end of 12 days of fishing, much of it in weather that froze lines to rods and started the first ice of the season creeping out from the shores of Sawyer County lakes, Tony and his partner had brought 17 muskies into the little Wisconsin town of Hayward. The smallest was a 25-pounder, many were over 30 pounds, and one of them, at 43 1/8 pounds, was the largest musky reported from the Hayward sector that year.

Almost from the first day of their fishing, October 30, when they caught a 31 3/4-pounder and a 38 1/2-pounder, the Burmek brothers had Hayward popping with excitement That's quite an achievement, for Hayward calls itself "the musky capital of the world." Day after day the Burmeks fished often in freezing winds which made it impossible to hold a boat over a bar long enough to get in two casts. And each evening they came back to town with their fish, mostly of trophy size.

Haywardites wondered how long the Burmek luck would hold. And they speculated, as fishermen will, that the Burmeks might be getting their monsters with setlines or by using suckers for bait, a deadly method that's quite legal but considered unsporting by many.

Having been directed to the Rivkin general store in Hayward to weigh their first day's catch, the Burmeks thereafter weighed all their muskies at Rivkin's. Fred and Tony drove to and from the dock in a station wagon, and folks soon began flocking to the store when the station wagon pulled in each night.

When the 12 days were over the Burmek musky take totaled 533 1/4 pounds, plus 26 pounds for a single northern pike. They gave fish away as they caught them ...

The statistics of the Burmek catch can be had from almost anyone in Hayward, or from the newspapers. But over and above the statistics, impressive as they are, is the story of a real fisherman, Tony Burmek. Tony, who makes most of his living guiding fishermen on the waters around Hayward, is 43 years old. For 20-odd years he has done little else but fish for muskies.

There are any number who are "crazy about fishing," but almost always these anglers vary their sport by pursuit of different species. Not Tony. Tony

Tony Burmek coming off the water during one of the "Twelve Days."

fishes for muskies, nothing else. I have known this shy, courteous guide for 10 years, and if he had the literary ability of an Ernest Hemingway, he could write a book about muskies that would be a classic of its kind.

Tony got interested in muskies in 1934 while visiting relations in the Hayward country. Since then he's devoted most of each summer to studying these fish, especially those in Sawyer County lakes. If he spots a good fish, he'll keep after it for weeks.

He believes that the best fishing is when the barometer is rising. There's nothing new in that. But there is in the way Tony carries out the barometer's orders. When it starts a sensational climb, Tony will drop anything to get on musky water.

He also uses contour maps. These, too, are available to all anglers. Of the more than 8,000 lakes in Wisconsin, some 1,200 have been contoured, a fine job done back in the C.C.C. days. But in 20 years there have been slight changes from silting, so Tony, the perfectionist, makes annual airplane flights over the lakes to study variations in the bars. Once he found a productive reef that wasn't shown on a contour map.

When Tony and Fred left Milwaukee late that October night, they had no idea they were going to write a startling page in Wisconsin musky fishing. On the way north they ran into a little snow. When they got to Hayward the barometer was low.

By noon of that first day the barometer climbed from 29.75 to 29.90, temperature was 39, wind west, sky overcast. That was enough for Tony. He and Fred put a boat in Round Lake, six miles east of Hayward. This is a "name" musky lake of 3,276 acres, in a class with neighboring lakes such as Grindstone, Lac Courte Oreilles, Teal, Lost Land, and Ghost.

It was to be drift fishing in mid-lake over bars Tony knows well and which few others bother with. Fred chose a homemade plug whittled out by Tony two years before. In its few earlier tests this plug had failed, so it had been forgotten in a tackle box.

On his third cast Fred hooked a small musky and released it. In the time it took the boat to drift 20 feet or so, Tony, casting with the same plug, hooked a musky which weighed 38 1/2 pounds. That fish shook the hook as it lay exhausted alongside the boat, but Fred got a net under the fish and heaved it aboard.

You'll get no long stories from Tony about fights with fish. He says, "You get one hooked solid and you play him instinctively. The big moment in musky fishing is when you get the fish to strike."

Back over a mid-lake bar they went. It was Fred's turn with the homemade plug. He took a musky that went 31 3/4 pounds — the biggest male, Tony says, he's ever seen. Big muskies are females, usually.

Most of the fish taken on this trip struck upward in deep water, sometimes in spots where the bottom was 25 feet straight down. The plug, which has a violent tail action, was kept three or four feet below the surface. Tony says maybe other lures would have worked as well. He doesn't know. He and Fred stayed with the one that was producing.

There' s a theory in the North that muskies go on feeding sprees in late autumn, and Tony is a strong supporter of this idea. But, as he says, "Just try to get the general public out on those lakes in late October or November."

Here in Wisconsin it's well known that after Labor Day, and the opening of schools, the fishing lakes are deserted. You could rake the Chippewa Flowage with cannon fire and endanger nary a fisherman.

The second day found the Burmeks back on Round Lake — barometer higher, wind still west, temperature 38. Tony's diary records laconically that they didn't get onto the lake until noon because "All the Hayward folks were around us talking musky fishing."

Over the mid-lake bars in the first half hour they each released muskies. The wind picked up, the boat pounded. They went inshore, and off a point in deep water Tony hooked one. "It didn't rush toward the bait on the surface like you see 'em do in summer," says Tony. "Just one lunge up from the bottom, then, boom." Tony boated that fish. It weighed 28 pounds.

The third day was warmer. It was cloudy, with an east wind. Over the bars in the middle of Round Lake they drifted for two hours, releasing three fish weighing more than 12 pounds apiece. They moved in to the point of the previous day, caught an 18-pounder and released it.

Tony Burmek with one of the 17 big muskies kept during the "Twelve Days."

The next fish hit a long way out from the boat. It was big. Tony saw the whole plug outside the musky's mouth. He knew it was lightly hooked, and for 15 minutes he sweated it out. Fred saved the show. He got a gaff into the fish just as the plug dropped out. This one weighed 41 1/2 pounds.

It was the biggest musky of the Hayward area for the season — up to that moment. They took that fish right into Hayward left it there, and returned to Big Round after lunch.

That afternoon over a mid-lake bar Fred felt that familiar jolt of a fish coming up from below. "We had quite a time with this one," Tony's diary records. "He wouldn't surface. I rowed quite a way with him. Then he came up, Fred worked him in close and I shot him with a pistol. The fish weighed 36 pounds."

By the end of the third day, all Hayward was talking of the Burmek brothers. Publisher Gingras made a date to go with them next day, then had to cancel it.

For the fourth straight day they tried Round Lake. Fred lost a medium-sized fish and then, over those same mid-lake bars, caught a 26 pound northern pike. (Both the Burmeks will tell you that big northerns fight as hard as muskies.) After the northern, Fred got an 18-pound musky and released it. It was one of their coldest days, the day knuckles started to bleed from chapping. Tony further battered his knuckles playing a 31-pounder up that beat up his numbed fingers with the reel handle.

Snow shoveling was the order of the fifth day. The Burmeks scooped the snow out of their boat on Round Lake and worked Leder's Bay. Each hooked and released small fish. Tony had decided to rest the mid-lake bars. Off White's Point Fred hooked, played, and shot a 29-pounder. At the entrance to Hidden Bay, Tony hooked and released a small one. Then, well inside the bay, Tony took a 26 1/4-pounder.

Monotonous? "No," says Tony. "There was extra fun in getting into Hayward every night with those fish. We had the skeptics looking pretty sick."

On the sixth day the Burmeks almost surrendered to the cold. They worked Round Lake for two hours. Fred caught and released a small musky and they went ashore and started a fire. In later afternoon Tony took a musky off Pine Point that weighed 33 pounds. Fred released a small one. They quit.

On the seventh day Fred put back a musky he estimated at 25 pounds. The fish was played a long time and was exhausted. To revive it they slipped it into a wet gunny sack and sloshed the sack back and forth in the water to make the gills open and shut, thus forcing oxygen to the fish.

This was Fred's last day with his brother. He took one more musky of about 14 pounds, returned it, and called it quits. Shortly afterward Tony wound up The day with a 25-pounder. It was the smallest of the muskies the Burmeks displayed in Hayward.

On the eighth day Fred was on his way back to Milwaukee. With the barometer at 30, highest of the entire period, Tony went alone to the sprawling Chippewa flowage, the famous "Big Chip" known to musky madmen from many states. It holds the world musky record, a 69-pound 11-ounce fish taken in October of 1949, and is one of the great musky-producing waters of the continent.

Using the same plug and system to fish over the Church bars of the flowage, Tony caught and released a little one. Then he motored to the narrows, took a 30-pounder, and was back in Hayward by suppertime.

At this juncture Tony was wishing he had 100 all-out musky fishermen with him. "I'd have assigned them to different lakes," he says, "so we could run a real test. I suspect the muskies were hitting everywhere."

Again alone on the ninth day, Tony tried Lac Court Oreilles, a 4,827-acre lake famous among the musky faithful since before the turn of the century. There was six inches of snow on the ground. Tony remembers that day very well: "There's a point on this lake — Winter's Point — and it looked like it was named right that day. I drifted across the point once, hooked and released a small one. On the next drift I took a 27-pounder."

That night there was a hard freeze and on the following day Tony didn't fish. But he was back at the musky bars the next day, this time with Clayton (Sergeant) Slack, resort operator, for a partner.

Over Andres Bar, Slack took a 38 3/4-pound musky. Tony released one hooked off Musky Point and on the next drift across the same point boated a 28-pounder.

By now Hayward was buzzing, if not seething, over the fantastic Burmek campaign. The nightly weighing at the general store was drawing onlookers like a circus sideshow. Burmek muskies were displayed on ice in the glass case at the Moccasin Bar. And people were talking. A few thought Tony might be violating the law by having too many fish "in possession," the possession limit being only one musky a day. But Tony — and Fred too- gave away each day's trophy before going after another. Some skeptics still thought the Burmek haul was the result of some mysterious and unsporting system. However, most people, among them George Curran,

A large hybrid taken by Tony Burmek from Big Round Lake during the "Twelve Days."

state game manager at Hayward, simply accepted it as a run of good luck by persistent and expert fishermen.

On the 11th day the barometer was rising. Again Slack was Tony's partner and again they fished the big flowage. In the first hour Tony released three fish. He thinks one weighed about 20 pounds. Then he hooked and shot a 28 1/2-pounder.

He and Slack went ashore for lunch. Back at it again in the afternoon, Slack hooked and lost a really big one. Tony doesn't know how big it was. He never saw it. Slack kept on casting and before the end of the afternoon had boated a 37 1/2-pounder.

At this point the Burmek diary gets about as emotional as the Burmek diary gets. Tony recorded: " Slack was beside himself with excitement."

Tony was getting tired. The daily routine of bucking wind and waves, the constant cold, the wet, cracked hands, the bleeding knuckles — all were taking their toll.

Tony didn't want to go out that final 12th day. But Slack was keyed up and Tony agreed to one hour of fishing, no more. It was so cold they welcomed chances to trade off casting and warm up with the oars. Slack's young son was with them and it got too cold for him to fish. The hour passed but Slack persuaded Tony to stay a bit longer.

The next and final fish of the trip was caught by Tony. It weighed 43 1/2 pounds, biggest musky of the season in the Hayward region.

Final score was 17 muskies boated in 12 days. The men released 22 and counted a total of 42 that struck, either to be killed, lost, or released.

It's not hard in Hayward today to find people who question the Burmek feats in one way or another. Tony' s own good reputation is the best answer to those who whisper. I have to go along with Tony, knowing him as I do.

Tony and Fred had a lot of things on their side. They know these waters. They know how to make a plug run the gamut of its possibilities — shallow, deep, slow, fast, side-to-side, up and-down. They had the musky grounds almost entirely to themselves, and that's important. These were fish that hadn't been showered with hardware day in, and day out. And the fish were obviously on the feed just before the freeze-up.

Most important of all, the Burmeks had the benefit of Tony's 20-odd years of devotion to the sport. A man like Tony Burmek develops a knowledge of fish and fishing that he finds difficult to transmit to others.

Chapter 7:
Big Muskies:
When? Where?
And Why?

If you have reached the point where you have caught several muskies but have yet to get that big one, or perhaps have tasted victory on your first lunker and don't wish to regress, where are the best places to go to increase your percentages?

I would like to mention Eagle Lake, Ontario. Eagle didn't show up in the *Field & Stream* contest list until 1937. One of the main factors was that there were no roads to it until 1933. Since then it has consistently produced muskies over 40 pounds and has produced two of only three 60-pound muskies ever to come out of Canada, the second one being the Ontario record for 48 years.

In the 1940s, it took a musky in the upper 40s to even make the top ten in the *F&S* contest!! I think the primary reason being that there were fewer musky fishermen, and the muskies had more of a chance to grow to a large size before being caught.

Wisconsin's record-producing Chippewa Flowage started producing consistently after its formation in 1924, but didn't really come of age until 1938. From then until 1959 the "Chip" had 16 fish in the *F&S* contest, one being Louis Spray's world record of 69 pounds 11 ounces.

Which waters have been the consistent producers of hog muskies?

For the best of the world musky waters, Lake of the Woods stands head and shoulders above the rest for size and consistency, with Eagle Lake close behind. Just those muskies on record in the *F&S* contest would make your hair stand on end. From 1918 to 1972 there is on record 56 between 40 and 50 pounds, 17 from 50 to 58 pounds 4 ounces, which ironically enough is the largest taken there. Three of these were world record fish.

Eagle Lake has produced dozens over 40 pounds and seven verified over 50 pounds.

Eagle Lake Honor Roll
Muskies Over 50 Pounds

Weight	Angler	Date	Lure (Type)	Rank
61-9*	Edward Walden	1/08/40	#12 Pflueger Muskill (A)	7
60-8**	John J. Coleman	10/03/39	Creek Chub Pikie (B)	8
55-0	Steve Albers	09/22/85	Whopper Stopper Hellcat (B)	21 (tie)
54-0	Karl Ghaster	09/21/54	Marathon Musky-Houn (A)	30 (tie)
51-8	Lewis Hilfer	10/10/38	South Bend Musky-O-Reno (C)	55
51-4	Joseph Bertoncini	10/01/57	Marathon Musky Hawk (A)	59 (tie)
50-8	Russell Baker	09/03/51	Marathon Musky-Houn (A)	69 (tie)

* Beat previous year's world records and was Ontario record for 48 years
** First-ever verified 60-pounder and world record when caught
(A) Bucktail
(B) Crankbait
(C) Surface bait

Ontario, Canada
Moon River — many over 40 pounds; 3 over 50 pounds; 1 over 60 pounds
Pipestone Lake — 3 over 40 pounds; 2 over 50 pounds
Dryberry Lake — 3 over 40 pounds; 1 over 50 pounds
French River — 5 over 40 pounds; 2 over 50 pounds
Rainy Lake — 5 over 40 pounds

Wisconsin
Chippewa Flowage — many over 40 pounds; 3 over 50 pounds; 1 over 60 pounds; 1 world record

Big Muskies: When? Where? And Why?

Grindstone Lake — 2 over 40 pounds; 2 over 50 pounds; 1 world record

Lac Courte Oreilles — 2 over 40 pounds; 2 over 60 pounds; 1 world record

Minocqua-Tomahawk — 6 over 40 pounds; 1 over 50 pounds

Lac Vieux Desert — 9 over 40 pounds; 2 over 50 pounds (both hybrids)

North Twin — 3 over 40 pounds; 1 over 50 pounds

Butternut Lake — 5 over 40 pounds

Flambeau Flowage — 5 over 40 pounds; 2 over 50 pounds

Minnesota

Leech Lake — 7 over 40 pounds; 2 over 50 pounds

Lake Winnibigoshish — 2 over 40 pounds; 1 over 50 pounds

Lake Bemidji — 1 over 40 pounds; 1 over 50 pounds

New York

Lake Chautauqua — 4 over 40 pounds

New York/Quebec

St. Lawrence River — many over 40 pounds; 3 over 50 pounds.

I would like to mention that the majority of these records came from the *F&S* contest records. Undoubtedly, there are several other lakes that have produced large muskies now and then, but the above names keep coming up in the records. Also, I'm sure additional fish over 40 pounds have been caught from most of these waters.

The results listed above tend to prove out the theory I have had in the past — big water big muskies!! I would like to pass on a theory from my late friend, Gil Hamm, founder of Muskies, Inc. It has much merit: "If you buy a small goldfish and put him in a small bowl and feed him regularly he will grow to a certain size and stop. Put him in a larger bowl and continue the same feeding pattern and he will grow larger! Each time he is transferred to a larger bowl or tank he will grow! Have you ever seen a goldfish that was released in a lake? They grow as big as carp ..."

Perhaps this is why the largest musky waters produce the most and the biggest muskies, in addition to containing the larger species of muskies. I have continued researching the subject and have obtained additional information that further expands some of the facts and accomplishments of the *F&S* records, and further demonstrates the rarity of muskies over 50 pounds, not only in the "good old days" but currently. One theory I have long expounded "big water big muskies," is backed up fully by the records. I will further delve into this subject and relate new information I have uncovered that I believe lends itself to why only certain waters can and have produced record muskellunge.

One fact I would like for you to keep in mind is that in all of the following statistics, the catches and weights are on record and are verified! There may be other records and verified catches that I haven't been able to locate to date, but since muskies over 50 pounds usually create much publicity, especially in recent years, I will proceed on the basis that my records cover the vast majority. Should any reader have additional verified information, I would appreciate hearing from you.

The 50-Pound Club
Compiled by Larry Ramsell as of March 5, 1997

The morning of September 22, 1953, was overcast with a brisk west wind, and Myrl McFaul started out on Vilas County, Wisconsin's, North Twin Lake. McFaul was pleased with what he considered "good musky weather," as he drifted alongside a large weedbed nearly a mile from the nearest shore. Three times in the past five days he had raised a huge musky from the eastern end of this weedbed. He had placed a bobber on the spot to mark it. Following are McFaul's own words, as he described what happened that fateful day:

"Drifting toward the bobber, I was casting all around it. Nothing doing. After I had drifted about thirty feet past it, I played a hunch and took one last shot back toward the bobber; my Worth Musky Fin suddenly looked like somebody had touched off a depth charge underneath it. The lake literally exploded before my eyes! The big fish cleared the water on the strike; he nearly took the rod from my hands with that first wallop, and the sight of him in mid-air took my breath away.

"He broke water again and then sounded, heading for the weeds.

I thought he was going away — and according to my dwindling reel spool, he was — but just as I started to put the pressure on him he came roaring out of the water not thirty feet from the boat. Then he was down into the weeds again. I had the slack in by that time, and he kept tearing up and down the length of the weedbed, cutting off the weeds with my line until the whole section looked like somebody was going over the lake bottom with a mowing machine.

"The wind was carrying us out into open water, and a fellow in another boat came over to lend me a hand. The musky ducked under the approaching boat and came out the other side. I thought he was gone, but after I cleared the line and he broke the surface again I knew we were still hooked up. He was tiring by this time. Me? Why, I was just as fresh as a daisy — one of last year's crop of daisies. But shortly after this I managed to get my gaff into his jaw and wrestle him into the boat. He was a beautiful fish, and I was grateful to him for giving me my own private thrill of a lifetime.

Myrl McFaul's big musky weighed in at 53 pounds 12 ounces, and is tied for thirty-fifth spot on the all-time big musky list here in the 50-Pound Club. Just recently, *Musky Hunter* magazine Historical Editor John Dettloff proclaimed McFaul's musky to be the largest ever taken (verified) from Vilas County waters after another fish that had been claimed to be bigger was disqualified.

The following list of 50-pound and larger muskies are, to date, the only muskies that have been caught in recorded history whose weight can be verified through supporting documentation and/or pictures that support the weight. Additionally, those listed currently have no doubt cast upon them at this time. Others of questionable value or proven to be falsified have been left off the list.

In 1996, only two muskies over 50 pounds, to my knowledge, were caught and weighed. Both, amazingly enough, came from the state of Minnesota. Minnesota is not known for producing muskies of this size, since it had produced only four fish that reached these proportions before 1996! One of these, a 51-pound 14-ouncer from Bemidji Lake, was caught by Karl Dobmeier and made the No. 52 spot in the *1997 Musky Hunter's Almanac* listing. The second was a 52-pound 4-ounce beauty out of Leech Lake. It was caught, weighed on a certified scale and then released on October 5 by Dave Unzeitig.

While Lake Bemidji has only had muskies in it for 14 years, Leech has long been a superlative producer of muskies. It would have to be thought that perhaps the release program had something to do with 1996 producing one-third of Minnesota's muskies over 50 pounds! What does the future offer?

No.	Weight	Angler	Date	Lure	Water
1.	70-0	Robert Malo	6/6/54	Live Sucker	Middle Eau Claire, WI
2.	69-11	Louie Spray	10/20/49	Spray Sucker Harness/sucker	Chippewa Flowage, WI
3.	67-8	Cal Johnson	7/24/49	South Bend Pike-Oreno	Lac Courte Oreilles, WI
4.	65-0	Ken O'Brien	10/16/88	Countdown Rapala	Moon River, ON
5.	61-13	Louie Spray	8/19/40	True Temper Bass Pop	Lac Courte Oreilles, WI
6.	61-9	Edward Walden	10/8/40	#12 Pflueger Muskill	Eagle Lake, ON
7.	60-8	John Coleman	10/3/39	Creek Chub Pikie Minnow	Eagle Lake, ON
8.	59-11	Art Barefoot	6/5/89	Cisco Kid Diver	French River, ON
9.	59-8	Louie Spray	7/27/39	Marathon Musky Houn	Grindstone Lake, WI
10.	58-8	Ruben Green	7/25/45	Ottertail Spinner	McGregor Bay-Georgian Bay, ON
11.	58-4	G.E. Neimuth	9/24/32	Creek Chub Pikie	Lake of the Woods, ON
12.	57-10	William Fulton	1917	Unknown	French River, ON
13.	56-11	Gene Borucki	8/30/84	Rapala	Manitou Lake, ON
14.	56-8	Jack W. Collins	7/24/31	Pflueger Muskill	Lake of the Woods, ON
Tie	56-8	R.D. Shawvan	9/4/41	Heddon Giant Vamp	Lake of the Woods, ON
16.	56-0	Fred Reinhart	9/12/44	Reinhart Jinx	Lake of the Woods, ON
17.	55-11	Sam Finsky	6/20/63	#3 Mepps Gold Spinner	Lake Kakagi, ON
18.	55-2	Neal Crawford	9/13/46	Marathon Musky Houn	Lake of the Woods, ON
Tie	55-2	Joe Lykins	4/1/72	Creek Chub Pikie Minnow	Piedmont Lake, OH
20.	55-0	Arthur J. Ross	9/28/42	Marathon Musky Houn	Chippewa Flowage, WI
Tie	55-0	Herman Reber	10/4/42	Heddon Vamp Spook	Pipestone Lake, ON
Tie	55-0	Stanley Baker	9/16/49	Big Spoon (spinner)	St. Lawrence River

Big Muskies: When? Where? And Why?

No.	Weight	Angler	Date	Lure	Water
Tie	55-0	Charles Fawcett	10/2/54	Heddon River Runt	English River, ON
Tie	55-0	Gary Ishii	10/11/81	LeBlanc Swim Whizz	Moon River, ON
Tie	55-0	Steve Albers	9/22/85	Whopper Stopper Hell Cat	Eagle Lake, ON
Tie	55-0	John P. Ryan	8/25/92	Radke Pike Minnow	English River, ON
27.	54-8.5	Mark Kontianen	10/15/77	LeBlanc Swim Whizz	Moon River, ON
28.	54-3	Lewis Walker Jr.	9/30/24	Dead 8" Red Chub	Conneaut Lake, PA
Tie	54-3	Jim Carrol	7/16/87	Lindy Rig & Worm	Restoule Lake, ON
30.	54-0	William Walshe	8/22/43	Willow Spinner	St. Lawrence River
Tie	54-0	C.W. Frale	9/8/50	Johnson Silver Minnow	Lake of the Woods, ON
Tie	54-0	Karl Ghaster	9/21/54	Marathon Musky Houn	Eagle Lake, ON
Tie	54-0	Michael Pederson	10/21/55	Cisco Kid	Honey Harbour-Georgian Bay, ON
Tie	54-0	Art Lyons	8/28/57	Dardevle	Winnibigoshish, MN
35.	53-12	Gordon M. Curtis	8/25/29	#7 Skinner Spoon (spinner)	Lake of the Woods, ON
Tie	53-12	Myrl McFaul	9/22/53	Worth Musky Fin	North Twin Lake, WI
37.	53-8	W.L. Kirkpatrick	9/8/32	Creek Chub Pikie Minnow	Lake of the Woods, ON
Tie.	53-8	Adolph Bockus	9/16/40	Marathon Musky Houn	Lake of the Woods, ON
Tie	53-8	Lew Morgan	9/27/44	Marathon Musky Houn	Big Vermilion Lake, ON
40.	53-0	George Collins	7/10/46	Johnson Spoon	Lake of the Woods, ON
Tie	53-0	E.W. Flint	8/29/46	Marathon Musky Houn	St. Lawrence River
42.	52-12	Emanuel A. Oberland	7/1/29	Pflueger Spoon (spinner)	Pokegama Lake, WI
43.	52-8.75	Rita Hillenbrand	11/11/69	Live Sucker	Flambeau Flowage, WI
44.	52-8	Gerry Winteregg	9/22/41	Roberts Mud Puppy	Lake of the Woods, ON
44.	52-8	Harry Faulkerson	6/24/50	Unknown	Lac Courte Oreilles, WI
46.	52-4	Harry Gardner	8/16/49	Roberts Mud Puppy	Eagle Lake, ON
Tie	52-4	George McQuillen	11/12/94	Kwikfish	Lake of Two Mountains, PQ

A Compendium of Musky Angling History

No.	Weight	Angler	Date	Lure	Water
Tie	52-4	Dave Unzeitig	10/5/96	Northland Bucktail	Leech Lake, MN
49.	52-0	Gust Peterson	10/10/35	Pfleuger Spoon (spinner)	White Sand Lake, WI
Tie	52-0	William Dashley	10/9/42	Creek Chub Pikie Minnow	St. Lawrence River
Tie	52-0	Charles Rothermal	8/18/45	Heddon Plug	Trout Lake, WI
Tie	52-0	Harold Ferguson	10/1/54	Creek Chub Pikie Minnow	St. Lawrence River
53.	51-14	Karl Dobmeier	9/14/96	Northland Bucktail	Lake Bemidji, MN
54.	51-12	Joseph Mathis Jr.	7/22/48	Casco Slo-jo	Lake Winnebago, WI
Tie	51-12	Eugene Avrill	10/12/64	South Bend Bass-Oreno	Lake of the Woods, ON
56.	51-11	George Moore	8/5/37	Marathon Musky Houn	Lake of the Woods, ON
57.	51-8	Lewis Hilfer	10/10/38	South Bend Musk-Oreno	Eagle Lake, ON
Tie	51-8	Robert Geister	9/23/75	Creek Chub Giant Pikie	Pipestone Lake, ON
59.	51-8	Don Reed	7/23/82	Lindy Musky Tandem	Wabigoon Lake, ON
60.	51-6	Eugene Eggert	10/19/63	Bucktail Spinner	Manitou Lake, ON
61.	51-4	Dennis Kestner	9/18/53	Heddon River Runt	Lake of the Woods, ON
Tie	51-4	Joseph Bertoncini	10/1/57	Marathon Musky Hawk	Eagle Lake, ON
63.	51-3**	John Knobla	7/16/19	Skinner Spinner	L. Vieux Desert, WI-MI
64.	51-1	Mike Kelner	5/19/73	Fathead Minnow	Leech Lake, MN
65.	51-0	F.J. Swint	9/13/16	#8 Skinner Trolling Spoon & Frog	Chief Lake, WI
Tie	51-0	Ed J. Smith	9/30/63	Creek Chub Pikie Minnow	Moon River, ON
Tie	51-0	Gene Allen	9/21/75	Bobbie Bait	Lac du Flambeau, WI
68.	50-14	Henry J. Bianco	8/21/46	Heddon Vamp	Lake of the Woods, ON
69.	50-12	Dr. H.C. Remele	9/25/46	Creek Chub	Woman Lake, MN
Tie	50-12	Stewart Levere	1968	Unknown	St. Lawrence River
71.	50-8	Melvin Westlake	7/21/37	Marathon Musky Houn	Lake of the Woods, ON

Big Muskies: When? Where? And Why?

No.	Weight	Angler	Date	Lure	Water
Tie	50-8	Lee Handley	10/10/37	South Bend Flash-Oreno	Dryberry Lake, ON
Tie	50-8	Russel Baker	9/3/51	Marathon Musky Houn	Eagle Lake, ON
Tie	50-8	Dennis Denman	10/1/81	Unknown	Mille Illes River, PQ
75.	50-7	Gordon Lawton	9/1/51	#9 Buffalo Spoon (spinner)	St. Lawrence River
76.	50-4	J.C. Nichols	8/12/25	11" Sucker	Columbus Lake, WI
Tie	50-4**	Delores Lapp	6/28/51	Marathon Musky Houn	Lac Vieux Desert, WI/MI
Tie	50-4	Emmett Ostlund	9/11/51	Imitation Frog	Lake of the Woods, ON
Tie	50-4	Robert Grutt	6/10/89	Buchertail Willow Buck	Big Round Lake, WI
80.	50-3	A.D. Hudson	NA	Lowe Star Bait	Conneaut Lake, PA
Tie	50-3	John Vaughn	6/5/90	Mepps Aglia & Twister	St. Lawrence River
82.	50-2	Dominic Tasone	1/2/64	Creek Chub Pikie Minnow	St. Lawrence River
83.	50-1	Mrs. E. Reinardy	10/27/62	Live Sucker	Flambeau Flowage, WI
84.	50-0	Herbert Kerr	8/23/36	Pfleuger Bearcat Spinner	St. Lawrence River
Tie	50-0	Theodore Meisner	8/30/41	Marathon Musky Houn	Grindstone Lake, WI
Tie	50-0	Nicholas Dire	7/22/42	Spinner	Lac du Flambeau, WI
Tie	50-0	Alfred Adolphsen	8/28/42	Unknown	Lake of the Woods, ON
Tie	50-0	Joseph Blazis	6/20/48	Heddon Queen	Rowan Lake, ON
Tie	50-0	Stanley Kroll	8/22/51	Creek Chub Pikie Minnow	L. Winnibigoshish, MN
Tie	50-0	Ray Kennedy	8/6/56	Marathon Musky Houn	Minocqua, WI
Tie	50-0	H. Marcus	8/4/57	Creek Chub Pikie	St. Lawrence River
Tie	50-0	Terry Bachman	9/21/83	Dardevle	Lake Nosbonsing, ON
Tie	50-0	Robert LaMay	10/18/83	Crane Bait	High Falls Flowage, WI

** *Hybrids*

As you examine the all-time top 93 list for waters that produce the largest muskies, my long-held theory, "Big water big muskies," becomes fact. Of the top 25 or so, there is only one lake that is small — Middle Eau Claire Lake in Wisconsin is credited with producing a 60-plus-pounder. However, when we further examine the facts, we find circumstances that could allow the unusual weight. The fish was caught very early in the season on June 6, and was found to still contain 8 1/4 pounds of eggs and a partly digested pike that weighed 3 pounds. I am not trying to discredit the angler or his fish, but rather point out that small waters do not produce record class muskies normally.

As we further delve into the subject, other facts present themselves. Not only must the musky waters be big, but several other criteria are present:

1. These waters are in the northern part of the musky distribution range in close proximity to the Great Lakes.

2. They are natural musky waters containing northern pike and the larger species of muskellunge.

3. They are on the Canadian Shield.

4. They have (or had) adequate forage.

5. They have areas of deep water for protection and feeding.

6. They are or were basically "geologically young" waters with adequate (but not excessive) spawning areas.

Let us further expand on the above statements. Consider that because these waters are in the northern part of the range it takes longer to grow record class fish. It takes approximately 30 years to grow a 70-pound fish there. However, waters in the southern part of the range which have longer growing seasons, which allow faster growth, fail to produce 50-pound muskies, let alone a 60- or 70-pound fish. One reason could be they don't live as long in the fast growth regions. This has been determined to be the case in Bone Lake, Wisconsin, from State DNR research.

The northern waters are also in what is known as the zero soil erosion area. Glaciers, the last of which was the Laurentide Ice Sheet, pushed most of Canada's and extreme North America's top soil to the south.

The abundant and easy to obtain forage, usually ciscos and alewives, lead to low expended energy to obtain a meal. Large water provided the ability to feed deep and obtain full growth potential and maximum survival.

It is my contention that practically all of the possible record fish have been and are continually being removed from these potential record class waters. Angling pressure has increased severely over the years, and equipment is far superior to that of early days. The records back this statement up also when you consider that our current world and Wisconsin state record has stood for 48 years (since 1949). The Minnesota state record has stood for 43 years. The West Virginia state record was broken in 1997 under unusual circumstances — it was caught from a lake that is heavily stocked with trout. And the Pennsylvania record has stood for 73 years (since 1924)! The world record for tiger (hybrid) muskellunge has also stood for 78 years (since 1919)! The final coup de grace from the records is the fact that there has been only one musky over 60 pounds caught since 1949 when a 65-0 was caught from Georgian Bay, Ontario. Only 22 muskies have been caught over 50 pounds since 1964!

What conclusions can we draw from the above facts? Are the days of the big muskies over? I will pass on further information from my research and will also include some theories currently being developed.

Following are a few quotes from a letter I received from the Ministry of Natural Resources of Ontario. "No doubt Lake of the Woods does have some monster musky swimming in it, but they are very hard to catch." (Due to available natural forage). "Realistically, we think Georgian Bay may have the largest musky of them all. It is a very large area of water, has an abundance of natural food, and contains some pretty fair musky habitat."

A couple of quotes from Al Lindner's *In-Fisherman*: "The Great Lakes themselves contain muskellunge, but no consistent means has yet been found to locate them. What may be the home of more muskies than any other waters in the world remains, therefore, an untapped resource." Also, "Since muskies suspend, they are able to feed on the cold water forage species (ciscos, tullibees, etc.) that suspend over the deep humps or sunken islands. For this reason, the muskies in such lakes have the best chance of growing to their full potential."

What am I leading up to? As I see it, there are a few possibilities yet available to us to find a record musky. The possibility in the Great Lakes will take time and equipment. At times a large boat will be necessary. A change of tactics is also in order. Musky fishermen are traditionally shallow water (5 to 15 feet) fishermen. Perhaps angling pressure has either changed the musky's feeding patterns or perhaps deep water muskies have always been available, but no techniques have been developed to successfully catch them except by a few.

Another tactic seldom pursued is very late fall fishing. At this time the ciscos make a shallow water run to spawn and for a short period large muskies move in to feed. For some muskies, it is the only time of the season that they are vulnerable to the angler.

So, being the eternal optimist and ignoring my own facts as dictated by the records, I will still look forward to a new musky world record in the near future.

No. 1, Robert Malo, 70-0   *No. 2, Louis Spray, 69-11*

No. 3, Cal Johnson, 67-8

No. 4, Ken O'Brien, 65-0

No. 5, Louis Spray, 61-13

No. 6, Edward Walden, 61

No. 7, John Coleman, 60-8

No. 8, Art Barefoot, 59-11

No. 10, Ruben Green, 58-8

No. 12, William Fulton, 57-10

No. 9, Louis Spray, 59-8
(held by Alton Van Camp)

No. 14, Jack Collins, 56-8

No. 11, George Neimuth, 58-4

No. 13, Gene Borucki, 56-11

No. 14 (tie), R.D. Shawvan, 56-8

No. 18, Neal Crawford, 55-2

No. 18 (tie), Joe Lykins, 55-2

No. 20 (tie), Herman Reber,
55-0

No. 20 (tie), Arthur Ross, 55-0

No. 20 (tie) Charles Fawcett,
55-0

No. 20 (tie) Gary Ishii, 55-0

No. 20 (tie) Steve Albers, 55-0

No. 20 (tie), John Ryan, 55-0

No. 28 (tie) Jim & Scott Carroll, 54-3

No. 27, Mark Kontianen, 54-8.5

*No. 28 (tie), Lewis Walker Jr.,
54-3*

No. 30 (tie), C.W. Frale, 54-0

No. 30 (tie), Karl Ghaster, 54-0

No. 30 (tie), Art Lyons, 54-0

No. 30 (tie), William Walshe,
54-0

No. 35 (tie), Gordon Curtis,
53-12

No. 37 (tie), W.L. Kirkpatrick, 53-8

No. 35 (tie) Myrl McFaul,
53-12

No. 44 (tie), Harry Faulkerson, 52-8

No. 37 (tie), Adolph Bockus, 53-8

No. 37 (tie), Lew Morgan, 53-8

No. 42, E.A. Oberland, 52-12

No. 43, Rita Hillenbrand, 52-8.75

No. 46 (tie), George McQuillen, 52-4

No. 49 (tie), William Dashley, 52-0

No. 44 (tie), Gerry Winteregg, 52-8

No. 46 (tie), Dave Unzeitig (left), 52-4

No. 49 (tie), Gust Peterson, 52-0

No. 49 (tie), Clay Ferguson Sr., 52-0

No. 53, Karl Dobmeier, 51-14

*No. 54 (tie), Eugene Avrill,
51-12*

*No. 54 (tie), Joseph
Mathis Jr., 51-12*

*No. 56, George
Moore, 51-11*

*No. 57 (tie), Lewis
Hilfer, 51-8*

No. 57 (tie), Robert Geister, 51-8

No. 64 Mike Kelner, 51-1

No. 57 (tie), Don Reed, 51-8

No. 63, John Knobla, 51-3
World record hybrid

No. 65 (tie), F.J. Swint, 51-0

No. 65 (tie), Ed J. Smith, 51-0

No. 65 (tie), Gene Allen, 51-0

No. 71 (tie), Dennis Denman, 50-8

No. 71 (tie), Lee Handley, 50-8

No. 76 (tie) Bob Grutt, 50-4

No. 76 (tie) Delores Lapp, 50-4

No. 76 (tie) J.C. Nichols, 50-4

*No. 80, A.D. Hudson,
50-3*

No. 80 (tie), John Vaughn, 50-3

No. 82, Dominic Tasone, 50-2

No. 83, Mrs. E. Reinardy, 50-1

*No. 84 (tie), Terry Bachman,
50-0*

No. 84 (tie), Nicholas Dire, 50-0

No. 84 (tie), Ray Kennedy, 50-0

No. 84 (tie), Theodore Meisner, 50-0

No. 84 (tie), Robert LaMay, 50-0

Chapter 8:
The Importance
Of Releasing
Muskies

In the past several years, an exciting trend has started to become an accepted norm in musky angling. I am referring to the releasing of legal non-trophy muskies — and yes, some trophy-sized fish as well! It has not come about calmly — but rather has, at times, caused some hard feelings. Why has this new trend come about? Why are more and more musky anglers releasing legal fish? More musky anglers are realizing that the only way to return to the days of many big muskies is that fish must be released to reach their full size potential. In this final chapter we will review history and learn that the problem of declining big muskies is not new — it is finally being recognized and admitted that perhaps the current problem is increasing numbers of expert anglers and greatly increased leisure time, enhanced by very efficient, modern equipment and quick, easy access to top musky waters. Let us now review some quotes from days gone by:

It was not an uncommon experience some years ago to catch this species weighing up to and over one hundred pounds; at least old-timers and commercial fishermen operating on the Great Lakes and tributaries vouch for this. The St Lawrence River Between the Thousand Islands and Montreal Bay of Quinte in Lake Ontario, and Georgian Bay in Lake Huron have produced over a period of a great many years the world's largest muskalonge.

Next:

The Hayward Lakes Region has always been famous for its fishing waters. What was fishing really like in the days when its lakes and streams had few fishermen and these waters reportedly abounded with fabled big lunkers who had never seen a lure? Were the " big ones" as plentiful as we are led to believe? The answer to these questions is without a doubt an affirmative according to what records I can find of these times.

In September of 1892, a Fishing and Hunting Guide of Northern Wisconsin, a twenty page booklet authored by O.E. Rice, was being printed by the Hayward Journal-News. We will quote from it, with some editing: "Near the terminus of a splendid turnpike carriage road built from Hayward in 1891 one justly celebrated Lost (Lost Land) and Tea [Teal] lakes. Here is destined to be the favorite fishing resort of this section, as the waters are filled with the ordinary lake fish before named ... In these waters the lover of sport realizes his greatest expectations, for the famous muskallonge fish are caught here in numbers. These cannot be landed with a pole because of their great size and strength. They run all the way from seven to sixty pounds and are taken on a trolling hook. Six hundred pounds of fish were caught in two days by a party of three about the middle of August, 1892 ...

Accompanying this article was a photo from an 1897 plat book showing four anglers with twelve muskies taken in one day!

"Angling in the Middle West" by Emereson Hough in the August 1901 issue of *Outing* magazine indicated that already in 1901, the handwriting was on the wall. To quote:

In regard to the angling for muscallunge, one is obliged to write somewhat in the past tense. We still have muscallunge fishing in Wisconsin, though little or none in Michigan. Minnesota has a number of muscallunge waters within her borders and indeed is today attracting the greater portion of the attention of the trolling cult. Yet prolific as are these waters, there is no comparing the results of today which were common ten, fifteen or twenty years ago. Pen cannot chronicle the unspeakable butchery which took place over all the Wisconsin wilderness when the railroads first penetrated that virgin country. Never has the brutishness of human nature been more fully exemplified than it was up in the dark forests of the pine country, which was at that time but little known. It was exceedingly simple. One went up the railroad to almost any little logging town, took a little used trail to almost any little lake tributary to the Mississippi River system, any where in the Manitowish, Turtle Lake, Tomahawk Lake, or St. Germain region, indeed on any one of those lakes which drain into the Wisconsin or the Flambeau River, and having secured any kind of a boat from a birch bark to a lumbering bateau, he simply took to trolling almost any kind of a spoon hook in almost any part of the lake. The merest novice might take a dozen, a score, indeed two scores of magnificent muscallunge in a day's fishing, if he did not tire out. One party composed of men from Louisville, Kentucky and from Chicago, on one trip piled up over a ton of muscallunge on the sandy shores of one of the lakes near Three Rivers, Wisconsin. They returned year after year and repeated their shameless performances, until at length even the guides revolted and told them that they must come there no more. A great deal of this was hand line fishing, without the first element of sport attached to it. One learned gentleman, who adorns the medical fraternity in the city of Chicago, invented a sort of spring box, so arranged in the stern of the boat that when a muscallunge struck the spoon he found himself played automatically on a big coiled spring, like a mammoth watch spring. By means of this contrivance, with the hand line in one hand and a couple of poles sticking out over the side of the boat, this gentleman angler managed to satisfy his idea of sport. No one can tell how many tons of fish this one party of ruffians have killed. Members of the party used to boast of their performances, up to within a few years back, at which time they began to hear so much plain talk regarding themselves that they now never refer to those distant days.

Dave Johnson was slightly ahead of his time, releasing this (over) 50-pounder in 1985.

Today we do not hear of thirty and forty pound muscallunge as a common thing in Wisconsin. The fish run very much smaller and very much fewer. It is the same old story. If a good fish, say an eighteen or twenty pounder, is taken at any of the summer resorts, the news is multiplied by two and sent to the newspapers and sporting goods stores of the city. Really I doubt if there was a fish taken over forty pounds in Wisconsin last season, and perhaps not a half a dozen, recorded and unrecorded, that went over thirty pounds. The largest muscallunge of which I have heard in these waters weighed fifty-five pounds and it was taken some fifteen years ago (1886)."

Next:

In the Spring of 1895 it was not unusual to capture individuals weighing from 40 to 50 pounds, and 20 to 30 pounds was a common weight.

Again, under the heading of Eagle Waters, Wisconsin:

Each of the ladies of the party had the good fortune to hook muscallunge, and with some coaching and little assistance each one killed her fish. Miss Josephine DeMott handled her tackle with skill borne of experience and with the coolness of a veteran.

The Importance of Releasing Muskies

It is interesting to note that these members of the "Acme Rod and Gun Club" who camped on Stone Lake, made a big issue of sport as evidenced by the following statement:

> The Acmes don't fish with hand line and drag these (fish) into the boat by brute strength. Every mascalonge hooked by us that can beat the steady spring of a 9 oz. rod and gentle persuasion of an F or G silk line is welcome to his liberty. It takes time to kill fish in this way before they can be beaten. Greater numbers can be taken by hand lines — mere pot fishing — and we do not care to compete with that style of slaughter." Also, all of their fish were weighed "in presence of witnesses on a Fairbanks Standard scale."

It would appear that members of this club were far ahead of their day in both sportsmanship and honesty! If only someone would have realized that there was not a never-ending supply of muskies and started a release program; as they *This dandy, over 55 pounds, was released by Ed Barbosa in 1994.* killed many muskies!

Next we have an extensive quote from Al Lindner's *In-Fisherman*:

> No complete study of muskellunge and musky fishing could be made without first delving into the colorful history of this exciting and challenging sport. In digging through the archives, the In-Fisherman found that almost from the beginning of civilization's advance across the continent, the fortunes of the muskellunge began to wane, and that the seeds of mystery, myth and misconception were sown early.
>
> As early as April 5, 1891, the depopulation of the musky began. In an article in Minnesota's Hubbard County Clipper, the "sand lake trout" (muskellunge) was hailed as the "king of fresh water fish" by a local group of avid sportsmen led by a Colonel Harding. Harding's two claims to fame were the capture of Jefferson Davis at the close of the Civil War and a phenomenal catch

of musky.

On July 7, 1889, Colonel Harding and a group of other anglers, including Deuvitt Carlson of Osage and John Liesenfeldt of Pard Rapids, caught 300 musky from the Mantrap chain of lakes. From the accounts of this feat, it appears that most of these fish were under 10 pounds, a far cry from today's release program procedure. The larger fish were salted down to be "used as needed later."

This was not just an isolated incident In July of 1891, a Dr. Kidly and a party of four from Marshalltown, Iowa, also visited the Park Rapids area. In a report sent back to his local newspaper, Dr. Kidly described his experiences:

Denise Wachelka's released beauty weighed in the mid-40s.

"I know that many men have been killed for telling outlandish fish stories, but it is impossible to give the reader much of an idea of the fishing in the Park Rapids, Minnesota area, as it can hardly be compared to anything we know of in Iowa. I've been in all the better fishing grounds in the U. S. and it beats anything I have ever seen.

"The good fishing grounds are practically unlimited. Hubbard Co. has many lakes, all of which are full of fish, almost each lake containing different fish. However, Big Sand Lake of the Mantrap chain contains the largest and the best fish in the neighborhood. The sand lake trout is somewhat similar to the muskellunge, yet there is a marked difference and the natural history books of the government do not properly describe it (This refers to the barred variety).

"It is the most perfect and beautiful fish that swims the fresh water and the flesh is simply delicious. It truly is king of the fresh water fish.

"It is a large fish ranging from six to thirty pounds. The largest one caught by our party weighed twenty pounds. Several others weighed fifteen and seventeen pounds and ten pounders are caught by the score ... We consider a hundred of three, four and six pounders a good day's work. We have 1,500 pounds salted down."

Interestingly, the old timers had difficulty in landing the really big fish due to inadequate equipment.

The Importance of Releasing Muskies

In the early 1900s, Park Rapids and surrounding resort areas recognized an influx of visitors wanting to fish, particularly for the muskellunge. So the region began advertising, featuring pictures of large muskies. But large catches eventually began taking their toll.

By the 1920s, muskies were still being caught, but not as frequently, and large specimens were getting scarce. Thirty pounders were not being taken and 15 to 20 pounders were considered exceptional fish. People who had fished musky for years firmly believed that the "big ones were still down there, but just too crafty to be caught." This is the stuff of which legends and myths are made.

Following this early depletion, the Park Rapids area was never the same for musky fishing. Today, a 15 or 18 pound fish wins the local Fuller's Fishermen's Golden Book contest. The region's lakes are small and despite a musky propagation station at nearby Nevis, they have never regained their early musky population levels or large-sized fish.

Will Ian Buchanan's 40-plus-pound release be the next 60-pounder from Canada?

This sadly, is a story repeated many times across the nation.

In Ohio the story was much the same. The early French settlers told of catches of piconeau (muskellunge) which were stacked like cordwood along the shore. In the mid 1880s, Union soldiers stationed at the mouth of Maumee Bay of Lake Erie (now Toledo) described the number of muskies caught in a single day in the hundreds. In contrast, the Wise Fisherman's Encyclopedia, published in 1951, says:

"The fishing importance of the streams flowing into Lake Erie from Toledo to the Pennsylvania line could easily be exaggerated, and it generally is. The Maumee River may have muskellunge, but if one is taken in a blue moon it would be a surprise. Some of the tributaries of the Maumee are better than the stream itself ..."

The entry goes on to say, "The Ohio muskellunge (*Esox m. ohioensis*) is mostly found toward the eastern part of the state and will never be anything more than a scarce article in the state ..."

Today, through artificial propagation, a fishery of sorts has again been restored in Ohio but, as in other regions, nowhere near what it was once upon a time.

In the lakes of New York, the musky story followed similar lines. Howard

M. Levy, in his book, Man Against musky, tells about an afternoon catch in November, 1932, of more than 900 pounds by a market fisherman on Lake Chautauqua. Nearly 30 of the fish weighed almost 30 pounds each.

Levy says, "... during the Depression years and prior to that time, fishing for the market was allowed on Lake Chautauqua, with virtually no restrictions as to size, limit or season (rod and reel was, however, required). The market fisherman, while possibly realizing some enjoyment in his work was, nevertheless, primarily interested in the financial returns from his catch.

"Late fall and winter live bait fishing (in the 1930s), both from boats and through the ice, produced fabulous catches, most of the fish being heavy females, the backbone of the brood stock. It is no wonder, then, that the 'lunge population of Chautauqua Lake by the mid-1930s dwindled to the point of extinction .."

John Wozny released this 57 1/2-incher in 1994.

In Michigan, the musky was abundant enough to support a limited commercial fishery. In 1884, the Michigan State Board of Fish Commissioners said that the muskellunge was known to fishermen of the entire coast (Great Lakes and Lake St Clair). "It is," they said, "very large and it appears not plentiful in any certain locality. It commands the highest price of any of the fish." Yet, by 1955, other than Lake St. Clair, only 15 Michigan lakes and streams provided a marginal musky fishery. Many of them — with artificial propagation — were in Michigan's Upper Peninsula.

Canada, meanwhile, has had an interesting background. Being isolated and not easily accessible or developed, many lakes retained a muskellunge fishery despite a lack of regulations.

Although the musky was recognized as a distinct species in Ontario, it was treated as sort of a northern pike subspecies. The size of the fish and the quality of its flesh made it very acceptable commercially. Between 1870 and 1900, thousands of pounds were annually marketed in Quebec and Ontario. Statistics for 1890 listed a commercial musky catch of 651,409 pounds in Ontario alone and noted that most of it was from Lake Scugog. The commercial catch from Lake Simcoe in 1868 listed 229,050 pounds.

Commercial fishing for musky came to an end in Ontario by 1904 in the

The Importance of Releasing Muskies

face of a considerable surge in angling interest and drastic decrease in catch. In Quebec, commercial fishing continued until the mid 1930s. Over the years, legislation gradually added season, size, and daily bag and possession limits.

In the March, 1932, *Sports Afield*, the noted outdoor writer, Robert Page Lincoln, said:

Undoubtedly the Lake of the Woods section and a vast region north of it, chiefly the Lac Seul district, will be the last great stamping ground of the species (muskellunge) in North America. Fortunately, much of this region yet remains to be fished by anglers for the sport of it; therefore, it will produce potential fish for the next seventy-five years ...

One reason for the unusual number of the muskellunge species in the Lake of the Woods region is the immense water area that the fish has as its hunting ground and habitat. It must necessarily take an area as vast as this to keep so many huge fish within its limits. When one considers the great amount of food that it takes to keep one of these huge fish well fed and in the swim, one can readily realize that food and a lot of it is in demand and that an ordinary lake would not easily harbor very many of these assimilators of finny provender.

Given a lake as large as Lake of the Woods, however, with a vast supply of food to its credit, the muskellunge is able to hold its own in amazing fashion, baffling the scientists and amazing the anglers alike by the very numbers of these great fellows, whereas, in other sections of North America, they are found but sparingly and probably never were as numerous as they are in the present day in this northern region. Added to this, the muskies in Lake of the Woods are huge in size compared to the average taken elsewhere ...

Elsewhere in that 1932 article, Lincoln says:

... authorities, however, have looked upon this condition with no little alarm, the belief being advanced that the parent stock is being caught off since very few fish of this species under 20 pounds in weight are taken by the anglers. It would seem from this that the muskellunge is gradually being trimmed down with few young muskies in varying stages of growth coming on to fill the depleted ranks ...

How true this is. Fishermen just seem to ignore the lessons they learn from history until it is too late.

Wisconsin, of course, has a long and varied musky history. Artificial propagation started early there and has been the source of much of our material. It seems that musky rearing began in 1899 and well that it did. Wisconsin lakes are small when compared with other musky waters and the "skimming the cream" came early and hard. In a 1901 publication of the American Fisheries Society, James Nevin said alarmingly:

> For many years since the wilderness of northern Wisconsin was opened by the railways and by lumbering operations; with the advent of the comforts and conveniences which the railroad takes into a new country, and the encroachment of the settler and summer hotel on the primitive banks of our northern lakes, the pursuit of the muskellunge has been constant and relentless. Its utter extermination has been well nigh accomplished in many of our lakes to which it is indigenous and nearly all of our waters have been cleared of this fish to such an extent that it s future has become a matter of much concern to sportsmen, fish culturists and others interested in keeping our waters well-stocked with superior game fish.

Depletion of the musky stock can take place fast. For the most part, the good 'ol boys had little thought about tomorrow. In September 1892, an article in the *Fishing and Hunting Guide of Northern Wisconsin* said:

> ... Perhaps better known than any other lake in northern Wisconsin is Lac Courte Oreilles because of the Indian Reservation established there in an early day. In addition to an abundance of lake fish, here are found plenty of muskellunge. Thousands of pounds of fish are shipped from this lake every summer ...

That fish were as plentiful as such reports claimed, there is little doubt. It is possible that some of these writers were "hacks" who were mostly promoting the area, but articles written by C.H. Crane, a respected writer-angler in the *American Field* and the *Sportsman's Journal,* and reinforced locally in the *Hayward* (Wis.) *Republican* of August 1884, attest to their abundance. Crane said that "exaggeration was not the case." Many barrels of fish, he reported, were shipped while his party of sportsmen were there and other stories of huge catches and consequent shipments of fish appeared in newspapers of the day.

In one article, Crane disclosed:

> ... Monday we set out by team over a splendid forest road for Teal Lake, five miles away, where we put in a very enjoyable day with muscallunge ... small but gamy from two to fifteen pounds. The catch for five rods for the day was seventy eight fishes: weight three hundred and seventeen pounds. These were packed and sent to the "heathen" — we did not know what else to do with them ...

The *In-Fisherman* has piles of stories about muskies wherever they were found. From the material it is clear that as the population moved westward, the musky population plummeted accordingly.

What's the point of all this background? Well, such stories are helpful in dispelling one long-standing myth — that the musky is crafty and difficult to catch. It was so elusive that it was — except for artificial propagation — almost fished to extinction! That's not a very good recommendation for such a cunning creature: In fact, the musky is probably the most vulnerable of our five major inland game fish. Remember that the anglers of yore were not known for their sophisticated techniques.

Thick black fishing lines, heavy steel leaders and cane poles all were part of the accepted method of musky fishing. Deep water angling was unknown. And despite this, it was almost "good-by, musky!"

Make no mistake, musky fishing is a trophy game. Although the old timers had no compunction about stringing up a six-pounder, they did appreciate and seek out lunkers.

However, the release program is exciting! From it I have developed:

The 45-Pound Release Club
Compiled by Larry Ramsell as of March 5, 1997

It would be redundant to say that the live release program has been a resounding success. The record speaks for itself, and it is no accident that larger average size fish are being caught each year. This, coupled with new frontiers being found and explored, has resulted in muskies being released that otherwise would have been trophies for the wall. These facts are bringing us closer to the day when a new world record would be hung on the scale.

While some zealots claim they would release even a world record fish, I think the moment of truth would find otherwise. What, I ask, would be the point? To release a fish of that caliber would deny the musky world what it has been waiting for — proof that such a fish is possible and does exist! With the clouds of doubt that surrounded every record musky since 1939, I can't believe anyone would release such a creature and then try to claim it! Nor can I believe anyone would release such a creature and keep quiet about it.

The purpose of this club is to acknowledge those anglers who have released super trophy fish, one of which could ultimately be recaught as a world record.

While I will be relying on angler honesty for fish placed in this listing, a few criteria will need to be met:

1. A picture will be required.
2. Length and girth measurement (To nearest 1/4-inch) required.
3. A witness to the release and measurement is required.

Estimated weight for each fish listed is calculated using the revised

estimated weight formula: (Girth - .75") X (Girth - .75") X Length / 800 = Estimated Weight. (See the estimated weight chart in the *Musky Hunters Almanac* for a complete explanation of this formula.) It is possible, however, that some of these fish, if extremely stocky, could be even heavier than listed.

Mark Maghran with a twin to his 1995 monster "honorable mention" fish. Mark has now released two fish in the 45-pound class.

I have added a column that shows what the weight would be by the standard formula as well as the revised formula. It is interesting to note, that two of 1996's and one of 1997's were weighed prior to release, and that weight was closest to the weight developed by the revised formula.

The live release program continues to return huge trophy size muskies to the water to grow even larger. The 1997 update adds nine more giants to the list, and I'm sure that even more were caught and released. Should you or someone you know have released a fish that meets the requirements of this club: 45 pounds estimated using the standard formula of GxGxL/800 (or weighed on a certified scale), you may submit it for recognition.

The fish will be listed by both the standard estimate and by the new revised formula, that subtracts 3/4-inch from the girth before the formula is applied. This girth reduction has been found to more accurately reflect the "true" weight of the fish had it been killed. Due to the differences in musky shapes, and the differing forage bases throughout the musky range, this deduction may not be necessary in all cases, hence the dual listing.

An Honorable Mention category has been added to include fish that may just miss the esteemed 45-pound mark by the formula, but in reality could have scale weighed 45 pounds. I'm sure all anglers appreciate the safe live release of any huge musky, even if it falls somewhat short of the goal of this 45-Pound Club. Naturally, fish that make the weight by the original standard formula, will be included.

The 45-Pound Release Club

No.	Angler	Date	Length	Adj. Girth	Live Girth	Est. Weight	Standard Form. Weight
1.	Alan Martinson	8/23/96	60.38	27.31	28.06	56.29	59.43
2.	Ed Barbosa	10/20/94	58	27.75	28.5	55.83	58.89
3.	Gary Sedlak	7/27/96	59	27.25	28	54.76	57.82
4.	John Wozny	12/4/94	57.5	27.25	28	53.37	56.35
5.	Wally Bednarz	11/6/94	57	27	27.75	51.94	54.87
6.	Dave Johnson	9/29/85	55	27.25	28	51.05	53.90
7.	Dave Unzeitig	10/5/96	55	27.25	28	51.05*	53.90
8.	Jocelyn LaPointe	12/8/96	60	26.25	27	51.68	54.68
9.	Bob Mehsikomer	1996	54.5	27.25	28	50.59	53.41
10.	Janet Garrol	10/16/93	50.5	28	28.75	49.49	52.18
11.	Janet Garrol	9/24/94	54.5	26.75	27.5	48.75**	51.52
12.	Dr. Tom Ring	10/7/92	56.5	26.25	27	48.67***	51.49
13.	Rich Wren	11/13/94	54	26.75	27.5	48.30	51.05
14.	Jeff Corbrin	10/16/94	57.5	25.5	26.25	46.74	49.53
15.	Mike Langhammer	10/7/94	55.5	25.75	26.5	46.00	48.72
16.	Gale Radtke	11/16/96	55	25.75	26.5	45.59	48.28
17.	Shawn McCarthy	8/16/92	57	25.25	26	45.43	48.17
18.	Ralph Cook	4/21/96	50	26.875	27.625	45.14	47.70

* This fish was weighed before release at 52.25 pounds (certified scale).
** This fish was weighed before release at 49.65 pounds.
***This fish was weighed before release at 49 pounds.

A Compendium of Musky Angling History

Honorable Mention

No.	Angler	Date	Length	Adj. Girth	Live Girth	Est. Weight	Standard Form. Weight
1.	Mark Maghran	11/14/94	52	26.25	27	44.79	47.39
2.	Mark Maghran	11/29/96	52	26.25	27	44.79	47.39
3.	Denise Wachelka	10/29/94	56	25.25	26	44.63	47.32
4.	Don Hunt	10/12/94	52.5	26	26.75	44.36	46.96
5.	Bob Mehsikomer	1988	56	24.75	25.5	42.88	45.52
6.	Todd Maragas	10/13/96	51 1/4	25.75	26.5	42.48	44.99
7.	Peter Lucani	10/13/95	53	25.25	26	42.24	44.79
8.	John Novak*	6/9/96	51.5	25.25	26	41.04	43.52

* Hybrid

The last item I would like to use is a short story by Dennis J. Van Patter:

I Watched Him Swim Away

Late last week I caught my first sizeable musky. It was an experience I will never forget.

In only the fifteenth day of my musky fishing career (spread out over two years), my first real goal in this great sport came true.

We were casting large bucktails over a shallow reef-weedbed in Ontario's Eagle Lake on a dark, windy evening The sixth day of our seven-day trip was nearing an end and only one musky has been landed by our party — a fine 23-pounder which fought savagely before losing its battle earlier in the day.

Suddenly a musky swirled behind my bucktail without touching it. I retrieved normally, knowing the fish could be following in. Sure enough, he appeared moments later behind another lure only to disappear under the boat. I began a furious figure-8 only to be rewarded with a smashing strike almost immediately.

The strong fish ran a long way, stopped, then moved out again. Keeping strong pressure and hoping it was well hooked, I fought to keep it out of the weeds. The fish gradually came closer and was landed — 21-plus pounds, 42 1/2 inches of musky.

To lunker fishermen, it would not have seemed like much. To me, it was everything.

For a moment, there was a question in my mind about whether or not to keep him. I greedily knew it would have made a beautiful mount beside a slightly smaller northern pike I caught earlier in the trip.

But he fought so well and so desperately that, despite the fact I won this round, it seemed to me as though it had finished in a draw.

He rewarded me with the satisfaction of landing him, and it was up to me to give him something in return — the chance to live and perhaps give someone else what he had given me.

As he was returned to the water unhurt and as he quickly swam away, I felt overwhelmingly grateful. I know now that this act of release will always be my biggest thrill in musky fishing.

About The Author

L arry Ramsell brings 43 years of musky hunting experience together in his presentations. Included in those 43 years are hundreds of muskies caught, including dozens of trophy-sized fish both caught and released, topped off by a 44-pound 4-ounce trophy which is a line class world record and 45- and 40-pound class releases.

His musky hunting has carried him to most of North America's big fish waters, such as Georgian Bay, Eagle Lake, Lake of the Woods and the Ottawa and St. Lawrence rivers in Ontario; Wabedo, Little Boy, Inguadona and Leech Lakes in Minnesota; The Chippewa and Flambeau flowages, Lac Courte Oreilles, Round, Moose, Lac Vieux Desert, Minocqua, Tomahawk, North Twin and many others in Wisconsin where he has been a guide over the years since the mid-1960s; Lake Okoboji in Iowa; Pomme de Terre in Missouri; Cave Run and Green River in Kentucky; Dale Hollow on the Kentucky/Tennessee border; The Niagara and St. Lawrence rivers and

The author released this beauty, which weighed 43 pounds with its tail still in the cradle.

Lake Chautauqua in New York; Lakes LeBouf and Conneaut in Pennsylvania; and Clear Fork, Pymatuning and West Branch in Ohio. In addition, he has fished dozens of other waters throughout 12 states and two provinces.

Larry developed the world records program as world records secretary for the National Fresh Water Fishing Hall of Fame and was a representative of the International Game Fish Association for 16 years. Among many other positions, Larry is a two-term past International President of Muskies, Inc. He is currently the fish historian for the Hall of Fame and world record adviser.

Larry is a well known international freelance writer on the subject of muskies. His work has appeared in such well known publications as: *In-Fisherman, Fishing Facts, Musky Hunter, Fish and Fang* (Germany), *North American Fisherman* and *Fishing World*, among others.

In 1982 Larry published his book *A Compendium of Muskie Angling History*, recognized internationally as a reference encyclopedia on the sport and its big fish. It has been updated and revised and reprinted in 1997. In addition, Larry and Canadian guide friend Bill Hamblin co-edited the *Musky Hunter's Almanac* in 1996. It was

The author struggles to hold his 44-pound, 4-ounce monster from Ontario's Eagle Lake.

377

widely accepted and was repeated in 1997. It will again be published for 1998.

In 1986, Larry spent the summer as a volunteer on Bernard Lebeau's musky research team in northwestern Ontario, where his primary responsibility was the radio tracking of huge muskies on Eagle and Wabigoon Lakes.

Larry presented a photo historical display at the Cool Water Symposium in St. Paul, Minnesota and the musky symposium at LaCrosse, Wisconsin.

Larry is a popular and frequent speaker at sport shows, banquets, seminars and club meetings on a variety of topics regarding muskies. He guides for muskies in the Hayward, Wisconsin, area.

Larry can be contacted at: P.O. Box 306; Knoxville, IL 61448, phone: (309) 289-4259 winter and (715) 462-9953 in summer.

It appears the author is about to kiss this mid 30-pound musky (I don't think so!) before letting it return to its watery home.

Surface Bait Subtleties

Surface Bait Subtleties
Topwater Tactics For Muskies

By John Dettloff

Surface baits are arguably the most exciting technique for muskies. Author John Dettloff specializes in their use and provides detailed instruction on how to fish them. Dettloff, the historical editor of *Musky Hunter* magazine, is a Chippewa Flowage musky guide and historian.

This book is a must for those who fish topwaters for muskies and/or have fallen in love with the Chip!

TO ORDER:
Mail this form with your payment to:
Musky Hunter Magazine
P.O. Box 340
St. Germain, WI 54558

VISA & MasterCard users
may call toll free
1-800-23-MUSKY

Enclosed is my check in the amount of $ _____ for _____ copies of "Surface Bait Subtleties."

Name _____

Address _____

City _____ State _____ ZIP _____

VISA _____ M/C _____ Exp. Date _____

Card No. _____

Signature _____

Daytime telephone _____

Note: Add $2 shipping per book when ordering multiple copies. Wisconsin residents must add 5.5% sales tax (total of $13.66 plus shipping per book).